THE OLD
TESTAMENT
WORLD

THE OLD TESTAMENT WORLD

JOHN ROGERSON · PHILIP DAVIES

University of Sheffield

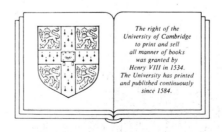

The right of the
University of Cambridge
to print and sell
all manner of books
was granted by
Henry VIII in 1534.
The University has printed
and published continuously
since 1584.

CAMBRIDGE UNIVERSITY PRESS

Cambridge   New York
New Rochelle Melbourne Sydney

Frontispiece: Abraham and the Three Angels,
a page from the St Louis Psalter, 1523–70.

First published in Great Britain and Australia in 1989
by the Press Syndicate of the University of Cambridge
The Pitt Building, Trumpington Street, Cambridge CB2 1RP
and at 10 Stamford Road, Oakleigh, Melbourne 3166.

British Library Cataloguing in Publication Data

Rogerson, J.W.
  The Old Testament world.
  1. Bible. O.T. — Critical studies
  2. Palestine, ancient period
  I. Title II. Davies, Philip R.
  221.6

A John Calmann and King book.

ISBN 0-521-34006-3

This book was designed and produced by
JOHN CALMANN AND KING LTD, LONDON

Designed by Behram Kapadia
Typeset by ⚒ Tek-Art Ltd., Croydon.
Printed and bound in Hong Kong

CONTENTS

Preface

PART I   THE SETTING   13

1   Geography and Ecology of the Land of Israel *John Rogerson*   14

The Land 16; *The coastal plain 16*; *The Shephelah 18*; *The Highlands 19*; *The Jordan
Valley 22*; *The Transjordanian Highlands 23*; *The desert 23*; Climate and Vegetation
24; Population and Agriculture in 1200 BCE 28; Land and Land Use 1200 to 587
BCE 35; Land and Land Use 587 to 63 BCE 41; The Theological Significance of the
Land 43

2   Social Organization *John Rogerson*   45

Blood Ties 45; Conflicting Loyalties 48; The Function of Genealogies 51; Social
Groupings 56; *The bet av 56*; *The mišpaḥah 56*; *The ševet 57*; *The power structure 58*;
The bet avot 59; *Other post-exilic groups 61*

3   Israel's Neighbours *Philip Davies*   63

Nations sharing Israel's territory 63; *Nations on Israel's borders 64*; *Empires 70*; *Canaanites
70*; *Amorites 71*; *Phoenicians 72*; *Philistines 72*; *Canaanite religion and culture 73*; *Political
and social organization in Canaan 75*; *Transjordan 77*; *Ammonites 78*; *Moabites 79*; *Edom
80*; *Amalekites and Midianites 81*; *Amalekites 81*; *Midianites 82*; *Nabateans 83*;
Arameans 84; Empires 90; *Egypt 90*; *Hittites and Hurrians 94*; *Assyria 97*; *Babylon 102*;
Persians and Medes 109; *Greece 113*

PART II   THE HISTORY AND RELIGION OF ISRAEL   115

4   Until the Time of Solomon *John Rogerson*   116

The Early Israelites 117; The Philistines 120; Saul 122; David and Solomon 123;
Patriarchal Traditions 132; The Exodus 132

5   From the Division of the Kingdom to the Babylonian Exile
     John Rogerson   134

Jeroboam's Rebellion 134; The Divided Kingdom 139; The House of Omri 141;
Internal and External Conflicts 144; Kings of Judah 149; Assyrian Aggression 149;
The Invasion 152

6   Israel under the Persians and Ptolemies *Philip Davies*   158

Exile 158; The Situation in Judah 160; The "Return" 161; Ezra and Nehemiah
163; Elephantine 171; Alexander and the Ptolemies 172

7   From the Maccabees to Herod the Great *Philip Davies*   174

The "Hellenistic Crisis" (c. 175–140 BCE) 174; *Development of the crisis 178*; *The Maccabean Revolt 180*; The Hasmonean Dynasty 182; *Jonathan and Simon 182*; *John Hyrcanus 184*; *Aristobulus I and Alexander 184*; *Salome Alexandra (Shelomzion) and her sons 189*; Herod the Great 191

PART III   LITERATURE AND LIFE   195

8   Creation and Origin Stories   *John Rogerson*   196

Sumerian and Akkadian Texts 198; The Problem of Sources 199; The Meaning of "Myth" 200; Genesis 1:1–2:4a 201; Genesis 2:4b–25 204; Genesis 3 205; Genesis 4 208; Genesis 5 209; Genesis 6–9 210; Genesis 11:1–9 212; Conclusions 216

9   Narratives   *Philip Davies*   217

"Factual" versus "Fictional" Narrative 217; *Historiography 218*; Simple and Complex Narratives 218; Complex Narratives 220; *Historiography 220*; *Old Testament Historiography 221*; *The Chronicler 223*; *The first and second books of Maccabees 224*; Simple Narratives 225; *Folk forms 225*; *Saga 225*; *Legend 227*; *Folk tale 227*; *Non-folk forms 228*

10   Legal Texts   *John Rogerson*   233

Administration of Justice 235; *Direct appeal to God, or use of an oracle or ordeal procedure 236*; *Making an ad-hoc decision in a particular case 237*; *Laws collected, systematized, and administered by established authorities 237*; *Law making and drafting by professional lawyers or scribes 238*; The Book of the Covenant 238; Leviticus 17–26 242; *Priestly families 243*; *Sexual relations 243*; *Religious life 244*; *Social relationships 245*; Deuteronomy 245; *Religious practice 247*; *Women 248*; *Regulations about war 248*; *Humanitarian provisions 249*; The Decalogue (Ten Commandments) 250

11   Sacrifices and Psalms   *John Rogerson*   253

Sacrifices 253; Sacrifice in Ancient Israel 255; *Regular and special offerings 256*; *The history of Old Testament sacrifice 257*; The world-view of Leviticus 1–16 259; *Defilement and purification of the sanctuary 260*; *Rites of passage 260*; *Atonement for the whole people 261*; The Psalms 263; *The royal ceremonies of the psalms 263*; *Form-critical study of the psalms 270*; *The collection and editing of the psalms 271*; *Conclusion 273*

12   Prophetic Literature   *Philip Davies*   274

"What is "Prophecy"? 274; Prophecy as a Social Institution 275; Prophets in the Ancient Near East 275; Prophets in Ancient Israel 276; Prophecy in the Old Testament 278; *A largely literary product 278*; *"True" and "false" prophecy 279*; *The purpose of Old Testament prophecy 281*; Individual Prophets and Prophetic Books 282; *Prophetic speech 282*; Isaiah 285; *Second Isaiah 287*; *Third Isaiah 288*; *The Latter Prophets as historical figures 288*; *Hosea 289*; *Amos 289*; *Micah 290*; *Jeremiah 290*; *Ezekiel 291*; *Haggai 291*; *Zechariah 292*

13 Wisdom Literature *Philip Davies*   293

What is "Wisdom"? 293; Types of Wisdom Literature 294; *"Instructions" 294*;
Argument 296; *Narrative 296*; *Manticism 296*; Who were the "Wise"? 297; *Wisdom
and scribal class 297*; *Wisdom as an intellectual tradition 297*; *Folk wisdom 297*; The
Book of Proverbs 298; *Types of proverb 298*; The Book of Job 301; The Book of
Qoheleth 303; Wisdom Psalms 305; Ben Sira 306; The Wisdom of Solomon 307

14 Apocalyptic Literature *Philip Davies*   310

The Meaning of "Apocalyptic" 310; Apocalyptic Subject Matter 311; Divination
313; *Babylonian mantics 313*; *Divination in Israel 313*; *Mantic wisdom 314*; Jewish
Apocalypses 315; *Enoch 315*; *Daniel 320*

15 Beyond the Old Testament *Philip Davies*   323

"Judaism" 323; "Early" Judaism 324; *The idea of a "normative" Judaism 324*;
"Apocalyptic" versus "Rabbinic" Judaism 329; *"Palestinian" versus "Hellenistic"
Judaism 329*; *Four Jewish "parties" 329*; Outward Characteristics of Early Judaism
330; *Circumcision 331*; *Anti-Idolatry 331*; *Diet 332*; Times and Seasons 332; The
Holy Place: Temple and Priesthood 334; *Temple 334*; *Priesthood 334*; Scripture,
Law, and Scribes 335; *Scriptures 335*; *The Law 336*; *Scribes 337*; The Identity of
"Israel" in Early Judaism 337; *Sadducees 339*; *Pharisees 339*; *Essenes 340*; *The "fourth
philosophy" 342*; *Other Jews 342*; *Samaritans 343*; Messianism 343

PART IV THE FORMATION OF THE OLD TESTAMENT   345

16 Oral Tradition and Pre-exilic Collections *John Rogerson*   346

A Variety of Oral Traditions 349; *The book of Judges 349*; *The books of Samuel 350*;
Genesis 351; *Exodus 354*; Written Forms of the Old Testament 355; *Political considerations 356*; *The edition of the reign of Josiah 357*

17 Post-exilic Collections and the Formation of the Canon
    Philip Davies   360

The Pentateuch 360; *Some possible outlines 361*; The Adoption of the "Law of
Moses" 363; The Prophetic Collections 364; The Books of the Latter Prophets
365; *Jeremiah 365*; *Ezekiel 367*; The Minor Prophets 369; Writings 370; The Canon
371; Text and Versions 373

Bibliography   376
Index   380

PREFACE

This introduction, although fairly conventional in form, aims to reflect the way in which the Old Testament is being explored and discussed in present-day scholarship.

We have not attempted to put forward any particular religious or theological point of view; rather, we have tried to describe the many ideas and attitudes offered in the Old Testament and to set these in their geographical and social contexts. In no sense was the nation of ancient Israel radically different from its neighbours. It was unique only in the sense that every nation is unique. The Old Testament, on the other hand, is a collection of literature unlike any other.

The two most important recent developments in Old Testament studies are an increased use of social-scientific methods, and a greater interest in taking literature as *literature* rather than as doctrine or as history. These two interests may seem contradictory, the one focusing on the real world *behind* the text (with the danger of concentrating only on historical matters), the other focusing on the world *in* the text (with the danger that we disregard history and interpret the literature in any way we like). The two approaches serve as mutual correctives, and must be prominent to be representative of current scholarship.

In conformity with current usage we have used BCE (Before the Common Era) and CE (Common Era) instead of BC and AD respectively, but we have also disregarded current usage by using "Old Testament" as opposed to "Hebrew Bible". We recognise that "Old Testament" is a Christian designation and that it differs from the "Hebrew Bible" in the way in which its books are ordered. The retention of "Old Testament", however, in no way contradicts our aim to avoid any particular theological or religious point of view.

A further point requiring clarification is our use of *Yhwh*. These four consonants constitute the proper name of the God of Israel. Traditionally, Jews do not pronounce this name, and Christians have followed their example by substituting for it the word "Lord". Our compromise is to use the consonants but not to vocalise them.

We would like to thank our colleagues and students in Sheffield, both past and present, and in particular David Clines. John Rogerson wishes to acknowledge a grant from the Heinrich-Herz-Stiftung which enabled him to work on the book in Bochum in 1987, as well as the hospitality of the Evangelisch-theologische Fakultät and Professors H. Graf Reventlow and Siegfried Herrmann. Finally, our thanks go to the staff of John Calmann and King who have patiently and courteously facilitated our endeavours, and to Rebecca Maskell for preparing the index.

JOHN ROGERSON   PHILIP DAVIES

OPPOSITE In biblical times, the road from Jerusalem to Jericho was about 13 miles (20 kilometres) long, in the course of which it descended 3500 feet (1100 metres), passing through lonely and frightening landscape, much eroded by wind and rain. The modern road is about 22 miles (35 kilometres) long, and the lower section of the old road has recently been re-metalled. The whole area is covered with vegetation in the winter months, and is grazed by the sheep, goats and camels of the bedouin.

OVERLEAF, ABOVE From Azekah, a Judean city in the Shephelah (lowlands), there is a good view of the valley of Elah, the setting for the encounter between David and Goliath (1 Samuel 17). One gets an excellent impression of the low, rolling hills and gentle valleys of the area. On the horizon it is possible to make out the higher hills of the Judean heartland.

PART I

THE SETTING

ABOVE The wilderness of Judea, in spring.

OPPOSITE The Kidron valley or brook is mentioned in the Old Testament as the eastern boundary of Jerusalem (1 Samuel 15:23). It is part of a long watercourse that begins to the north of Jerusalem, and conducts the winter rains to the Dead Sea.

PREVIOUS PAGES This view across the Valley of Jezreel from Megiddo looking east-north-east gives a fine impression of the great expanse of flat space which it creates in an otherwise hilly country. Megiddo was one of the most important strategic sites on the southwest side of the valley. In the distance on the far left are the hills of Lower Galilee; to their right is the isolated Mount Tabor.

CHAPTER 1

GEOGRAPHY AND ECOLOGY
OF THE LAND OF ISRAEL

"A certain man went down from Jerusalem to Jericho" (Luke 10: 30). Although these words are from the New Testament, rather than the Old, they well illustrate how much the study of the Bible can be enriched by a knowledge of its geography and social setting. The story of the Good Samaritan can be understood by someone who knows absolutely nothing about the world of the Bible; it concerns three travellers, one of whom did and two of whom did not come to the aid of a man who had been robbed and beaten up as he journeyed. A knowledge of the background, however, not only illuminates the story, but invites readers to use their imagination as they read it.

The road from Jerusalem to Jericho descends over 3,000 feet (900 metres) in the space of 15 miles (24 kilometres). It passes through wilderness — that is, land which supports sheep, goats, and camels for the five or six months of the rainy winter season (October to March), but which is bare in the summer. This landscape is weird and unfriendly, the result of erosion of the hills by rain and wind over thousands of years. The road winds along valleys overlooked by hills which have many caves — caves that served as refuges for robbers until quite recent times. This bleak and dangerous landscape is referred to in the simple words, "went down from Jerusalem to Jericho". With this sort of picture in our minds, we use our imagination as we read the story. We are not surprised that a man should be robbed on such a road, nor are we surprised that two travellers did not want to linger, even though they saw a man in need. The action of the man who stopped to help becomes even more praiseworthy; he was running quite a risk by stopping.

But it is not only a knowledge of geography that we need to grasp the full meaning of the story. If we know something about Old Testament purity laws — for example, the regulations concerning priests in Leviticus 22: 4–7 — we may interpret the action of the priest and levite as follows: they may have been on their way up to the temple to officiate there. If the man by the roadside were dead, and they touched him, they would become unclean and would not be able to officiate that day. The full power of the story is, however, conveyed by the fact that the traveller who helped the wounded man was a Samaritan, and that rela-

tions between Jews and Samaritans were far from cordial. The story therefore challenges its readers to act in a way that puts the needs of a human being above the enmities that separate races; but this point would be lost if we had no idea who Samaritans were, and that they were disliked, if not hated, by many Jews. In the first two chapters of this book, we shall try to write about the land and social organization of the Old Testament in a way designed to illuminate the text, and to stimulate the imagination of readers.

The hills of the Shephelah (lowlands) form a transition between the coastal plain and the central Judean hills. The coastal plain opposite the Shephelah was occupied by the Philistines, while the tribe of Judah occupied the Shephelah.

THE LAND

By far the best way of visualizing the land of Israel was suggested by George Adam Smith (1931, p. 48). We are to think of six strips placed side by side, and going from the top to the bottom of a page (north to south), as in Map 1, opposite.

The coastal plain

The first strip, on the extreme left (the west), is the coastal plain. It begins about 15 miles (24 kilometres) south of Tyre and is a narrow strip with the sea on one side and mountains on the other. As it comes south it merges into the broad valley of Jezreel on its eastern side, while to the west it becomes the beautiful bay that sweeps in a semicircle from Akko to Haifa. At this point it ends, because the hills that make up Mt. Carmel block its progress any further south. To continue along the coastal plain you must either go round the edge of Mt. Carmel where it almost reaches the sea, or you must cross the Carmel ridge by one of two or three passes.

Of all the parts of Israel, the area around Haifa has probably undergone the greatest changes in the centuries between Old Testament times and the present. Then, the coastline was about half a mile (less than one kilometre) farther to the east; along the southern edge of the bay, the delta of the river Kishon made it impossible to travel farther south. The modern town of Haifa, which lies at the foot of Mt. Carmel and extends up its side, did not exist. This part of the coastal plain is hardly mentioned in the Old Testament.

South of the place where Mt. Carmel meets the sea, the coastal plain continues, at first as a very narrow strip between sea and mountains, then broadening out and running on until it merges into the Negev region. In Old Testament times parts of this section of the coastal plain were covered with pine forests, the last of which were used by the Turks during the First World War. Other parts of the plain were swampy. This was because the river channels that carried the waters from the central hills to the Mediterranean Sea could not cope with the volume of water, particularly in the winter. Their passage was partially blocked by the two barriers of hard limestone which were formed in geological time when the sea twice receded and returned, each time to a lower level.

Like the northern part of the coastal plain, the section to the south of Mt. Carmel is rarely mentioned in the Old Testament. It had only one natural harbour, at Joppa (Hebrew Yafo), from which Jonah set sail in his attempt to avoid going on a mission to Nineveh (Jonah 1: 3). To the south of Joppa, the coastal plain was occupied by the Philistines. Their cities of Gaza, Ashdod, and Ekron are the scene of the exploits of Samson (Judges 16) and of the disastrous effects of their capturing the Israelites' Ark of the Covenant (1 Samuel 5). Otherwise, the lack of mention of this area is probably due to the fact that it contained part of the major international route from Egypt to Damascus and beyond, known as the Way of the Sea (Isaiah 8: 23). This was generally controlled by Egypt or by one of the northern powers, such

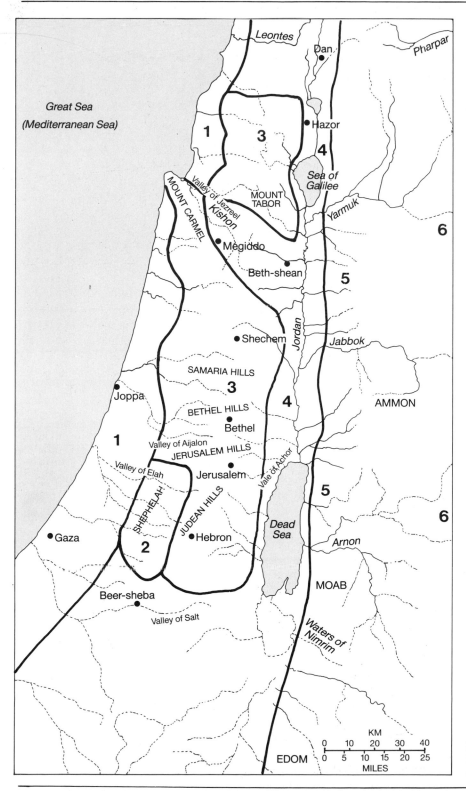

MAP 1 The ''six strips'' of Israel, according to George Adam Smith (1931).

The city of Lachish was the chief city of the Shephelah (lowlands) in Judah. After its capture by the Assyrian king Sennacherib in 701 BCE, the victory was commemorated in the famous reliefs now in the British Museum. Here, Israelite prisoners are being led away; the representation of date or fig trees at the bottom may be an indication of the type of trees growing in this area at the time.

as Assyria. Only rarely did the Israelites exert any effective authority in this region, and few Israelites lived there.

The Shephelah

The second strip is really only half a strip, and is to be found separating the part of the coastal plain where the Philistines were settled, from the hill country of Judah. It is almost level at top and bottom with the Dead Sea, two strips to its right. Called the Shephelah, which in Hebrew means lowlands, it is a transitional area between the coastal plain and the central hills, and rises to 1,500 feet (460 metres) at its highest points.

Today, this area is one of the most beautiful parts of Israel, especially where it has been planted with forests, even if the trees are different species from those that were there in Old Testament times. Then, the region was well known for its sycamore trees (1 Kings 10: 27) and for sheep farming (2 Chronicles 26: 10). It is mentioned in the Old Testament first of all as the scene of encounters between Samson and the Philistines, and between Judah and the Philistines (Judges 14–15; 1 Samuel 17). It was quite natural that the Philistines, as they tried to expand their territory, should concentrate on the lowlands immediately to their east. There must have been a lot of fighting between them and the tribe of Judah, a conflict of which we have only hints (Judges 15: 9–19). In the period of the monarchy, the route running along the western edge of the Shephelah, from Beth-shemesh to Lachish was fortified, so as to prevent potential enemies from attacking Judah by way of the Shephelah. Its capital, Lachish, was the second most important city in

Judah after Jerusalem, and when the Assyrian king Sennacherib captured the town in 701 BCE, he regarded this as a feat worthy to be depicted in the massive stone reliefs shown opposite.

The Highlands

The third strip is the central hill country. It is the most important and the most varied of the six strips, and can be divided into three main areas: Galilee, the Samaria and Bethel hills, and the Hebron Hills. Galilee itself is usually divided into Upper and Lower Galilee, a division based on the fact that the hills of Upper Galilee are on average 1,000 feet (300 metres) higher than those of Lower Galilee. This is not the only difference. Upper Galilee is made up of high peaks and narrow gorges. No routes cross it in any direction, and it was hardly suitable for settlement in Old Testament times. Thus, it does not really figure in the Old Testament. Lower Galilee is quite different; its mountains are more isolated from each other, and there are broad valleys and basins which offer natural routes. One of its mountains, Mt. Tabor, has become completely isolated from the surrounding hill country, and stands in a plain like a giant upturned bowl. Conditions for settlement were much more favourable compared with Upper Galilee, although there was no really important city in the region. Yet even Lower Galilee is rarely mentioned in the Old Testament, whereas in the New Testament it figures prominently as the place where Jesus spent most of his life and where he concentrated his ministry. The reason for this is that Galilee was always under threat from Israel's northern neighbours, Syria and Assyria. In about 900 BCE, the king of Damascus invaded Galilee and destroyed some of the towns on the edges of its hill country (1 Kings 15: 20). Although the region was later recovered, it was lost again around 740 BCE to the Assyrians. Galilee's prominence in the New Testament was the result of its conquest in 103 BCE by King Aristobulus I, and its re-incorporation into the Jewish kingdom.

The progress of the central hill country southwards is interrupted by the valley of Jezreel. The word "valley" is misleading, because the area is in fact a triangular plain nearly 50 miles (80 kilometres) wide from the coast to the Jordan Valley and 20 miles (32 kilometres) across from north to south. It is a large catchment area for the rains that come from the surrounding hills, and these waters are conducted to the sea by the river Kishon. In Old Testament times the Kishon could not cope with heavy rain, and the plain was liable to flooding. This made it marshy and partly unsuitable for travel or settlement. It did, however, contain important routes, and it was an area where horses and chariots could be deployed in battle. Judges 4–5 records a victory won by Deborah and Barak over a Canaanite army, the outcome being decided by a cloud-burst that flooded the plain and bogged down the Canaanite chariots (Judges 5: 21). It was also in the valley of Jezreel that Saul tried in vain to defeat the Philistine chariots, and lost his life on the nearby mountain range of Gilboa (1 Samuel 31: 1–6; 2 Samuel 1: 6).

Jerusalem is situated close to the point where the Judean hills merge on their eastern side with the Judean wilderness. To the east of the city, the hills topped by the Russian Church of the Ascension, the Victorian Augusta Hospital (on the far right), and the Mount Scopus campus of the Hebrew University form the ridge from which the hills fall away into the wilderness. These are visible for several miles as one approaches from the south east.

The journey from Lower Galilee into the valley of Jezreel involves even today a steep descent down a twisting and turning road. On the other side of the valley, however, the ascent into the Samaria hills is quite gentle, and the hills enclose other broad basins or valleys. Finally, the road enters a long narrow plain running roughly north to south, and where this is crossed almost at right angles by a valley which runs from the coastal plain to the Jordan Valley, the heartland of the Samaria Hills is reached. Where the valleys intersect stood the city of Shechem, flanked on either side by Mt. Ebal and Mt. Gerizim. Shechem was the first capital of the northern kingdom after the death of Solomon (c. 931 BCE) and is mentioned in Genesis in connection with Abraham (Genesis 12: 6) and Jacob (Genesis 33: 19–20).

As the road continues to the south, the broad valleys enclosed by the hills become rarer, until the road enters the Bethel Hills and begins to twist and turn along valleys at the foot of them. Here the hills seem to be packed tightly together, and there are no obvious routes in any direction. In Old Testament times the settlements were not far from what served as the main north-south route.

The Hebron Hills are separated from the Bethel Hills by the Jerusalem saddle. This country is lower than the Bethel or Hebron hills, and has broad valleys and a plain on which an airstrip was built in this century. It also provides a number of routes from the coastal plain to the central

hills, being flanked on the coastal side by the Lod triangle, a wedge of land running into the hills from the coastal plain. Towards the southern end of the Jerusalem saddle is Jerusalem itself, at 2,400 feet (730 metres), a strategically located city at the crossing of routes from north to south and west to east. It is to be noticed that Jerusalem is more or less level with the northern end of the Dead Sea, and therefore commands the most southerly route across the Jordan Valley and into Transjordan. Any farther south travel is blocked by the Dead Sea.

The Hebron Hills begin just south of Bethlehem. They rise to over

The present Old City of Jerusalem, enclosed by its sixteenth-century walls, lies to the north of where the city was located in Old Testament times. The Jebusite city which was captured by David was built on the spur immediately below the rectangular Noble Sanctuary (*Haram esh-sharif*).

3,000 feet (900 metres) and then fall away into the Negev region. They are much less wide than the Bethel Hills, because they are flanked on the west by the Shephelah, or lowlands. Access was always far more difficult from the coastal plain on to the Bethel Hills, compared with access to the Jerusalem saddle and the Hebron Hills via the Shephelah.

The Jordan Valley

The fourth strip is the Jordan Valley, part of a geological fault that extends into East Africa, and which is the lowest natural surface in the world. At its most northern end in Israel was the city of Dan, at one of the several sources of the River Jordan. To the south of Dan was the Lake Huleh region, an area of swamps and pools, which today has been drained. To the south of Lake Huleh and on the edge of Upper Galilee was the city of Hazor, which controlled north-south and east-west routes. Almost exactly opposite the Bay of Haifa on the coast, the Jordan Valley broadens out to become the Sea of Galilee. This is about 12 miles (19 kilometres) long and 5 miles (8 kilometres) wide, the surface of the lake being 600 feet (180 metres) below sea level. Again, it is remarkable that this lake, so prominent in the New Testament in the

Although the hills that make up the Judean wilderness have been deeply riven by the rains that flow to the Dead Sea, they also form a series of terraces descending from west to east. In the winter months these provide adequate grazing for sheep and goats, but become more barren the nearer they get to the Dead Sea.

ministry of Jesus, is hardly mentioned in the Old Testament. The hills around the Sea of Galilee were volcanic in geological time, with the result that much black basalt stone is found on its western and northern sides.

South of the Sea of Galilee the River Jordan resumes the journey down the valley, following a very tortuous path until it flows into the Dead Sea, about 65 miles (105 kilometres) away. In biblical times, the Dead Sea did not extend as far to the south as it does today. It is 1,200 feet (370 metres) below sea level and has a very high salt content, in spite of being fed constantly by the fresh waters of the Jordan. It figures hardly at all in the Old Testament, a notable exception being the vision in Ezekiel 47, where the prophet sees a stream issuing from the Jerusalem Temple and running down into the Dead Sea, making its waters fresh and life-supporting. South of the Dead Sea, the rift valley continues, and it eventually rises to 650 feet (198 metres) above sea level before sloping down to meet the Red Sea at the Gulf of Aqabah.

The Transjordanian Highlands

The fifth strip, to the east of the Jordan Valley, consists of the hills of Transjordan (Hebrew *Ever Hayarden*, "the land beyond the Jordan") which rise like a steep wall out of the Jordan Valley to heights of 4,000 feet (1,220 metres). Opposite Galilee was the region of Bashan, with a plateau which enjoyed good agricultural conditions. In the Old Testament, bulls or cows of Bashan are regarded as fierce (Psalm 22: 13) or well-fed (Amos 4: 1). South of the River Yarmuk, which enters the Jordan Valley at the south end of the Sea of Galilee, is the area of Gilead. Here, in hilly, forested country, some Israelites related to the tribe of Ephraim settled. It was the country of Jephthah (Judges 11), and it was also here that David's forces defeated those led by his rebellious son Absalom (2 Samuel 18: 6–18). To the south of Gilead and towards the east was the territory of the Ammonites, on the site of whose capital, Ammon, now stands Amman, the capital of Jordan. To the south of the Ammonites, level with the lower half of the Dead Sea, was the kingdom of Moab, dominated by a broad plateau which was good for agriculture and for sheep farming. The story of Ruth reflects the agricultural advantages of Moab over the Judean hills, when it depicts the family of Naomi leaving Bethlehem for Moab in order to find food (Ruth 1: 1). Finally, in strip five was the territory of Edom, to the south of the Dead Sea.

The desert

About strip six there is little to say. It is the desert extending eastwards into what is now Saudi Arabia.

It will be clear from this description that the geographical features of the land of Israel make it very unusual, if not unique. Where else in the world is there a large inland sea whose surface is 1,200 feet (370 metres) below sea level? Where else can you go, in the space of 15 miles (24 kilometres), from the cool climate of Jerusalem in winter to the summer-like warmth of the Jordan Valley? In fact, the geography of Israel left its mark on the language to a surprising degree. Although there is a general Hebrew verb meaning ''to go'', there are also verbs specifically meaning ''to go up'' and ''to go down'', and these were used advisedly in a land where there was a lot of going up and down. For example, in 2 Samuel 2: 1 David enquired of God whether he should ''go up'' to one of the cities of Judah. At the time, David was in Ziklag, at the southern edge of the Shephelah. Any move from there to the heartland of Judah would involve ''going up'' at least 500 feet (150 metres); and it would involve travelling along one of the few routes that managed to cut through the hills. As we have seen, in some parts of the land there were no routes in any direction, and where obvious routes existed, they were controlled by fortified cities, such as Hazor, Shechem, and Jerusalem.

CLIMATE AND VEGETATION

Visitors who go to Israel in the summer (June to September) are sometimes surprised to discover a landscape bare of grass and flowers, except where there has been artificial watering. In fact, the growing cycle in Israel is very different from that of Europe or North America, where the winter months are ''dead'' months because of the cold. It is cold in the winter months in Israel, too, although the average temperature in Jerusalem in January is around 50°F (10°C), compared with an average for Sheffield, England of 36°F (3°C). What is decisive in Israel is the fact that rains fall only from October to April, and that the temperature in these months is high enough to encourage growth. From May to September there is no rain, and the soil dries out completely under the hot sun, producing the brown and bare effect that sometimes disappoints visitors in those months.

The distribution of rain varies in the different regions in Israel. In the Dead Sea area annual rainfall is 4 inches (100 mm), whereas in Jerusalem it is 22 inches (550 mm). The southern end of the Hebron Hills receives about 16 inches (400 mm), while Upper Galilee has an annual rainfall of 28 inches (700 mm). Thus there is a tendency for rain to increase as one goes northwards. In the story of Joseph and his brothers, Joseph is sent by his father from Hebron to look for his brothers and the flock. He initially goes as far as Shechem, where he discovers that his brothers have gone even farther north to Dothan. This movement from a region whose rainfall is 16 inches (400 mm), to one where it is over 20 inches (500 mm), makes geographical sense. Furthermore, there is evidence to suggest that the rains were more unreliable in areas of lower rainfall than in areas of higher rainfall (Hopkins 1985, p. 90).

Reliability of rainfall is also an important factor in Israel. Ideally, for agriculture, the early rains (Hebrew *yoreh*) come in October, softening the hard-baked earth sufficiently for ploughing and planting. The main rains, 70 per cent of the total, then fall in December to February, and the season ends with the latter rains (Hebrew *malqosh*), which give

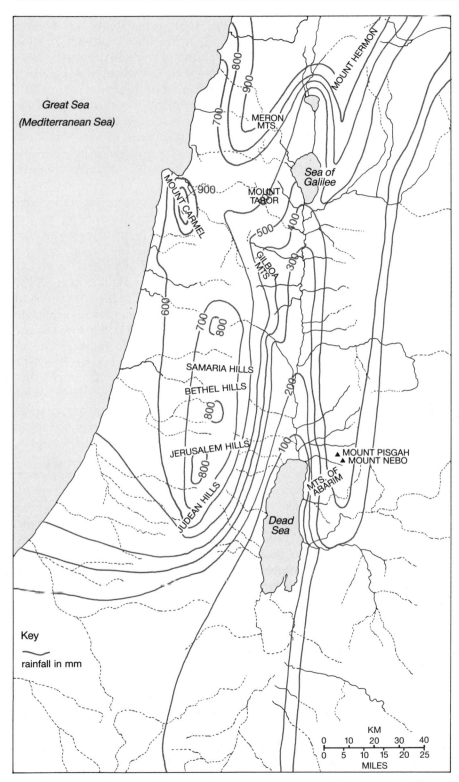

MAP 2 Israel: the annual rainfall.

a final boost to the maturing of the crops. Unfortunately, this ideal occurs only a third of the time (Hopkins p. 87). For about another third of the time the winter consists of the alternation of wet and dry spells; other patterns include a wet early season followed by dry weather and an early dry season followed by a late wet season. The latter is particularly unhelpful to agriculture, as it is almost impossible, or was in Old Testament times, to plough the hard-baked soil until the first rains had softened it. In view of the variability of rainfall from year to year, it is not surprising that "rain at the proper times" was considered to be a blessing from God (Leviticus 26: 4), and that the word "famine" occurs frequently (Genesis 12: 10; Ruth 1: 1).

Given that 70 per cent of the rainfall is ideally concentrated into three months, it is clear that the rains, when they do fall, are heavy. For example, Sheffield, located in one of the rainier areas of England, has an average annual rainfall of just over 31½ inches (800 mm), but this is distributed over twelve months. If 70 per cent of Jerusalem's 21½ inches (550 mm), falls in three months, this gives about 5 inches (130 mm) for each of those months, compared with 3½ inches (86 mm) for Sheffield's wettest month. Furthermore, even that amount in Jerusalem is concentrated into no more than 50 days. Thus, when it rains in the wettest months, the rain is very heavy indeed; this has implications for the soil and for the retention of moisture in a land characterized mainly by hills and valleys.

The modern visitor to Israel and the West Bank sees a land whose hills are often bare, except where forests have been planted in recent times, or where terracing is in use. In Old Testament times the land-scape looked very different. In the hills of Galilee and in the Samaria, Bethel, and Hebron hills there were forests of the evergreen oak *Quercus calliprinos*, the deciduous oak *Quercus ithaburensis*, and the pine *Pinus halepensis*, along with their associated undergrowth. Of these trees, the evergreen oak predominated especially in mountainous areas. Thus, the initial force of the heavy rains was broken by the leaves of the evergreen oaks, and the moisture was retained by the root systems of the undergrowth. With the clearing of the forests, however, there was nothing to prevent the heavy rains from washing the soil from the side of the hills into the valleys, thus producing the sort of bare landscape familiar to modern visitors to some parts of the country.

We do not know exactly how extensive the forests still were at the beginning of the Old Testament period (c. 1200 BCE). The text itself certainly has many references to forests and woods, and to the wild animals such as lions and bears that lived in them. Joshua 17: 14–18 records a complaint of the people of Ephraim and Manasseh that the land allocated to them (essentially the Samaria and Bethel hills) was too small and that its surrounding valleys were occupied by strongly garrisoned Canaanite cities. The reply given to them by Joshua is that they should clear the forests in their area and settle there. In 2 Samuel 18: 8, the battle between the forces of David and Absalom takes place

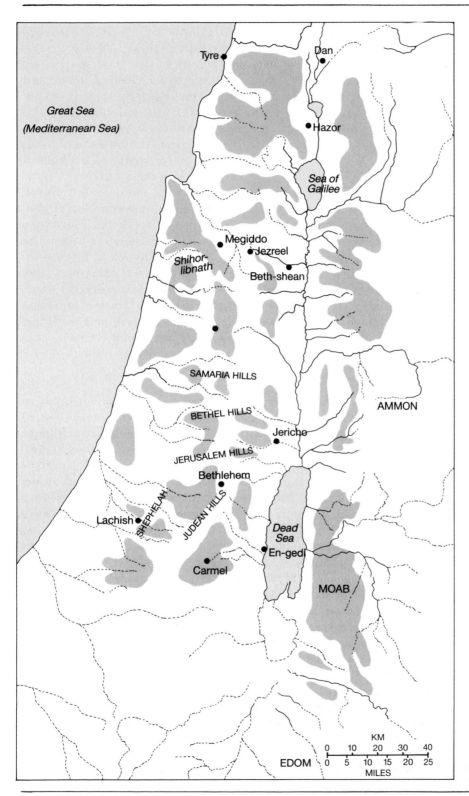

Map 3 Forested areas of Israel, c. 1200 BCE.

OPPOSITE, ABOVE The flat and broad Golan Heights preserve some instances of the kind of evergreen oak forest that covered the hill country of Israel in Old Testament times. Although the climatic conditions of the Golan differ a little from those of the hill country (there is a higher rainfall on the Golan, and snow remains there in winter), we get some idea from this view of the density of growth and undergrowth that characterized the Old Testament landscape where the forests had not been cleared.

OPPOSITE, BELOW The landscape of Israel has changed many times over the millennia. In Old Testament times, the hills around Hebron were forested with evergreen oaks, and valleys were cleared for growing grain, olives and vines. In the sixth century BCE, there may well have been an abundance of olives and vines, which diminished with the Moslem conquest of the seventh century CE when the consumption of wine was banned among Moslems. Even today, vines are grown in predominantly Christian or Jewish areas — these vineyards are near Hebron.

in a forest in the area of Gilead in Transjordan, and the forest is said to have killed more people than the sword. In 2 Kings 2:23–4 two bears are said to have come out from a forest near Bethel and savaged a group of children. In 2 Kings 17: 25 God is said to have sent lions against the people of Samaria, a claim that would make sense if the recent exiling of the population to Assyria had enabled forest cover to regenerate, and had brought an end to lion hunting. Although we can only guess about the extent of the forests in 1200 BCE, it is likely that the central core of Upper Galilee was completely forested (remains of the ancient forest can still be found here). In Lower Galilee the basins and valleys had been cleared, as had the areas around the main routes. In the Samaria Hills, the basins and valleys and main routes were cleared, but away from settlements the forests remained. The Bethel Hills were probably still largely forested, especially on their western side. The Jerusalem saddle, on the other hand, was probably much more open country, while the Hebron Hills were not so densely covered as those of Bethel. Parts of the Shephelah had probably been cleared of trees. Whether or not this guesswork is correct, it is important to realize that modern visitors to Israel and the West Bank see a very different landscape from that of Old Testament times.

POPULATION AND AGRICULTURE IN 1200 BCE

Research into the ethno-archaeology of Old Testament times is only just beginning, and therefore what is said here is a generalization of complex matters which scholarship does not yet fully understand. (Hopkins (1985, pp. 137–170) gives a cautious review of the whole subject area.)

The beginning of the biblical period in Israel in the Early Iron Age is marked by the establishment of new, small settlements, and by the re-occupation of sites that had been abandoned during the Late Bronze Age. The overall impression is of the dispersion of settlements, not of their concentration in particular areas. Some of the new settlements were located in remote parts of the countryside, where conditions for agriculture were not always ideal. Perhaps remoteness, and therefore the unlikelihood of being attacked by enemies, was more important to these communities than good agricultural conditions.

The villages or small towns in which the Israelites lived had populations ranging from about 150 to 1,000. The people lived in houses that were often variations on the so-called four-roomed house, of which the central ''room'' was probably a courtyard. There may have been an upper storey on the rear part of the house. Each house would contain a nuclear family of about five people, although this might vary from three to seven or even eight persons. In the case of large and strategically located settlements, there would be defensive walls, public buildings, and a square where public transactions could take place.

The life of a village revolved around the agricultural cycle, for each settlement produced all its own food needs. We possess, in the shape

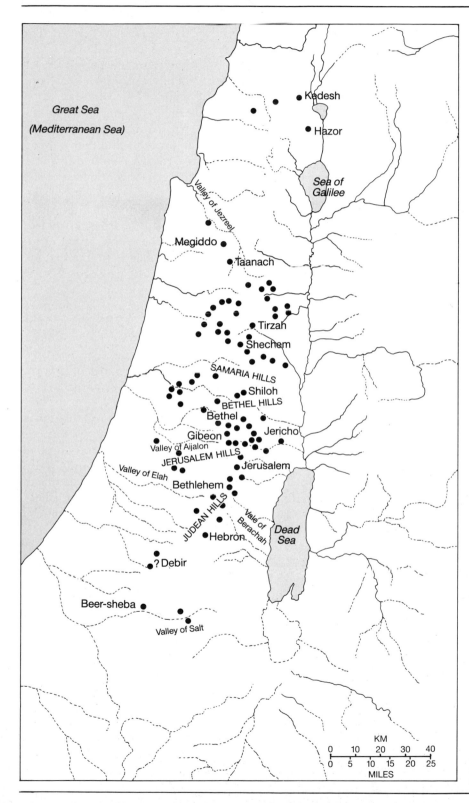

SAMARIA HILLS

BETHEL HILLS

JERUSALEM HILLS

JUDEAN HILLS

Valley of Jezreel

Valley of Aijalon

Valley of Elah

Vale of Berachah

Valley of Salt

Great Sea
(Mediterranean Sea)

Kedesh

Hazor

Sea of Galilee

Megiddo

Taanach

Tirzah

Shechem

Shiloh

Bethel

Gibeon

Jericho

Jerusalem

Bethlehem

Hebron

?Debir

Beer-sheba

Dead Sea

KM
0   10   20   30   40
0   5   10   15   20   25
MILES

PREVIOUS PAGES The Wadi Qelt is fed by two other wadis as well as collecting the rains that fall on the eastern side of the watershed and conducting them to the Jordan valley. The result is a spectacular gorge which from the fifth century CE became a centre for Christian monks. St. George's monastery, founded in the fifth century and several times rebuilt, remains today. The wadi is also supplied by three springs, and a small aqueduct conveys water to the former refugee camp near the site of New Testament Jericho.

OPPOSITE The Dead Sea fills part of the rift valley that runs from the southwest foot of the Hermon range to the Gulf of Akaba. The Sea itself is about 50 miles long by 9 miles wide (80 by 14 kilometres) although its size has varied over the millennia, and it was probably smaller in biblical times than it is today. At 1250 feet (390 metres) below sea level its shore is the lowest natural point on the earth's surface, and the sea has a depth of 1300 feet (400 metres). On its eastern side the mountains of Moab are clearly visible.

MAP 4 Settlements in early Iron Age Israel, c 1200 BCE.

of the so-called Gezer Calendar, (found in the remains of that ancient city), a list of agricultural duties that needed to be attended to year-by-year, and although it is some 300 years later than the period under examination, it can be briefly considered here (Borowski, 1987, pp. 32–44). The first activity listed is olive harvesting. This would be done in September and October, and presumably the gathering-in would include the pressing of the olives, which were grown mainly for their oil.

The second and third activities were sowing cereals and then sowing pulses, such as lentils and chickpeas, with two months allotted to each. Precisely when this was done depended on the arrival of the first rains, without which the hard soil could not be ploughed prior to sowing. Also, given the unpredictability of the pattern of the rainfall, as described above, the farmers probably prolonged the planting season in order to see how the weather developed before planting the whole of the crop. The next activity is hoeing weeds (one month). This was probably done between February and March and involved collecting grasses and other weeds to be used as hay. The next task, also requiring a month, is harvesting barley. This grain was widely grown, because it was more tolerant of harsh conditions than wheat, and it matured earlier. This harvest occurred during April, and was followed six weeks or so later by the harvest of wheat (although this crop may not have been grown in the hill country). The final activities were the harvesting of grapes, probably in July and August, and the harvesting of figs and dates in September.

These activities demanded some coordination of effort, and they raise questions about social organization. Most obviously, the harvest periods required as many men, women, and children as possible to complete the task. For the harvests that took place in the dry months the main hazard was not, as in northern Europe, for example, rain or storms, but heat. Again, the ploughing demanded some cooperation, especially if the oxen used were owned by the village as a whole, rather than by individual families.

A much-debated question is whether, around 1200 BCE, the settlements in the hill country had begun to construct the terraces that certainly existed on a large scale two or three centuries later, and remains of which can be seen today. The advantages of terraces were that they prevented the heavy rains from washing the soil down the slopes, and provided well-drained beds for planting crops. If terraces did exist from this period, they are further evidence of a cooperative type of social organization, for there was much hard work involved in their building and maintenance (Hopkins 1985, pp. 173–186). Whether or not they did exist, it is likely that crops were strategically placed in relation to the settlements. Those closest at hand would be pulses, such as beans and lentils; then would come the orchards, with the barley or wheat areas farthest away. The size of the area in which crops were grown was determined by the amount of walking that could be reasonably done from the settlement and back, usually a mile or so each way.

With the life of settlements largely devoted to agriculture, and given the importance of the various harvests, it is to be expected that the completions of harvests were marked by communal celebrations. We have some glimpses of these celebrations from later periods in the Old Testament. The book of Ruth, for example, suggests that the barley harvest was a communal activity, which was followed by drinking, wooing, and lovemaking (Ruth 3). From the point of view of Israel's later developed religion, agricultural celebrations were linked to key events in Israel's faith. The barley harvest was the Festival of Unleavened Bread, the wheat harvest was the Festival of Weeks (Pentecost), and the fruit harvest was the Festival of Booths or Ingathering (Sukkôth).

LAND AND LAND USE 1200 TO 587 BCE

Israel in 1200 BCE consisted of villages and small towns in the Hebron Hills, the Shephelah, the Jerusalem Hills, the Bethel Hills, the Samaria Hills, Lower Galilee, and possibly the Negev, to the south of Hebron. The Philistines occupied the coastal plain level with the Shephelah, while in parts of the region occupied by the Israelites were cities, such as Jerusalem and Beth Shean, that can, for the sake of simplicity, be called Canaanite. We must not think that the whole of the land was occupied. In fact, large parts of it were covered with forests, some of which had reached the peak of their growth, others of which were in various stages of degeneration because of fires, or because of partial clearing for the purposes of settlement. Israel's social and political organization will be discussed in detail in chapter 2; here it can simply be noted that the individual village was the basic unit of social life at the level above the family. Each village aimed to be self-sufficient, but villages were linked by marriage ties, and would come together to face common enemies. The main point that needs to be made here is that there was no central or local government that required the villages to produce a surplus which could be taken as a form of taxation.

During the period of the ''judges'', the situation changed for those settlements that were closest to main routes. Judges 3 records that a coalition of Moabites, Ammonites, and Amalekites captured Jericho and forced the tribe of Benjamin to pay tribute for eighteen years. This would have taken the form of agricultural products and would have entailed the production and delivery of surplus grain and fruit. In Judges 6 the Midianites, a nomadic people from the Negev region, are said to have invaded the land at harvest time for seven years, in order to take the harvest for themselves. These raids were probably restricted to areas near the main routes, for Judges 6: 2 records that the Israelites tried to withdraw into the less accessible regions. Nonetheless, a considerable disruption of normal agricultural life is indicated.

The most serious and successful threat to Israel's agricultural life in this period came from the Philistines. From a geographical point of view, it was to be expected that the Philistines should first expand at the ex-

pense of the tribes of Dan and Judah, and this is what we find in Judges
13–16. The story of the Danite hero Samson implies that the people of
Dan were under Philistine control, and this would certainly have meant
the payment of tribute in the form of agricultural surpluses. Judges 15:
9–13 also claims that the people of Judah (probably those in the
Shephelah) had lost their independence to the Philistines. Following the
defeat of the combined Israelite forces by the Philistines at the battles
of Aphek, the Philistines seem to have established garrisons in Israelite
territory. A passage in 1 Samuel (13:16–18) mentions a garrison in
Michmash, and says that three parties of Philistines left the garrison,
going in different directions to collect produce. The following verses,
19–22 (a passage whose Hebrew text may be partly corrupt) says that
there was no smith in Israel and that the Israelites had to go to the
Philistines to get their agricultural implements sharpened.

This passage has often been interpreted to mean that the Philistines
had a monopoly of iron and that this gave them a technological advantage over the Israelites, an advantage that the Philistines exploited to
the point where they let the Israelites have iron agricultural tools to
increase the surpluses that the Philistines could then take. In fact, the
passage says nothing about iron; and recent research (summarized by
Frick 1985, pp. 173–189) suggests that the Philistines did not have a
monopoly of iron and that, in any case, iron was not initially superior
to bronze. Also, both bronze and iron plough-points were used in settlements after iron became more widely available.

In fact, 1 Samuel 13: 19–22 is concerned mainly with a Philistine
strategy, designed to prevent the Israelites from having military weapons.
To this end, the Philistines restricted the activities of travelling groups
of metal-workers, with the result that, whatever the metal involved, the
Israelites could get agricultural tools sharpened and repaired only on
Philistine terms. However, this indicates a vastly different situation in
Israelite life compared with the period when villages were mostly
independent and self-supporting. Agricultural surpluses had to be produced for the Philistine overlords, and in bad years this almost certainly
meant that the villages did not have enough for their own needs.

A new situation arose when Saul was appointed to lead the Israelites
against the Philistines. Saul needed some kind of regular army, and this
meant that men had to be taken from villages and that surpluses had
to be organized to feed the army. First Samuel 14: 52 says that whenever
Saul saw a strong man fit for war he took him into his service. Light
is further thrown on the new situation by 1 Samuel 17: 12–18, which
recounts how David's three eldest brothers joined Saul's army. Whatever
may be the difficulty of reconciling 1 Samuel 17 with the fact that in
1 Samuel 16: 22 David is already Saul's armour-bearer, verses 12–18
possibly indicate the problems of recruitment and supplies for Saul's
army. The departure of David's brothers for the army would reduce
the manpower available for agricultural production. David is told by
his father to go to the scene of battle to deliver parched corn (wheat)

and bread to his brothers, and cheese to the commanders. It may be that, at this stage in Israel's development, each family or village was responsible for supplying food for those of its members in Saul's army. This would depend, however, on how far away the fighting was from the homes of the soldiers. In the story of 1 Samuel 17, the fighting was some 20 miles (32 kilometres) from David's home, Bethlehem.

The length and character of Saul's reign will be discussed in chapter 4, but if we assume that Saul initially defeated the Philistines and gave relief to his people, this does not mean that conditions returned to the tranquillity that we have assumed for 1200 BCE. A permanent change had occurred, and this would develop to the point where the independence and self-sufficiency of the Israelite villages and towns would vanish.

When, in 1 Samuel 8: 5, the elders of Israel ask Samuel to appoint a king over them he replies (verses 11-17):

[a king] will take your sons and will use them for his chariot and his horses, and they will run before his chariot. He will make them commanders of fifties; they will have to plough his land and harvest his harvest and make his weapons of war and of riding . . . . He will take the best of your fields and vineyards and olive trees and give them to his officials; he will take a tenth of your grain and your vines and will give it to his courtiers and officials . . . . He will take a tenth of your flocks; and you will become his slaves.

Although this passage in its present form was written much later than the time of Saul, it accurately spells out the implications of having a centrally controlled state. Already in Saul's time, enlisted soldiers were rewarded by gifts of land, as indicated in Saul's mocking remark, ''Will the son of Jesse [i.e. David] give you fields and vineyards and make you commanders of thousands and hundreds?'' (1 Samuel 22: 7). The implication is that the king can and does reward his servants with gifts of land, although at this time such gifts were probably of unowned land.

The reign of David saw an increased concentration of land in the hands of people close to the king. David acquired Jerusalem by right of conquest, and also inherited Saul's possessions. Second Samuel 9:7 records that David summoned Saul's grandson Mephibosheth and promised to restore to him the property of Saul. David also ordered Siba, Saul's servant, to administer the property, and to give enough of its produce to Mephibosheth to enable the latter to live at David's court (2 Samuel 9: 10). Siba apparently had fifteen sons and twenty servants. The latter were not necessarily slaves, but probably men who had freely entered the service of Saul. Nonetheless, they had to be supported or they had to work, and therefore Saul had acquired property. It is also to be noted, from 1 Samuel 14: 28–32, that David's son Absalom and David's commander-in-chief Joab had adjacent property which, in Absalom's case, was worked by his servants. This again suggests gifts of land by the king to his family and commanders, and the employment of people who entered their service to look after the agriculture of the land. A further development in the reign of David was the establishment of an elite bodyguard, the Cerethim and Pelethim commanded by Benaiah (2 Samuel 8: 18). Here was another group of agriculturally non-productive people who had to be supported and who, on retirement, would expect to be rewarded with land.

It is in the reign of Solomon, however, that the agricultural implications of centralization reach their climax. In 1 Kings 4: 7–19 twelve officials are named, who were put in charge of twelve regions, each of which had to provide for the king and his court for a month. 1 Kings 5: 2–3 lists what was required daily to maintain the luxury of the king and his household. It is noticeable that some of the officials in charge of the districts were Solomon's sons-in-law — for example, the son of Abinadab (1 Kings 4: 11) and Ahimaaz (1 Kings 4: 15). It would be a mistake to suppose that the demands of the court were imposed upon an agricultural base that remained constant in size or got smaller. The likelihood is that, under the early monarchy, new towns were built and many terraces were constructed. These were also royal estates and managers; 1 Chronicles lists officers of David who were in charge of fields, vineyards, orchards, and olive groves and herds of sheep, goats, and camels. Also, David had conquered neighbouring peoples, such as those of Ammon, Moab, Edom, and Damascus, and these subject peoples paid tribute to David, and to Solomon for some of his reign.

Solomon's building works placed additional burdens upon the agricultural population. According to 1 Kings 5: 13–16, Solomon conscripted 30,000 workers who worked a shift system whereby in any month 10,000 worked in Lebanon, presumably preparing timber, and the other 20,000 were at home. This pattern of one month on duty and two months at home was probably designed to minimize the effect of such programmes upon the manpower needed to produce agricultural goods. No such shift arrangements are recorded, however, for the 70,000 porters, the 80,000 quarriers, and the 3,600 supervisors mentioned in 2 Chronicles 2: 2. Although these numbers are, of course, enormously inflated, they remind us of the obvious but necessary fact that extensive building projects involved the recruiting of workers, and that even if these were paid for their work, they were absent from the land, and had to be fed from central resources while they were away from home.

A little later, it will be necessary to ask how the kings acquired land, and how the picture so far presented can be reconciled with the Old Testament insistence that the land belonging to a family was not to be disposed of. First, however, we must complete this sketch of the effects of the monarchy upon land use.

Returning to Solomon, we note that in addition to maintaining a lavish court and engaging in building projects, he also imported luxury items, which are recorded in 1 Kings 10. He also incurred debts, which he paid off by ceding twenty cities in Galilee to Hiram (1 Kings 9: 1–13). It is not thus surprising that when he was succeeded by Rehoboam, the elders of the northern tribes asked the new king to lighten the burden that his father had imposed upon them (1 Kings 12: 4). Rehoboam's refusal was one of the causes of the revolt of the northern tribes and the establishment of the northern kingdom of Israel (1 Kings 12: 16–19).

The loss of the northern kingdom of Israel to the Assyrians in 734–721 BCE brought changes to land ownership and use in the Samaria and Bethel hills. The prominent families were taken to Assyria and were replaced by clients of the Assyrian king. The land given to them was probably a reward for services rendered (2 Kings 17: 6, 24). We are not to think of the wholesale transfer of populations to and from Assyria; many ordinary Israelites remained, but they were now the servants of foreign landowners. In the southern kingdom, Judah, it is recorded of King Uzziah (c. 767–739 BCE) that he loved the land, and that he sponsored agriculture in the Negev region, besides possessing herds of cattle in the coastal plain and the Shephelah and fields and vineyards in the hill country (2 Chronicles 26: 10).

How did the kings acquire land? Whenever possible, they bought it or acquired it by exchange. David purchased a threshing floor in Jerusalem for the site of the Temple (2 Samuel 24: 18–25). Omri purchased a site from Shemer, on which to build his capital, Samaria (1 Kings 16: 24). And Ahab, though regarded as a particularly evil king by the Old Testament writers, tried initially to acquire a vineyard belonging to his neighbour Naboth by purchase or exchange (1 Kings 21: 2). When he failed, however, he resorted to another method: that of taking possession of the land of anyone put to death for a capital offence. This was the fate of Naboth's vineyard, after Queen Jezebel had arranged for Naboth to be wrongly accused, tried, and executed (1 Kings 21: 14–16). Also, all land conquered by the king — for example the coastal plain occupied by the Philistines — or land which was not otherwise owned — became the property of the crown. As was indicated earlier, many parts of the Samaria, Bethel, and Hebron hills were forested and unoccupied at the beginning of David's reign, and such areas could be given to royal servants, or might become royal estates, to be cleared and developed by royal officials.

What about the Old Testament ideal that a family's land should not be disposed of? Naboth's refusal to sell or exchange his vineyard was based on the conviction that he should not dispose of the "inheritance of the fathers" (1 Kings 21: 3). Jeremiah, while he was detained in Jerusalem in the year of its destruction (587 BCE), bought a field from his cousin Hanamel in accordance with his duty as nearest relative to keep the land in the family (Jeremiah 32: 6–13). In the book of Ruth, the land still belonging to Naomi, in spite of her ten-year absence from her home, Bethlehem, is purchased by Boaz after Naomi's closest relative refuses to carry out his duty (Ruth 4).

These passages indicate that during the monarchy land was owned by individual families, and that it was the duty of relatives to help any members of the family that found themselves in difficulties. In the case of Jeremiah's cousin Hanamel, we can suppose that he had been unable to produce sufficient grain and fruit to feed his family and to provide surpluses required by the state. Several dry winters could have this effect. He was therefore forced to borrow either grain or its equivalent in silver, for which he may have paid interest of 60 per cent. Another bad harvest would have left him short of food, and unable to repay the debt and its interest. In this situation he sold his land to his nearest relative, Jeremiah. This did not mean that Hanamel would now vacate the land and that Jeremiah would work it. Rather, Hanamel would use the purchase price to pay off his debts, and Jeremiah would become Hanamel's landlord, entitled to some of the surplus. As soon as possible, Hanamel would re-purchase the land.

In principle, this was an excellent social mechanism, designed to preserve the independence of families on their own landholdings. In practice, it sometimes worked out differently. Isaiah 5: 8 attacks those who join house to house, and field to field until there is nowhere left in the land for anyone else's property. Amos (8: 4–6) condemns those who exploit the poor by selling grain at exorbitant prices and who force the poor to sell themselves into slavery. What do such passages imply?

Let us go back to Hanamel and suppose that neither Jeremiah nor any other relative was in a position to buy the land. Hanamel would then have been forced to sell to someone outside the family, who might well have evicted him and his dependants, obliging him to become a day-labourer. If this failed to produce a living wage — and day-labouring was a precarious occupation — he might then have been obliged to sell his children or himself into slavery. More will be said of this in the next section. It is clear, however, that because of exorbitant rates of interest and high prices for grain (Amos 8: 5), families that could not grow enough food to support themselves and provide the necessary surpluses would quickly be in difficulties that relatives could not necessarily help them to overcome. Also, we must not rule out the possibility that some landowners did not hesitate to deal harshly with their own relatives, and even to dispossess or enslave them.

In social terms, the situation that existed, and which was criticized by Isaiah and Amos, was one in which there were two classes, the landed and the landless. Among the landed were those who exploited the landless poor by hiring them as day-labourers for low wages, by selling them food at inflated prices, and by charging exorbitant interest if they made a loan. The wealth accumulated by these exploiters was spent on luxury items. Amos mentions that such people had winter houses (probably in the warmer zones of the Jordan Valley) and summer houses, and rooms or furniture inlaid with ivory (Amos 3: 15). Their women were well-fed and fat (a desirable attribute in ancient Israel) like Bashan cows (Amos 4: 1). Their days were spent feasting, drinking wine, and singing songs (Amos 6: 4–6). Isaiah 3: 16–23 lists the luxury ornaments and clothes possessed by the women of well-to-do families in Jerusalem.

This exploitation, which resulted in a landed wealthy class and an impoverished landless class, has been called rent capitalism (Lang 1985, pp. 93–99). It is interesting that none of the prophets' criticism of these abuses was directed specifically at the monarchy. However, the development of rent capitalism had been made possible by the rise of the monarchy, which had brought about drastic changes in land ownership and use compared with the situation around 1200 BCE (Alt 1970, pp. 367–391).

LAND AND LAND USE 587–63 BCE

In 587 BCE Jerusalem fell to the Babylonians for the second time in ten years, and the king and other prominent Judahites joined those who had been taken into exile in Babylon in 597 (2 Kings 24: 14–16, 25: 18–21, cp. Jeremiah 52: 28–30). Gedaliah was appointed governor of Judah by the Babylonians in Mizpah and he encouraged the people remaining in that land, as well as those who had fled for safety across the Jordan Valley, to get on with the harvest (Jeremiah 40: 10–12). Jerusalem had fallen in the month of March, and thus there was an abundant harvest of grapes and figs that year (Jeremiah 40: 12). With Babylonian armies in the land, there would have been little possibility of planting grain in the previous winter whereas mature vines and fig trees needed little attention.

Jeremiah 41–2 records the murder of Gedaliah by Ishmael and the flight of many of the people to Egypt. Also, the southern part of Judah was occupied by the Edomites, who probably appropriated the land for themselves. We know nothing about the situation in Judah between 582 and 539 BCE, but we can guess that many of the wealthy landowners had been exiled, and that the poorer people who remained may have been able to repossess their own land, or land that was abandoned.

According to Ezra 1: 1ff., a decree of Cyrus, king of Persia, in 539 allowed the Jews to return from Babylon to Judah in order to rebuild the Temple. We do not know how many people returned. The list of returning Jews in Ezra 2: 1–70 does not date from that period, as the same passage is connected with the situation in 445 in Nehemiah 7: 6–72; in any case, it is difficult to see how more than 50,000 people (Ezra 2: 64–5) could have been received, accommodated, and provided for in a land that probably barely met the needs of the existing inhabitants. The picture presented in Haggai 2: 10 and Zechariah 1–8, in prophecies dating around 520 BCE, is one of massive agricultural failure, with disappointing yields caused by poor weather (Haggai 2: 16–17). The prophets attributed these disasters to the failure of the people to rebuild the Temple, and they promised that when this was done, the fertility of the land would be restored (Haggai 2: 19; Zechariah 8: 12).

Hans Kippenberg (1982, p. 47) has suggested that in the period beginning in 539 BCE, when Judah was administered as a Persian province, agriculture was diverted from cereals to vines and olives. Judah certainly was now confined, territorially, to a small area roughly 30 by 30 miles (48 by 48 kilometres) comprising the southern part of the Bethel Hills, the Jerusalem Saddle, and the northern part of the Hebron Hills, together with a small part of the Shephelah. This was not an area especially suited for cereals, and it certainly is plausible that the population intensified their production of wine and olive oil so as to make surpluses that could be sold in return for cereals.

Only at the time of Nehemiah (445–420 BCE) do we get detailed information about the situation in Judah. Nehemiah 5 records the complaints brought by some of the people against their relatives. One group complained that they had to pledge their children in order to get cereals to eat. Another group had to pledge fields, vineyards, and houses in order to get cereals. A third group complained about the taxes that they had to pay to the king. This probably meant that they had to produce surpluses to trade for coinage in which the taxes were paid.

The culprits in this situation were the wealthier Jews and officials. Indeed, Nehemiah 5: 8 implies that Nehemiah had been purchasing the freedom of Jews who had become the slaves of foreigners, while wealthy people were actually selling fellow Jews to foreigners. Nehemiah called a meeting of the culprits and confronted them with what they were doing. They agreed to his demand that they should cancel the debts owed to them, and that they should return the fields, houses, and vineyards that they had acquired to their former owners. Nehemiah himself agreed to cancel the debts owed to him.

This reform raises the question of the origin of Leviticus 25. The chapter begins with the Sabbath year law, according to which the land must lie fallow once every seven years. (Recent research [Hopkins 1985, pp. 200–202] indicates that the custom of fallowing was actually much more frequent than this, at any rate in the Iron Age.) The chapter then introduces the custom of the jubilee year, that is, every fiftieth year, in which all land must revert to its original owners. (The year would be opened by the blowing of a trumpet, or *yōbhēl*, from which the word ''jubilee'' is derived.) The chapter further enjoins that no interest must be charged on loans (verses 35–38). In the jubilee year, those who have been forced to sell themselves into slavery not only will become free, together with their wives and children, but will return and take possesison of their lands (verses 39–43).

Were these laws formulated in order to confirm Nehemiah's reform? Certainly if they existed before Nehemiah's time, they were disregarded; and it is strange that Nehemiah did not appeal to these laws — for example the law forbidding the charging of interest — when confronting those who had exploited their kin. It is probably safe to say that, in its present form, Leviticus 25 presupposes Nehemiah's reforms and represents an attempt to subordinate economic interests to theological convictions. The land must be allowed to rest in the seventh year as a reminder to the Jews that they are Yhwh's people, and that it was he who gave them the land in the first place (Leviticus 25: 38). He did not give it to his people so that they could exploit those who had fallen on hard times; and slavery was an unacceptable permanent situation for Jews to be in, because God had delivered his people from slavery in Egypt (Leviticus 25: 55).

These noble ideas were practised only so long as they could be enforced by someone in authority. In the late fourth century BCE Judah became part of the Egyptian empire of the successors of Alexander the Great, and then, about 200 BCE, became part of the Syrian empire of Alexander's successors. Although these events left little trace in the Old Testament (cp. Daniel 11) and will not be discussed in detail here, the new rulers of Judah exacted taxes, which were collected by powerful members of the Jewish aristocracy, and permitted slavery (Kippenberg 1982, pp. 79–81). Although the revolt of the Jews led by the Maccabees in 167 BCE was, among other things, an attempt to throw off foreign domination so that Jewish laws could be obeyed, the Hasmonean dynasty that thus became established took on the form of an oriental despotic monarchy. It was as a protest against such government that groups such as those at Qumran were established as an attempt to re-establish the people of God on the basis of his laws.

THE THEOLOGICAL SIGNIFICANCE OF THE LAND

The aim of this chapter has been to sketch the appearance of the land of Israel, and to give an outline of how the people used it in Old Testament times. Up to this point we have presented a social and historical view, and have shown how, following the rise of the monarchy, the story is mainly one of the exploitation of the weak by the strong. Even the exile in Babylon did not bring any fundamental changes; indeed, the situation described in Nehemiah 5 is one of exploitation quite as bad as anything criticized by the eighth-century prophets. The reforms of Nehemiah, and their reflection in Leviticus 25, represented an ideal which was scarcely ever realized in the Old Testament period.

But there is another direction from which this subject can be approached: the theological direction. For whatever the social realities may have been in Israel, when the Old Testament is read as a whole, the land is an important symbol, in terms of which Israel's understanding of God is expressed (see Brueggeman 1977).

The story of the Hebrews begins in Genesis 12: 1–8, with the story of Abraham, who became landless in response to the call of God to leave his present home in Haran, north Mesopotamia, and to the promise of God that he will be given a new home. That new home, the land of Canaan, will not be for Abraham only, but also for his descendants (Genesis 13: 14–18). Between the promise and its fulfilment, however, there are many stumbling blocks. His grandson Jacob flees to Haran, because of Esau's anger (Genesis 27: 42–5), although on the way he also is promised the land of Canaan (Genesis 28: 13–14). Later, Jacob and all his family go down to Egypt at the beginning of a sojourn that lasts, according to the story, for 430 years (Exodus 12: 40).

The Exodus from Egypt is the movement of a landless people towards a land of their own — although again, there are many hazards involved, not least some of the people's despairing belief that slavery in Egypt was preferable to freedom in the wilderness (Exodus 16: 2–3). When the goal is finally reached, two new dangers arise. The first is that the Israelites will become self-sufficient in their land and will forget God (Deuteronomy 8: 7–18). The second is that they will forsake their God in favour of the gods of the peoples already in Canaan (Deuteronomy 7: 1–5).

The land as the place where Israel lives in the presence of God now becomes a testing ground. Will Israel live faithful to God's commandments or not? According to the prophetic witness, the people do not live faithfully, and so a new element appears: that of the threat of exile. There will be a movement from possessing the land to being once more landless. This idea is found particularly strongly in the book of Jeremiah, who lived through the period of the destruction of the Temple and the exiles of 597 and 587 (Jeremiah 25). Jeremiah also proclaimed, however, that there would be a return (Jeremiah 32: 14–15), and in the words of the prophet of the return (Isaiah 40–55), the movement back to the land is seen as a new exodus and a return across the desert (Isaiah 43: 14–21).

Yet the return to the land was, in fact, a time of disappointment. One of the most moving passages in the whole of the Old Testament is the prayer of the people in Nehemiah 9. This ends with the words:

> You gave this land to our fathers so that we could enjoy its fruits and its riches; but now we live in it as slaves. Its rich produce goes to the kings, whom you have set up over us because of our sins. They rule over us and our cattle according to their desires: therefore we are in great need.

In view of such a sentiment, it is no surprise that in the years that followed Nehemiah, there were attempts to regain Israel's control over the land and hopes that God would intervene to restore the land fully in accordance with his ancient promises.

The Old Testament cannot be fully understood without an appreciation of the land of Israel. Geography, social history, and theology combine to assist our reading and to stimulate our imagination.

CHAPTER 2

SOCIAL ORGANIZATION

Anyone who reads the Old Testament soon comes across a phrase such as, "X the son of Y". Normally we pass over such information without paying too much attention to it. Most of us do not know very much about our families farther back than our grandparents; nor would it make much difference to our lives, although it might be interesting, if we could trace our ancestry back over many generations. In the Old Testament, the situation is different, and if we can think ourselves into the Old Testament way of viewing social relationships, this will certainly assist our reading.

In Britain and North America men identify themselves by a surname, such as Smith, and a forename, such as John. Women either adopt their husband's surname or retain their own. In our society, with its focus upon the individual, a person tends to think of his or her surname as something belonging to himself or herself. Even though a surname is a family name, that fact does not mean very much to most of us. There are, of course, a few family names that convey, first and foremost, the idea of a family; one example is Kennedy; another is Windsor; but these are the exceptions.

In the Old Testament there is no such thing as a surname. However, this does not mean that families cannot be identified or that they lack importance. On the contrary, the Old Testament way of identifying a person allows his (the word is used deliberately) family connections to be established in a more comprehensive fashion than the British or North American system allows.

BLOOD TIES

In 1 Samuel 9: 1 Saul is introduced as the son of Kish, the son of Abiel, the son of Zeror, the son of Bechorath, the son of Aphiah. It may seem excessive to us, and it is slightly unusual even in the Old Testament to identify a person in terms of his descent back to his great-great-grandfather. Moreover, it is almost impossible for us today to know what sort of an impact this introduction was intended to make upon the readers. The passage does, however, enable us to see the advantage of the Israelite way of identifying people.

What we have in 1 Samuel 9: 1 is a *maximal lineage* — that is, a quick way of linking Saul back to Aphiach, whom we can take to be the person after whom the maximal lineage is named. However, Saul not only had a maximal lineage; he had an *ordinary lineage* as well — that is, one that linked him to his immediate family. We can deduce from 1 Samuel 14: 49–51 that Saul's grandfather Abiel had another son, named Ner, whose son Abner (Saul's cousin) was Saul's commander-in-chief:

However, Abiel may well have had brothers, and so may have Zeror, Bechorath, and Aphiah. Saul's maximal lineage might be set out as follows:

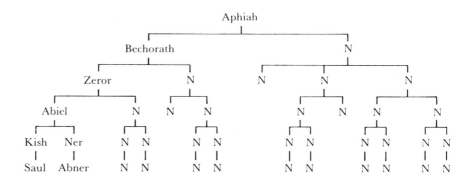

Although this reconstruction is purely artificial, it will help to make the point that each of the persons named in Saul's maximal lineage had descendants, who were therefore Saul's relatives, and the farther back the maximal lineage goes, the greater the number of relatives.

In early Israelite society it was important to know who one's relatives were. There was no centrally-organized police force to maintain law and order and to punish wrongdoers. A person's safety was a function of the group to which he or she belonged, and in terms of war it was the duty of those who were related to each other to stand together. There are two illustrations of this in the Old Testament, both dealing with Saul's tribe, that of Benjamin.

The first incident concerns Saul himself. In 1 Samuel 11, it is recorded that the Ammonite king Nahash threatened the inhabitants of Jabesh-gilead, a village in Transjordan to the north of Ammon. The villagers sent messengers to Israel requesting help, and when they reached Saul, he immediately sprang into action; he organized an army of Israelites and eventually defeated the Ammonite king. We might say that Saul reacted as he did because he was the king, although it is doubtful whether we should think of Saul as being the same sort of king as Solomon and his successors, with their highly developed government. Be that as it may, the possibility is that Saul was distantly related to the people of Jabesh-gilead. According to Judges 21: 10–14, four hundred virgins had once been taken from Jabesh-gilead and given as wives to the men of Benjamin, following a vow by the rest of the tribes that they would not give their women to the Benjamites as wives. Admittedly, we have only one instance in the Old Testament of a descent group based on the female line (Judges 9: 1); but unless a woman was expected to sever all ties with her family when she married, we can suppose that links established through marriages also had social implications in Israel. Thus, Saul may well have been going to the aid of relatives.

The other incident precedes that in which the virgins of Jabesh-gilead were given to the Benjaminites. It is the account in Judges 20 of a violent confrontation between Benjamin and the eleven other tribes, in which the latter gained the upper hand only with some difficulty. The reason for the confrontation was that the tribes wanted to punish the Benjaminite town of Gibeah for an outrage that it had committed against a traveller's concubine (Judges 19). The Benjaminites refused to allow the other tribes to punish Gibeah, and stood by their fellow tribesmen, at great cost to themselves. Whatever we may think about the historicity of this narrative, its social attitudes underline the concept of solidarity — in this case, the solidarity of the tribe of Benjamin with a threatened Benjaminite village.

So far, we have stressed the importance of blood ties between families for the purposes of mutual defence. Two other social mechanisms that depend on blood ties in the Old Testament are blood revenge and the redemption of land and persons.

In the absence of a central authority with a police force and powers of arrest and trial, justice is organized on a local basis through social groups and their representatives. Some crimes, however — and, in particular, homicide — call for drastic and immediate action against the wrongdoer. In ancient Israel this action was taken by the "avenger of blood", a close relative of the murdered person, whose duty it was to find and kill the murderer. It would appear from the Old Testament that orginally the avenger of blood was entitled to pursue a killer even if the killing had been accidental. In Numbers 35: 9–29 certain "cities of refuge" are designated, to which persons can flee if they have accidentally killed someone. If such a killer gets to the "city of refuge" without being killed by the "avenger of blood', and the inhabitants of that city accept that the killing was an accident, the killer can remain there in safety. However, the "avenger of blood" is entitled to take the killer's life if the latter leaves the "city of refuge". This state of affairs lasts until the death of the high priest, after which the killer can leave the "city of refuge" and return to a normal life. As a social mechanism, the law of blood revenge was not peculiar to Israel (Bohanan 1967, pp. 303ff.). It was not only a device for punishing murderers; it was also a powerful sanction. Anyone contemplating a murder would have to reckon with the fact that the intended victim's relatives had the duty to avenge the killing.

We have already touched, in the previous chapter, upon the redemption of land and persons. If a man fell onto hard times, and was forced to sell either himself or his family in order to pay his debts, it was the duty of his relatives to come to his aid, and to buy the land or the man and his family, with a view to the situation being reversed as soon as possible (cp. Leviticus 25: 14–31, 35–43, 47–55). Of course, this ideal, as we have noted, often did not work out in practice. Quarrels between members of a family were as common in ancient Israel as in any other society. Two familiar stories in the Old Testament tell of the conflict between the brothers Cain and Abel (Genesis 4: 1–16) and between Jacob and Esau (Genesis 27). Even if these characters belong more to the realm of legend than to history, the stories reflect something of filial rivalry in those distant times. Such lapses from the ideal, however, do not diminish the importance of kinship networks as powerful social mechanisms in ancient Israel.

CONFLICTING LOYALTIES

So far, this chapter has stressed that there was a different perception in ancient Israel about the relation of individuals to the social groups to which they belonged, compared with attitudes in modern Western society. The next section will show how Old Testament narratives can be illuminated if we take the trouble to work out the social networks that they imply.

We have already seen that Saul appointed his cousin Abner as his commander. In the case of David, this patronage within the family was to continue (see 1 Chronicles 2: 13–17).

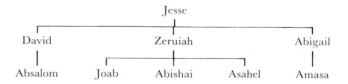

Joab, who was David's commander, was also his nephew. Moreover, Joab and David's son Absalom were first cousins. Thus, when we read about a certain amount of collusion between Joab and Absalom in 2 Samuel 14, when the latter had been banished from court, we are not dealing merely with relations between a royal prince and the top-ranking professional soldier but with members of the same family. When Absalom rebelled against David and forced him to flee from Jerusalem (2 Samuel 15–18), Absalom appointed another first cousin, Amasa, as commander-in-chief in Joab's place (2 Samuel 17–25). In the battle between the forces of David and Absalom, Absalom was deliberately killed by Joab (2 Samuel 18: 14–15), despite David's forbidding this; Joab also later killed Amasa (2 Samuel 20: 8–10). Whatever Joab's motives may have been, we read the narrative in a new light when we realize that his victims were his first cousins.

Family relationships may also help us to understand David's apparent inability to control Joab. Repeatedly, Joab disobeys David and gets away with it, at least during David's lifetime. For example, David disapproves of Joab's murder of Abner, even though this is in revenge for Abner's killing of Joab's brother Asahel (2 Samuel 2: 19–23; 3: 22–27.) David sings a lament at Abner's funeral about the stupidity and waste of Abner's murder, and then says the astonishing words.

Although I am anointed king I am today too weak, and these men the sons of Zeruiah are too strong for me (2 Samuel 3: 39).

As we have seen, Joab even killed Absalom against David's instructions, as well as Amasa, whom David had confirmed as commander-in-chief after Absalom's death.

In trying to understand the relationship between David and Joab we may at first conclude that David was unwilling to punish a relative, even though Joab evidently had no such scruples. If we try to probe more deeply, we are struck by the fact that Joab's father is never named. Joab and his brothers are always called the sons of Zeruiah, their mother. Who was Joab's father? All that we are told is that he was a Bethlehemite (2 Samuel 2: 32). A fragment of genealogy in 2 Samuel 17: 25 suggests that his grandfather may have been the Ammonite king Nahash.

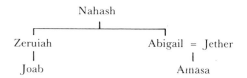

On the face of it, this seems absurd, because Zeruiah was David's sister, or half-sister, and we can only reconcile 2 Samuel 17: 25 with 1 Chronicles 2: 13–17 by supposing either (a) that Abigail's mother was married to Nahash before she married Jesse, or (b) that this same woman was the mother of both Abigail and Zeruiah by Nahash before she married Jesse.

The mention of Nahash in the text could be rejected as a corruption of the text, were it not for indications elsewhere that David was in fact on good terms with Nahash the Ammonite king. When Nahash died, David sent messengers to his son to console him. "I will show favour to Hanun the son of Nahash even as his father showed favour to me" (2 Samuel 10: 2). The fact that Hanun misinterpreted this action and insulted David's messengers could have been based on a suspicion that David wanted to lay claim to the Ammonite throne on the basis of being Nahash's wife's son, and thus a sort of half-brother to Hanun.

Again, when David fled from Absalom, he crossed the River Jordan to the west of Ammonite territory, and there he was supplied with food by Shobi the son of Nahash (2 Samuel 17: 27). A close connection between David and Nahash cannot therefore be ruled out; and if it is likely, it not only suggests an explanation for Joab's power over David (an agreement to try to conceal their Ammonite connection?) but also sheds light on the relationship between David and Saul. Saul, after all, had delivered the people of Jabesh-gilead from Nahash (1 Samuel 11).

Another narrative in which it helps to work out who was related to whom is that of Jeremiah 36–41. A good starting-point is 2 Kings 22: 3–13, the account of the finding of the book of the law in the reign of Josiah (622/1 BCE). Two of the people involved with the discovery are the state-secretary Shaphan and his son Ahikam. Also mentioned is Achbor. We now turn to Jeremiah 26, which records events that took place around 608 BCE — that is, about fourteen years after the discovery of the law book. Here we find that the son of Achbor, namely Elnathan, was entrusted with pursuing the prophet Uriah to Egypt and bringing him back to Jerusalem to be executed (Jeremiah 26: 20–23). We are also told that Jeremiah himself escaped a similar fate, being protected by Ahikam, son of Shaphan.

Jeremiah's support by the family of Shaphan is further indicated by the fact that Jeremiah's letter to the exiles in Babylon (Jeremiah 29) was conveyed by another son of Shaphan, Elasah (29: 3). If we turn to Jeremiah 36, dated around 605 BCE, we find that when Jeremiah's secretary, Baruch, read from the scroll that Jeremiah had dictated, he did it in a chamber that another son of Shaphan, Gemariah, had in the Temple. Among the officials to whom the news was brought that Baruch had read the scroll were the state-secretary Elishamah; Gemariah, son of Shaphan; and Elnathan, son of Achbor. If we now move to Jeremiah 39, dated to 587 BCE, we find that Gedaliah, to whom was entrusted the administration of Judah by the Babylonians, was the son of Ahikam (who had protected Jeremiah) son of Shaphan; and it was to Gedaliah's charge that Jeremiah was committed (Jeremiah 39: 13–14, 40: 6). Gedaliah was murdered, however, by Ishmael, son of Nethaniah, son of Elishamah — presumably the Elishamah who was presiding as state-secretary when the scroll was read by Baruch eighteen years earlier. We can represent some of these relationships as follows:

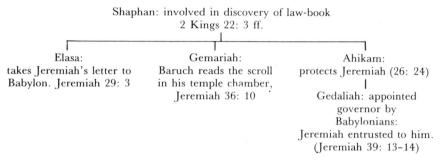

On the basis of this, we see that with the ranks of the officials who ran the administration of Judah — at any rate from 630 to 587 BCE — there were powerful families with conflicting interests. The family of Shaphan was supportive to Jeremiah, and may, therefore, have agreed with his policy, which favoured submission to Babylon. The family of Elishamah, on the other hand, took a different view, and after the fall of Jerusalem, the grandson of Elishamah assassinated the grandson of Shaphan. This was, perhaps, in the eyes of the Elishamah family, a way of punishing the Shaphan family for its pro-Babylonian sympathies. Such a reading of the text helps to place Jeremiah's activity in the context of the politics of his day, as well as making sense of the lists of names with which Jeremiah 36–41 abounds.

THE FUNCTION OF GENEALOGIES

The next aim in this chapter is to consider the function of the genealogies, especially those in Genesis and 1 Chronicles. When this has been done we shall be in a position to describe in a more technical manner the social organization of Israel and the history of its development in the Old Testament.

We have already noted that in the Old Testament a person is defined in terms of the group to which he or she belongs. This is an indication of a desire to construct an orderly social world in which each individual and each larger social unit can be plotted and therefore classified. It is the social equivalent to the mapping and classifying of the objects of the natural world which will be discussed below in chapters 8 and 11, which deal with creation and sacrifice. Without such classifying, the world would be a chaos of unrelated phenomena; classifying brings the chaos into order and helps a society and its members to locate themselves within a meaningful framework.

This is the function of the genealogies in Genesis chapters 5, 10, and 11: 10–31. They place the family of Abraham on a genealogical map that indicates how the whole of the human race had grown and divided since the days of Adam and Eve, the supposed first human beings. These parts of Genesis, greatly abbreviated and simplified, can be represented as follows:

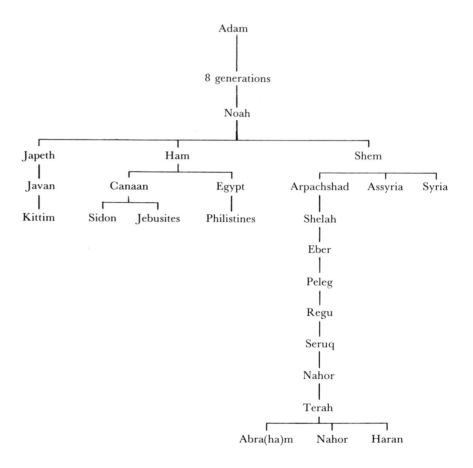

This genealogical map not only locates Abraham in relation to the rest of the human race; it expresses the affinities and distances in relation to other peoples that were felt by the Old Testament writers. There is a closer affinity with Assyria and Syria than with Egypt; and it is noticeable that peoples such as the Jebusites and the Philistines, with whom the Israelites competed for the land of Israel, are perceived as belonging to a different branch of the human race from the family of Abraham.

As the narrative of Genesis proceeds, further genealogies express perceived relationships with Israel's immediate neighbours.

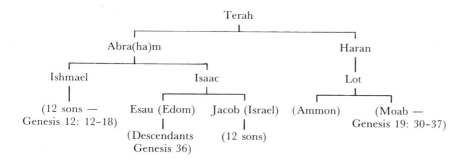

The peoples of Ammon and Moab are seen as Israel's second cousins, whereas the Edomites are brothers, and the Ishmaelites (inhabitants of the Negev, to the south of Judah) are first cousins. Along with these perceived affinities are elements in the narrative that serve to stress the "purity" of Israel as against the "mixed" or "impure" origins of the adjacent peoples. Thus, Ishmael is Abraham's son by Sarah's Egyptian maidservant Hagar (Genesis 16: 1–14); Esau married various foreign women (Genesis 26: 34–5); and Lot's children were born of an incestuous relationship between him and his two daughters (Genesis 19: 30–37). Israel is related to the neighbouring peoples, but it alone has preserved the "purity" of the family of Terah.

This point brings us to a consideration of the genealogies of Isaac and Jacob. They can be shown as follows:

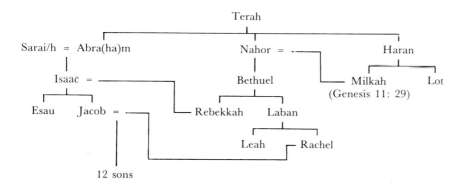

An interesting feature of the genealogy is a tendency to marry across the generations. Nahor married his niece; Isaac married his cousin's daughter; and although Jacob married his uncle's daughters, they are a generation farther away from the common ancestor than Jacob. In fact, the genealogy is probably a "fiction" designed to link the

17.190.1804

Joseph receiving his brothers.

families of Abraham and Jacob to a common ancestor via the shadowy figure of Isaac. Although the matter cannot be discussed here, it has long been recognized that the Abraham and Jacob cycles of stories developed independently of each other — a fact re-emphasized by the most recent research on the origins of the Pentateuch. "Israel" was probably an association of groups of diverse origins, around whose ancestors various traditions collected. One of the purposes of Genesis was to link these ancestors together by means of genealogy and story and then to plot this unified story onto a larger genealogical canvas. To call this ''fiction'' is not to describe it as deceit or fraud. Genealogies, for ancient Israel as for many other peoples, were not a type of history; rather, they were the expression of a need to plot existing local social realities onto a chart that explained them in terms of a comprehensive scheme, So far as we can tell, the genealogies and stories of Abraham and Jacob date from the late monarchy (seventh–sixth centuries BCE), whereas genealogies in the early chapters of Genesis did not reach their present form until probably the fifth century BCE. This does not mean, however, that this material was simply invented at those times. What we now have almost certainly contains earlier attempts to map the genealogical relationships of the Israelites. In their present and final form the genealogies reflect the social realities of the time of their final redaction.

The genealogies in 1 Chronicles 1–9 reproduce much of the material in Genesis, adding to them genealogies of eleven tribes. In one case, that of Naphthali, the information is very sparse, and simply lists four sons of Naphthali, the information being taken from Genesis 46: 24. In the case of the tribe of Dan, 1 Chronicles had no information at all. Probably, the compiler did not think that it was worthwhile listing the one son of Dan recorded in Genesis 46: 23! There is also no mention of Zebulon. The reason probably is that these tribes, which occupied Upper Galilee, had been absorbed into the kingdom of Syria since the ninth century, and little or no information about their families had been preserved.

If some tribes have no mention or scant mention, other groups are treated at length. This is especially true of the tribe of Judah, the family of David, and the tribe of Levi, and this is exactly what we would expect. The writer of Chronicles lived in Jerusalem round about 350 BCE, in a community dominated by the Temple and its clergy. There was no longer a Davidic king on the throne. However, the family of David still existed, and its maximal lineage is recorded in 1 Chronicles 3: 10–24. There are seven generations following King Jehoiachin (exiled in Babylon in the sixth century BCE) which probably brings the family down into the early part of the fourth century. Furthermore, the writer of Chronicles attributes to David rather than Solomon the setting-up of the Temple institutions, particularly where the musicians were concerned (1 Chronicles 6: 31). Thus the chronicler not only wanted to map the social realities of his day onto a chart that went back to the first human being, Adam; he wanted also to establish links with the past. This he did by recording the names of families of northern tribes, even though some of these tribes no longer existed (see 1 Chronicles 5: 22, 26). But principally, he made links with the past by listing David's descendants down to his own time, and by depicting the Temple worship of his day as worship that had been initiated by David himself (1 Chronicles 23–26).

SOCIAL GROUPINGS

As we now turn to discuss actual social organization in ancient Israel,
it is necessary to appreciate that the evidence contained in the Old Testament is not easy to interpret. The Hebrew terms for various social groupings are not the precise language of a modern social anthropologist but,
rather, are terms in the natural language of the people, and they often
lack precision. For example the Hebrew *bet av* literally means "father's
house" and is usually held to be a smaller social unit than Hebrew *mišpah
ah*, which is often translated as "clan". The actual usage of the terms
is not so straightforward, however. In Judges 17: 7 the tribe of Judah
is described as a *mišpahah*; but in Amos 3: 1 the whole people of Israel
is called a *mišpahah* (see further Rogerson 1978, pp. 94–96). The
reconstruction that follows is presented with caution.

The bet av

We begin with the smallest unit, the *bet av*, or "father's house". This
probably had two senses in pre-exilic Israel. First, it denoted a family
residing together. Israelite families numbered around five or six persons, even allowing for the fact that more children would be born than
survived into adulthood. The *bet av* of an unmarried man or woman
would be that of their father, and in this case the term would refer to
a nuclear family. A good example would be Genesis 50: 8, where Joseph's
"house" can refer only to the nuclear family of which he is head. Recent
research (Lemche 1985, pp. 231–2, 250–1) suggests that nuclear families
were more frequent in ancient Israel than extended families — that is,
groups consisting of a father and mother and married sons and their
children living together and acting as a single unit. Such an extended
family is that of Noah, in Genesis 7: 1. Noah enters the ark with his
entire "house" (Hebrew *bayit*), which includes three married sons.

The second main use of *bet av* is to denote *descent*. A good example
is Genesis 24: 38, where Abraham's servant has been instructed to travel
to Mesopotamia to Abraham's "father's house" to seek a wife for Isaac.
Obviously *bet av* here refers not to a residential group but to a descent
group. It is probably best understood as a lineage, from which Abraham
had separated himself but within which he wished his son to marry.

The mišpahah

Mišpahah is usually translated as "clan" in recent versions of the
Bible. This is probably not helpful, because "clan" has a number
of meanings in anthropological literature (Fox 1967 pp. 49–50, 59,
134–6). Non-specialists are probably most familiar with Scottish clans,
which are groups sharing a common surname on either their father's
or mother's side. This does not fit very well with the Old Testament,
where there are no surnames. Indeed, the Hebrew tribe, sharing a
common name such as Judah or Benjamin, was probably closer to clans
sharing a common name, such as Cameron. A *mišpahah* was probably

a maximal lineage — that is, a descent group which established ties of kinship between families through a common ancestor who was no longer living. However, maximal lineages, unlike Scottish clans, could divide to form new maximal lineages, which would then bear different names from those they had borne earlier. *Mišpaḥah* is best thought of as a descent group. This explains references such as Judges 17: 7:

There was a man from Bethlehem of the *mišpaḥah* of Judah . . .

and Amos 3: 1:

Hear this word which the Lord has spoken against you, children of Israel, against the whole *mišpaḥah* which I brought up from the land of Egypt. . . .

In the first case, the whole of the tribe of Judah is seen as a group descended from its ancestor, Judah. In the second case, Amos addresses the Israelites as descended from their ancestor Jacob.

If *mišpaḥah* is primarily a descent group, this raises the question whether it owned and apportioned land, as some have argued (Kippenberg 25–6). There are no unambiguous references to a *mišpaḥah* as owning land. It is clear that people within the *mišpaḥah* were expected to buy land from impoverished relatives; but this is not the same thing as the *mišpaḥah* actually owning the land. In fact, the case of the daughters of Zelophehad (Numbers 27: 1–11, 36: 1–9) seems to indicate that a *bet av* and a tribe (*ševet*) possessed land, and that the *mišpaḥah* ensured that it stayed in the family. Zelophehad had died in the wilderness, leaving only three unmarried daughters. These appeal to Moses to give them some land, so that their father's name does not die out. Moses agrees to this, and land is given to what is in effect a nuclear family without a male head. In Numbers 36, the men of the tribe (*ševet*) argue to Moses that if the daughters of Zelophehad marry men of other tribes, the land held by these women will belong to the tribes of their husbands and will be lost to Zelophehad's tribe. Moses therefore commands the women to marry only within their *mišpaḥah*, thus ensuring that the land stays within the tribe. The implication is that if Zelophehad's daughters married men of other tribes, their land would become the property of the nuclear family (*bet av*) of their husband. If the *mišpaḥah* owned the land, the daughters of Zelophehad could presumably marry whomever they pleased without affecting such ownership. This is not the scenario assumed in Numbers 36.

The *ševet*

The *ševet*, or tribe, is the most difficult term to define (see further Rogerson 1978, pp. 36–89), because social groups can be bound together in so many different ways; by descent, by residence, by a common dialect, or by a common religion. In the Old Testament, tribes were certainly groups bound by residence *and* descent, and also, if we are to believe Judges 12: 6, according to which Ephraimites could not pronounce the word "shibboleth", by common dialects. There is much that we do not

know about the Israelite tribes, simply because we do not have sufficient evidence to work on. A minimal definition of *ševet* would be: the
largest social unit for mutual defence against other Israelite social units.
This would explain the fact that in the book of Judges, tribes fight against
each other on at least two occasions (Judges 12, 20, and 21).

If we test out these tentative definitions against Joshua 7: 14–17, we
shall see how they work in practice. In this passage, the people are
assembled so that the culprit who has taken some of the spoils of Jericho
can be discovered. This will be done by the manipulation of a ''lot''
(perhaps the casting of stones onto the ground), which will identify which
tribe (*ševet*) is to be taken, then which *mišpaḥah*, then which family (*bet
av*) and then which man (Joshua 7: 14). It is important that the sequel
be read in the Revised Version, for it accurately represents what the
Hebrew text includes, whereas many more recent translations do not.

So Joshua rose up early in the morning, and brought Israel near by their
tribes; and the tribe (*ševet*) of Judah was taken; and he brought near the
family (*mišpaḥah*) of Judah; and he took the family (*mišpaḥah*) of the Zerahites;
and he brought near the family of the Zerahites man by man; and Zabdi
was taken; And he brought near his household (*bayit*) man by man; and
Achan, the son of Carmi, the son of Zabdi, the son of Zerah, of the tribe
of Judah was taken.

We notice first of all the fluidity of the terminology. Judah is called both
a tribe and a *mišpaḥah*. This is best explained by assuming that when
Judah is called a tribe (*ševet*) it is viewed as a residential group, and when
it is called a *mišpaḥah* it is viewed as a descent group. We next note that
after the maximal lineage of the Zerahites was taken (Zerah was one
of the two sons of Judah; see Genesis 38: 30) the living heads of the
lineages that composed this maximal lineage were brought forward.
Zabdi, the grandfather of the culprit Achan, was taken. The next step
is important. It was not Zabdi's *sons* who were next brought forward,
but the heads of all the nuclear families that belonged to his lineage,
including his sons and his grandsons. This is why the text says that Achan
was taken, without recording that his father Carmi was taken first. Thus,
in this passage, *bayit* (house) means lineage in the case of Zabdi, and
the traditional Hebrew text makes perfect sense once we recognize that
terms such as *bayit* and *bet av* have more than one meaning.

The power structure

So far, we have considered social networks, but have not asked how power
was exercised in them. This has become an important question recently,
especially in the wake of Gottwald's massive and important book on the
origins of Israel (Gottwald 1979). He argues that in the period 1250 to
1050 BCE the Israelite tribes emerged as egalitarian social units, consciously opposed to the oppressive rule of the Canaanite city-states. Other
studies (Wilson 1977) have compared Israelite tribes to the segmentary
societies found in parts of present-day Africa — that is, societies made

up of groups in which power is shared equally among its members.

It must be said that the evidence for the nature of Israelite social organization before the monarchy in the eleventh century BCE is very sparse indeed, and that what evidence there is seems to point in a different direction from that of egalitarian segmentary societies. In what has been said above about *bet av* and *mišpaḥah*, with examples taken from Genesis and Joshua, the assumption has been that these narratives reflect the social realities of the times of the writers, i.e. the period of the monarchy. If it is possible to rely on parts of Judges for information about social organization prior to the monarchy, the picture that emerges is one in which the tribes were led by men who belonged to dominant lineages, and who enjoyed a higher-than-average level of prosperity. Judges 8: 30 records of Gideon that he had seventy sons, born to him by many wives. This suggests that he was a powerful member of a dominant lineage, and that his protestation of belonging to an insignificant lineage (Judges 6: 15; note the similar disclaimer by Saul in 1 Samuel 9: 21) is not to be taken literally. In Judges 10: 3–4 we are told that Jair had thirty sons (and by implication, more than one wife), that they rode on asses and possessed thirty cities named after their father. Ibzan (Judges 12:8–10) also had thirty sons, and Abdon (Judges 12: 13–14) had forty. Whatever we make of these figures, the text means us to understand that these ''judges'' of Israel were men of power and influence. Scanty as our information therefore is, it seems safer to conclude that prior to the monarchy, Israelite tribes had dominant lineages which provided judges and military leaders when necessary. There is no evidence that Israel at this period was a segmentary society (Rogerson 1986). Certainly, with the rise of the monarchy, powerful families and lineages established themselves in the court, as we saw above when discussing the background to Jeremiah 36–41. We also saw how both Saul and David gave key posts to their relatives, thus consolidating power within their families.

The bet avot

The exile brought about far-reaching changes in Israel's social organization. In texts that can be dated with certainty to the Second Temple period, such as the books of Chronicles, a new term is found; *bet avot*. This is not simply the plural of *bet av* but a term literally meaning ''house of fathers''. In practice it is a descent group similar or identical to a *mišpaḥah*, but with the difference that it bears a name, and to that extent can be compared with a Scottish clan.

In Nehemiah 7: 7–38 (paralleled in Ezra 2: 2–35) there is a list of the people who returned from exile. It takes the following form:

> sons of Parosh, 2, 172
> sons of Shephatiah, 372
> sons of Arach, 652
> sons of Pahat-Moab belonging
>   to the sons of Joshua and Joab, 2,818 . . .

The list gives eighteen such units, whose sizes range from 95 to 2,818, the average size being between 600 and 800. Then follow ten geographical units of the form:

> men of Bethlehem and Netopha, 188
> men of Anathoth, 128
> men of Beth-asmaweth, 42

At the end of the list are two or three more groups of the form:

> sons of Harim, 320.

This list is probably to be dated in the first half of the fifth century BCE, and it gives the numbers of the lay persons who belonged to the post-exilic community in Judah at that time. Other lists in the same chapter record the numbers of priests, Levites, and temple servants. The lay people who are listed under place names are probably those who were not taken into exile by the Babylonians. The rest were descended from exiles, and had developed a type of social organization that bound groups together by allegiance to or descent from the men, such as Parosh, Shephatiah, and Arach, who are named in Nehemiah 7. We do not know anything about Parosh, Shephatiah, and Arach, etc., apart from having their names in Nehemiah and Ezra. We can hazard the guess that, while in exile, extended families were broken up and settled in different parts of Babylon, thus necessitating new social groupings, which named themselves after men such as Parosh and Shephatiah. The purpose of these new social groupings was to maintain the identity of the Israelites, who were living in an alien culture. Nehemiah 7: 61–2 records that some of those who returned to Israel could not prove that they belonged to such a *bet avot*, although it is not clear how this affected them. Priestly descendants who were in the same position (Nehemiah 7: 63–5) were excluded from the priesthood.

Whatever the origins of these groups, it is clear that they were the basic units of social organization in the post-exilic community, a community whose centre was the Jerusalem Temple, and of whose population perhaps over a third were priests, Levites, and temple servants. We find these same units occurring, with minor variations, in the account of the rebuilding of Jerusalem in Nehemiah 3, and the dissolution of mixed marriages in Ezra 10: 18–44. No doubt these units were each responsible for the collecting and payments of dues to the Persian government (the new masters, following Persia's conquest of Babylon). It may also be that the leaders of these units were the people responsible for making their fellow Jews debtors and slaves, as described in Nehemiah 5. We may suppose that the creation of new social units had weakened the duties of mutual support that had been characteristic of the *mišpaḥah*, and we may interpret Nehemiah's action, described in that chapter, as an attempt to reassert those duties. At the same time, we find in Leviticus 25 a new basis for this duty of mutual support. It is a religious basis, grounded in God's redemption of Israel from slavery in Egypt (Leviticus

25: 55). The old social ties are reinforced by a religious ideology appropriate to a community whose life is focused around the Jerusalem Temple. As we shall see in the remainder of this chapter, the history of Judah from 400 to 63 BCE was, to a great extent, a struggle between the demands of authoritarian rulers and the ideals of this religious community.

Other post-exilic groups

In 332 BCE Alexander the Great brought Persian rule in Judah to an end, and from 323 to 198 BCE the country was part of the Egyptian empire established by one of Alexander's generals, Ptolemy. Under the Ptolemies, the selling of people into slavery for debt was legalized (Kippenberg pp. 79–80) and towards the end of the third century a certain Joseph, of the family of the Tobiads (see Nehemiah 6: 1, 17–19, 13: 4), gained the right to collect taxes. Joseph doubled the amount collected. In order to meet these new demands, the peasants in Judah had either to sell some of their family into slavery or to switch their production to crops that earned greater income, such as olive orchards. Under the Seleucids, the successors of Alexander who ruled Syria, and who became the overlords of Judah in 198 BCE, there arose in Judah a new aristocracy, who wished to change the basis of the life of the people. Jerusalem became a *polis* based upon Greek models, whose name was Antiocheia and of which only the aristocracy could become citizens. A gymnasium was built, and Greek sports were encouraged (2 Maccabees 4: 1–17). Whatever else may have been the reasons for the banning of Judaism by the Seleucid king Antiochus IV in 167 BCE, he only brought to a logical conclusion an attack upon Judaism that had been mounted from within its own ranks. The subsequent Maccabean revolt can be seen as an attempt by the ordinary peasants not only to defend their religion but also to defend the freedom from slavery and impoverishment that was enshrined in its laws.

The revolt, led by the Maccabean family, liberated the Temple in 164 BCE, and after many ups and downs struggled to a final victory. However, the dynasty of rulers that emerged appropriated the high-priesthood (142 BCE), took the title of king (103–102 BCE), enlarged the territory of Judah, so as to include Galilee once more, and generally turned into despotic rulers little better than those whom the revolt had overthrown. In 63 BCE, with two rival claimants to the throne locked in a bitter struggle, Rome took over the rule and administration of the province.

Against this background there were formed religious parties who sought in different ways to practise and preserve the ideology of Judaism. One such group was the community known to us from the so-called Damascus Document, whose ideology owed much to that of the immediate post-exilic community (Davies 1982). The aim of the groups was to found a new type of social and religious life based not upon kinship but upon free acceptance of a new covenant made with God. The group had "camps" in various towns, whose members were households, including servants and day labourers. The organization of each "camp" was based upon the leadership of priests and Levites, and Israelites had precedence over proselytes. Mutual responsibilities included the support of orphans and the poor, and the redemption of those threatened with or fallen into slavery. Thus we see here the attempt to form an alternative society to that which prevailed in Judah and to achieve by means of acceptance of a religious covenant what, in earlier times, kinship ties through the *mišpaḥah* had been intended to achieve. Some members of this group later formed the community known to us from the discoveries at Qumran (Dead Sea Scrolls).

Another group that must be briefly mentioned is the Pharisees. Although little is known about their origins, they became what can best be described as a movement for the education of the people in the knowledge and practice of the Jewish law. This became all the more important after the conquests of the Maccabean kings had greatly enlarged the territory that was ruled from Jerusalem. Although the Pharisees had their own fellowship groups, they did not attempt to be a self-contained community after the fashion of the covenanters of the Damascus Document.

It is also important to mention the Samaritans, for whatever may have been their origins, they represent another attempt to maintain a religious community, free if at all possible from the depredations of tyrannical government. In the Judean-influenced documents that are preserved in the Old Testament and the Apocrypha, the Samaritans are viewed unfavourably, no doubt because their existence was a threat to Judean claims to be exclusive heirs of the religion of Moses. From the social point of view, however, they constituted a temple-based community in the heartland of the old northern kingdom; an alternative temple-based community to that in Jerusalem. Given that their scriptures were the first five books of the Old Testament, we can say that their religious ideology, too, was based upon God's election of his people, an election that had profound implications about how social organization should support the poor and prevent their degradation into slavery.

When we read the Old Testament and encounter genealogies or find people introduced by means of specifying their descent, we must remember the two features of ancient Israelite life that may seem foreign to us today. The first is a feeling of solidarity between individuals and their social group, in which the group has obligations to protect individuals from harm, injustice, and poverty. The second is a religious ideology which established links of mutual responsiblity on the basis of common membership of a covenant community. Both conceptions were, in the pre-exilic and the post-exilic periods respectively, attacked by those who wished to use power for their own ends. The resultant conflicts gave rise to new forms of social and religious organization, as well as being the soil from which grew the messianic hopes and expectations of the people.

CHAPTER 3

ISRAEL'S NEIGHBOURS

The nations and peoples that surrounded ancient Israel helped to
shape its history and culture; without knowing them we do not
know Israel's world. They also play roles in Israel's narratives
and imagination, as revealed through the Old Testament. Edom is Esau;
Egypt, the "house of bondage"; the Canaanites, seven nations to be
driven out. We shall look at their character on both the stage of history
and the stage of the Old Testament, trying — insofar as is possible —
to demonstrate the relationship between the two.

We must accept at the outset that we shall not find in the Old Testament any dispassionate assessment of other nations; these exist, for the
most part, as agents of either punishment or rescue, in a divine plan
which always focuses on Israel. But we must also realize that this egocen-
tricity is not peculiar to the Israelites, but was shared by most of their
neighbours. Also shared was the convention of representing relationships between peoples and states in terms of ancestry and kinship.
Although such kinships often did reflect a recognition of genuine racial
affinity, they could also be used to depict political relationships. This
function of genealogies has long been realized by anthropologists. Thus,
for example, the descent of Ammon and Moab from an incestuous union
between Lot and his daughters and the descent of Edom from Esau imply
relationships betwen Israel and its Transjordanian neighbours of an am-
biguous nature — kin, yet illegitimate; or first-born, yet usurped. The
real world of Israel and its neighbours, and the literary world they inhabit
in the Old Testament are distinct, but not unrelated. The physical and
psychological worlds interact.

We can consider Israel's neighbours in three groups. First are those
who in fact lived alongside Israel within the same territory. Second are
nations adjacent to Israel's borders. The third group are those nations
whose homelands did not border upon Israel's but whose empires
stretched into Israel's land during the biblical period.

Nations sharing Israel's territory
The population of Palestine was already mixed before the time of Israel
and remained so afterwards. It was predominantly Semitic (Amorite and

Phoenician), but with Indo-European elements too; these included Hurrians, possibly Hittites, but chiefly Philistines. In the Persian and Greco-Roman periods Edomites moved into the southern Judean hill country, Nabateans and Arabs encroached in Transjordan, and Greek cities grew up along the coastal plains and in Galilee and Transjordan. Some of these elements were absorbed into Israel, some were ruled by Israel, and some remained outside Israel.

The Bible represents the problem of these nations in different ways. The attitude taken by the Deuteronomic literature — that is, the book of Deuteronomy, and other books influenced by its ideas and vocabulary; such as Joshua and Judges (see chapter 10) — is that the nations resident in Canaan when Israel arrived were formally dispossessed by their god Yhwh, though that decree was not fully executed by Israel. On the level of ideology, Israel's right to the land was by divine gift, the gift being validated by military conquest. Culturally, Canaan represents the antithesis of Israel, and constituted a permanent threat to Israel's covenant fidelity and thus to its rights over the land. This ideology seems to fit the time of Israel's independent statehood in the 10th–7th centuries BCE.

Other biblical attitudes to these nations surface elsewhere. In Ezekiel 47: 21–22 a different attitude is taken: non-Israelites who live in the "land of Israel" will not be dispossessed, but "they shall be to you as native-born sons of Israel; with you they shall be allotted an inheritance among the tribes of Israel". In the patriarchal stories, the claims of Israel (through the patriarchs) to the land are based on unfulfilled promise; the patriarchs live as gērîm ("resident aliens") among the mainly hospitable indigenous population. Like the passage from Ezekiel, but less optimistic and more realistic, this attitude fits plausibly with the realities of the Persian period (mid-sixth to late fourth centuries), when, under foreign dominion, the inhabitants of the province of Judah inhabited a small part of Palestine, while substantial Jewish communities lived in Babylon, Syria, and Egypt (all associated with the journeys of Abraham).

The three strategies towards other peoples represented in the Bible may be called elimination, integration, and coexistence. Although elimination is the best-known of the biblical solutions, there is no historical evidence that it ever occurred — unlike the other two.

Nations on Israel's borders

Israel's immediate neighbours include the Transjordanian states of Aram (Syria) to the northeast and the Transjordanian nations of Ammon, Moab, and Edom, together with the Midianites, Amalekites, and perhaps Ishmaelites, all nomadic peoples who dwelt principally in the territory of Moab and Edon. In the Persian and Greco-Roman periods Transjordan was dominated by Nabateans and Arabs, while Edomites moved into the Negev, where they are better known as Idumeans. Although the Phoenicians' heartland, too, lay on Israel's borders, to the northwest,

OPPOSITE, ABOVE Mount Carmel is, strictly speaking, a range of hills about 12 miles (20 kilometres) long and from just over 1 mile (2 kilometres) to 4 miles (7 kilometres) wide, reaching a height of 1800 feet (540 metres). At its northwestern tip it narrows and meets the sea at modern Haifa, thus obstructing passage northwards from the coastal plain.

OPPOSITE, BELOW Mount Tabor, in Lower Galilee, is a prominent and isolated hill about 10 miles (18 kilometres) to the west of the bottom of the Sea of Galilee. It reaches a height of about 1900 feet (575 metres) and is about 1½ miles (2½ kilometres) long and just under a mile (1½ kilometres) wide. As it had no water supply it did not become the site of an ancient city. It was, however, a rallying-point for Israelite tribes in time of war, and the site of an ancient sanctuary.

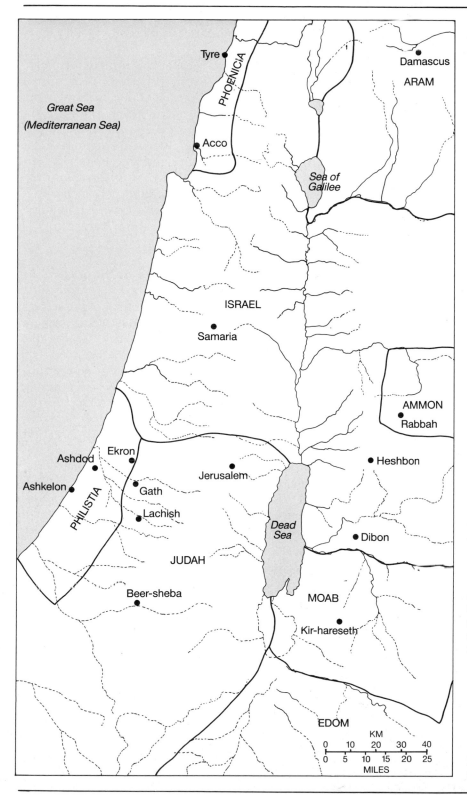

Great Sea
(Mediterranean Sea)

Tyre

PHOENICIA

Damascus

ARAM

Acco

Sea of
Galilee

ISRAEL

Samaria

AMMON

Rabbah

Ashdod

Ekron

Heshbon

Jerusalem

Ashkelon

Gath

PHILISTIA

Lachish

Dead
Sea

Dibon

JUDAH

Beer-sheba

MOAB

Kir-hareseth

EDOM

KM
0   10   20   30   40
0   5   10   15   20   25
MILES

PREVIOUS PAGES Tyre, the main seaport on the Phoenician coast, contained two harbours, one on the mainland, one on an island, linked by a causeway built during the period of the Israelite monarchy. The city dates from at least 2000 BCE, and became, with Sidon, the base of the huge Phoenician trading empire which spread across the Mediterranean in Old Testament times. From the fifth century BCE onwards, it was a centre of coinage, supplying the official coinage of the Temple in the Roman period. Besieged by Alexander the Great for seven months in 332 BCE, it recovered as a major Hellenistic city, and came to dominate the economy of the region, including Galilee.

OPPOSITE Bethshan is situated at the eastern end of the Valley of Jezreel, where it meets the Jordan Valley, and is thus a site of strategic importance. Already an Egyptian stronghold in the fifteenth century, it became a major Philistine garrison city, from whose walls the bodies of Saul and his sons were hung (1 Samuel 31: 10, 12). Few traces remain at the site from before the Hellenistic period, when the city of Scythopolis was founded on the site. Its most famous relic is a Roman amphitheatre (now largely restored).

MAP 5 Israel and its neighbours in the Iron Age.

their territory also included most of Palestine, so we shall consider them under "Canaanites"

The inhabitants of Transjordan were Semitic and practised circumcision. Hence in the Bible their descent is traced back to the family of Abraham. For this reason, Aram is also presented as the ancestral home of the patriarch (although he himself is said to come from Ur, in Mesopotamia). "Aram", in Genesis 22, was a grandson of Nahor, Abraham's brother; Har(r)an (Genesis 24) an Aramean kingdom. Most of these descendants of Abraham are therefore rightful occupants of their land, possibly even understood as heirs of promises to Abraham, the "father of nations" — in deliberate contrast to those nations occupying the "land of Israel" (even though many of these, too, were Semitic and practised circumcision, the mark of descent from Abraham).

Empires

The empires of which Israel became a part during its history are the Assyrian, Babylonian, Persian, Macedonian (with its successors, Ptolemaic and Seleucid), and Roman. Throughout much of the second millennium, Egypt had controlled Palestine, and in the Old Testament period it continued to exercise considerable influence. Under the Ptolemies Egypt again administered Palestine for over a century. The cultural influence of these nations upon Israel varied, but where such influence existed, it is rarely acknowledged in the Bible, and where it is acknowledged, deplored. The dominant role accorded such powerful nations in the Bible is as agents of Yhwh or as his opponents or rivals; whether employed by Yhwh in order to pursue his plans for Israel, or offering a futile challenge to his ordering of world affairs, these empires are often treated somewhat condescendingly (not least in the closing verses of Jonah, where the Ninevites are presented as mere creatures of God, just like cattle). Living in a vacuum between great powers, the victims of these powers' ambitions, Israel thus responded in its literature as it could not militarily — affirming a cultural and religious superiority which would in the end, however distant, be vindicated in political terms.

"CANAANITES"

The word "Canaanite" is used in the Bible (and today) to denote the non-Israelite population of the land of Canaan. Such a population, however, was neither racially nor politically homogeneous. Culturally and religiously the distinction between "Canaanites" and "Israelites" is hardly less problematic. No racial, material-cultural, or linguistic distinction between "Israelite" and "non-Israelite" is archaeologically or historically meaningful. The only possible definition, which is religious, poses huge problems, since many "Israelites" worshipped Baal, while many "Canaanites" may have worshipped Yhwh (e.g. Uriah the Hittite, 2 Samuel 12). The Bible acknowledges that the "Canaanites" did not disappear after the time of Joshua (Judges 1) but although it assumes

they would disappear gradually (Exodus 23: 29; Deuteronomy 7: 22),
it does not record when, or where, or how, they disappeared. The
"Canaanites", as biblically defined, are, frankly, a product of biblical
ideology, and they become a problematic entity outside that context.

The only workable definitions of "Canaanite" are (a) those born in
the land of Canaan (i.e. Palestine), whether Israelite or not; or (b) The
Phoenicians, who were the culturally dominant element in the land of
Canaan before the existence of Israel and a major element thereafter,
although they were centred outside the land, to the north (see below).
In this section we shall deal with the non-Israelite population of the land
of Canaan, since "Israel" is being dealt with separately. This population existed before, during, and after the period of the Israelite and
Judean monarchy, and consisted of many different racial elements.
"Canaan" never made up a political state but it did form prior to the
advent of Israel, a social and economic system.

The different racial elements in the land of Canaan are sometimes
simply called "Canaanites" (e.g. Judges 1), sometimes Amorites (Genesis
15: 16), and are sometimes enumerated in lists of seven (e.g. Deuteronomy 7: 1; Joshua 3: 10 — which gives the inclusive category of
"Canaanites" as one of the seven!) or even of ten (e.g. Genesis 10: 15;
15: 19 — including both Canaanites and Amorites as members of the
list!). Of most of the members of these lists, we know either little or
nothing. Of Girgashites and Perizzites, for instance, mention is totally
lacking outside the Bible. Jebusites, so far as we can tell, are the pre-
Judean inhabitants of Jerusalem. Hivites may be Hurrians (non-Semitic,
originally from far to the northeast); Horites may not be a racial term;
some think it derives from the Hebrew word for "cave" and denotes
cave-dwellers. Hittites, of whom we do know a good deal, seem to dwell
in the Judean hills and to have Semitic names (e.g. Uriah, the husband
of Bathsheba). Many scholars doubt whether they are the Anatolian
Hittites (see below). It is not impossible that Horite, Hivite, and Hittite
are somewhat confused in the Bible. We are left, out of this confusing
potpourri of names, with Amorites, Phoenicians, and Philistines as the
major elements of the population of Canaan.

Amorites

Amurru, which is agreed to lie behind "Amorite", is a term used in
Mesopotamian texts, meaning "Westerners". It refers to Semitic groups
who spread out over the Fertile Crescent at the end of the third millennium BCE, distinguishable to modern scholars by their common
language (identifiable in personal names). A group of Amurru entered
Canaan in 2100–1900 BCE; and in the fourteenth–thirteenth centuries
an Amorite kingdom existed in what is now Lebanon. But the relationship of these *Amurru* to the biblical Amorites of Palestine is unclear,
because although the latter term is used for the kingdoms of Og, and
Sihon in Transjordan in the stories of the Israelites' wanderings in the
wilderness, it also occurs to describe the Palestinian populace.

Phoenicians

However, it may be asserted (if the statement means anything) that the Phoenicians were historically the "real" Canaanites — certainly culturally and probably etymologically. It is still widely held that "Canaan" derives from an Akkadian term *kinaḫḫu*, meaning red-purple dye, which was extracted from the Mediterranean murex shell — this term then being extended to the cloth thus dyed and, further, to the region from which it came, north of Acco. Alternatively, or additionally, the term came to denote the merchants dealing in the cloth. (The meaning "traders" for "Canaanites" is also reflected in the Bible in Isaiah 23: 8; Proverbs 31: 24; Zephaniah 1: 11; and Zechariah 11: 7, 11). In this case, the Greek *phoinik-* has an almost identical history, and thus linguistically "Canaanite" and "Phoenician" would be synonymous. Other etymologies, however, have been proposed; for example, a connection with the Hebrew verb *qnˁ*, meaning "to be low", might imply a definition of "lowland dwellers".

Genesis 10: 15–19 represents the extent of Phoenician settlement as throughout Palestine and northwards to the Orontes River. Ugarit (see below) lay either at or just beyond the northern boundary of their homeland. At the other extreme, the fifteenth-century Egyptian Amarna letters written to the Pharaoh by the rulers of Canaanite cities, designate by "Canaan" the area between the Mediterranean and the Jordan from Gaza northwards. Already by the beginning of the second millennium the Phoenicians were trading at harbours such as Acco, Byblos (Gebal), and Sidon (perhaps their earliest settlement; see Genesis 10). Tyre, from about 1200 BCE, became their most important centre. Thence they spread into Palestine and stamped their culture upon the Amorite and other racial groups. Political alliance with David and Solomon gave the Phoenicians access to the Red Sea and produced a Phoenician-built and Phoenician-designed temple for Solomon in Jerusalem. Relations with the kingdom of Israel were generally friendly. Like all states in the region, the Phoenician cities suffered at the hands of the Assyrians, but from the sixth century onwards trade expanded, and colonies were founded in North Africa and Spain. During the Neo-Babylonian and Persian periods, Tyre remained independent; captured by Alexander the Great, it nevertheless recovered is status and became a dominant influence in the region, its economic hinterland extending into Galilee. It was Tyrian coinage that came to be required in the Jerusalem Temple (cp. Mark 11: 15).

Philistines

The third major population element in Canaan, the Philistines, migrated from Crete (according to Amos 9: 7) or possibly Asia Minor to the southwest coastal plain between Joppa and Gaza in about 1200 BCE. Having first failed to settle in Egypt, they emerged as the heirs of Egyptian imperial control in Palestine, probably installed there as Egyptian protégés. Three of the five known Philistine cities, Ashkelon, Ashdod, and Gaza, were ancient; Gath and possibly Ekron were new foundations. The reason for their expansion into the highlands is probably that they were professional warriors; need for more agricultural produce or greater control over the protection of trade routes are secondary possibilities. One direction of their expansion was along the coastal plain and via the Jezreel valley, where they established a presence at Bethshan, a former Egyptian garrison city. Near here they defeated Saul on Mt. Gilboa. Another direction of expansion, against Judah, came via the Shephelah, where they had built Ekron and Gath. The Samson cycle deals with the Philistine presence in the Shephelah west of Judahite territory, and the migration of the tribe of Dan from this region to the Hermon foothills was presumably a result of this pressure. It has often been suggested that it was the Philistine threat which created the Israelite state, through necessitating a permanent military leader. If it is true that David was a Philistine vassal, and as such ruled over Judah, with his own personal fief being Ziklag, (a town given him by the Philistine king Achish) the Philistines did indeed play a major role in the creation of the kingdoms of both Israel and Judah. At any rate, their initial progress in subduing the highlands was reversed by David, and with the emergence of the two kingdoms the Philistines remained confined to their own five cities and the surrounding coastal plain.

Canaanite religion and culture

It is plausible, if an oversimplification, to claim that the culture of Canaan was mainly that of the Phoenicians, overlying that of the Amorites — which in many respects may not have been much different. The Phoenicians both absorbed and passed on a variety of cultural influences through trade, which they dominated through their superior harbours. They also possessed raw materials, especially wood from the forests of the Lebanon range; and their craftsmanship in wood, stone, and metalwork was of a high standard. The arrival of the Philistines apparently made little cultural impact; these assimilated very quickly the indigenous Semitic culture. In reconstructing this culture, and in particular the religion, we can concentrate on the Phoenicians.

The Bible speaks of the Canaanites as worshipping at "high places"; remains of such sites have been identified, for example, at Hazor and Megiddo. Canaanite temples mainly seem to follow a basic plan comprising an anteroom and a shrine, the plan followed in Solomon's building. Another type was the "tower" shrine, of which examples have been found at Shechem and Megiddo; there is a possible reference to the use of such a tower for sacrifice in the Keret epic from Ugarit (Keret I 3 p. 53ff; see ANET pp. 142–149).

In 1929 excavations on the mound of Ras Shamra were commenced, revealing a site occupied until about 1200 BCE and housing a great city with a huge palace; this city was once known as Ugarit. Although well to the north of the main Phoenician cities, and regarded by some scholars as Aramean, it is very widely taken as a primary source of knowledge

Several small hewn limestone altars such as this were found at Megiddo, dating probably from about the tenth century BCE, and measuring between 18–20 inches (46–51cm) high. They may have been domestic or incense altars, and their raised corners — also found on larger altars — have suggested the "horns" of the Israelite altar as prescribed in Exodus 27: 2 and as grasped by Joab when seeking sanctuary (1 Kings 2: 28).

ABOVE A fourteenth-century BCE tablet from Ugarit (modern Ras Shamra).

about the Phoenicians. From its artefacts we can discover the extent of its trade and the wealth it engendered. But even more significant for most scholars is the impressive library of texts, from which we learn at first hand of its system of writing. These texts are chiefly Babylonian, but the local language was also written, and an important local innovation was a cuneiform system whose characters represented not syllables, as the Babylonian-Assyrian system, but consonants. Thus many fewer signs were required. The "alphabet" and the language are closely related to Hebrew; in particular, many Israelite cultic terms are explained from the Ugaritic texts — as would be only to be expected, since the Israelite-Judean Temple cult was Phoenician in all major respects except its deity.

Indeed, the religion revealed at Ugarit is recognizably that which the Bible so vehemently censures as the "abominations" of the Canaanites. Its senior deity is the high god El — who, however, plays little active part in Phoenician myths. In the Bible "El" is used as a general term for "God", and several divine titles compounded of El and an epithet (e.g. El Elyon, Psalm 78: 35; El Shaddai, Genesis 17: 1; and El Bethel, Genesis 31: 13) refer to Yhwh. It is possible that this usage represents one of many religious assimilations of Amorite-Phoenician religion by Israel. El's consort, Asherah, also appears (with her identity as a goddess obscured) as a Canaanite cult object (e.g. Judges 6: 25). Hadad, the storm god, was the most important deity, as he was also to the Arameans; he is better known to us by his honorific title "Baal" ("lord"), used in the Bible. The "Baal Epic" (or Epics; the reconstruction is uncertain) from Ugarit tells how he overcame Death (*Mot*), a story reflecting the cycle of rain and drought, seed and harvest, death and life (ANET pp. 129–142). His struggle with Yamm (the Sea) perhaps betrays the concerns of a maritime people, though it also echoes the Babylonian myth of creation as a conquest over the primeval chaotic waters. The corn god Dagon, adopted by the Philistines, was sometimes identified with him. His consort was Ashtart, the goddess of war. Another war goddess was Anat. Reshef was a god of the underworld, as was Horon. There were numerous other gods, some with duplicate functions and similar names. But the pantheon is not as well-organized as, for instance, the Babylonian, and this surely reflects a lack of political organization and a high level of syncretism.

The vitality of Canaanite private religion is attested by the large number of figurines found there — probably amulets or charms; in some cases they may represent the major deities. Otherwise, we know much less of private than of public religion. The temples of Canaan contained altars, sacred pillars (*masseboth*), and statues, and were often located on raised mounds (cp. 1 Kings 14: 23). Here, sacrifices of many different kinds were conducted (*shĕlamîm*, for example, or "peace-offerings", are mentioned at Ugarit). The examination of entrails as a means of prophesying was common, too, a practice widely used in the ancient Near East but referred to perhaps only once in the Old Testament (Ezekiel 21: 21).

It is difficult to discern any distinctive features of Philistine culture. We do not know their language, and from the few personal names available it is impossible to reach any firm conclusion about its type. Their gods all bear Semitic names — Ashtoreth, Dagon, Baal-Zebul. Their best-known artefactual remains are clay coffins with faces moulded on the heads, discovered at Bethshan and elsewhere. Even here Egyptian influence is strongly suspected, and the coffins tell us nothing of Philistine beliefs about the dead. We can identify Philistine decorated pottery, which survived for about two centuries before the local varieties entirely took over. Despite their military conquests in Canaan, the Philistines ultimately became the vanquished; their culture, such as it was, submitting rather easily to that of the peoples they defeated in battle. Their only major bequest was, by courtesy of Rome, the name of "Palestine" itself and a byword for a hostile attitude to culture.

Political and social organization in Canaan

For the whole of the Late Bronze Age (1550–1200 BCE) Canaan consisted of city-states. For centuries these had been under greater or lesser Egyptian control, but this weakened during the fourteenth century. The nature of the process of disintegration is disputed: it was helped by weak Egyptian policy, and resulted in many battles involving the cities in which outlaws called *habīrû* were used. The economic system that developed

ABOVE A gold pendant, probably of Ashtoreth, the Canaanite version of the Semitic goddess of fertility and of water — known also as Astarte and Ishtar.

A gold dagger, found at Gezer.

Among the most interesting finds from Bethshan are these clay coffins with lids upon which the face and crossed arms of the deceased are represented. These "anthropoid" coffins are now generally regarded as Philistine.

in Canaan was — as in most of the ancient Near East — feudal. Near-constant warfare between cities, using chariots and siege weaponry, concentrated populations in or near cities dominated by a ruling élite employing a highly specialized warrior caste, which was supported financially by the imposition of taxes on the peasantry. Some scholars (e.g. Gottwald, 1979) have seen in the "Amarna wars" a social revolution of the *ḥabīrû* against the feudal society; others see the process as a struggle for independence and supremacy between the cities, in which the *ḥabīrû* were hired mercenaries. Whatever the case, in 1284 BCE a

peace treaty between Egypt and the Hittites confirmed Egyptian
sovereignty over the land of Canaan, and this was presumably in effect
at the time of Israel's emergence there. But that control would have been
confined to the cities of the lowlands, with Israel's territory in the
highlands outside the domain of Egypt. The Egyptian military ruling
élite shortly yielded place to the Philistines, who formed a cohesive social
structure, geared to warfare, with iron-smelting technology (though not
necessarily a monopoly on this, as was once thought) and chariots. We
know little for certain of the Philistines' political organization. Their
leaders were called *seranim* — presumed to be related to the Greek word
tyrannos — but were these rulers of each of the cities (Judges 3: 3
enumerates five of them) or military officers (1 Samuel 29: 22)? Did
the Philistines create their own society or insert themselves as a class
within the existing feudal structure? Probably the latter; the Samson
stories, while narrating bitter conflict, also hint at a good deal of social
intercourse (Judges 14).

TRANSJORDAN

Ammon, Moab, and Edom were what can be called "nation-states";
unlike Canaan, they were racially homogeneous and monarchic. It is
unfortunate that we know so little of these nations, because their origins
and social and religious development were similar to Israel's in many
respects. Amalekites and Midianites, on the other hand, cannot be
geographically defined so precisely, though they lived and roamed in
Transjordan, and they figure in biblical traditions. But although we know
a little of the Midianites from their artefactual remains and can deduce
something from biblical tradition, we have no extra-biblical data on the
Amalekites, nor on the Ishmaelites.

The states of Ammon, Moab, and Edom did not originate with the
settling down of originally nomadic tribes into arable land, as was once
frequently asserted. Such a process no longer accords with what we know
of ancient nomadism. The emergence of Ammon and Moab, at least,
in about 1200 BCE, was due to other factors. At this time Egyptian control in Palestine was weakening, Philistines began to arrive in the
southwestern coastal plain, and Aramean migration into the region
around Damascus resulted in the establishing of another powerful state
in the region. Ammon and Moab may have been formed directly by
Aramean settlement. Or economic decline in Canaan may have provoked population movement eastward. Both explanations have also been
offered for the origin of Israel. Edom may have originated in similar
circumstances, but the balance of probability suggests a different origin,
somewhat later and from the southeast.

The three Transjordanian states appear to have developed more
quickly than Israel into monarchies. Genesis 36: 31ff, gives a list of "kings
who reigned in the land of Edom, before any king reigned over the
Israelites". This view, if suggesting an earlier origin for Edom than

archaeology implies, is consistent with the depiction of the "kings" Sihon and Og in Transjordan in Israel's "wilderness" traditions (Numbers 21: 21–35), Eglon "king" of Moab in Judges 3, and the "king" of the Ammonites in Judges 11. It has been argued that Israelite kingship was modelled on the non-hereditary kingship of these nations, a suggestion possibly true for Israel, but hardly for Judah, where David, probably starting as a vassal city-state ruler under the Philistines, occupied Jerusalem as his personal city and founded an hereditary dynasty.

The attitude towards Ammon expressed in the Bible, is everywhere ambivalent. Ammon and Moab are represented as kin, but dubbed as inferior or even the products of incest; found within Israelite society, and intermarrying with Israelites, but depicted as hostile nations; possibly containing worshippers of Yhwh, but excluded from membership of Israel's "congregation". Edom, traced from Esau, is a brother of "Israel" (Jacob), deprived of birthright. Yet here the parallels end, for the subsequent reconciliation between Jacob and Esau contrasts with a history of conflict, even enmity, between the two nations, as recorded in the old Testament. This ambiguity is not necessarily perplexing; the phenomenon is known to anthropologists who have studied "segmentary societies", among which the most frequent conflicts can take place between those groups most closely related genealogically. Almost certainly the Israelites and their Transjordanian neighbours were closely related in origin, and possibly also in social, political, and religious structure.

Ammonites

The Ammonites occupied territory between the Jabbok and the Arnon rivers. Their capital, Rabbath-Ammon (where Ammān, the capital of Jordan is now sited) is about 25 miles (40 kilometres) east of the Dead Sea. Their rightful territory, according to the Bible, included only the eastern part of this region, while the western part was settled by Israel. This part, together with the region north of the Jabbok, formed what Israel called Gilead, and Israelite claims to it begin in a description, in the "wilderness period", of an *Amorite* kingdom ruled by Sihon from Heshbon and given by Yhwh to Israel because of that king's intransigence. The assignment of this territory is detailed in Joshua 12 and 13 and forms the basis of the dispute between Ammon and the Israelites in Gilead in Judges 10–12. Perhaps this division of territory was fixed in the wake of wars with Ammon fought by Saul and David. Under Solomon, and for much of the pre-exilic period, Gilead remained part of Judah/Israel. By the end of the eighth century this territory was part of Ammon — now already, like Judah, an Assyrian vassal.

We may assume that the population of Gilead included both Israelites and Ammonites, and certainly relations between the two nations were not always hostile. David headed there during Absalom's revolt. One of the cults admitted by Solomon (1 Kings 11) was that of "Milcom (v. 5) or Molech (v. 7), the abomination of the Ammonites". The mother of Solomon's son Rehoboam was from Ammon (1 Kings 14: 21, 31).

According to 2 Kings 24: 2 Ammonites assisted Nebuchadrezzar; and the prophetic books express resentment at what must have been seen as Ammonite benefits from the destruction of Judah by the Babylonians (e.g. Jeremiah 27: 3; Ezekiel 21: 20; and Zephaniah 2: 8–9). But at this time many Judeans must have sought refuge in Ammon, since after Nebuchadrezzar had departed, they are reported as having returned (Jeremiah 40: 11), while a royal claimant, Ishmael, seems to have tried to promote his cause in Ammon (Jeremiah 41: 10).

We may assume that Judeans continued to live in Ammon, and Ammonites in Judah. During the exile in Babylon Judeans intermarried with Ammonites (and Moabites), and according to Ezra 9: 1 they had not, a century later, "separated from their abominations". This is one point of view; but Nehemiah's enemy, Tobiah, though an Ammonite, bore a Yhwistic name (a name containing the element 'Yah' [Yhwh]), and the Tobiads were the ruling family in Ammon during the Persian period. Subsequently, Ptolemy II changed the name of Rabbath-Ammon to Philadelphia and made it a Hellenistic city. It successfully resisted the siege of Alexander Jannaeus, who had conquered most of the territory, but in 63 BCE the Roman general Pompey added it to the league of ten cities called the Decapolis and granted it independence from Jewish rule. By now the area between the Arnon and Jabbok rivers, i.e. Ammon and Gilead, was known as Perea; disputes between Jews and non-Jews in this Hellenistic "development" were not uncommon.

The Old Testament acknowledges Ammon, like Moab, as kin, even if by means of Lot's incest with his daughter. By virtue of this descent, Ammonite territory is acknowledged (Deuteronomy 2: 19–20) to have been given to them by Yhwh. According to Jeremiah 9: 26 the Ammonites also practised circumcision. In fact, Ammonite language and religion were probably close to that of Judah/Israel, facilitating the interchange of religious and political (hence racial?) affiliation, and perhaps even amalgamation, in Gilead. The law that "No Ammonite or Moabite shall enter the assembly of the Lord; even to the tenth generation none belonging to them shall enter the assembly of the Lord ever" (Deuteronomy 23: 3) may claim, in the case of Ammon, lack of hospitality in the "wilderness period" though the culprit, Sihon, was Amorite according to the Bible, not Ammonite! We may suspect that Ammon's proximity in every way to Israel was the real problem.

Moabites

Moab was Ammon's southern neighbour, lying between the Arnon and the Zered rivers, though often stretching farther north. Several Moabite settlements are mentioned in the Bible, but less than half have so far been identified. Moab's wealth lay both in its sheep breeding (2 Kings 3: 4) and in its position on the great trade route of the "King's Highway" leading to Syria from the Red Sea. This may be the reason why David conquered Moab as he did Ammon (Gilead also lay on the route). Having gained freedom after the reign of Solomon, Moab then fell into the hands of the Israelite kings. Its successful escape from this yoke is narrated in the Mesha[c] Inscription (the "Moabite Stone", ANET 320–321), a black basalt inscription of its king Mesha[c] left at Dibon, to be dated to about 830 BCE, which confirms (though from a different viewpoint) the biblical version of events. Mesha[c] claims that by using Israelite slave labour he rebuilt many cities. Even more interestingly, the inscription reveals the script of Moab to have been identical to that used by the Israelites, and the language only dialectally different. Unfortunately, a stele from Balu[c]ah (still undeciphered) and a few fragments are the only other Moabite literary remains.

Moab was also placed under Assyrian tribute at some time during the eighth century, but joined with Ammon and Aram to invade Judah during the reign of Nebuchadrezzar. In the Persian period it ceased as an independent state; settlement appears to have declined, although as a race they persisted.

Place names in Moab containing the name Baal suggest that Moabite religion was influenced by, or derived from, that of Canaan. The Mesha[c] inscription refers to a "high place" for Chemosh, a god who also appears in many personal names. The language Mesha[c] uses of Chemosh and of warfare resembles that found in the Old Testament. The inscription also mentions Yhwh, Gad (the tribe occupying Gilead in Transjordan according to Joshua 22 for example), the word ḥrm ("ban", or wholesale slaughter of a defeated population, as in the book of Joshua), and a curious " 'r'ldwd [David?]", some kind of cult object).

The same pattern of kinship and enmity as existed between Israel and Ammon is found here between Israel and Moab; descended from the offspring of Lot's incest. Moab is hostile to Israel in the wilderness period; and Moabites are excluded, like Ammonites, from the "congregation of Israel". It is from Moabite territory that the Israelites are presented as crossing into Canaan; during the Judges period, Ehud delivered Israel from Eglon, king of Moab. But on the other hand, the story of Ruth not only adopts a Moabite as heroine, but also traces her descendants to David. According to 1 Samuel 22, David's parents lived in Moab. There are grounds, then, for suspecting that David was more than distantly Moabite. Perhaps much of what was said above about the racial, religious, and linguistic affinity of Israelites and Ammonites pertains here also.

Edom

The territory of Edom lay to the south of Moab, from the Zered River to the Gulf of Aqaba, but it also crossed the Wadi Arabah, or Rift Valley. Archaeological evidence places Edomite origins in the early Iron Age; no Edomite sites earlier than the eighth century BCE have been discovered, and these all lie east of the Arabah. Although it is possible that Edom's origins are connected with those of Ammon and Moab, they may belong, rather, in northern Arabia, and at a slightly later period. According to the Bible, Edom was suppressed under David and Solomon; the latter built the port of Ezion-Geber at Aqaba, and Edom was thereafter periodically subject to Judah until it, too, became an Assyrian vassal in the 8th century.

In the exilic and Second Temple periods (587 BCE–70 CE) Edom, now referred to as Idumea, moved its territory west and north, while its original homelands were occupied by Arabs and Nabateans. In the Hasmonean period Idumeans were forcibly circumcised by the Jewish ruler John Hyrcanus and incorporated into the Jewish nation. The ironical outcome was Herod the Great, the Idumean king who finally exterminated the Hasmonean line (see chapter 7).

Edom has left no substantial literary remains. Its position and some of the sites excavated suggest wide trade contacts, for it was, like Moab, on an important north–south trading route, the "King's Highway". However, this does not necessarily mean that the Edomites were wealthy. The name of its chief deity was Qaus, a name probably Arabian in origin, which appears on jar-handles from the two major Edomite sites at Umm el-Biyara and Tell el-Kheleifeh, and in Edomite personal names attested in Assyria and Egypt. Eloah is another possible name for Edom's god, used also in the Bible for the God of Israel, and frequently in Job, which has been suggested to be of Edomite provenance.

The identification of Edom and Esau, the elder brother of Jacob whose birthright was usurped, suggests a close relationship between Edom and Israel, perhaps reinforced by Amos's reference to a "covenant of brothers" (1: 11). The Esau = Edom equation is often thought to be artificial and secondary, but it still requires explanation, though possibly on a political rather than a racial basis. Such a bond seems already taken for granted in biblical texts from the Persian period and is thus likely to be older, since no basis can be found for it after the exile. Perhaps it dates to the period after David's conquest, when attempts to bring the two kingdoms of Judah and Edom together may have taken place. A further explanation, perhaps complementary, builds on traditions that associate Yhwh with the Edomite homeland (e.g. Judges 5: 4). Yet another explanation proceeds from the fact that the Bible nowhere mentions the Edomite gods, and that in Deuteronomy 2: 5 Yhwh is said to have given Edom its land. Perhaps there was an ancient religious bond between Edom and Israel, but this remains speculative. Yet the forced circumcision of Idumeans by the Jewish ruler in the second century BCE suggests a continuing awareness of the sort of affinity implied by the brotherhood of Israel and Esau.

AMALEKITES AND MIDIANITES

Amalekites

The Amalekites' homeland is located in the southern Negev. Genesis 36: 12, 16 (and 1 Chronicles 1: 36) trace Amalek from Esau (= Edom), and v. 12 names his mother as Timnah, also the name of a city in the northeast of the Sinai Peninsula; Israelites fight with Amalekites en route to Canaan from Egypt (Exodus 17). The Kenites, who inhabited the

Negev, are also said to have lived among them (1 Samuel 14–15), and David fought them near Ziklag (1 Samuel 39) — both references pointing to the northern Negev. Genesis 14 also seems to locate them in this general region. There are, however, some curious hints of Amalekite presence in the hill country, probably of Ephraim: Numbers 14: 45 links them with Canaanites in the "hill country"; Saul's encounter with them (1 Samuel 15) makes better sense in the Ephraimite hill country, and the judge Abdon (Judges 12: 15) is buried "in the hill country of the Amalekites, in the land of Ephraim". There are, finally, accounts of Amalekites in league with Moabites (in Judges 3) and Midianites (Judges 6 and 7; they were defeated by Gideon). Chronologically, the Bible traces them from the time of Abraham (Genesis 14) to Hezekiah (1 Chronicles 4: 43). We have no extra-biblical data about them. It has been suggested that they occupied the city of Hormah (Tel Masos), but this is uncertain. It is more generally assumed that they were nomadic, though this also is a guess. Their encounters with Israel or Judah take place either in the Negev area, or when they fight for others (as mercenaries?). The best guess is that their activity against Israel/Judah was confined to the time of Saul and David.

Despite only sporadic opposition to Israel on their part, Amalekites seem to be particularly abhorred in the Bible. They are threatened with eternal divine hostility (Exodus 17), with ultimate destruction (Numbers 24: 20), and with a blotting-out of their memory (Deuteronomy 25). Ostensibly the reason is their unprovoked attack on Israel in the wilderness (Exodus 17), but this story may be a pretext. They appear as foes in the "Judges period", in the time of Saul and David, and then, finally, in the time of Hezekiah in an isolated report in 1 Chronicles 4: 43 — but as victims, not aggressors. The most interesting of the biblical references is in Balaam's oracle, which calls them the "earliest" or "greatest" of the nations. Whichever is the better translation, neither sense is easily explained.

Midianites

The Midianites occupied territory southeast of Moab and Edom, where they can first be traced from about the twelfth century BCE. The most important site connected with them is Timnah, where, on the site of an older Egyptian shrine to Hathor, stood a tent-shrine, containing in its sanctum a copper snake. This suggests an intriguing parallel with the life of Moses (see below). Midianite pottery has also been identified, and was apparently produced from a single site.

Little else is known, however, of the Midianites, apart from what can be inferred from the biblical traditions. They are traced to Abraham (Genesis 25: 1–2), and a close connection binds Moses to them; he married the daughter of a Midianite priest, Jethro, who subsequently became a priest of Yhwh. It is interesting to speculate on the link between this Midianite connection and the connections with Edom, which also might suggest an ancient religious bond (see above); both Edomites and

Midianites occupied the same general area — where, in fact, the Sinai of the biblical accounts is often placed by scholars, rather than the traditional location in the Sinai peninsula. (In Numbers 22 and 25 Midian is located farther north, with Moab; but this may be in fact a confusion between Moab and Midian). In Numbers 31 Midian is massacred by Israel; in Judges it is the oppressor of Israel, and is vanquished by Gideon. Midianites are usually described as living in tents and travelling (Genesis 37, Judges 6). To pin down any firm historical connection from these traditions is tricky; an early struggle between Israel and Midian for control over Transjordan is a possibility, no more. We have to reckon with the possibility that at the time of writing down the relevant accounts, the identity and character of the Midianites, perhaps like those of the Amalekites, were no longer clearly remembered.

Another Transjordanian neighbour worth mentioning is the tribe of the Ishmaelites. However, despite the importance of Ishmael as the first-born of Abraham, these people play a very small part in the Old Testament, being possibly involved in the Joseph story (Genesis 37: 25–28; but see also v. 36) and mentioned alongside other neighbours in Psalm 83: 6. According to Genesis 25: 18, they dwelt in Arabia.

Nabateans

The beginnings of the Nabateans as a nation cannot be traced; possibly Asshurbanipal's inscriptions refer to them (c. 650 BCE). But they emerge for certain as a tribe of Arab nomads at the time of Alexander the Great. They settled down where Edom had been in pre-exilic times, in lower Transjordan and south of the Dead Sea. Their empire, as it came to be, was built on their trading and the trading of others who passed through their region — which lay, of course, across the major caravan route from the Mediterranean to Arabia and the Red Sea. Their capital city was Petra, about 50 miles (80 kilometres) south of the Dead Sea where the trade routes from both east and west of the Jordan converged towards Aqaba. But the Nabateans were not mere nomadic traders. They were powerful enough to repel the forces of the Macedonian king of Syria, Antigonus, in 312 BCE. They also settled in villages and practised agriculture, thanks to irrigation systems and the necessary stout fortifications against the plundering Arabs, which can still be seen.

The first Nabatean king to be known is Aretas I (c. 170 BCE), under whom the Nabateans first showed interest in the politics of the region. In particular, Aretas attempted to gain control of the trade routes farther north, towards Damascus, and west, towards Gaza. However, in Transjordan, the Hasmonean kings of Israel had secured large tracts of territory. One of them, Alexander Jannaeus, came into conflict with Aretas provoking a Nabatean invasion, which had to be bought off. Dealings with the Hasmoneans continued as Aretas looked for territory in Transjordan in return for aid to Hyrcanus II in regaining power. Accordingly, Aretas defeated Aristobulus somewhere in Judea, and proceeded to besiege Jerusalem. Only the arrival of Pompey saved the situation. Under Herod the Great Judea lay on the frontier of the Empire, with the Nabateans beyond it, and Herod was obliged to fight the Nabateans. Later, Herod Antipas married the daughter of the Nabatean king, whom he subsequently wished to replace with Herodias. This policy led to war with the Nabateans, which he lost. A Roman force had to be sent against the Nabateans to retrieve the situation. It was, however, not until the time of Trajan that the Romans finally conquered the Nabateans, when their capital (by then moved to Bostra) became the centre of the Roman province of Arabia. Thereafter the Nabateans declined and were (re-?)absorbed by the surrounding Arabs.

The most famous relic of the Nabateans is Petra, whose most impressive remains, however, are of Greco-Roman style and date from the second century CE (see p. 105). Like many other trading nations (such as the Phoenicians), they produced notable artistic achievements, especially pottery. Their language was a dialect of Aramaic, written in a distinctive form of the standard script, possibly an ancestor of the classical Arabic script. Their deities were Dusharat and his consort Allat, deities of weather and fertility, like the major Syrian deities.

The Nabateans came to the attention of biblical scholars when Albrecht Alt proposed that their religion of the "god of the fathers" offered a close analogy to the religion of early Israel — a theory now less widely held than previously. But direct contacts between Nabateans and Jews, as we have seen, belong to the Greco-Roman period.

Arameans

The Arameans were descended from Amorites who settled at first in the mountains at the northern and northeastern fringes of the Fertile Crescent. Hence in Genesis 10: 22–23 Aram is listed, along with Elam and Asshu, as sons of Shem; and Amos asserts that they came from Qir — an unknown region, but one linked again in Isaiah 22: 6 with Assyria and Elam. These Amorites mingled with non-Semitic Hurrian stock, and at the end of the second millennium some descended into Syria, whence they can properly be called Arameans, since Aram denotes the Syrian region, not the racial group. The Arameans established a number of states here and in northwest Mesopotamia (e.g. Aram-Zobah, whose king, Hadadezer, is mentioned in 2 Samuel 8: 10).

But the state referred to as "Aram" in the Bible is the one centred on Damascus, which in fact became paramount in the biblical period. Its relations with Israel, with whom it struggled for territory and local supremacy, were largely determined by the power and presence of Assyria. When Assyria was weak, Aram was Israel's main enemy; when Assyria was relatively strong, Aram's concerns were directed eastward, and Israel could be allowed to flourish in peace; when Assyria was a threat to the entire region, Aram and Israel could form an alliance. Fortunes fluctuated: under the Israelite king Jehu, Hazael, the king of Damascus, attacked Israel; but the Judean Joash recovered lands from Aram. Under Jeroboam II Damascus came under Israelite control; but

OPPOSITE Gezer: A row of ten monoliths (some over nine feet tall), forming a north-south wall just inside the inner wall of the city. The structure, which was once thought to be a Canaanite "high place", dates from the sixteenth century BCE, when, free from Egyptian control, the city enjoyed its greatest prosperity.

OVERLEAF Megiddo. On the middle left of the picture is the Solomonic gate and on the raised area to the left of the palm tree is the Israelite casemate wall. In the foreground is the area with the stables or storage areas of the reign of Ahab, and to their right the ninth-century water system.

Rezin, allied with Israel, threatened Judah in the so-called Syro-Ephraimite war, and Ahaz brought in Tiglath-Pileser, who defeated and slew Rezin in 732 BCE (II Kings 16: 5–9). The Arameans were then deported (back to Qir?). Damascus lost its status, being included in the Assyrian province of Hamath. Thereafter Damascus remained an important economic, but not political, centre. Thus it remained during the Babylonian and Persian periods. In the Greco-Roman period it changed hands from the Seleucids to the Nabateans, to the Armenians, and finally to the Romans. From at least the sixth century onwards, and possibly from earlier, the city contained a Jewish community.

The Arameans occupied an important area, controlling trade routes along the Fertile Crescent and between Mesopotamia and Anatolia. The neighbouring Assyrians, who were racially akin to them, sought control over precisely this area. The result was an empire in which Aramean culture played a large role. In particular, the Aramaic language was widely used alongside Akkadian, as it was also under the Babylonians and under the Persians, when it was the recognized *lingua franca* of the western part of their empire. In 2 Kings 18: 26 the Assyrian *Rab-shakeh* is implored to speak in Aramaic rather than Hebrew, since Judean officials could speak it, but not the rest of the people. It became the language of Palestine, including Judah, from the sixth century BCE.

The chief gods of the Arameans were Baal and Hadad. Ashtar, Marduk, and Shamash were also worshipped, as in Mesopotamia. We have several inscriptions from these Aramean states, the best-known of which are from rulers named Zakkur, Kilamuwa, Bar-rakib, Panammuwa, and Azitawadda. These mainly recite the history of the king and, in most cases, his dealings with the Assyrians and give us little insight into the material culture of these states; they occasionally reveal the existence of dynastic gods.

Various connections are made in the Bible between Israelites and Arameans. In Deuteronomy 26: 5 Israel is described as descended from a "wandering Aramean" (or an "Aramean about to perish") — probably a reference to Jacob. According to Genesis 24 Jacob was sent to Abraham's "country and kindred", to "Aram Naharaim" ("Aram of the two rivers"), to the "city of Nahor", which was probably Harran (Genesis 27: 43), where lived Laban "the Aramean". Genesis 28 calls the territory "Paddan-Aram". It lay between the rivers Habor and Euphrates, bounded on the west by the cities of Carchemish and Aleppo. The area was occupied by the Aramean state of Bit-adini (2 Kings 19: 12; Amos 1: 5), which was absorbed into Assyria in 855 BCE. It was, of course, from Harran that, according to Genesis 12, Abraham had travelled to Canaan. The assertion of close kinship between the patriarchs and Arameans suggests that Israel contained racial elements that regarded themselves as Aramean by descent — as distinct from Canaanites. The possibility that this connection reflects political or economic affinities — as such connections often do — seems remote; there was little such affinity, and the geographical links with the Harran region suggest

OPPOSITE, ABOVE The Wadi Mojib (the ancient river Arnon) shown here marks the northern boundary of the territory of Moab, which comprised a plateau about 300 feet above the surrounding terrain (3000 feet above sea level). Deep gorges carried the rainwater into the Dead Sea, which lies beyond the hills in the background. Moab was well-watered and provided land for both agriculture and the grazing of animals, particularly sheep — according to 2 Kings 3: 4, Mesha, King of Moab, had to deliver in tribute to Israel the wool of "a hundred thousand lambs and a hundred thousand rams".

OPPOSITE, BELOW The heartland of Edom is in the mountainous range extending south from the Dead Sea, through which the ancient King's Highway ran from Aqabah in the south toward Damascus. Despite this apparently forbidding terrain, Edom was well populated in Old Testament times, and reasonably prosperous from trade, mining and agriculture. In the Greco-Roman period this area was inhabited by Nabateans, whose capital Petra lies at the southern end of this mountain range.

something more. The stories of Elijah and Elisha further connect Aram and Israel. They take place against the background of war between the two, but the cultural affinity is strongly suggested: Elijah comes from Gilead and Elisha anoints an Aramean king; Na'man the Aramean seeks help from Yhwh. Dangerous as it would be to insist on the historical accuracy of all of these stories, the implication of cultural and religious affinity remains strong.

EMPIRES

Palestine was the victim of imperial ambitions for most of the biblical period, and unavoidably so, since it lay in the path of both trade and military routes. In this respect its fate was no different from that of the Syrian or Transjordanian states, whose pretensions to autonomy were first denied by Assyria, which prepared the ground for the empires that were to follow. Additionally, Palestine stood between Egypt and Mesopotamia, between the Red Sea and the Mediterranean, and was regarded by Egypt as part of its own "sphere of influence". Inevitably, it could hardly be independent of the fortunes of Egypt.

On the eve of the Israelites' appearance there, Palestine was under Egyptian control, which passed, with Egyptian consent or encouragement, to the Philistines. The reigns of David and Solomon witnessed a brief spell of Israelite rule over Palestine and much of Transjordan. Under the divided monarchy the struggle for local supremacy lay between the two Israelite kingdoms and their neighbours, particularly Aram — but under the looming shadow of Assyria, whose ambitions had long been clear. One part after another of Syria-Palestine either fell under their vassalage or became absorbed into the Assyrian empire, as did Judah and Israel, respectively. From the Assyrian yoke Judah passed briefly to the Neo-Babylonian, and thence to the Persian. Thereafter it lay under the Hellenistic (Greek-Oriental) Ptolemies (Egypt), then the Seleucids (Syria). This was followed by the greatest era of Jewish political history, when the boundaries of the independent Jewish state briefly exceeded even those claimed for David. But this could never have been more than an interlude. After the advent of Rome, the Jordan became a boundary of the Empire, whose centre lay far to the west; and Judea, a buffer state or buffer province.

Egypt
Egypt was the immediate imperial neighbour of Palestine, though it exercised no direct control during the biblical period until the time of the Ptolemies. The Egyptians were not Semitic and their cultural affinities with their neighbours in the Fertile Crescent were much less strong than those among these peoples. Egypt enjoyed a stable political structure, based on a strong monarchy and elaborate bureaucracy, and helped by the artery of the Nile, which fed and unified the country. Relative isolation secured Egypt from continual invasion and occupation until the

seventh century and fostered a conservative mentality. Even in the Greco-Roman period, Egypt's Hellenistic culture preserved much of the indigenous character.

At the end of the Late Bronze Age (c. 1200 BCE) Egypt had control of Palestine, thanks to a peace treaty with the Hittites, concluded under Rameses II. Under his successor, Merneptah, the "sea peoples" invaded Egypt but were repulsed and in celebration of that event the pharaoh erected a stela on which the earliest mention of "Israel" occurs. The same pharaoh repulsed the "sea peoples", some of whom (Philistines) settled in Canaan, probably under Egyptian patronage. Egyptian intervention resumed with Sheshonk I, to whose court Jereboam I fled, and who invaded Palestine in the time of Rehoboam (1 Kings 14: 25–26). Egypt thereafter remained a necessary ally of both Israel and Judah. It was not only a potential (if usually ineffective) counterweight to Assyria, but also close and powerful enough to require appeasement. It provided a refuge for the inhabitants of Palestine in time of famine and also asylum for refugees fleeing before Assyria and Babylon. Such Jewish refugees provided the beginnings of what became a large Jewish population in Egypt in the Greco-Roman period. Egypt also recruited Jewish soldiers to guard its borders. One such colony was established at Elephantine, probably in the seventh or sixth century. Its archives, containing texts from the Persian period and written in Aramaic, refer to a Jewish temple and to other deities beside Yhwh (whom they refer to as Yahu) and contain some legal documents and a letter to Jerusalem about the celebration of Passover.

However, Egypt itself was invaded by the Assyrian kings Esarhaddon and Ashurbanipal between 670 and 660 BCE. It regained independence, and during the death-throes of Assyria, the pharaoh Necho took his army through Palestine to confront the Neo-Babylonians and Medes and presumably to lay claim to Palestine. Josiah's attempt to block him at Megiddo resulted in his own death. But Egypt won nothing: Nebuchadrezzar's victory at Carchemish opened up Palestine to him.

Egypt remained independent until Cambyses invaded in 525 BCE. Occasional revolts during the Persian period were unsuccessful, except for a spell of independence in 404–341. The arrival of Alexander the Great in 332 led eventually to a Macedonian dynasty, founded by Alexander's general Ptolemy, which administered Palestine until 199 BCE, when the dynasty of another of Alexander's generals, Seleucus, wrested it from the Ptolemies. During the strife that built up in Jerusalem under Seleucus's successors, one high priest, according to Josephus, fled with his supporters to Leontopolis, in Egypt, and built another temple there. It was also in Egypt, probably around this time, that the Hebrew scriptures were translated into Greek for the Greek-speaking Jewish population in Egypt, many of whom resided in the city of Alexandria.

In 30 BCE Egypt became a province of the Roman Empire. But whether under Persians, Macedonians, or Romans, Egypt's culture remained recognisably Egyptian. Three dominant factors in this culture

OPPOSITE The Egyptian
Pharaoh Amenhotep IV
(Akhenaten), with his
consort Nefertiti and
daughter, is sacrificing to the
sun-god Aten in the form of
a disk whose rays end in
hands, symbolizing his
many-sided creative activity.

are the Nile, the sun, and the bureaucracy. There is also the distinctive
Egyptian obsession with death. Subsistence — peasant existence and
the national economy — depended on the reliable annual flooding of
the Nile, which inundated a strip of land to either side of its banks. Hence,
the land of Egypt consisted of the Delta and a thin strip of land along
the Nile banks; beyond this, settled life, civilization, and administration
were not possible. Another regular phenomenon, and one that caught
the Egyptian imagination, was the daily passage of the sun: across the
sky, down through the underworld, and back up the other side (naturally
on a boat, the obvious means of travel). The chief gods of the official
pantheon were represented by the sun: Re or Atum, or both, and for
a brief spell, Aten. Bureaucracy is manifested not only in actual records,
but also in paintings of everyday scenes and, most memorably and
ubiquitously, of the judgment of the dead, in which the deeds of the
soul are recorded and weighed by divine bureaucrats. There was, of
course, a god of bureaucracy, called Thoth. Texts of instruction for
bureaucrats abound, too; and there was a goddess of justice, truth, and
order (Ma'at), personifying royal and scribal ideals — one might say,
the goddess of administration. Next to pharaohs, chief officials received
the best burials. The afterlife was taken for granted, and elaborate care
taken to preserve the bodies of the illustrious. At the popular level, the
most important god was Osiris, the god of the underworld, along with
his wife Isis and son Horus. The story of this family combined a
vegetation myth with a belief in personal immortality: Osiris was a king,
murdered by his brother Seth, descending to the realm of the dead, but
being avenged by his son Horus with the aid of Isis. Horus himself,
the all-seeing (his symbols were the eye and the hawk), was also killed
and his parts scattered, only to be recovered by Isis, who then restored

BELOW An Egyptian
judgement scene, where the
recently deceased (far left) is
brought to judgement by the
god Anubis. Anubis weighs
his heart; under the scales
sits the hybrid creature who
devours the heart which is
too heavy (centre). To the
right stands Thoth the
scribe, recording the
judgement, and on the far
right Horus presents the
deceased before the throne of
the god of the dead, Osiris.

Horus to life. It was this cult that became prominent in the Greco-Roman period, with Isis being revered even in distant parts of the Roman Empire.

Contacts between Egypt and Israel were long and varied. Although Egypt figures in the Bible most prominently in the Exodus story, we cannot locate that event historically. The tradition symbolizes Egypt as a "house of bondage", a place to be escaped from. But this was apparently not Egypt's role during Israel's history; oppression came more usually from the north, and Egypt was, rather, a place to escape *to*.

The influence of Egyptian religion on Israel is difficult to assess. The Bible betrays no interest at all in Egyptian religion and mentions none of its gods. Some cases of possible influence can, however, be cited. A once-popular fancy was the quasi-monotheistic religion of Aten introduced by Amenhotep IV (Akenaten); some scholars used to suggest that this development may have influenced Moses' discovery of monotheism. Akhenaten's hymn to Aten (see ANET pp. 369–70) is quite similar to Psalm 104, and some direct borrowing is possible. The "Theology of Memphis" (ANET pp. 4–6), which glorifies the god Ptah as creating the world by his word, has also been suggested as an influence on Genesis 1, but this is dubious. A more probable case of borrowing exists between the *Instruction of Amen-em-ope* (ANET p. 421–424) and Proverbs 22: 17–24; more generally, the influence of Egyptian wisdom, copiously attested in books of Instructions, which gave advice on how to behave and succeed in life, often expressed in short sentences or epigrams, may be seen in Proverbs, where the lurking principle of an automatic retribution for folly may reflect the principle of justice personified by the goddess Ma'at.

Egyptian influence in the Greco-Roman period must also be taken into consideration; but such influence — as, for example, upon Jewish apocalyptic literature and upon the Wisdom of Solomon, II Maccabees, and (possibly) Tobit — stems not from indigenous Egyptian culture but from Hellenized Egyptian culture or even Hellenistic culture merely located in Egypt. The status of Jews in Alexandria is disputed; however, they were extremely numerous, and seem to have formed a distinct citizenry. Riots here between Jews and non-Jews are recorded, and the Wisdom of Solomon exhibits bitterness towards the author's host nation.

Hittites and Hurrians

The Hittites and Hurrians were both Indo-European peoples; they both established empires in the vicinity of Syria during the Middle Bronze and Late Bronze periods. The Hittite "new kingdom", which just preceded the emergence of Israel, was really Hittite-Hurrian; the dynasty was Hurrian, as were the major deities, and the Hurrian language was widely used.

By "Hittites" what are generally referred to are the people of the central Anatolian plain, whose state developed in Asia Minor between 2000 and 1700 BCE, centred on the city of Hattusa (modern Boğhazköy, in Turkey), and grew after 1700 into a network of allied and vassal states extending into Syria and beyond. Hittite control in Syria later gave way to the Hurrian kingdom of Mitanni, until about 1450, when the second period of Hittite, or Hittite-Hurrian, power ensued, reaching its zenith under Suppiluliumas (c. 1380–1350). Thereafter Syria was under Hittite control for two centuries. The treaty of 1284 between Hatti (as their nation was called) and Egypt set the boundary between them just south of Damascus. But Hattusa was overrun in 1190, and since no written record of the event survives, we do not know by whom. Seven Hittite city-states (such as Hamath) remained in Syria alongside Aramean states; the Assyrians knew the region as "Hatti-land". These cities are often called Neo-Hittite, and their language (Luvian) differed from that of the earlier Hittite empire.

The Hittites were chiefly agriculturalists, at the summit of whose feudal society was the king, the effective proprietor of the land, though in theory the deputy of the real owner, the storm god. In war, the king was the commander; in religion, the chief priest. Of the numerous deities of the Hittites (several borrowed from the Hurrians), many were attached to particular cities, according to the typical Near Eastern pattern. In the state cult the leading deities were the storm god, Wurusima, and the sun goddess, Taru; but these and other deities were supplanted in the

An eighth-century Hittite relief showing a procession of officials from Carchemish.

fifteenth century by their Hurrian counterparts, the chief of these being the storm god Teššup and his consort Hebat.

Hittite laws are of special interest, since they not only are extensively preserved but also, like the Hurrian texts from Nuzu, reflect Indo-European, rather than Semitic principles — in particular that of compensation, rather than of talion, or punishment in kind ("an eye for an eye . . ."). There are also numerous treaty texts; whether this betrays a feature of Hittite diplomacy or an accident of preservation, we cannot know. Also preserved are royal annals and proclamations. However, many extant Hittite texts are in Akkadian, and both the covenant treaties and annals conform broadly to the ancient Near Eastern pattern exemplified in numerous Assyrian texts.

The Bible does not allude to the Anatolian Hittites, but does mention the probably unrelated Palestinian "Hittites", whose identity is unknown (Uriah, the husband of Bathsheba may be one such; note his Yahwistic name and service in the Judean militia). Passages in 1 Kings (10: 29) and 2 Kings (7: 6) must refer to the Hittite states of Syria. Some cultural influence upon Israel from the Anatolian Hittites has nevertheless been claimed. A correspondence has been seen between the international treaty form used by the Hittites and both the structure of the Sinai covenant and the book of Deuteronomy. Individual laws in the Bible also parallel Hittite laws (e.g. the heifer-sacrificing ceremony of Deuteronomy 21: 1–9; the scapegoat ceremony of Leviticus 16; the drawing off of a sandal to indicate non-discharge of responsibility, as in Ruth 4 and Deuteronomy 25: 5–10). Another area of possible Hittite influence is historiography; but this remains controversial. Some other phenomena in the Bible may be explained from the Hittites, for example the ōbôt ("mediums"?), available, according to 1 Samuel 28: 3, to enquirers of God. The Hittite aybi was a pit which served as access to or for a spirit of the lower world. Also, teraphîm, apparently devices for predicting the future, are probably related to the Hittite tarpi, or "demon". Yet it is difficult to characterize or explain any cultural-religious Hittite influence, much of which must, in any case, remain hypothetical.

The Hurrians, who can be traced in Mesopotamia from about 2100 BCE, spread into northwest Mesopotamia and northern Syria between 1700 and 1600. In Mitanni, upper Mesopotamia, early in the fifteenth century, a dynasty of kings established a brief empire, which dominated Syria and Assyria. There was also an allied Hurrian kingdom in Cilicia, in Asia Minor. After Mitanni had fallen to Assyrians and Hittites, in 1350, the Hurrians, their language, and their culture, remained influential in northern Syria and apparently even in Palestine. The most important Hurrian archive is from Nuzi, on the upper Tigris. From the legal texts discovered here several parallels to episodes in the patriarchal narratives have been suggested; among these are the adoption of slaves by childless couples (Genesis 15: 2–3), the giving of a concubine to her husband by a childless wife; and the selling of a birthright. These parallels, if they do demonstrate Hurrian influence, have no bearing on the authenticity or date of the patriarchal stories, but more likely attest the survival of Hurrian practices in Canaan well into the Israelite period.

Assyria

More than any other foreign nation, Assyria defined the political shape of the ancient Near East during the biblical period. The city of Asshur lay on the Tigris River about 200 miles (320 kilometres) north of Babylon, near the edge of the northern Mesopotamian plain. Other major cities of Assyria were Calah and Nineveh. Assyria was bordered on the west by the Syrian desert and on the north and east by mountains separating it from the ancient kingdoms of Urartu and Media respectively.

As a biblical tradition (Genesis 10: 11) supposes, Assyria was originally settled by people from farther down the Tigris-Euphrates basin, in Babylonia. It is from this direction that Assyria is most easily accessible; the Akkadian language of Assyria is virtually a dialect of Babylonian; and many of the gods of Assyria are also Babylonian. The script is derived from the older inhabitants of Southern Mesopotamia, the Sumerians. It appears that after Sumerian and Babylonian occupation, Assyria assumed independence sometime about 2000 BCE, when we find it trading with Asia Minor, an activity that was later to govern Assyrian imperial policy during the biblical period.

Assyria emerged as a military power in the fourteenth century BCE under Ashur-uballit I and his immediate successors; again they marched west, to Carchemish and Haran. Their first forays as far as the Mediterranean coast of Phoenicia were under Tiglath-Pileser I (c. 1100) who

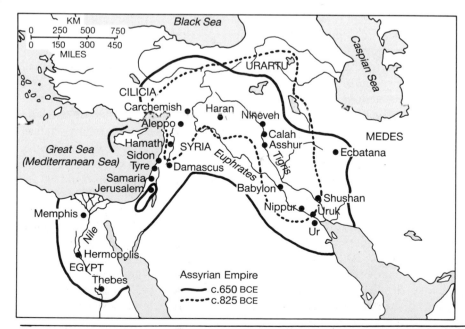

Map 6 The Assyrian Empire, c. 825 BCE and c. 650 BCE.

The Black Obelisk of Shalmaneser III (859–824 BCE) was erected in the city of Nimrud (Calah) to commemorate, in words and pictures, the victories of the Assyrian king. One of its panels depicts the Israelite monarch "Jehu son of Omri" (or possibly his representative) offering tribute.

took tribute from Gebal, Sidon, and Arvad. After two centuries of involvement elsewhere, Assyria again pushed towards the Mediterranean in the ninth century under Ashurnasirpal II, in a series of sporadic but vicious campaigns, celebrated in contemporary Assyrian accounts. His successor, Shalmaneser III, developed a more consistent policy of annual campaigns in all directions. In 853 he fought at Qarqar a coalition of twelve states, led by Damascus and including other Arameans, Israel, some Phoenician ports, a token Egyptian force, Arabians, and Ammonites. The battle was inconclusive, but in 841, Shalmaneser defeated Hazael of Damascus and received tribute from Tyre, Sidon, and King Jehu of Israel, as depicted on the Black Obelisk, which he had erected in his own honour.

Shalmaneser's policy and aims contrast markedly with those of his predecessors, who had represented themselves simply as predators. His annals stress the economic and material gains of his campaigns — in particular raw materials, luxury items, and manpower for building projects. Assyria now had access to the Mediterranean coast, and especially to Cilicia, a source of iron and silver. These and other goods accrued from yearly tribute and from one-sided trade agreements. Assyrian-populated colonies were established in distant places, which obviated the need for annual campaigns for tribute, as well as providing potential military bases.

After another respite for Syria, Tiglath-Pileser III re-launched the westward drive in 744 BCE, exacting tribute from many states, including Israel. When Damascus and Israel formed an alliance against Judah, presumably in an anti-Assyrian move, Ahaz of Judah appealed to Tiglath-Pileser who annexed Damascus to his empire and reduced Israel to a small area around the city of Samaria. Sargon II's annexation, in 721, of Samaria and evacuation of its inhabitants were not solely punitive, but also served a policy of resettling areas of the empire depopulated by the removal of slaves for building projects under Ashurnasirpal II and Shalmaneser III. Furthermore, the Assyrian population was too small to sustain its empire, and so was enlarged by forced immigration. The Assyrians drafted defeated soldiers into their ranks and imported craftsmen for building programmes these assimilated as Assyrians. The names of officials called *limmu*, by whose terms of office years were dated, contain many foreign names; Israelites do not appear here, but many may have become Assyrians. Had it not been for a last-minute settlement — or, as Isaiah 37: 8–37 describes, a miraculous intervention — Judeans would doubtless have joined them in 701 BCE, when Sennacherib captured all of Judah but Jerusalem itself. Before this campaign, and his assassination shortly afterwards, he had rebuilt Nineveh, and, indeed, prisoners from his campaigns (doubtless including Israelites) are depicted at work there.

In 672 BCE Esarhaddon was able to conquer part of Egypt — a victory reasserted (after an Egyptian coup) by his successor, Ashurbanipal, under whom the Assyrian empire reached its greatest extent.

An Assyrian relief from Sennacherib's palace at Nineveh (c. 700 BCE). It shows slaves engaged in building the palace. To erect the many monumental buildings, for which Assyria itself had too little manpower, the Assyrian rulers often resorted to transporting populations from subjugated lands.

But within only a few years it was to be obliterated by the resurgence of Media and Babylon from the south and east, and Scythians from the north. Asshur fell in 614, Nineveh in 612, and finally Harran in 610. Assyria no longer existed, except as a geographical region.

The Assyrians have earned for themselves a reputation as warlike and vicious — a reputation which their own graphic art seems to confirm. The great Lachish frieze, for instance, shows an efficient and cruel war machine. Assyrian kings also took trouble in their annals to record in self-glowing detail their military exploits. Other favoured subjects of Assyrian friezes are hunting, in which the slaughter of animals (as well as their muscular strength) is emphasized. Nevertheless, the cruelty and militarism of Assyria form only part of the picture. The Assyrians' geographical position made them vulnerable, for they did not live on profitable trade routes, and were surrounded by powerful states like Mitanni, Urartu, Mari, and Babylon. Their military aggression is partly explained by a feeling of miliary and economic insecurity (and perhaps also of cultural inferiority). The main aim of Assyrian expansion was in fact trade, of which Syria was always the hub and the Arameans the proprietors. Assyria subdued its empire by an ideology of terror, including exemplary ruthlessness and exaggerated accounts of exploits.

Yet there are also impressive cultural achievements to chronicle. The Assyrians were far from uncultured, and their role in the transmission of Mesopotamian civilization was considerable, although distinctive characteristics are not easy to isolate. Victims of foreign campaigns were conscripted to work on magnificent building programmes in cities such as Calah (modern Nimrud), where, for example, Ashurnasirpal had botan-

The siege and capture of the Judean city of Lachish by Sennacherib (700 BCE) is depicted in a frieze on the wall of the palace at Nineveh. Here a siege engine can be seen at the walls alongside Assyrian archers, while firebrands and stones are being hurled down by the defenders, and some Judeans can be seen coming through the gateway.

ical and zoological gardens constructed. The many different kinds of sculpture and relief work undertaken include glazed panels, ivory carvings, metalwork, and murals. Ashurbanipal, in the seventh century, created a library, collecting and copying texts from Assyrian and non-Assyrian archives, as a result of which many otherwise unknown texts have been recovered. Assyrian administration is extensively recorded in numerous texts, including not only the royal annals but also building inscriptions, letters, and legal texts. The literary bequest also includes religious texts, including myths and legends, hymns, proverbs, and records of observations of entrails, astronomical bodies, and omens. From such observations arose the rudiments of anatomy, astronomy, botany, and mathematics.

The administration of the Assyrian empire was headed by the king, who was both religious and military leader of the nation and regent for the god Asshur. Tribute was collected by local governors, where these were appointed (e.g. the *rab-shakeh*, Isaiah 36). It is important to distinguish between territories ruled by vassal kings and those annexed to Assyria. The former were expected to pay tribute but little else. Although the Assyrians deliberately aimed to control their empire by terror, much of their military activity was in response to revolt. It was

common to remove cult statues from defeated lands at the time of conquest, but once the vassal status had been formally acknowledged and instituted by the appropriate oaths, these statues were usually returned and the local cults continued unmolested. There is no evidence of Assyrian interference in the cult of vassal states. In territories formally annexed, however, it seems that the population, now regarded as citizens of Assyria, were obliged to support the Assyrian cult. Thus, it seems, there would have been no imposition of Assyrian religion on either Israel or Judah under Assyrian vassalage. Even after the annexation of Samaria in 720, although the worship of other gods entered with the colonists, the worship of Yhwh continued alongside these cults. The probability is that some syncretism between Asshur and local deities frequently took place in annexed territories. But the Assyrian empire, in destroying the political power of the Aramean states nevertheless acquired a strongly Aramaic character, at least in the areas to the west of its own heartland. Aramaic was the *lingua franca* of most of the region between the Tigris and the Mediterranean, and Arameans the traders who provided the economic blood-supply. Aramean scribes were drafted into the Assyrian administration alongside Assyrians. In the eighth-seventh centuries we should speak of an Assyrian-Aramaic culture, and

These friezes from the palace at Nineveh of Ashurbanipal (668–629 BCE), last of the great Assyrian kings, depict lion-hunting. In the upper panel the king is holding a rampant lion by the tail, while in the lower panel he is pouring a libation over the carcases. The decoration of palaces with friezes depicting slaughter, whether in war or recreation, conveys the aura of power which Assyrian monarchs cultivated to subdue their vassals.

this is no doubt how Israel and Judah experienced it, as far as religion and language were concerned. Such a state of affairs may be reflected in Genesis 10: 22 where Aram is presented as the brother of Asshur.

The religion of Assyria was in many respects like that of Babylonia. However, there was apparently an especially strong allegiance to the national deity Asshur. The Assyrian annals represent the king consistently as a subject of Asshur, in whose service Assyria's enemies are overcome and whose name recurs frequently in the annals as the giver of victory. Assyrian wars were holy wars. Yet the Assyrians did not claim their victories as triumphs of Asshur over other gods but as the result of support for Assyria by those other gods. The speech of the *rab-shakeh* in 2 Kings 18: 25 is a plausible construction of Assyrian propaganda in this respect — Yhwh, he claims, is on Assyria's side. In Assyria, although Asshur was the national god and supreme patron of the king, other deities were also worshipped. Many of these were particularly associated with certain cities, as in Babylonia, where their cult was celebrated in temples and ziggurats. Most of these deities — for example, Anu, Hadad, Ishtar, Nabu, and Sin — were also worshipped by Babylonians and Arameans.

By the time the Bible was written down, which took place almost entirely in the Persian period, Assyria had passed into history, though its memory remained powerful. That part of the world, unlike Egypt, or even Babylon, was unknown; Jews taken there from Samaria apparently never returned. Although it was once supposed that under Manasseh, in particular, Assyrian religion was introduced into Judah, it now seems that the biblical denunciation implying reversion to *Canaanite* practice may be nearer the truth; it was apparently not towards Assyrian but Syrian (i.e. Aramean) cults — including the cult of Moleh — that Judeans turned in the seventh century. The Assyrians presented themselves to Israel and Judah not as a foreign culture or religion but as a military predator, and one to be feared (see Isaiah 10: 13–14). This hatred is expressed in the prophet Nahum's jubilation over the fall of Nineveh (Nahum 3). In the case of Jonah's mission Nineveh probably serves as an ironic example of repentance from the most hated nation and the concern of Yhwh for human beings.

Babylon

Babylon is a city on the Euphrates (in Hebrew and Akkadian "gate of God") which has given its name to lower Mesopotamia, the Tigris-Euphrates basin. It was open to invasion on all sides, and aspired only briefly to widespread military conquest, though it remained a cultural centre. Because of its close ties with Assyria, it was treated respectfully, despite its frequent revolts against Assyrian rule. The city may go back as early as the third millennium BCE, but it came to prominence in the eighteenth century BCE with the Amorite dynasty of Hammurabi. However, between the sixteenth century and the sixth, Babylon enjoyed independence only intermittently. It became a major power with the rise of the Chaldean (also called Neo-Babylonian) dynasty under

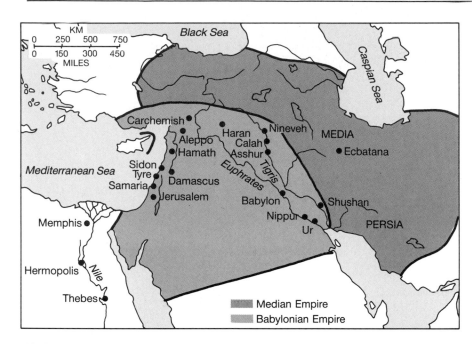

MAP 7 The Median and Babylonian Empires, sixth century BCE.

Nabopolassar, when it finally overthrew Assyria. Its prominence was short-lived; it was, in turn, captured by Cyrus the Persian. However, under successive foreign empires it flourished as a major cultural and economic centre. It was an important city of the Persian empire until it was captured by Alexander the Great, who died there in 323. Subsequently it belonged to the Seleucids until 64 BCE, when it passed into the control of the Parthians.

Religion and society are difficult to separate in Babylon, as in most ancient Near Eastern societies. The king was the supreme priest, under whom were numerous priestly castes. Priestly activities ranged from temple maintenance, sacrifice, and liturgy to the casting of spells, diagnosis of medical complaints, and the reading of various kinds of omen. The major cities had their own festivals and sacred days, the best known (held for example at Babylon, Ur, and Asshur) was the *akitu* festival, which, in local variations, featured the ritual re-enthronement of the king by the god, possibly accompanied by a ritual combat celebrating the creation of the world and a "sacred marriage". Babylonian religion (like Assyrian) operated at three levels: national, city, and private. At the national level we find the supreme triad of Babylonian gods, consisting of Anu, the heaven god (principal temple at Uruk); Enlil (chief temple at Nippur), the storm and air god; and Ea, the god of water and of wisdom (chief temple at Eridu). Their consorts were Inanna, Ninlil, and Damgal respectively. These gods had been borrowed from the earlier Sumerians; others making up the pantheon included Marduk (of Babylon); Bel (= Baal); Ishtar, the fertility goddess; Sin, the moon god (of Ur and Harran, consort Ningal); Shamash, the sun god (of Sippar and Larsa, consort Aya); and Nebo, the god of science,

RIGHT The refurbishing of the Ishtar gate of Babylon (dating from c. 580 BCE, i.e. during the Jewish exile) formed part of Nebuchadrezzar's extensive building programme. The gate was situated in the northern wall of the city, on the east bank of the Euphrates. At the New Year enthronement festival the images of the gods were carried through it along the "Processional Way" to the Akitu-Temple. The restored gate, decorated with glazed enamel bricks depicting bulls and dragons, now stands in the Vorderasiastisches Museum in Berlin.

OPPOSITE Petra, the capital of the Nabateans (fourth century BCE-second century CE). The kingdom was founded mainly on trade, and the city made viable by a well-engineered system of reservoirs. The impressive remains of this desert city belong almost entirely to the first century CE. Many of them are the work of Greek masons, but tombs like these exhibit an eclectic native style.

who was especially popular in Assyria. The goddess of war and hunting was Ninurta; Nergal (consort Ereshkigal) ruled the underworld. Gods of foreign origin included the storm god Hadad (Adad), Dagon, and Dumuzi (Tammuz), a god of vegetation. Some syncretism took place: Marduk and Bel replaced Enlil in some formulations, and Ishtar could be identified with Inanna. It seems that although each of the major gods was patron of a different city, there was little overlap, and thus some form of rationalization between cults of the city-states may have occurred.

At the city level, the local god was paramount in the cult; its temple would be the focus of the city's religious life and festivities, supporting a large priesthood and playing a central role in the city's economy; it owned most of the land. At the private level, there was a host of minor deities, Babylonian cosmology divided the cosmos into the upper and lower worlds, each populated by a host of minor deities; in the upper world by the *Igigu*, in the lower by the *Annunaku*. These, in company

with numerous spirits, both good and evil, played a larger part in every-day private life than the major gods.

The language of Babylonia, Akkadian, was Semitic, and was written in syllables, usually on clay with a wedge-shaped stylus (*cuneus* — hence cuneiform writing). Literary remains range from grammar books through love songs, fables, incantations, and omen lists, to myths about the creation of the world and the Flood. The Babylonian Chronicle, from the Chaldean period, is widely regarded as a remarkably objective account of political events. Also in the Chaldean, Persian, and Greek periods, an increased interest in astrology and horoscopes is observable.

Babylon's dealings with Judah were brief but highly consequential. Second Kings 20 tells of an apparent attempt by Merodach-Baladan (Marduk-apla-iddina) to achieve independence from Assyria with help from Judah. Some Babylonians were deported by Sargon II to Samaria (2 Kings 17). After Babylon secured hegemony over Palestine, and follow-ing a series of inept gestures of protest and rebellion, Nebuchadrezzar had Jerusalem besieged and captured, the Temple razed, and a section of the population deported. Yet a generation or two later most Jews exiled there preferred to remain rather than return, forming communities which grew larger and more important throughout the biblical period; their academies formed the centre of rabbinic Judaism from the third century CE. The influence of Babylon on monarchic Israel is moot. The *akitu*-festival has been used as a basis for reconstructing a New Year festival at Jerusalem, but the occasion for such influence is uncertain. The hypothesis of a general ancient Near Eastern religious pattern is equally dubious.

The influence of the Babylonian exile and diaspora upon the character of Judaism ought not to be underestimated. We ought to attribute to this experience not only the emergence or at least the increased prominence of a number of basic characteristics of Judaism, such as synagogue, circumcision, and sabbath, but also of law and its interpreta-tion, the political and economic power of the priesthood, and the understanding of the world as a system of signs (manticism). As for the biblical literature, most of which was composed during and after the exile, here the influence is also great. The stories of creation and flood in Genesis 1–11 show close parallels to stories and themes in Babylo-nian mythology; the literature about Enoch (collected in 1 Enoch; see chapter 14) betrays a good deal of Babylonian influence, as do parts of Daniel. What is not certain is how much of this cultural, literary, and religious influence was exerted during the sixth-century exile and how much was mediated afterwards via the large Jewish communities in Babylonia, and notably by their academies.

Persians and Medes

The arrival of the Persians in the land now called Iran was the result of that Indo-European migration early in the second millennium which also produced the Hurrians. Some of these Indo-Europeans settled east

PREVIOUS PAGES This rather simple limestone tomb in Pasargadae in Persia (modern Iran) is reputedly the burial place of Cyrus (550–530 BCE), who, by conquering his father-in-law the Median king, Astyages, founded the Persian empire. He subsequently took Babylon and authorized the resettlement of Jewish exiles to Judea, for which he was acclaimed as Yhwh's "messiah" ("anointed") by the Jewish poet known as Second Isaiah (Isaiah 45: 1).

OPPOSITE The high cliffs and narrow gorges surrounding Petra made the city almost impregnable.

of the Tigris, and are referred to in the annals of Shalmaneser II around 836 BCE as paying tribute to him. Their territory, called Parsuash, was also ''visited'' (in the words of the Assyrian historian) by Tiglath-Pileser III, who paid a similar visit to a related and neighbouring Indo-European tribe, the Medes. Some years before the fall of Nineveh, both regions became fully independent. At this period, the Medes were the more powerful, and in alliance with the Babylonians they sacked Nineveh under their king Cyaxares, whose son Astyages gave his daughter in marriage to the son of the Persian king, Anshan. This son, named Cyrus, united the two tribes. In so doing, he waged war against his father-in-law and sacked the Median capital of Ecbatana. Media then became the first satrapy of the Persian empire. Henceforth ''Medes'' (as they were better known to the Greeks) and ''Persians'' constituted one empire.

The Persian empire grew westwards into Armenia and much of Asia Minor, and eastwards towards India, before Cyrus turned his attention to Babylon, to whose subjects he presented himself as the legitimate sucessor of the old dynasty. He effected a minimum of change in the administration of that country. The innovation and liberalism of his policy of allowing exiles to return and sponsoring local religion have been much overemphasized; it was neither new, nor disinterested.

Cyrus' successor, Cambyses, added Egypt to the empire. But on Cambyses' death in 522 BCE there was the first of the palace revolutions that were to plague the history of the empire, especially at moments of royal succession. Darius won this struggle and imposed his rule over the empire, including Egypt. Already in this period, however, we should note the presence of Greek traders and mercenaries and the fact that much of our best information on the Persian empire comes from Greek

MAP 8 The Persian Empire, sixth to fourth century BCE.

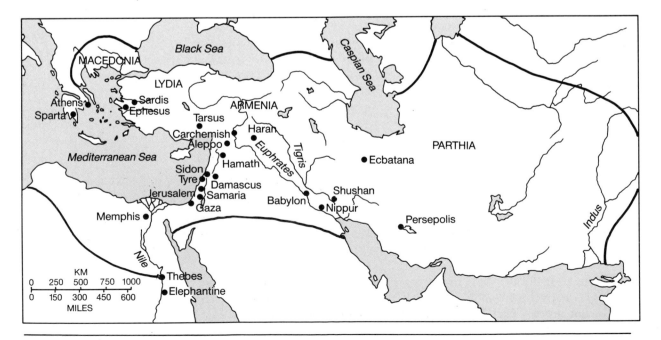

This impression, made from a cylinder seal of agate found at Thebes in Egypt shows the Persian king Darius I (522–486) hunting lions. Although the artistic style, as well as the winged disk of the god Ahura-Mazda above are both distinctively Persian, the scene incorporates many motifs from earlier Assyrian friezes, such as those of Ashurbanipal.

writers — Herodotus, and also Xenophon, who led a mercenary force to aid an unsuccessful revolt against the Persian king. With Darius began the 200-year struggle between Persia and Greece which Alexander the Great finally ended. Artaxerxes (465–423), probably Nehemiah's monarch (see chapter 6), was succeeded by Darius II, after the usual struggle; and he, in turn, by Artaxerxes II, who also had to cope with a rebellious Egypt. It was his successor, Artaxerxes III, who accomplished this. After Arses, Darius II (335–330) had to face the revenge of the Greeks, now united under a Macedonian, Alexander the Great.

The conquest of the entire Persian empire by Alexander was not the end of Persia. Another Persian empire was to rise under the Parthians centuries later. Although existing much later than the biblical period, this empire saw the essential completion of the Talmud within its large Jewish communities — outside the orbit of Christianity — before yielding to the forces of Islam.

The Persians were a relatively small warrior society; its warriors belonged to guilds each of which had a master. The army was based, like the Roman army later, upon units of fifty and multiples thereof. The famous road system which the Persians developed was designed especially for military movement — again, like the Romans; there were stores at intervals on the route. Of course, these also facilitated trade. Land was owned largely by vassals, who received them from the king. Usually the vassals were soldiers, who in return offered their service.

The empire was divided into satrapies, usually about twenty at any given period, and each was subdivided into provinces and then into districts. Each satrap had an elaborate financial and military administrative system at his disposal. Although the satrap was Persian, his subordinates would be local. The Persians were too small a nation to control the empire, except by allowing local structures and personnel to govern under Persian overall organization. This created a flexible empire, but one conducive to nationalistic revolt and which, when broken up, could revert to previous structures, as it did under Alexander's successors. An empire-wide system of scrutiny was maintained by the king's "eyes", who visited parts of the empire unannounced. However, despite good communications, the cohesion of the empire was frequently strained; satraps were in command of large areas which they often treated as minor domains of their own, and satrapies often became hereditary (as did fiefs, often held in the end by militarily untrained and unwilling persons).

Much of Persian art, certainly royal art, is in the Assyrian tradition, especially the excellent stone carvings. Babylonian influence is weak, except in enamelled brickwork. Greek influence is also seen, and Greek craftsmen were employed in the Persian court. The language of the Persians, Old Persian, was written in cuneiform. Throughout the western part of the empire, Aramaic was the language of bureaucracy, as well as of most of the population. Of literature other than royal inscriptions we know very little.

The deity most often mentioned by Darius in his inscriptions is Ahura Mazda, whose principal priests were the Median tribe of Magi. In the religion of Mazda the king played a major part as supreme priest and supreme warrior (though the latter title was honorary; the king did not always engage in combat. Other deities were Ahita and Mithra, who was especially venerated by soldiers. In the late Roman Empire the cult of Mithra was widely followed, especially by soldiers, and was a serious rival to Christianity. According to Herodotus the Persians worshipped heaven, the sun and moon, and the elements of air, fire and water. But although the Persian prophet Zoroaster (c. 1000 BCE) pre-dated the empire, it is not certain whether the religion of the Persian kings was Zoroastrian. Darius I is often thought to have adopted the prophet's teachings, which proclaimed Mazda as a single, good god, represented by fire and water, and opposed by an evil force. This system later developed into a full dualism. Importantly, Zoroastrianism was not a nationalistic religion and did not play a role in imperialistic ideology.

The Persians are portrayed rather favourably in the Bible. Cyrus is proclaimed Yhwh's agent by Second Isaiah (2 Isaiah 44: 28–45: 7); Nehemiah, his cupbearer, is given a commission to rebuild Jerusalem; and the Temple is rebuilt by Persian decree. In Daniel 6, which is set in the reign of Darius ("the Mede"), the king is on the side of Daniel. Most remarkably, perhaps, we find a Jew, Esther, as a Persian queen, a circumstance presented as quite natural. Does all this indicate some kind of respect for Persian culture? It is difficult, in fact, to illustrate the extent of contact between the province of Judah and the Persians, of whose empire it formed a part. Artefactual remains suggest rather little Persian influence compared to the lowlands and the coastal plain. Angelology and eschatology have often been thought to derive from Persian religion, together with several traits of apocalyptic literature. The correspondences are wide and impressive, but it is difficult to specify very many direct connections. However, there can be little doubt of the presence of Persian dualism in the Dead Sea Scrolls, which remains without an entirely satisfactory explanation. Such dualism is hard to find in other contemporary Jewish literature.

Greece

The long struggle between Persia and Greece ended when Alexander the Great (died 323) marched victorious through its empire. Although technically one might call his victory and the resulting empire Macedonian, Macedonia was but the agent of Greek culture; Alexander had been a pupil of Aristotle and saw himself as champion of the Greeks. But he created no single political empire. The semi-autonomous satrapies, often old kingdoms in new forms, became Greek kingdoms; after decades of fighting between Alexander's successors, the *diadochi*, two realms emerged in the Near East: the kingdom of Ptolemy, which comprised Egypt and Palestine, and that of Seleucus, including Mesopotamia and Syria; each king ruled from a newly-built Hellenistic city (Alexandria and Antioch, respectively). Many other cities were founded as settlements for Greek soldiers and traders; but in the spirit of Hellenism they embraced many of the local populace, too.

In 198 BCE Antiochus III defeated Ptolemy V and gained control of Palestine. The change of sovereign marked, and possibly contributed to, an intensification of strife between two Judean families, those of Onias and Tobias, which led to civil war and then to war between the Selucids and Judeans (see chapter 7). The rapid decay of both Hellenistic kingdoms permitted a revival of Judean imperialism under the Hasmonean dynasty, which itself ended in civil war. These events were all played out against the backdrop of an encroaching Rome. Yet from the time of Alexander the Great onwards, we can rightly speak of the Greco-Roman period, for while Rome later assumed political sovereignty, the character of the Empire owed most to the Greek ethos, which, combined with elements of Oriental culture, produced "Hellenism"; the Greek

MAP 9 The Empire of Alexander the Great and his successors, fourth to first century BCE.

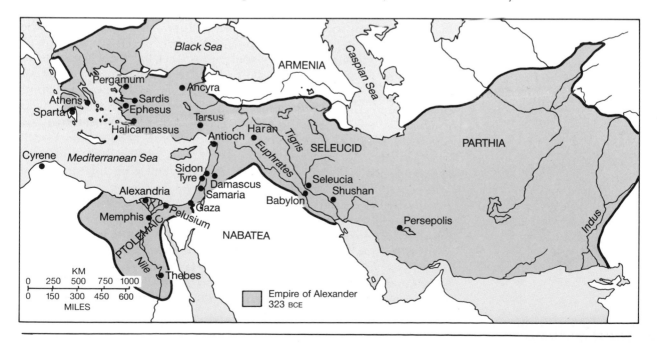

empire, therefore, was a cultural, not a political, entity.

There are essential differences between the Greek and the preceding Oriental states, and hence in their respective empires. The earlier empires were monarchic and reinforced by divine sanction. Assyria, Babylon, and Persia were essentially a product of Oriental feudalism, with the conquering nations ruling over vassal states. The replacement of local rulers created an administratively cohesive empire, as with Persia; but in fact regional cultural autonomy persisted in either case. Although the Persian empire introduced a measure of concern for the welfare of all its subjects, the satraps' essential function was the gathering of taxes. Like its predecessors, this empire consisted of the ruling nation and the ruled nations.

The system was different in Greece, where cities were smaller and were ruled by élite democracy. No monarchy existed, and the gods were not invoked in the political process. The ideological corollaries of a system in which citizenship replaces aristocracy are as follows: rational decision-making by equals replaces royal decree; politics becomes the responsibility and duty of the individual citizen. As John Marks puts it, the three "lines of Greek thought" are humanism, politics, and justice — each insisting on the value and responsibility of the individual, balanced against the demands of society. These values were enshrined in the Greek system of education, which taught that philosophy was an integral part of political life. Thus Hellenism was a way of life open to all or any, and not reserved for Greeks. It was *anti*-nationalistic and secular. Judaism, accordingly, survived either through preserving its own sovereignty (temporarily) or by defining itself as a philosophy, in which it succeeded on many levels.

Hellenism is not explicitly addressed as an issue in the Old Testament, though it looms in the books of 1 and 2 Maccabees in the Apocrypha. Greece (Yawan, "Ionia"?) is, however, mentioned — e.g. in Genesis 10 (1 Chronicles 1), Joel 3: 6 (Greeks as traders alongside Phoenicians), and Second Isaiah 66: 19 (as a place far off). But in the book of Daniel, Greece is named three times as the world empire succeeding Persia. Antiochus IV, the Seleucid "king of the north" who issues the final challenge to the sovereignty of the "Most High" is portrayed by Daniel as a horn growing on the head of the Greek beast, but not as representing the beast itself. Since both Ptolemies and Seleucids had previously administered Palestine tolerantly, no condemnation of Greece itself is implied.

Although the Roman Empire intervenes in the eastern Mediterranean during our period, its direct cultural, as opposed to political, influence is not considerable, and many scholars choose to speak of the "Greco-Roman" as a period of continuous cultural identity. Since, too, the major centres of the Roman Empire lay elsewhere, and since the Old Testament takes no account of it, the Roman world most appropriately belongs in a discussion of the New Testament and of early and rabbinic Judaism.

PART II

THE HISTORY AND RELIGION
OF ISRAEL

Jericho in the Jordan Valley, west of the river, is perhaps the oldest inhabited
city yet uncovered, its occupation dating from about 7000 BCE. This urn in
the shape of a head was unearthed from a burial chamber and dates from the
eighteen–sixteenth century BCE. Although this is well before the emergence of
Israel, the Canaanite culture it represents lasted until 1200 BCE.

CHAPTER 4

UNTIL THE TIME
OF SOLOMON

Where does the history of Israel begin? The obvious, simple answer to this question may seem tautological, but it is an answer with far-reaching implications. The history of Israel begins with Israel. That is, it begins with an association of tribes that were occupying the Samaria and Bethel Hills and possibly parts of Lower Galilee around 1230 BCE. But this simple answer raises a whole host of questions. Surely the Old Testament account begins much earlier, with Abraham (c. 1900 BCE)? What about the Exodus, the wanderings in the wilderness, and the conquest of Canaan?

In order to answer these questions it is necessary first to distinguish between the actual history of Israel, so far as it can be known, and the Old Testament narratives *about* that history. The history of Israel is something reconstructed by scholars on the basis of various types of evidence, which includes the Old Testament, the results of archaeological surveys, and the historical records of Israel's neighbours. Any particular reconstruction will reflect the interests and biases of the author(s), it will be open to correction or modification in the light of new discoveries, and it may well contradict reconstructions of Israel's history by other scholars at certain points.

The narratives about Israel's history in the Old Testament belong to a different category of writing. Although they have an interest in Israel's past, their main purpose is religious. They are concerned to tell the story of Israel, the people of God, and thus to show how God brought the people into being and blessed, punished, exiled, and restored them. They are based upon stories that circulated among the people orally, upon ancient hymns and poems, and upon state chronicles; but they are not researched history in the modern sense. They were compiled, in some cases, many hundreds of years after the events that they portray, and if they are based on oral traditions, these traditions will have been telescoped, idealized, and structured into dramatic episodes in the course of transmission (see chapter 16).

It is not being suggested here that Abraham did not exist or that the Exodus never happened; nor is it being suggested that it is impossible to try to set Abraham and the Exodus somewhere within the history of the ancient Near East. The point is that for the purposes of modern

TIME CHART		
c. 1230		Israel mentioned in Merneptah stela
	1190	Philistines settle on coastal plain west of the Shephelah
?	1130	Deborah and Barak defeat Canaanite coalition commanded by Sisera
?	1100	Gideon defeats the Midianites
?	1080	''Kingship'' of Abimelech
?	1040	Philistine pressure upon Judah and Dan
c. 1020–1000		Saul
c. 1000–960		David

historical reconstruction, narratives such as those about Abraham and the Exodus do not provide sufficient information to enable us to incorporate them into a history of Israel.

To say this is to focus attention upon the real purpose of the narratives in the Old Testament; this purpose is not to provide information useful to an historian of the late twentieth century but to witness to the religious faith of their authors. Moreover, this religious faith was expressed by means of literary and narrative conventions such as plot structure and character contrasts. This is why, in part III of this book, Old Testament narratives will be treated from a literary point of view. From the historical point of view these narratives are of value insofar as they complement knowledge gained from other sources, and thus enable us to construct a more complete picture of the Old Testament world than would otherwise be possible. In what follows, the narratives that tell Israel's story prior to the existence of the people in the northern hills around 1230 BCE will not be totally ignored; but they will be considered only after the attempt to reconstruct Israel's history up to Solomon has been made. The reason for doing this will be clear by the end of the chapter.

THE EARLY ISRAELITES

Israel's history, then, begins around 1230 BCE, for the simple reason that this is the earliest known reference to Israel in a text that can be dated with confidence. The reference occurs in the stela that records victories of the pharaoh Merneptah:

> Plundered is the Canaan with every evil;
> Carried off is Ashkelon; seized upon is Gezer;
> Yanoam is made as that which does not exist;
> Israel is laid waste, his seed is not.

> (ANET p. 378)

In this text, "Israel" is preceded by a sign that indicates that what is being referred to is a people, not a geographical area.

If we ask where "Israel" was located, and what it consisted of, the probable answers are that it was primarily in the Samaria and Bethel hills and consisted of villages that were scattered along the routes or overlooking valleys, and in several cases in fairly remote areas where the forests had been partly cleared. It may also have included villages in parts of Jezreel and Lower Galilee and the northern part of the Jerusalem Saddle. The information about the villages comes as a result of archaeological surveys, which have now established that at the beginning of the Iron Age (c. 1200 BCE) there was a marked increase in the number of village settlements in the highlands of Canaan (see Map 4, p. 33). The location of Israel primarily in the Bethel and Samaria hills is indicated in the book of Judges (and also in the Jacob traditions of Genesis, 28–36). A large part of Judges is set in this region. Ehud (Judges 3) is a Benjaminite; Gideon is from Manasseh (Judges 6–9); Abimelech's activity is concentrated upon Shechem (Judges 9); and the outrage at Gibeah and its aftermath (Judges 17–21) take place on the southern fringe of the Bethel Hills. The main exceptions are the Deborah-Barak story, whose action takes place in the Jezreel Valley, although Deborah's home is in the Bethel Hills (Judges 4: 5); the Jephthah story (Judges 11–12), which is located in Gilead, the area of Transjordan opposite the Samaria Hills; and the Samson cycle (Judges 13–16), which is located on the western fringe of the tribal areas of Benjamin and Ephraim. However, these exceptions confirm, rather than contradict, the view that the Israelite heartland was, in fact the hills of Samaria and Bethel. It is striking that there is hardly any mention of Judah in the book of Judges, despite its being, eventually, the dominant part of the nation.

The villages that were the basic territorial units of Israel were linked by means of kinship, which was expressed in terms of ordinary maximal lineages (see chapter 2). We do not know how many lineages would be found in an average village, or how many villages would be embraced by a maximal lineage. The largest territorial unit was the tribe, which we have defined as the largest social unit for mutual defence against other Israelite social units. Within each tribal area there were dominant lineages, which provided leaders who were able to rally the people together when the tribe was threatened. There is also some evidence that there were individuals who were the heads of groups of fighters, whose presence could be either disruptive, as in the case of Abimelech (Judges 9), or beneficial, as in the case of Jephthah (Judges 11–12).

Some, at least, of the tribes worshipped a god of war, whom they called Yhwh, although we must not conclude from this that their conception of Yhwh was identical to that later proclaimed by Israel's eighth century prophets. Indeed, Judges suggests that some conceptions of Yhwh at this period were crude. For example, Jephthah is presented as vowing to Yhwh that he will sacrifice the first human being that he meets, if and when he returns home victoriously (Judges 11: 30). Again, the

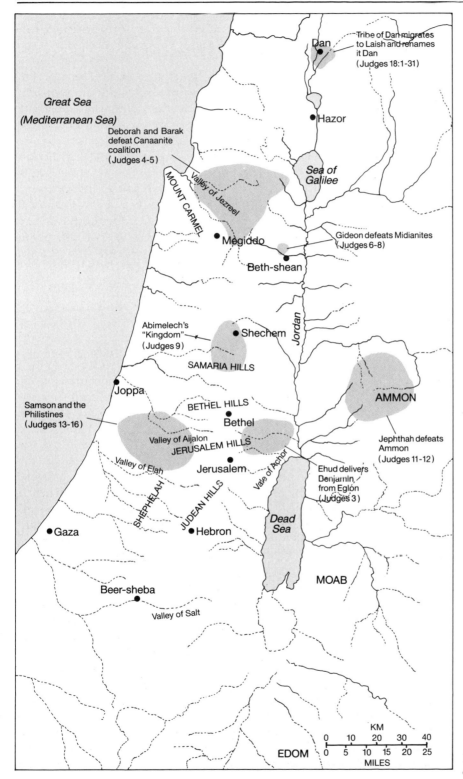

Great Sea
(Mediterranean Sea)

Tribe of Dan migrates
to Laish and renames
it Dan
(Judges 18:1-31)

Dan

Hazor

Deborah and Barak
defeat Canaanite
coalition
(Judges 4-5)

MOUNT CARMEL

Valley of Jezreel

Sea of
Galilee

Megiddo

Beth-shean

Gideon defeats Midianites
(Judges 6-8)

Jordan

Abimelech's
"Kingdom"
(Judges 9)

Shechem

SAMARIA HILLS

AMMON

Joppa

BETHEL HILLS

Bethel

Samson and the
Philistines
(Judges 13-16)

Valley of Aijalon
JERUSALEM HILLS

Jephthah defeats
Ammon
(Judges 11-12)

Valley of Elah

Jerusalem

Vale of Achor

Ehud delivers
Benjamin
from Eglon
(Judges 3)

SHEPHELAH

JUDEAN HILLS

Dead
Sea

Gaza

Hebron

Beer-sheba

MOAB

Valley of Salt

KM

0   10   20   30   40

0   5   10   15   20   25

EDOM

MILES

MAP 10 Israel in the period
of the Judges.

conduct of Samson, especially his amorous adventures, surprise us when we remember that he was a Nazirite — that is, someone pledged in some way to the service of Yhwh (Judges 13: 7; 16: 17).

The most important evidence about Israel's religion of this period comes from Judges 5, which is almost certainly based upon an ancient poem of triumph following Israel's victory over a coalition of Canaanite city-states in the Jezreel Valley. In the poem Yhwh is described as the God of Israel (5: 3), whose home is in the south (5: 4), and whose coming to aid the people causes the forces of nature to tremble (5: 4). Although the victory is achieved by the bravery of the fighters (5: 14–15, 18) and the shrewd courage of Joel (5: 24–7), it is Yhwh who ensures victory. The stars fight against the Canaanites, and the heavens pour down rain upon them (5: 21). Those Israelites who did not join the battle are criticized for not having come to the help of Yhwh (5: 23). The poem closes with the prayer:

> Let all your enemies perish, Yhwh;
> but let all who love you be like the sun, when it rises in
>   its strength, (5: 31).

Judges does not indicate how or where Yhwh was worshipped. Gideon is told (Judges 6) to build an altar to Yhwh in his village. In Judges 17: 1–5 a pious man who lives in the Bethel Hills has an image of Yhwh made for his own household and recruits a Levite to be his priest. Alas for this pious man, both his image and his priest are later appropriated by members of the tribe of Dan and transported to the far north of the land (Judges 18: 15–27). On the other hand, we learn from Judges 21: 19 that there was an annual festival in hour of Yhwh at Shiloh, on the northern edge of the Bethel Hills. It does not follow that this was the main or only Yhwh sanctuary. We learn later of a sanctuary at Nob, for example (1 Samuel 21: 2). It is safest to conclude that Yhwh was worshipped at various local shrines, and that there was no centralized priesthood. A difficult question to decide is whether there were, literally, ''judges'' in this society, or, rather, an institution that administered justice on a local or larger scale. The lists of so-called minor judges at 10: 1–5 and 12: 8–15 may be no more than the names of prominent members of dominant lineages who acted as arbitrators. Deborah was certainly a judge (Judges 4: 4–5), but this must have been because she possessed outstanding gifts which were widely recognized and trusted. We do not really know whether, above the level of village or tribe, there were any institutions that belonged peculiarly to Israel.

THE PHILISTINES

The period of the Judges, which lasted from around 1250 to 1020 BCE, was one in which the territory of Israel was invaded by peoples from outside the land. In only one case was there a battle with the Canaanites, who shared the land with Israel (Judges 4–5). Towards the end of this period, Israel was faced by an enemy that was apparently intent upon taking over the land and making the Israelites a subject people.

The Philistines were part of a group called in Egyptian texts the "sea peoples", who settled in the coastal region of Canaan alongside the Shephelah, in the latter part of the thirteenth century BCE. For well over a hundred years they lived peaceably with their neighbours. Towards the end of the period of the Judges, however, they began to expand into parts of the Jerusalem saddle and Shephelah that were occupied by the tribe of Dan, eventually forcing the Danites out of this area. This is the background to the Samson cycle (Judges 13–16) and the account of the Danite migration to the far north (Judges 17–18).

At the same time that Dan was under pressure, the tribe of Judah was also being confronted by the Philistines. The reference in Judges 15: 9–17 to a Philistine attack upon Judah makes perfect geographical sense. The heartland of Judah was separated from the Philistines by the Shephelah, a transitional area bound to be disputed territory if one group wanted to expand at the expense of the other. At this point, a word must be said about the origins of Judah.

It has already been remarked that Judah is hardly mentioned in Judges. In Judges 5, where some tribes are criticized for not coming to the assistance of Yhwh, Judah is not mentioned at all. The evidence indicates that in the period of the Judges the tribe of Judah did not belong to the Israel association. In fact, as will be suggested at the end of the chapter, Judah may have had a closer affinity with the peoples of Moab and Ammon than with the Israelite tribes.

The Old Testament tells us nothing about fighting between Judah and the Philistines; but there must have been such fighting, and it was possibly during this phase that the young David killed a Philistine champion in the event that has been elaborated into the highly stylized account of the slaying of Goliath in 1 Samuel 17. We must assume that the Philistines made little headway against Judah, for only by doing so can we make sense of the next Philistine move, namely, their battles against the Israel tribes, who were to their northeast and less accessible than Judah.

The Israel tribes were defeated by the Philistines in two battles at a place controlling access to the heartland of Israel. The Philistines placed garrisons at least in parts of the Jerusalem Saddle and southern Bethel Hills (1 Samuel 13: 16) and denied Israel the services of travelling metalworkers, so that they could not make weapons (1 Samuel 13: 19–22).The Israelite leader at this time was Samuel, who is presented in 1 Samuel 1–15 as a combination of priest, prophet, and judge, and who is not easy to locate beneath the layers of tradition. It is not impossible that he inspired some local or bigger victories against the Philistines (1 Samuel 7: 2–17), and he was certainly trusted as a judge (1 Samuel 7: 17; 8: 1–3) and was also the spiritual leader of groups of ecstatic prophets (1 Samuel 19: 18–24). We remember that Deborah was both prophetess and judge (Judges 4: 4). What Samuel was evidently not able to give to the tribes was a permanent victory. For this, a new type of leadership and organization was required.

Recent studies of the rise of the monarchy in Israel (e.g. Frick 1985; Flanagan 1981) have drawn attention to the cultural evolutionary aspects of this development. Their work is a timely reminder that history is not created simply by great individuals — or, more precisely, that it should not be written as though it were. After all, Israel had faced and defeated enemies before, and had not found it necessary to establish some form of permanent leadership (although the matter is aired in Judges 8). What was different about the Philistine threat? The difference was probably that the Philistine occupation(s) of the land, and their demand for agricultural surpluses led to a temporary breakdown of social organization. 1 Samuel 13: 6–7 tells of Israelites hiding in holes, crevices, and cisterns, and of others fleeing across the Jordan in the face of a Philistine advance. There were only three possibilities open to the Israelites: permanent flight from their homes, complete submission to the Philistines, or the acceptance of a new social order that would concentrate power in the hands of one lineage and lead to some loss of personal freedoms (cp. 1 Samuel 8: 10–18).

SAUL

Of the mode of Saul's emergence to kingship (if kingship is the right word), we have, in 1 Samuel 8–11, three conflicting accounts. According to one account, Saul was secretly anointed by Samuel on the instructions of Yhwh (1 Samuel 10: 1). Another version has Saul chosen by lot (1 Samuel 10: 20–24); while the third account presents Saul as a military leader after the manner of the deliverer-judges of the book of Judges, after whose victory the kingdom is "renewed" (1 Samuel 11). It is probable that this movement to permanent leadership was gradual rather than sudden. Saul may have led the Israelites to initial victories over the Philistines (1 Samuel 13–14), as well as victories over the Ammonites (1 Samuel 11) and the Amalekites (1 Samuel 15), but the Philistine pressure was constant, and towards the end of his reign it had become such a threat that even Judah was now allied to Israel under Saul's leadership (1 Samuel 23: 6–13). What began as leadership in the form familiar from the book of Judges became permanent leadership under constant pressure from the Philistines.

How long did this process of consolidation take? Here we encounter the difficulty that we do not know how long Saul reigned. In 1 Samuel 13: 1 the length of the reign is given as two years; but the text is almost certainly corrupt, for it gives Saul's age at the time of this "accession" as one year. A figure before the "two" has evidently been lost; but whether the complete figure was twelve, twenty-two, or thirty-two we do not know. In any case, twelve years would probably be long enough for constant Philistine pressure to bring about the social changes implied by permanent leadership.

Saul himself seems to have been an ardent adherent of Yhwh. The fact that one of his sons, Eshbaal, had a name that included the divine

In the first of these two scenes from the life of David, the king is probably instructing Solomon to build the Temple (1 Chronicles 28: 9–20). In the second, the aged David is nursed by Abishag (1 Kings 1: 3–4).

name "Baal" can probably be explained by the fact that "baal" means "lord" and that in Saul's day the struggle between the worshippers of Yhwh and the fertility god Baal was not an issue within Israel. It was to be quite a different matter, of course, in the ninth or eighth century (see chapter 5). Saul may well have been a protégé of Samuel at some point, and even a member of a prophetic group (1 Samuel 10: 10–12). As king, he carried out religious reforms such as the suppression of consulting with the dead via mediums (1 Samuel 28: 3). As time went on, however, the pressures became too much for him. He had to contend not only with the Philistines but also with the opposition of Samuel (1 Samuel 13: 13; 15: 26) and with his own jealousy at the prowess and popularity of David (1 Samuel 18: 7–8). He was finally overwhelmed by the Philistines in a battle on the eastern edge of the Jezreel Valley (1 Samuel 29, 31), and took his own life rather than become a prisoner of the Philistines. David knew a brave man when he saw one, and the deaths of Saul and his son Jonathan drew from David one of the most sublime tributes to human bravery in the whole of the Old Testament (2 Samuel 1: 18–27).

DAVID AND SOLOMON

David, to whom fell the task of reversing the Philistine triumph over Israel, is something of a mystery. It was noted in chapter 2 that David's mother may have been married at one point to the Ammonite king Nahash. There are also indications that David's lineage had Moabite connections. The book of Ruth credits him with a Moabite great-grandmother (Ruth 4: 18–20), and it was to the king of Moab that David took his parents to safety when he was fleeing from the wrath of Saul (1 Samuel 22: 3–4). Given that Judah is scarcely mentioned in the book of Judges, we must consider the possibility that prior to sustained Philistine pressure upon Israel, Judah had been allied for decades with Moab and Ammon, and that there were kinship ties between them. In this case, it was the Philistine threat that brought Judah and Israel together. If David belonged to the dominant lineage in Judah, his introduction into the court of Saul and his marriage to Saul's daughter Michal (1 Samuel 16: 18–21; 18: 17–29) may have marked the formal alliance between Israel and Judah against the Philistines.

What had David done prior to coming to Saul's court; and did he come alone? These questions remind us that the traditions in 1 Samuel are primarily religious in intention and are not a history of the period. They leave much unsaid and offer only tantalizing hints, which can be interpreted in several different ways. What follows is no more than intelligent, but important, guesswork. In 2 Samuel 21: 15–22 and 23: 8–39 there is an account of the deeds of David's warriors and a list of their names. At least one of these incidents must be dated towards the end of David's kingship (2 Samuel 21: 15–17), but this need not necessarily be done for all of them. One of the heroes mentioned here, David's nephew, Asahel (2 Samuel 23: 24), was killed by Abner before David became king over the northern tribes of Israel; thus David's band of thirty warriors must have existed then. Furthermore, it is tempting to date the story about David's heroes bringing water from the Philistine-occupied Bethlehem to David's hide-out (2 Samuel 23: 13–17) to the period of Judah-Philistine fighting prior to David's entry into Saul's court. If this is correct, then David was already the leader of a group of fighters with Philistine scalps to their credit when he joined Saul's court, bringing his heroes with him. The bizarre story of David's collecting the foreskins of 200 dead Philistines as the bride-price for Saul's daughter (1 Samuel 18: 24–29) indicates that the task of dispatching the victims was performed by David and his men (1 Samuel 18: 27)

If David was the leader of a small private group of warriors, it is not surprising that Saul became increasingly wary of him, in spite of the deep friendship between David and Saul's son Jonathan (1 Samuel 18: 1–5). David was eventually forced to leave Saul's court and probably returned to Judah, where he protected villages from the Philistines in return for provisions for his men (cp. 1 Samuel 23: 1–5; 25: 2–19). Saul's power, however, had now grown to the extent that he was able to operate in Judah, and to command some loyalty from Judahites in opposition to David (1 Samuel 23: 11–12). David's only course was to desert to the Philistines. He became a vassal of Achish, king of Gath (1 Samuel 27: 1–7), and was allowed to settle in Ziklag. Here he played a shrewd double game. He raided the peoples of the northern Negev, pretending to his overlord that he was raiding his own people. In fact, he was sending

gifts to them, preparing the way for his reacceptance by them (1 Samuel 27: 8–12; 30: 26–31).

Following Saul's death (David was spared from fighting on the Philistine side against him; 1 Samuel 29: 1–11), David moved to Hebron, where he was made king over Judah. That this was done with Philistine permission is not surprising. David, after all, was seen as a loyal Philistine ally, and no doubt he was expected to provide tribute for the Philistines, in the form of agricultural surpluses. Moreover, if Judah had so far been mainly independent of Israel, David's kingship in Judah constituted no particular threat to the Philistines. Indeed, the account of the battle between the forces of David and Saul's son Eshbaal, in 2 Samuel 2: 12–31, indicates rivalry between Israel and Judah. Probably, the Philistines encouraged David to police certain parts of Israel and to engage any Israelite forces that crossed over the Jordan River from the Israelite capital-in-exile at Mahanaim (2 Samuel 2: 8–11).

The Israelite commander, Abner, who was the power behind Eshbaal's throne, saw no future in this hostile relationship and was prepared to make an alliance with David (2 Samuel 3: 1–21). However, while Abner was visiting David in Hebron, he was killed by David's commander-in-chief, Joab (see chapter 2), in revenge for Abner's killing of Joab's brother Asahel. Abner's death hastened the collapse of Eshbaal's rule, and the elders of Israel came to David to offer him their nation's throne. By the time the Philistines realized what had happened, David was strong enough to defeat them and to free the land from their control. From his new capital of Jerusalem (even then an ancient city), David ruled over both Judah and Israel, uniting them into one kingdom. There followed the conquests of neighbouring peoples such as Edom, Moab, Ammon, and Syria. David had reversed the fortunes of Judah and Israel from humiliation by the Philistines to control of a small empire. From now on, moreover, the dominant religious viewpoint and the one that would find expression in the Old Testament, was that of Judah, which had not originally been part of Israel.

So far as we can tell from available sources, David was probably a sincere believer in Yhwh as god of war. Following the capture of Jerusalem and the defeat of the Philistines, he brought to Jerusalem the Ark of the Covenant, an object associated with Yhwh's warlike presence among the people (2 Samuel 6). Again, however, we must not cast David in the role of believer in Yhwh in the sense that later prophets were believers in Yhwh's exclusive claims over Israel. David appears to have allowed the worship of the Canaanite god El Elyon (see chapter 3) to be combined in Jerusalem with the worship of Yhwh; and Zadok, the high priest under David, had probably been the Jebusite high priest in Jerusalem prior to David's capture of the city. The acquisition of Jerusalem as the religious (as well as political) capital of Judah and Israel was to have a profound influence upon the development of Old Testament religion.

David was probably a better soldier than a ruler; in any case, it was

OPPOSITE The upper city of Hazor was built in the third millennium BCE. After its destruction in the thirteen century (claimed in Joshua 11: 10 to have been the work of the Israelites) it was rebuilt by Solomon, and further fortified by Omri and Ahab. At the bottom right of the picture is the Solomonic gate of the city, to the left of which can be seen the (double) casemate wall. The shadows cast by the pillars of Ahab's storehouse are above the casemate wall.

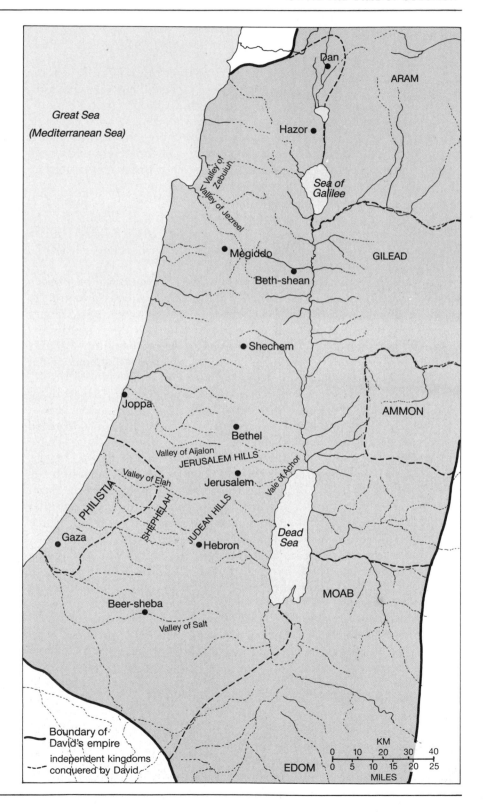

MAP 11 David's Empire.

asking a lot of one man suddenly to govern a small empire. During his reign, David had to face two revolts. One, led by his son Absalom, appears to have been supported by both Israel and Judah, and to have been suppressed only by the expertise of David's private army fighting in deliberately chosen wooded country (2 Samuel 15–18). The second revolt involved only Israel led by Sheba, who probably belonged to Saul's maximal lineage (2 Samuel 20). We do not know the causes of these revolts, and can only guess that underlying them was the discontent of the people, who had to provide young men for a large standing army and surpluses for a necessarily growing number of administrators.

David was succeeded by his son Solomon, after an undignified scramble for the succession between Solomon and his brother Adonijah, supported by interested parties (1 Kings 1: 5–53). Under the new king, more towns were built and fortified, trade links were developed, a palace and the splendid Temple were built in Jerusalem, and even greater

Solomon fortified key cities such as Gezer, Megiddo and Hazor. The gate at Hazor was provided with chambers that probably served as guard rooms. The casemate wall was a double wall which could be divided into sections which served as dwellings.

demands were made upon the ordinary people to provide labour and agricultural surpluses. That Solomon was able to prevent a revolt against his rule may be due to the fact that he was gradually forced to relinquish control over the peoples whom David had conquered (1 Kings 11: 14–25). This would have reduced the call on manpower for the army and would have concentrated resources more in Israel and Judah. Nevertheless, when Solomon's son Rehoboam went to Shechem to seek confirmation as king over Israel, he was asked to lighten the burdens that his father had laid upon the people (1 Kings 12: 4; see also chapter 1, pp. 38–9).

PATRIARCHAL TRADITIONS

So far, this chapter has traced the history of Israel from an association of tribes, centred in the Samaria and Bethel hills, to a state controlled by a lineage that probably came from outside Israel, in Judah. It is in the light of this knowledge that we must consider the traditions about the patriarchs, the Exodus, and the conquest of Canaan.

If Judah and Israel were not united until the time of David, the Old Testament narratives that present Israel as a league of twelve tribes, including Judah, cannot be dated earlier than the time of David, and were intended to reflect the political reality of the unification. The same is true of the genealogies and narratives that link Abraham and Jacob as father and grandson via Isaac (see chapter 2, p. 53). Jacob was almost certainly an ancestor about whom traditions circulated in the Israel of the Bethel and Samaria hills (Hosea 12: 3–8), while Abraham, whom the traditions connect strongly with Hebron (Genesis 23), was remembered in Judah. It is likely that both of these ancestors had links with northern Mesopotamia — a probability strongly re-emphasized in the case of Jacob (Genesis 28–31). Their families were probably involved in one or more of the various migrations of peoples from northern Mesopotamia to Syria and Canaan between the eighteenth and fourteenth centuries BCE, although it is doubtful whether they were connected. The tradition that Abraham's nephew Lot was the (incestuous) father of Moab and Ammon (Genesis 19: 30–38) also suggests that the peoples later called Moab, Ammon, and Judah were part of the same movement. All that we can confidently assert about Abraham and Jacob is that they were ancestors of the people of Judah and Israel, respectively, around whom traditions collected. In their present form, however, the narratives reflect the political realities of the period of the monarchy in depicting Abraham and Jacob as members of one and the same family. As *literature*, these narratives witness to the beliefs of their authors, and are treated accordingly in chapter 9.

THE EXODUS

In what we have so far written about the religion of Israel and Judah, we have described Yhwh as principally a god of war. What is surprising is that nowhere in the sources that we have used for the period up to Solomon is there any mention of the Exodus from Egypt, apart from passages that are clearly the result of later editing (e.g. Judges 11: 16; 1 Samuel 12: 8). In Judges 5, for example, Yhwh is said to have dwelt in Edom, in the south, but there is no mention of the Exodus. Among the earliest references is that in Hosea 11: 1:

> When Israel was a child I loved him,
> and out of Egypt I called my son.

These words date only from the second half of the eighth century BCE.

So far as we can tell, only a small group of semites, which later joined Israel, successfully fled from Egypt, avoiding recapture through what they believed was the miraculous intervention of Yhwh. They then crossed the Sinai Desert and the Negev, bringing with them Yhwh's portable shrine, the Ark of the Covenant. Travelling along the land to the east of the Jordan Valley, they crossed onto the western side above the Dead Sea and settled in the Bethel Hills. Here, they either met with people to whom they were distantly related — people whose ancestors had, like theirs, come from the north but who had not subsequently migrated to Egypt — or developed links with an indigenous people (to whom they were not related) through marriage. The conquest of Canaan may have been less a fight to enable the newcomers to settle, as presented in Joshua, than a number of battles between the Israel tribes and Canaanite city-states that wished to subjugate them. There is an example of such a conflict, from a slightly later period, in Judges 4–5. By the time that we reach the period of the Judges, Yhwh is the God of Israel, and the Ark of the Covenant is situated in the Bethel Hills, at Shiloh — although we know nothing of how this came about.

In their present form, the narratives of Genesis to Joshua reflect the political realities of the kingdom that David had created. Not only have the originally separate traditions about Abraham and Jacob been united, but Israel as a *twelve-tribe entity* is depicted as going down to Egypt and subsequently being delivered out of it in the Exodus. This reflects the fact that Yhwh was now the God of both Israel and Judah. The story of Yhwh's deliverance of the people from Egypt needed to embrace the ancestors of all those who now accepted Yhwh. Furthermore, because the narratives depicted Israel as a twelve-tribe unity leaving Egypt and journeying to Canaan, the occupation of the land had to be presented in terms of driving out its previous inhabitants, even though the book of Joshua, in fact, limits the campaigns of Joshua to comparatively restricted areas.

It is precisely because the books of Genesis through Joshua reflect the situation of the united kingdom that they are very difficult indeed to use for the purpose of historical reconstruction, and why they can be considered only at the end, rather than at the beginning, of an opening chapter on the history of Israel.

CHAPTER 5

FROM THE DIVISION OF THE KINGDOM TO THE BABYLONIAN EXILE

JEROBOAM'S REBELLION

Following the death of Solomon (c. 931 BCE), his son Rehoboam went to Shechem in order to be made king over Israel. When Solomon had succeeded David, after an admittedly untidy scramble for power, we are not told whether his Jerusalem anointing was followed by a subsequent election as king over the northern tribes. However, we must not rule this out. It would be odd for Rehoboam to seek northern confirmation if his father had created the precedent of making this unnecessary. We can assume, then, that even under the so-called united monarchy, Judah and Israel maintained separate identities, at least when it came to electing a king.

The story of Rehoboam rejecting the request of the northern tribes to lighten their burdens ("My little finger is thicker than my father's loins", was his reply [1 Kings 12: 10]), and of the subsequent rebellion of the tribes under the leadership of Jeroboam is a familiar one. However, it invites closer examination and a certain amount of speculation. The leader of the revolt, Jeroboam, belonged to the tribe of Ephraim, and thus came from the heartland of Israel. He had also been an official of Solomon and was in charge of the men who were recruited or conscripted from the house of Joseph — that is, the tribes of Ephraim and Manasseh (1 Kings 11: 28). This suggests that he belonged to a dominant Ephraimite lineage which was able to demand allegiance from other members of the tribe. The alternative account of events at that time, in the Greek translation at 3 Kings 12: 24b, suggests that it was Jeroboam, and not Solomon, who fortified Jerusalem. (The Hebrew text of 1 Kings 11: 27 attributes this work to Solomon.) Jeroboam "lifted up his hand against the king" (1 Kings 11: 26), as a result of which he was forced to flee from Solomon, finding refuge in Egypt until Solomon's death (1 Kings 11: 40). The Greek version claims that Jeroboam married the pharaoh's daughter, and that she was "great among the king's daughters" (3 Kings 24e).

So far, Jeroboam can be considered simply an ambitious young man from a dominant Ephraimite lineage whose job put men at his disposal and who looked for the chance to topple Solomon from his throne. But we can go deeper than this. Jeroboam could well have shared the resentment felt by his fellow countrymen at the burdens they were carrying in order to enable Solomon to complete his grandiose designs. This would be particularly true if it was Jeroboam who actually carried out the building work in Jerusalem; and his ''lifting up of his hand'' against Solomon could have been a refusal to treat his fellow tribesmen as Solomon's slaves. He would thus be a natural spokesman for the grievances that were put to Rehoboam at Shechem.

But there may have been a religious dimension also. In 1 Kings 11: 29–38 we find the famous story of Ahijah, the prophet from Shiloh, symbolizing the revolt by tearing his garment into twelve pieces and giving ten of them to Jeroboam. In the Greek account, at 3 Kings 12: 24o a different prophet, Shemaiah, acts out this piece of symbolism, and at a different point in the story. Ahijah's action takes place *before* Jeroboam flees to refuge in Egypt; whereas Shemaiah's action is at the meeting of the tribes in Shechem following Solomon's death. Either way, the revolt is prophetically inspired, and this too, calls for some reflection. We know, from 1 Samuel 10 and elsewhere, that there were groups of prophets in the northern territory; they will appear again during the reign of Ahab. We also know that their leader, Samuel, first supported and then opposed Saul's leadership. We therefore have to take into account prophetic groups in the north that were not afraid to play their part in determining who should and who should not lead Israel. Their support of Jeroboam against the house of David was therefore one factor in the rebellion. What was the reason for their opposition?

We have already suggested that the northern tribal area was where those Israelites settled whose ancestors had escaped from Egypt and whose cultic object was the Ark of the Covenant. We must admit that we know practically nothing about the form that their religion took, although its content probably included stories about Yhwh's deliverance of the people, and asserted Yhwh's right to the exclusive loyalty of Israel (cp. Deuteronomy 32: 1–43). Judah, in the form of the house of David, had appropriated the Ark and set it in a temple designed by a semi-Israelite (12 Kings 7: 13ff) and had fused the worship of Yhwh with some of the religious traditions of Jebusite (pre-Israelite) Jerusalem, especially with those that emphasized the role of the king as a mediator between Yhwh and the people (see below, chapter 11).

When Jeroboam had successfully completed his revolt and been made ruler of the northern kingdom of Israel, he set up images of bulls in the shrines of Bethel and Dan, saying to the people:

> Behold O Israel, your God
> who brought you up out of the land of Egypt.
>
> (1 Kings 12: 28).

Modern scholars are agreed that Jeroboam's bull images were no more idolatrous than the objects that filled Solomon's Temple, including the cherubim which were regarded as the throne of God (1 Kings 6: 23–8). We must accept that if Jeroboam's revolt was inspired by, among other

TIME CHART

961–931 — Solomon

		Israel		Judah	
		931–910	Jeroboam	931–914	Rehoboam
924	Invasion by Shishak			914–912	Abijah
				911–871	Asa
		909	Nadab		
		909–886	Baasha		
		885	Elah		
		885	Zimri		
		885–874	Omri		
		873–853	Ahab		
859–824	Shalmaneser III of Assyria			871–848	Jehoshaphat
		853–852	Ahaziah		
		852–841	Joram	848–841	Joram (probably the Israelite king)
		841–813	Jehu	841	Ahaziah
				840–835	Athaliah
				835–796	Joash
		813–797	Jehoahaz		
		797–782	Joash		
				796–767	Amaziah
		782–747	Jeroboam II		
				767–739	Uzziah
		747	Zechariah		
		747	Shallum		
745–727	Tiglath-Pileser III of Assyria	747–742	Menahem		
		742–740	Pekahiah		
		740–731	Pekah		
				739–734	Jotham
				734–728	Ahaz
722–705	Sargon II of Assyria	731–722	Hoshea		
705–681	Sennacherib of Assyria	(Fall of Northern Kingdom 722/1)		728–699	Hezekiah
				699–643	Manasseh
				642–640	Amon
				640–609	Josiah
605–562	Nebuchadrezzar of Babylon			609	Jehoahaz
				609–598	Jehoiakim
				597	Jehoiachin
				597–587	Zedekiah
				(Destruction of Jerusalem 587/6)	

OPPOSITE This fifteenth-century French artistic portrayal of the building of the Temple, for all its beauty, makes the common mistake of likening it to a great Christian cathedral. In fact, an important feature of the Temple was its courtyard, and only the most sacred parts of the Temple were housed in a building.

Auid en ainsi de quan-
tes uertus et de quantz
biens il a este aucteur
a ceulr de sa ligniee. et
combien plain de grant aage il est
mort nous lauons declairie ou li-

ure deuant dit. Quoud salomo
son filz ancores ieune enfant eut
pins le royaume de son pere. et fu
assis ou siege royal. toutle peuple
solennelment faueur. comme on
seult faire a un roy au commence

things, prophetic elements that wanted him to restore the "old" Yhwh religion of the northern tribes, he would not have deliberately set out to introduce new practices that had no basis in the past. Accordingly, the setting up of the bull images may be an important clue to the worship of Yhwh by the groups that had come from Egypt and the wilderness: it may have included the worship of Yhwh enthroned on a bull. This hypothesis seems to be supported by the story of the Golden Calf in Exodus 32, although in its present form, that narrative claims that worship involving the bull image was an act of apostasy; and it is certainly meant to prepare the reader of Genesis through 2 Kings to understand Jeroboam's actions as apostasy also.

If we bring together the various strands that have been outlined so far, and ask why and for what end the northern tribes rebelled, we can answer as follows. (1) Judah and Israel had never been united except briefly under Saul and during the reigns of David and Solomon. In David's reign there were two revolts and in Solomon's reign possibly one, that of Jeroboam. (2) The reigns of David and Solomon had made enormous demands upon Israel to provide manpower for the army and for building projects, at the same time that large agricultural surpluses were required. (3) The capture of Jerusalem, the building of the Temple to house the Ark, and the beginning of a type of Yhwh-religion stressing the importance of the house of David offended those in the north who saw Yhwh as Israel's deliverer from Egypt and its protector in Canaan. Insofar as Jeroboam's revolt had a manifesto, it stressed Israel's right to determine its own future as the people of Yhwh, freed from obligation to the house of David.

THE DIVIDED KINGDOM

For the next 350 years (200 years in the case of Israel), the two kingdoms would seldom be in a position to determine their own futures. The period of Israelite dominance of the surrounding area under David and Solomon had been made possible partly by the comparative weakness of Egypt, which was soon to flex its muscles and to give a tangible reminder to both kingdoms that it was again strong enough to affect their affairs significantly. In the north, first Syria, then Assyria, then Babylon would make their presence felt, sometimes with direst consequences.

Egypt intervened in the affairs of both kingdoms in the form of the campaign of Sheshonk I in 924 BCE. In 1 Kings 14: 25-7, where the pharaoh's name is given as Shishak, the effect of the campaign upon Judah only is recorded. Shishak is said to have taken away the temple and palace treasures, including objects made of gold. From what can be guessed of Shishak's movements from the list of cities that he claimed to have destroyed, it seems that he did not actually come to Jerusalem (Rehoboam probably sent him much gold in order to spare the city), and that Israel suffered more from his depredations than Judah. This must have been a blow to Israel. For them, Yhwh was, after all, a god

Opposite Around 880 BCE, Omri, king of Israel established a new capital on a virgin site. The city was named Samaria, and it served as a royal residence until its destruction by the Assyrians in 721 BCE. The city was rebuilt in 26 BCE by Herod the Great and named Sebaste, the Greek name of his patron, the Roman emperor Augustus. The western gate dates from the time of Herod although the remains visible here date from the second century CE.

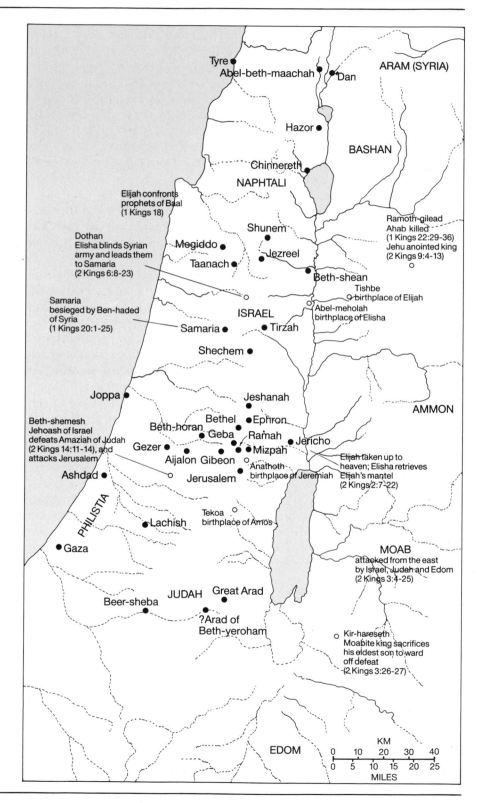

Tyre

Abel-beth-maachah ● ● Dan

ARAM (SYRIA)

Hazor ●

BASHAN

Chinnereth ●

NAPHTALI

Elijah confronts
prophets of Baal
(1 Kings 18)

Shunem ●

Ramoth-gilead
Ahab killed
(1 Kings 22:29-36)
Jehu anointed king
(2 Kings 9:4-13) ○

Dothan
Elisha blinds Syrian
army and leads them
to Samaria
(2 Kings 6:8-23)

Megiddo ●

Jezreel ●

Taanach ●

Beth-shean ●

Tishbe
○ birthplace of Elijah

Samaria
besieged by Ben-haded
of Syria
(1 Kings 20:1-25)

ISRAEL

Abel-meholah
birthplace of Elisha

Samaria ●   Tirzah ●

Shechem ●

Joppa ●

Jeshanah ●

AMMON

Beth-shemesh
Jehoash of Israel
defeats Amaziah of Judah
(2 Kings 14:11-14), and
attacks Jerusalem

Beth-horan

Bethel ●

Ephron ●

Geba ●

Ramah ●

Jericho ●

Gezer ●

Mizpah ●

Aijalon Gibeon

Anathoth
birthplace of Jeremiah

Elijah taken up to
heaven; Elisha retrieves
Elijah's mantel
(2 Kings 2:7-22)

Ashdad ●

Jerusalem ○

PHILISTIA

Tekoa ○
birthplace of Amos

Lachish ●

Gaza ●

MOAB
attacked from the east
by Israel, Judah and Edom
(2 Kings 3:4-25)

JUDAH   Great Arad ●

Beer-sheba ●

?Arad of
Beth-yeroham ●

Kir-hareseth ○
Moabite king sacrifices
his eldest son to ward
off defeat
(2 Kings 3:26-27)

EDOM

KM
0   10   20   30   40
0   5   10   15   20   25
MILES

Map 12 Events of the
divided monarchy.

of war, and defeat raised difficult questions. Although this setback occurred early in Jeroboam's reign, and he ruled for twenty-two years, it is possible that he began to lose the support of the prophetic groups from early in his reign. First Kings 14 records that the prophet who had encouraged his revolt now predicted a speedy end to his dynasty, although in its present form the story is the work of Judahite editors, who attribute Jeroboam's predicted misfortune to his apostasy in rebelling against Judah.

Jeroboam's son Nadab ruled for only two years before being killed by Baasha, whose tribe is given as Issachar (1 Kings 15: 27). Issachar occupied the Jezreel Valley and southern Lower Galilee. Baasha's rebellion may have been caused by inter-tribal rivalry, although the text gives no reason for his takeover. His extermination of Jeroboam's house (1 Kings 15: 29) probably affected the whole of what was probably, as suggested above, a dominant lineage.

Baasha soon proved himself to be an aggressive king. He moved against Judah and fortified the town of Ramah, in the Jerusalem Saddle, with the intention of making it, not Jerusalem, the town that controlled the north-south and east-west routes (1 Kings 15: 17). As a result, Asa, the king of Judah, sent a massive bribe to the king of Syria, with the request that he attack the northernmost towns of Israel, thus relieving the pressure on Judah (1 Kings 18: 18–20). In his message, Asa implied that there was already a treaty between Syria and Israel, which Syria was encouraged to break. This treaty had presumably been made when Israel feared that Judah would try to reconquer her, following the revolt. It would be in Syria's interests to have two smaller neighbours, rather than one larger one, to the south. It now suited Syria to weaken the immediate southern neighbour; it invaded the area around Dan and as far down as the Sea of Galilee.

According to 1 Kings 16: 1–4, Baasha, like Jeroboam before him, found himself on the receiving end of a prophetic announcement that his dynasty would not endure, and this prophesy, too, proved correct. This time, the takeover was much messier; but when things eventually stablized, there was established a dynasty that gave Israel an unprecedented period of power and influence, but also provoked the bitterest opposition from the prophetic groups.

THE HOUSE OF OMRI

Baasha's son Elah had scarcely been on the throne for a year when, around 885 BCE, he was assassinated by one of his own military leaders, Zimri, who now ascended the throne (1 Kings 16: 9–10). His rule lasted for only seven days before he took his own life when he was surrounded in his capital, Tirzeh, by the commander-in-chief of the army, Omri. Israel now found itself with two kings. Omri had been proclaimed king by the army that he was commanding at Gibbethon (1 Kings 16: 16), while another group made a certain Tibni, son of Ginath, king (1 Kings

16: 21). It is tempting to speculate that Tibni had the support of the prophetic groups, whereas Omri's power base was in the army. The fact that the biblical text says nothing about these matters is a sharp reminder that the books of Kings are theological, not historical, narratives, and that we know next to nothing about the history of Israel of this period. However, our hypothesis of an army-based versus a prophetic-led party would provide a reason for the division within Israel, and would make sense of the bitter hostility to the house of Omri on the part of the prophetic groups that becomes such a feature of 1 Kings from chapter 17 onwards.

The text of 1 Kings 16: 21–2 is so sparing in the information that it gives that we are not even told how long Tibni's rule lasted, whether or not there was a civil war, or whether Tibni died of natural causes or fell in combat. We can guess that Omri, backed by the army, soon gained the upper hand, and established his rule as the only effective regime. Tibni may have fled and been harboured by prophetic groups; but this is mere speculation. Politically speaking, Omri was the man of the hour, just as David had once been. He took over a weakened, divided Israel and quickly transformed it into the major power in the region, dominating Syria, Moab, and Judah. It is no accident that from 1 Kings 17 to 2 Kings 11, the text is concerned principally with Israel and that Judah receives only incidental mention.

The power of Omri is recorded in the Inscription of Mesha, king of Moab:

Omri, king of Israel . . . . humbled Moab many days . . . . Omri had occupied the whole land of Medeba and he dwelt in it during his days.
(ANET p. 320)

At the south west of the Megiddo site is a spring. In the tenth century Solomon constructed a gallery above the cave from which the spring could be reached. More impressive was the water tunnel shown here, constructed in the ninth century, probably by Ahab.

This probably means that Omri occupied the area to the north of the great gorge of the River Arnon and thus controlled the plateau of Moab famed for its sheep rearing. We also know from archaeological investigations that Omri (or his son) built new walls to replace those built by Solomon at Megiddo and Hazor, as well as impressive water tunnels at those cities. He established a new capital, Samaria, on a virgin site and began to make this a capital fit for a king. In the realm of foreign policy he created an alliance with Sidon, an alliance cemented by the marriage of his son Ahab to Jezebel, daughter of the king of Sidon (1 Kings 16: 31).

Omri's son Ahab, who succeeded him, was also a great builder and fortifier of cities, as he sought to consolidate the small empire bequeathed by his father. It is probable that during Ahab's reign, Jehoshaphat, king of Judah, was a vassal of the king of Israel. He, too, is credited with building projects and administrative reorganizations (2 Chronicles 19: 1–18), and these were probably carried out with Ahab's blessing. The reigns of Omri and Ahab were therefore, from the material point of view, a period of peace and prosperity, at least so far as the wealthy were concerned.

The picture sketched above in fact contradicts the biblical record. From the latter we must infer, first, that the king of Syria conquered some of the territory held by Omri, and that he set up trading outlets for Syrian merchants in Omri's capital, Samaria (1 Kings 20: 34). Furthermore, the biblical narrative records three campaigns of the Syrian king against Ahab. In the first (1 Kings 20: 1–21), Ahab won a victory, but only after his opponent had penetrated as far south as Samaria and laid siege to the capital. On the second occasion battle was joined at Aphek, and the Syrian king was forced to give himself up to Ahab. This was the occasion on which he promised to give back to Ahab the cities that had been taken from Omri (1 Kings 20: 22–34). The third campaign led to the death of Ahab at the battle of Ramoth-gilead (1 Kings 22: 1–40). In the light of these narratives, the reigns of both Omri and Ahab were characterized by defeats at the hands of Syria, one of which lead to the death of Ahab.

We do not deny that it is possible to defend the order of events as they are presented in 1 Kings 20 to 2 Kings 8, although in our view there are insuperable difficulties that tell against accepting the narrative at face value. The difficulties are fully set out by Hayes and Miller (1986, pp. 259–64. 290–1, 297–302) and will be briefly indicated here. First, the king of Syria who was Ahab's foe is given in 1 Kings 20 and 22 as Ben-hadad, whereas Assyrian records indicate that the Syrian king was Hadadezer. The same problem occurs with regard to Ahab's son Jehoram. His foe also is Ben-hadad (2 Kings 6: 24; 8: 7), whereas according to Assyrian records Hadadezer was still the Syrian king. Moreover, 2 Kings 8: 7–15 reports that Elisha encouraged Hazael to rebel against Ben-hadad. An Assyrian account strongly indicates that Hazael overthrew Hadadezer (ANET p. 280). The second main difficulty is that Ahab is said to have "slept with his fathers" (1 Kings 22: 40), normally the description of a peaceful death, although, according to 1 Kings 22: 37, Ahab died in battle. Thirdly, the account of the death of Ahab in battle at Ramoth-gilead is paralleled by the account of his son fighting a battle at Ramoth-gilead and receiving severe wounds in the fighting (2 Kings 8: 25–29). Finally, there was a Ben-hadad, king of Syria, who was a contemporary of Jehoahaz (813–797 BCE). This king was the son of Jehu, who led a prophetically inspired revolt against the house of Omri and Ahab. The mention of the prophets who were on the side of the king of Israel in passages such as 1 Kings 20: 13, 28 would fit in better with a member of Jehu's dynasty than with Ahab, who was bitterly opposed by the prophetic groups.

In adopting here a reconstruction of Israel's history that is at variance with the surface reading of the text, we remind readers of what was said at the beginning of chapter 4 regarding the distinction between the reconstructed history of Israel and the Old Testament narratives. Scholarly reconstructions of the history of Israel are always open to modification and correction, and are not undertaken without basic decisions that affect how the task is approached. Scholars who, for whatever reasons, hold that the order of events as related in the Old Testament must be correct, will reach different conclusions from those presented here. Obviously, in this instance, we do not set out from the view that the Old Testament order of events is above criticism. But we would also stress a point that has been made earlier, that these narratives are theological rather than historical, and that they must therefore be evaluated by different criteria, as they are in chapter 9. For the moment, we can say simply that the biblical writers had to do the best they could with the traditions available to them, without having Assyrian records and archaeological investigations to help them (see Rogerson 1983, pp. 47–54).

INTERNAL AND EXTERNAL CONFLICTS

We return then, to Omri and Ahab, and to the view that their reigns enabled Israel to enjoy a spell of material prosperity and dominance over their immediate neighbours. This tranquillity was spoiled by only two features. The first was the appearance on the scene of the Assyrian king Shalmaneser III. In 853 BCE, he fought a coalition of kings from Syria, Israel, and neighbouring countries at Qarqar on the river Orontes. The Old Testament says nothing about this battle, whose outcome was indecisive, but which probably indicated to Shalmaneser that he should go no farther south on this occasion. His opponents included Hadadezer, the Syrian king, who provided 1,200 chariots and 20,000 foot soldiers, and Ahab, who provided 2,000 chariots and 10,000 foot soldiers. Ahab's total may well have included the forces of Judah, which are not separately mentioned in the Assyrian records (ANET p. 279).

The second negative factor was bitter opposition to the house of Omri by the prophets. We suggested above that Omri's rival Tibni may have had prophetic backing. What provoked special opposition, however, was the ardent championing of the fertility god Baal by Ahab's foreign wife Jezebel. First Kings 18: 4 says that Jezebel tried to destroy the prophets of Yhwh, some of whom were hidden from her by one of Ahab's officials. In their place were put prophets of Baal. Elijah, the leader of the Yhwh prophets, used a prolonged drought as an occasion to proclaim that Yhwh was opposed to Ahab, and he also succeeded in defeating the Baal prophets at a confrontation to see who could call down fire on a sacrifice (1 Kings 18). Elijah's victory, however, was short-lived, and he was forced to flee from Jezebel's wrath (1 Kings 19). In the story of Naboth's vineyard (1 Kings 21) the values of the two sides are encapsulated. Jezebel abused royal power in deceitfully depriving Naboth of his vineyard; Elijah proclaimed that such behaviour was condemned by Yhwh.

Events during the years immediately following the death of Ahab are unclear, owing to contradictions in the biblical material itself. This can best be illustrated by the problematical succession of J(eh)oram.

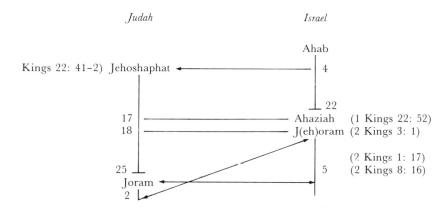

From this chart it will be seen that there are two dates for the accession of Joram (Jehoram), king of Israel: either Jehoshaphat's eighteenth year (2 Kings 3: 1) or the second year of the reign of Jehoshaphat's son Joram (2 Kings 1: 17) — that is, nine years later. Joram, son of Jehoshaphat, is said at 2 Kings 8: 16 to have acceded in the fifth year of Joram, son of Ahab. It is not possible here to discuss the problems of these figures (see Hayes and Miller, pp. 280–1), which touch on whether the traditional Hebrew text or the ancient Greek translations have better preserved what the original biblical writers actually set down. It will be noticed that, for a period, the name of the kings of Judah and Israel was identical. This raises the question whether one and the same man ruled both kingdoms. Hayes and Miller argue that this was so, suggesting that Joram, king of Judah, also became the king of Israel on the death of Ahaziah.

There is, however, another possibility: 2 Kings 8: 16 says that Joram, son of Jehoshaphat, became king of Judah while Jehoshaphat was still on the throne. This could, of course, indicate a co-regency between Jehoshaphat and his son; but if there was one and not two Jorams this text might indicate that Jehoshaphat was deposed by Joram, king of Israel.

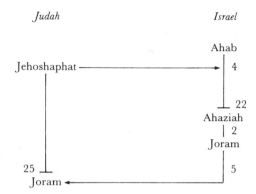

Thus Jehoshaphat's reign of twenty-five years tallies exactly with the eighteen remaining years of Ahab, two of Ahaziah, and five of Joram. It makes more sense to suppose that the dominant house of Omri usurped the throne of Jerusalem than that a relatively weak Judean king acceded also in Samaria. All this, of course, assumes that there was only one Joram.

The dynasty of Omri lasted for a little over forty years, from 885 to 841 BCE. It ended when Joram was badly wounded, by the prophet Elisha, in the battle of Ramoth-gilead against the Syrian king Hazael (2 Kings 8: 25–29), and Jehu, a commander used this opportunity to kill both him and Ahaziah, king of Judah, at the instigation of another prophet (2 Kings 9), while Joram lay recovering from his wounds in Jezreel. He shot Joram with an arrow as the latter tried to flee; Ahaziah was killed, also in flight, by one of Jehu's servants. Jehu now killed Jezebel, forced the officials in Samaria to destroy Ahab's lineage, and also killed the relatives of Ahaziah and all of the prophets of Baal (2 Kings 10). There remained of the family of Omri only Athaliah, who succeeded in consolidating her power in Jerusalem.

The dynasty of Jehu was destined to last for almost 100 years, from 841 to 747 BCE. For the first half of its existence, it was to suffer badly at the hands of its neighbours. Jehu was forced to pay tribute to the Assyrian Shalmaneser III in 841; and a few years later, the Syrian king Hazael began to humiliate Israel (2 Kings 10: 32–33). It is in this period (c. 830–805 BCE) that narratives such as those of 2 Kings 6, which describe Samaria's frequent sieges and consequent famine, are to be set. However, in the reign of Joash (c. 797–782) things began to swing in Israel's favour. Joash was able to defeat Hazael's son Ben-hadad and regain some of the cities that had been lost (2 Kings 13: 25; cp. 1 Kings 20, which may belong to the period). He was no doubt helped by the

OPPOSITE Shalmaneser III (859–824 BCE) was an aggressive Assyrian king who, in 853 BCE, met and claims to have defeated a coalition of kings including the kings of Damascus and of Israel (King Ahab). While the victory may not have been as decisive as Shalmaneser claimed, the king did force Ahab's successor and usurper Jehu to pay tribute in 840 BCE. Here, Jehu's representative bows before the Assyrian King.

pressure on Syria which was exerted by the Assyrian Adad-nirari III. From about 796 BCE, Syria ceased to be a menace, and for 50 years both Israel and Judah enjoyed a spell of peace.

KINGS OF JUDAH

Athaliah, who had held on to power in Jerusalem when Jehu rebelled in the north, lasted for seven years, before she was ousted by a revolt led by the Jerusalem priesthood. The aim of this revolt was simple: to restore the house of David to the throne of Judah and to establish Judah's independence once more. During Athaliah's reign Judah was little more than an outpost of the losing party in the struggle for power in Israel. Athaliah was replaced by the boy king Joash, who was no doubt subject to the wishes of the priesthood, except that he, not they, took the initiative in making repairs to the Temple (2 Kings 12: 5–17). During his reign, the rampant King Hazael of Syria made a raid against him, appropriating the temple and palace treasures as tribute (2 Kings 12: 18–19).

Joash was assassinated by two of his servants around about 796 BCE and was succeeded by Amaziah (2 Kings 12: 21; 14: 1–2). Amaziah enjoyed military success against Edom (2 Kings 14: 7) and was then unwise enough to challenge Joash, king of Israel, to a battle (2 Kings 14: 8). It was this Joash who had begun to turn the tide of Israel's fortunes against Hazael's son Ben-hadad, and he now defeated Amaziah, proceeded to Jerusalem, and tore down part of the wall. He also raided the treasuries and took hostages (2 Kings 14: 12–14). There is certainly something to be said for the suggestion (Hayes and Miller, p. 307) that Judah was, in fact, reduced to vassal status, and that this situation lasted for the next forty years or so. On the other hand, it is possible to argue from 2 Kings 14: 17–21 that Judah's vassal status lasted for only fifteen years. At the end of this period, Amaziah was assassinated, and replaced on the throne by Uzziah, in a gesture of independence by the people of Judah.

Of the long reigns of Uzziah (he is credited with fifty-two years at 2 Kings 15: 2) and Joash's successor in Israel, Jeroboam II, little is known. Jeroboam greatly enlarged Israel's borders (2 Kings 14: 25; but see Hayes and Miller, pp. 307–9), and Uzziah is said, at 2 Chronicles 26: 1–15, to have fortified Jerusalem, to have built up the army, and to have waged successful campaigns against Ammon and the Philistines. The end of the reigns of these two kings is the period of the prophetic activity of Hosea and Amos, which was directed against the luxury of the rich, the oppression of the poor, and the insincerity of the religion of the people.

ASSYRIAN AGGRESSION

From 745 BCE there was a sharp decline in the fortunes of Israel and Judah, brought about by the Assyrian king Tiglath-Pileser III (744–727).

OPPOSITE A detail of the bronze bands on the gates from the temple of Mamu built by Shalmaneser III (859–824 BCE) at his palace at Imgur-Enlil, now called Balawat . The top panel shows tribute from the cities of Tyre and Sidon, the bottom shows the capture of the city of Hazaza in North Syria.

ABOVE Tiglath-Pileser III, a
soldier prince, became king
of Assyria in 745 BCE. The
reliefs from his palace at
Numrud depict various
triumphs. The bottom of the
picture shows prisoners and
cattle leaving a defeated
Babylonian city, while at the
top right are depicted sheep
and goats captured from
'Arab' tribesmen. In the
middle of the relief, scribes
make a record and inventory
of these events.

ABOVE Tiglath-Pileser III,
744–727 BCE.

He strengthened his kingdom and embarked upon a policy of expansion that was to bring under his dominion the whole of Syria, Israel, Philistia, Judah, and Transjordan. The events of the years 745–721 BCE, which saw a rapid succession of kings in Israel (six of them in the fifteen years between 747 and 732) present some of the most difficult problems for historical reconstruction in the whole of the Old Testament (for a detailed discussion see Hayes and Miller, pp. 322–37). Coup was followed by counter-coup, as parties opposed to, or prepared to accept, Assyrian dominance struggled for the upper hand. One of the most famous incidents of this period is that of the alliance of the Israelite king Pekah and the king of Syria, Rezon, against Ahaz, the king of Judah, in an attempt to force Ahaz to join a coalition against Assyria. This happened in about 734 BCE (and cp. Isaiah 7: 1–14). Second Chronicles 28: 5–8; 16–18 reports that Ahaz suffered greatly at the hands of Pekah and the Philistines, the latter capturing parts of the Shephelah. Ahaz appealed to Tiglath-Pileser for help, and paid him tribute. In campaigns in 734–732, the Assyrian king conquered Syria, annexed the territory of Israel from the Jezreel Valley northwards, and reduced Israel to a client kingdom ruled by Hoshea. In 725 BCE, Hoshea rebelled against Shalmaneser V, whereupon the Assyrians besieged Samaria. It fell in 722 to Shalmaneser's successor, Sargon II, thus bringing to an end the history of the northern kingdom which Jeroboam's rebellion had founded in 931 BCE.

It is arguable that the fall of Israel to the Assyrians was one of the most important events for the development of the religion of the Old Testament. Here again, however, widely differing reconstructions are possible, given the meagre evidence. We know from archaeological investigations that the population of Jerusalem grew noticeably in the latter part of the eighth century BCE, and it is reasonable to assume that

This woodcut from the Lutheran Bible of 1534 depicts the siege of Samaria described in Second Kings chapters 6 to 7. Although the unscrupulous merchants seem to be better provided for than the text suggests, we can see the prophet Elisha at the top of the picture telling the king and his captain that God is about to lift the siege.

this was because of immigration from the former northern kingdom. Among these arrivals from the north may have been levitical or prophetic groups who brought with them traditions, written and oral, arising from Israel's Exodus-based faith. This made possible the beginnings of a fusion between the northern Exodus-based religion and the southern Jerusalem and house-of-David-oriented religion. Much depends on how the reign of Hezekiah (728–699 BCE) is interpreted.

A passage in 2 Kings (18: 3–8) presents Hezekiah as a religious reformer who destroyed the sanctuaries other than the Temple in Jerusalem. Second Chronicles 29–30 goes into much more detail about the religious reforms, and gives an account of Hezekiah sending messengers to parts of the northern kingdom inviting its people to celebrate the Passover in Jerusalem. In the account of that celebration, the narrative gives the impression that it was carried out in spite of uncertainties and irregularities; for example, it was held in the wrong month (2 Chronicles 30: 2, 15). It is necessary, of course, to use this material from Chronicles with a good deal of caution. The narrative is certainly strongly coloured by the theological bias of Chronicles; but there may be more than a grain of truth in its claim that Hezekiah ordered the Passover to be celebrated in Judah — probably for the first time in the south. If this is correct, then the influence of the arrivals from the north on the religion of Judah is evident. It is, of course, possible to interpret Hezekiah's actions mainly in political terms, with religious reforms being merely a way of achieving national unity (Hayes and Miller, p. 357).

Hezekiah was bent on achieving independence for Judah from the Assyrian rule under which it had existed since his father Ahaz appealed

In preparation for the siege of Jerusalem in 701 BCE by the Assyrian king Sennacherib, Hezekiah king of Judah built a tunnel some 1750 feet (533 metres) long to bring the waters of the spring on the eastern side of the city into the city on its western side. The "Siloam" inscription was discovered in 1880 and removed in 1890 to Istanbul. It records how two parties of tunnellers, working from opposite directions, met and completed the tunnel.

for help to Tiglath-Pileser III. Revolt was not easy, however. In 713–11 BCE, Hezekiah seems to have joined a revolt against Sargon, together with Philistia, Edom, and Moab; but this seems to have fizzled out (cp. Hayes and Miller, p. 352). With the death of Sargon in 705 Hezekiah made a determined effort at revolt, backed by careful preparations, which included the fortification of Jerusalem and other cities and the construction of the famous water tunnel that brought the waters of the Gihon spring from just outside the eastern walls of Jerusalem to within newly-built western walls (2 Kings 20: 20; 2 Chronicles 32: 4–5, 30). Then in 701 BCE, Judah was invaded by Sennacherib.

THE INVASION

The course of events during the invasion presents another body of evidence, which is far from easy to interpret. Scholars are divided over the dates of Hezekiah's reign, there being two possibilities, based upon 2 Kings 18: 1 and 2 Kings 18: 13. According to the first passage, Hezekiah became king in the third year of Hoshea, i.e. c. 728 BCE. According to the second passage, Sennacherib's invasion (of 701) took place in Hezekiah's fourteenth year. This would place his accession in 715 BCE. Moreover, some scholars have strongly championed the view (see Bright 1981, 298ff.) that 2 Kings 18: 13; 19: 37 telescopes *two* campaigns of Sennacherib against Hezekiah, one in 701 and the other in 689 BCE. If the higher chronology that makes Hezekiah's reign from c. 728 to 699 is correct, he would have been dead nine years before the second campaign. The view taken here is that the higher chronology *is* more likely to be correct and that there was only one campaign of Sennacherib. In any case, its effects were sufficiently drastic to teach

Hezekiah a lesson he was not likely to forget. Judah was occupied by the Assyrian army and Jerusalem was besieged. The fortified city of Lachish was forced to surrender, an event commemorated in the famous reliefs now in the British Museum. Hezekiah was forced to pay heavy tribute (2 Kings 18: 13–16); yet Jerusalem itself remained unconquered, a fact that gave rise to legends about its inviolability.

In reality, Judah had become once more an Assyrian vassal state, and this remained the state of affairs for the 55-year reign of Hezekiah's son Manasseh, who probably acceded soon after the debacle of his father's rebellion. Of Manasseh's reign we know very little. The assessment of

The city of Lachish was the chief city of the Shephelah (lowlands) in Judah. After its capture by the Assyrian king Sennacherib in 701 BCE, the victory was commemorated in the famous reliefs now in the British Museum. Here, Israelite prisoners are being led away.

him in 2 Kings 21: 1–9 is entirely in theological terms. He is said to have reversed his father's religious reforms, to have allowed child sacrifice, and to have encouraged occult practices such as communication with the dead. A passage in 2 Chronicles (33: 11–20) implies that at some point Manasseh rebelled against Assyria, was taken captive to Babylon (*sic*), turned in desperation to God, and on returning to Jerusalem carried out a reform of the cult. Scholars are divided over whether or not this is a reliable piece of information.

As Manasseh's reign wore on, so Assyrian power began to decline. Manasseh's son Amon, who acceded in 642 BCE, ruled for only two years before being assassinated by his servants. The "people of the land" now installed the boy Josiah on the throne. He was to enable Judah to enjoy its last spell of independence before the exile.

Josiah's reign, from 640/39 to 609 BCE, was probably the most important of any reign of a king of Israel or Judah for the development of the religion of the Old Testament. In 2 Kings 22: 8–20 we find the famous story of the discovery of the "book of law" in the Temple in 622 BCE. As a result of this "discovery", Josiah implemented a religious reform directed against the "high places" (the local sanctuaries) that were to be found in his kingdom, as well as involving a thoroughgoing purge of the personnel and fittings of the Jerusalem Temple. The reform culminated in a celebration of the Passover, of which 2 Kings 23: 22 records:

> Such a passover had not been celebrated since the days of the Judges, who ruled Israel, and not in the whole period of the kings of Israel and Judah.

This could mean no more than that this was the first Passover celebrated at the command of the king (in which case we must discount Hezekiah's observance of the feast). More radically, it may record the fact that this was the first Passover ever to be celebrated in Judah.

Whatever the truth is, we can detect behind the reform a victory of the bearers of the northern Exodus-based traditions who had fled from the north a century earlier and who had kept faith with their convictions during the difficult years of Manasseh's reign. They had probably put the "law book" into the possession of Hilkiah, the high priest of the Temple — the "law book" itself being part of, or an earlier draft of, what we now know as Deuteronomy. The book itself is dealt with in chapter 10; here, the important point to note is that it represented the final fusion of the Exodus and Jerusalem traditions. Deuteronomy speaks of a single sanctuary, at which alone sacrifice can be offered to Yhwh. Although never named in Deuteronomy, this place was accepted by its writers and by King Josiah to be Jerusalem. In regard to the concept of kingship, however, the book is most explicit (Deuteronomy 17: 14–20). The king must not accumulate wealth or a harem, but must devote his life to studying God's law so that he may better perform the duties of kingship.

Because of Assyrian weakness (Nineveh, the Assyrian capital, fell in

OPPOSITE Although the city of Samaria was originally established by Omri, it was his son Ahab who enhanced it architecturally. He enclosed the existing buildings within a casemate wall (shown here) and decorated his palace with ivories (1 Kings 22: 39). Many of these, dating from the time of Ahab and his successors, were discovered in the excavations of 1908–1910 and 1931–1935.

612 BCE, the latter part of Josiah's reign saw Judah enjoying a spell of independence and an extension of its territory. Josiah, however, was killed, when he went to meet or to fight the Egyptian pharaoh, Neco II, in 609 BCE, at Megiddo (2 Kings 23: 28–9). Of this incident, we know almost nothing. It is usually assumed that Josiah set out to prevent Neco from going to the assistance of the remnants of the Assyrian army, who were making a last stand at Haran against the Babylonians; and most modern translations of 2 Kings 23: 29 imply this, although the traditional Hebrew text (which may, of course, be corrupt) indicates that Josiah was going to Neco's aid. The result of the encounter was tragic for Judah, and initiated a brief period in which it was subservient to Egypt (2 Kings 23: 33). For the few remaining years of Judah's existence, the tiny state was a helpless spectator of the power struggle between Egypt and Babylon.

In 605 BCE the Babylonians, under the leadership of Nebuchadrezzar, defeated the Egyptians at the battle of Carchemish, and a year later he moved into Syria and Israel. The prophet Jeremiah saw in this movement the hand of God, and he declared the impending downfall of the state (Jeremiah 25: 1–14). The Judahite king Jehoiakim, who had been put on the throne by Neco, transferred his allegiance to Nebuchadrezzar (2 Kings 24: 1), but following a setback for Nebuchadrezzar in a battle against Egypt in 601 BCE, Jehoiakim rebelled. In 597 Nebuchadrezzar captured Jerusalem, and deported to Babylon King Jehoiachin, who had meanwhile acceded to the throne, along with a number of important officials (2 Kings 24: 8–17). The last king to rule in Jerusalem was the exiled Jehoiachin's uncle, who remained a loyal vassal for ten years before attempting another rebellion. This time, the Babylonian response resulted in the destruction of Jerusalem and its Temple, and the end of the kingdom founded by David.

OPPOSITE Jerusalem: the spring of Gihon which flows into Hezekiah's tunnel — 1750 feet (533 metres) long, dating from 701 BCE.

CHAPTER 6

ISRAEL UNDER THE PERSIANS AND PTOLEMIES

EXILE

After thirty-seven years of imprisonment in Babylon, Johoiachin and his sons were released by the Persians, as attested by both the Old Testament and cuneiform ration lists (ANET p. 308). The exiled Jews were located in certain sites; apparently many of these were ruined cities, called "tels" (cp. Ezra 2: 59; Ezekiel 1: 3), rather than dispersed. Thus some independent social organization was achievable. Jeremiah 29: 5–7, at any rate, recommends that the Jews build homes and farm the land. According to the book of Ezra, many of those who eventually returned to Judah were wealthy, with slaves (Ezra 1: 6; 2: 65). Exile, for most, did not mean captivity, and for many it actually brought prosperity. From a century later we have the archives of a firm from Nippur run by the Murašu family, containing names of Jewish business clients, showing Jewish ownership of land and housing, and employment as officials and administrators. Although the stories of Daniel 1–6 and the book of Esther are not to be taken as historical or literal in their details, they undoubtedly attest the attainment of high office by some of the Jews, at least under the Persians, and Nehemiah's position of royal cup-bearer offers a concrete example. Aspiration to political influence is encouraged here rather than condemned, and we may infer a Babylonian Jewish population who became generally positively disposed to their situation.

Nevertheless, the earliest recorded impressions of the Judean deportees are, of course, understandably negative, even hostile. Psalm 137 imparts a longing to return home, and the allusion to the "waters of Babylon" points up the great differences in terrain between the highlands of Judah and the flat Tigris-Euphrates basin, with its higher rainfall, wide rivers, and canals. Second Isaiah, also longing for the return, denounces the Babylonian gods and their statues, made by hands and carried about on the backs of animals (44: 9ff; 46: 1). Jeremiah 50: 36–38 sums up a Judean impression of Babylon: diviners, warriors, horses and chariots, treasures, waters, images, and idols. The feeling of political inferiority was countered by an assertion of religious superiority.

The development of political and economic aspirations did not entail complete social or religious assimilation, though doubtless many Jews

Time Chart

	Persian kings		Main events in Judah
		538–552	Various returns from exile, under Sheshbazzar, Zerubbabel and others (Ezra 1–2)
559–529	CYRUS 539–8 capture of Babylon and authorization of Temple rebuilding	538/7	Altar dedication (Ezra 3: 1–6)
529–522	CAMBYSES		
522–486	DARIUS I (Hystaspes)	520–515	Building of the Second Temple (Ezra 5–6)
486–465	XERXES I		
465–425	ARTAXERXES I (Longimanus)	458	Ezra's mission (first alternative date) (Ezra 7–10; Neh 8)
		448 (?)	Abortive attempt to rebuild the walls (Ezra 4. 7–23)
		445–433	Nehemiah's first term as governor (Neh 1–7)
		438/428	Ezra's mission (second alternative date)
		430 (?)	Nehemiah's second term as governor (Neh 13)
425–424	XERXES II		
424	SOGDIANUS		
424–405	DARIUS II (Ochus)		
405–359	ARTAXERXES II (Memnon)	398	Ezra's mission (third alternative date)
359–338	ARTAXERXES III (Ochus)		
338–336	ARSES		
336–331	DARIUS III (Codommanus)	332	Judah comes under Hellenistic rule

(Based on H G M Williamson, *Ezra and Nehemiah*, JSOT Press, 1987)

did assimilate entirely. We can attribute to the exile the emergence of, or the increased emphasis upon, a number of basic characteristics of Judaism which reinforced religious identity, such as the notion of holiness by separation, some forms of religious assembly, circumcision, observing the Sabbath, and the assembling, preserving, and codifying of religious (i.e. "national") literature. The Babylonian deportation perhaps marks the beginning of the history, as opposed to pre-history, of the Hebrew Bible. Two important developments, influenced by the Babylonian environment, are the political and economic power of the priesthood, and the absorption of elements of manticism. The authority and influence of the priesthood in Babylonia, for whatever reasons, persisted and even expanded in the province of Judah after the return of many priests to Jerusalem. Persian imperial policy reinforced an internal development. Manticism (divination) was a fundamental dimension of Babylonian religion, to which several priestly guilds were devoted. It implied an understanding of things unseen and in the future by means of an esoteric tradition of reading signs — be they dreams, animal entrails, astrological signs, the patterns of oil upon water, or, as in Daniel's case, writing on the wall (see chapter 14). Other specific items of Babylonian influence include the stories of creation and flood in Genesis 1–11 which reflect themes in Babylonian mythology. Much of this cultural, literary, and religious influence was exerted during the sixth-century exile: some of it was mediated during the Persian and Greco-Roman periods via the large Jewish communities established in Babylonia or by absorption from the general Hellenistic-Oriental milieu.

THE SITUATION IN JUDAH

The political map of Palestine through the late Assyrian, Babylonian, and Persian periods was essentially the same: the Assyrians had divided the territory of northern Israel into the three provinces of Megiddo (including most of Galilee), Dor (the Shephelah), and Samaria (the highlands). Samaria, despite repopulation by Assyria from elsewhere, was essentially Yahwistic in the Persian period, although defined as being outside "Israel" by Judeans and their Bible. The territory of Judah also remained the same from the late monarchy — extending from Bethel in the north to Bethzur in the south and from Jericho in the east to Azekah in the west. Under the Persians (and Babylonians?) it was divided into six administrative districts (see Nehemiah 3). No non-Judean immigrants were introduced, though an influx of Ammonites, Moabites, Edomites, and Samarians may have occurred. Relations between Samaria and Judah became closer.

The majority of Judeans, of course, were not taken to Babylon. These, called the "poor people of the land", were given vineyards and fields (2 Kings 25: 12; Jeremiah 39: 10), probably those once owned by the deportees. Although the capital of the district had been moved to Mizpah, some sort of cult probably persisted in Jerusalem at the site of the Temple, under those priests left behind. It has been suggested that they produced some of the literature often ascribed to the exile — prophetic traditions, even perhaps the Deuteronomistic history. This is not probable; but if it were the case, such writings would have been subject to revision by subsequent generations influenced by the ideology of the returned exiles, which became dominant. Only the book of Lamentations can be ascribed with some plausibility to those left in Judah. The "poor of the land" who comprised most of those left behind, were in any case not necessarily interested in theological vindication or explanation; they are more likely to have been concerned with physical survival, for their economic resources were not great; taxes still had to be paid and land worked. Even so, we must not be surprised that the population remaining in Judah opposed the 'returnees', for many of these were rich, were claiming land, and wished to add religious taxes for the upkeep of the Temple to those levied by the Persians. The prospect of reverting to serfdom or even landless labouring would not appeal.

THE "RETURN"

The biblical version of Israel's history asserts or implies that "Israel" went into "exile"; those who remained are of little or no interest or significance — an interesting reversal of prophetic traditions, which see the exile as punishment on wicked Israel, for now we find those exiled claiming to be the preserved line of the "righteous"! Behind this theological twist lies an important historical-social factor: the inevitable tension between those returning and those who had never left. The returnees claimed to be Israel, because this claim entitled them to control of the Temple, of the government (through the law), and of the possession of the land. They seem to have been claiming that their exile had preserved their purity, unlike those left behind, who were assumed to have intermarried with non-Judeans.

Tension between immigrants and the resident population is no more than hinted at in the biblical record, but it can be inferred from the Ezra-Nehemiah traditions, which represent it as opposition from outsiders, i.e. Samaria and other neighbouring peoples, who thus become, in a way, the successors of the "Canaanites" — an evil influence which will, unless strenuously rejected, corrupt the "people of God". Yet the real victims of the "return" were not outsiders, but the resident Judeans. Samarian opposition, where it occurred, was more probably representing the grievances of the "people of the land" (Ezra 3: 3) against the "sons of the exile" (Ezra 6: 16, 19–21; 10: 7, 16). The latter, defining themselves as the true Israel, succeeded in creating their own religious community by rebuilding the Temple, fortifying Jerusalem, and excluding other Judeans. The opposition they faced in pursuing these objectives is not surprising!

The incoherence and vagueness of the biblical account of the "restoration", as the return is also called, are due partly to the huge gap between the ideology of the literary sources and the social and political issues inherent in the real situation and partly to the fact that the account was compiled much later than the events, which, it must be concluded, the compiler either did not, or did not wish to, comprehend. Hence, we

The "Cyrus Cylinder", with cuneiform inscription, issued by Cyrus after his capture of Babylon, describing the ruler's repatriation of exiles, return of captured statues and images of gods and restoration of temples. The edict included the reestablishment of a Temple community in Judah (cf Ezra 1).

cannot identify precisely the historical details from these accounts. We can, however, identify the outcome which they are trying to justify. The starting point of the immigration, and of the major biblical account (the book of Ezra) is the edict of Cyrus allowing Judeans to "return", given in Ezra 1: 2–4 (in Hebrew) and 6: 3–5 (in Aramaic). The authenticity of the Aramaic decree is widely accepted; that of the Hebrew is disputed. Further letters in Aramaic in Ezra 4: 11–16, 17–22; 5: 7–17; 6: 6–12; and 7: 12–26 are generally taken also as authentic.

In the "Cyrus Cylinder" (ANET pp. 315–16) Cyrus presents himself as a restorer of local gods and temples and a repatriator of dispersed peoples. (Although often contrasted with that of Assyrian and Babylonian rulers, this self-description is very much in their tradition.) Cyrus announces how Marduk, the god of Babylon, looked through all the earth to find the righteous ruler to liberate Babylon. Another tablet, from Nippur, attributes this commission to the god Sin, and "Second Isaiah" attributes it to Yhwh. Such theological claims apart, the sources all agree in presenting the intiative for the reconstitution of the Judean community in accordance with religious law and ancestral cult as *Persian*. The sublimation of political nationalistic sentiments into religious nationalistic ones is not to be seen only in terms of an evolutionary process within Israelite-Jewish religion, but also, and perhaps decisively, as a Persian policy for the achievement of a politically passive empire. There is evidence of a consistent Persian policy to create religious communities instead of political ones — which in the case of Judah worked extremely well.

The process of "restoration", then, comprised three objectives, more or less in chronological order: the building of the Temple (cultic), the building of city walls (political-social), and membership of a culticallydetermined society (religious). All these objectives had economic implications. The two decrees in Ezra both focus on the rebuilding of the Temple, making that the purpose of the return. No wholesale immigration is here commanded or encouraged. There is a record of the Temple vessels being handed over to Sheshbazzar, the "prince" (nāsî), of Judah (Ezra 1: 7), and he is even said — this time bearing

A Babylonian cylinder seal and the impression it makes when rolled on wet clay. This example contains a prayer to the god Marduk.

the title *Peḥah* — to have started to rebuild the Temple as decreed (Ezra 5: 14–16). Then he disappears, and the remainder of the work of the Temple is attributed to Zerubbabel. As befits his name (''seed of Babylon''), Zerubbabel heads a list of returnees given in Nehemiah 7 — which is copied, with some differences of detail, in Ezra 2. Both versions are fairly certainly a record of several different groups of returnees (if indeed they are lists of returnees at all and not censuses from a later state). Certainly, these lists, on a genealogical basis, constitute a claim to Judean identity and entail a claim to ownership of property. The books of Haggai, Zechariah, and Ezra credit this Zerubbabel with laying the Temple foundations, which we can date to 520–516 BCE; and it is thus probable that he was the officially appointed governor of the province. He and the high priest Joshua (Jeshua) are described as two ''sons of oil'' (i.e. ''anointed ones'' or ''messiahs''; Zechariah 4: 14), anticipating the pattern of dual leadership, lay and priestly, which was to remain for some the theocratic ideal. If, as some scholars suppose, Haggai and Zechariah betrayed some political ambitions for a restored independent monarchy, perhaps encouraged by the revolts attending the death of the Persian king Cambyses, they were disappointed by the ultimate triumph of the strong king Darius.

EZRA AND NEHEMIAH

The political status of Judah within the Persian empire was that of a province of the satrapy of ''Beyond the River'' (i.e. west, from the Persian point of view, of the Euphrates). Of its governors we assume Zerubbabel to have been one, and Nehemiah was certainly another (in between we have no names, but that they were also Judeans seems probable). Both Ezra and Nehemiah are presented in the Bible as working under direct orders from the Persian administration. The aim of their activities, once the Temple had been built, was to control its cult, build Jerusalem's walls, and establish a community defined by racial purity and a covenanted religious-legal code. Ezra 4 relates that in response to complaints, King Artaxerxes intervened to stop the rebuilding of the

RIGHT Excavations at the "city of David", the Ophel hill south of the Temple mount, have revealed remains of pre-exilic houses destroyed by the Babylonians. Above these can also be seen parts of the wall rebuilt under Nehemiah, which enclosed a smaller city than the walls had previously contained. According to Nehemiah 3-6, sections of the wall and gates were built simultaneously by different families and communities to hasten its completion.

OPPOSITE The flat basin of the Tigris-Euphrates was prone to flooding, a phenomenon unknown in the highlands of Judah and Israel, although marshy areas existed in the vicinity of the Kidron (Judges 4 and 5) and parts of the coastal plain. Again unlike Palestine, the natural building material was mud-brick rather than stone, as accurately observed in the story of the "tower of Babel" (Genesis 11). Rivers like the Euphrates (pictured here), and the Nile, provided the communication and irrigation necessary for the growth of great civilizations.

city (not Nehemiah's effort, though Ezra is not mentioned either). But in trying to reconstruct the progress of these achievements we encounter the insoluble problem of dating the work of Ezra.

The date of Ezra's arrival in Jerusalem — and thus his relationship to Nehemiah — is the most notorious problem of biblical chronology. The date of Nehemiah's arrival is relatively firm: it can fairly confidently be placed in 445 BCE, under Artaxerxes I. The biblical tradition appears to place Ezra thirteen years earlier. However, the links between the two in the biblical narrative are tenuous and it is fairly certain that traditions about them were independently preserved, so that any chronological relationship is late and unreliable. Hence the widely supported opinion that Ezra's king was Artaxerxes II, and that Ezra thus came later than Nehemiah, in 398. A third proposal is that for the seventh year (of Artaxerxes I) we should read the thirty-seventh year, i.e. 428, between the first and second terms of Nehemiah. The safest course is to follow what the Bible largely does and treat each independently.

According to the Bible, Nehemiah was given permission to rebuild the walls of Jerusalem, and he returned to Judah accompanied by Persian troops, bearing official letters, and with provision of wood from the royal

estates. Despite this official backing, the commission was carried out under conditions of secrecy and speed, and against much local opposition. Nehemiah also introduced some reforms to alleviate the economic plight of the peasants, who complained of exploitation by other, rich Judeans which was driving them deeply into debt (Nehemiah 5: 1–5). The reported success of Nehemiah's action in enforcing remission of debts should not obscure two facts: first, the reforms were not part of his mission, but were enacted in response to complaints; second, although Nehemiah alleviated the worst effects of debt-slavery he did not reform the structure of land ownership. His renunciation of payment for his work is likewise cosmetic. Nehemiah's motives can be seen as pragmatic but not much else. Were these wealthy Jews recent immigrants, like himself? Another reform, probably Nehemiah's, was to increase the population of the city (Nehemiah 11: 1–2). No reason is given, but the decision makes sense as a means of consolidating around the Temple and around the "leaders of the people" a "Temple community", an enclave within the wider province. The biblical report reads as if few wanted to move: the choice was met by lot, and those who "volunteered" (if that term is not a euphemism for being chosen by lot!) were blessed.

After twelve years back at the Persian court (if the biblical account is reliable) Nehemiah returned with further reforms. Two dealt with the Temple: a certain Tobiah the Ammonite was removed from residence in the Temple, and those Levites who had no Temple status or income were given a role and provided with a tithe (more taxes!). A curfew on Sabbath trading in Jerusalem was imposed and mixed marriages banned. On this occasion Nehemiah's power seems greater, for the measures were said to be unpopular (Nehemiah 13: 25). Whose power lay behind Nehemiah? His measures all had the effect of consolidating a racially and religiously exclusive Temple-city-state. Persians, priests, and wealthy landowners benefitted, forming a trinity of power which remained a fairly constant factor until the Temple was itself destroyed in 70 CE.

The "temple-community" is a well-known social-economic model, especially for the ancient Near East. In some such societies the temple owns the land and permits some or all of it to be worked by community members. In others, the temple owns no land, and this was apparently the case in Judah, though we can see that the Temple did charge taxes (first fruits, tithes, portions of sacrifices, a one-third of a shekel payment) for its upkeep, including personnel. The Holiness Code (Leviticus 17–26), while allowing the poor to glean and promoting the sabbatical remission of debts, enhances, above all, the economic interests, and the ideology, of the priesthood. It prohibits, for example, animal slaughter unless offered as a sacrifice (a Temple tax on meat), and emphasizes the holiness of priests. Actual ownership of land was based on the household (extended family, "father's house"), a system which in fact allowed certain families to gain economic advantage over others by acquiring the land of "relatives", and turning surplus into cash. The Temple, by exacting tithes and by serving as a major customer for wood

PREVIOUS PAGES A view of the Ephraimite highlands looking west from the site of the Israelite capital city Samaria — later the Hellenistic city of Sebaste. Samaria was built on a virgin site by Omri, King of Israel (876–869 BCE; see 1 Kings 16: 24), and finally devastated by John Hyrcanus (c. 100 BCE). Sebaste was founded here by Herod the Great, and settled mainly by Greeks.

OPPOSITE The Herodium, built by Herod the Great about 7½ miles (12 kilometres) south of Jerusalem and 3 miles (5 kilometres) southeast of Bethlehem, is a largely artificial mound, hollow, with a palace at the top and a resort at its base.

and oil, could influence this process by the granting of franchises. The Persians demanded taxes not in crops but in cash — i.e. in precious metals. Hence, the crops grown needed to be saleable and in surplus. olives and vines consequently replaced cereals. The likely outcome is that the staple foods for the populace needed to be bought from outside, and the peasantry would not be able to sustain themselves from their own work. The exploitation of the peasantry, likewise, seems a fairly constant factor up to 70 CE and may have finally played a role in bringing the 'Second Temple' period to its destructive end.

The mission of Ezra is more difficult to understand than that of Nehemiah. Ezra himself appears only in Ezra 7–10 and Nehemiah 8, and the latter reference is widely held to belong originally between Ezra 8 and 9. His mission, moreover, consists of only one year's activity. He was not sent as a governor, or to rebuild Temple or walls. He is said to have had Persian authority specifically to take home fellow Jews, take gifts and grants for the national-ethnic cult, investigate the status of Jewish law, and appoint judges of the law over the entire satrapy of "Beyond the River". Ezra is described as a priest and "a scribe skilled in the law of Moses which the Lord, the God of Israel, had given", which may give a clue to his aims. But does the term "scribe" mean "administrator", from the Persian point of view, or "legal expert", from the Jewish? Or both? If Ezra's mission did include regularization of law throughout the satrapy, that law must have been seen as religious law, binding only on the Jews, but equally not a law by which the province of Judah should be ruled. If he were a kind of "minister for Jewish affairs", responsible for Jewish affairs in the empire, it is strange that he had no successors.

The nature of Ezra's mission may be clarified somewhat by a hieroglyphic inscription which relates the activities of another scribe, a certain Udjahorresne, a priest who sided with the Persians during the invasion of Egypt by Cambyses. Later, he was sent from the imperial court to Egypt to reorganize the "house of life" at the sanctuary in Sais, and part of this mission involved the codifying of religious laws (Hayes and Miller 1986, pp. 449–50).

What, then, did Ezra achieve? The biblical account concentrates on his reading of the law, celebration of the Feast of Tabernacles, and institution of a covenant (Nehemiah 8), which included the putting away of foreign wives — a course of action that was said not to have been carried through (Ezra 10: 44). He fulfilled the task of bringing returnees and gifts, but the parts of the commission relating to the law correspond only partly and vaguely to what Ezra did. A good guess is that the mission was initiated by the Persian King as a reaction to the revolt in Egypt, meeting the need to strengthen the loyalty of the neighbouring province. If so, perhaps it did succeed in its aims. Otherwise, we cannot ascertain that any of Ezra's activity had significant historical consequences even for Judaism, whether or not he "failed", as is commonly declared. The date of his mission is not a crucial lacuna in our knowledge.

Outside the books of Ezra and Nehemiah, he is ignored until the first century CE.

Between the time of Ezra and Nehemiah and that of Alexander the Great we know nothing from biblical sources except by inference. We do know that Egypt revolted against Persian rule and was finally subdued and that there was a widespread revolt of satraps. It has been suggested that in a further revolt of Phoenician cities Judah was involved, as is stated in some much later sources and may be supported by evidence of the destruction of cities in Palestine. The case is not impressive. The Jewish historian Josephus (first century CE) relates that — in the time of Artaxerxes II or III? — the high priest Johanan killed his brother, who had tried to secure the high priesthood for himself with the connivance of a high Persian official, Bagoas. This, if true, foreshadows a similar conflict in the reign of Antiochus IV (see below). Since the high priest was controller of the Temple, and hence the treasury, the office was worth trying to buy. In the Greco-Roman period the high priest ruled together with a council of elders (Greek *gerousia*), a development that may date from the Persian period. The Elephantine papyri (see below) reveal a Persian governor of Judah, a fact that might be significant, if one knew more. We also know that in the course of the fourth century, the province of "Yehud" minted its own coins, several of which have been preserved, as have jar handles stamped with *yhd* or *yršlym*. Coins were first introduced into the Persian empire from Lydia, and show some Attic influence. Their introduction had much to do with the growth in trade that occurred during the Persian period, especially with Greece — though Judah does not seem to have participated much in this. The jars may have been used for Temple taxation, which was partly in coin, though mostly in produce.

ELEPHANTINE

Babylonia was not the only site of Jewish settlement outside Judea, Isaiah and Jeremiah both refer to Jews living in Egypt. We also know of a Jewish military garrison which was probably stationed at Elephantine, on the upper Nile (modern Assuan) as early as the seventh or sixth century BCE, and which has left papyri written during the fifth century. From these papyri we learn that they had a temple in which they worshipped Yahu, Bethel, Harambethel, Ašambethel, and Anat. This temple had been recently destroyed by Egyptians, and a letter was written, presumably to the satrap, requesting permission to rebuild it. A further letter went to Bagohi, the Persian governor of Judah, repeating the request, and also to Johanan and other priests in Jerusalem. This request to Bagohi was also repeated, while yet another went to the sons of Sanballat, governor of Samaria and opponent of Nehemiah. These bore Yahwistic names, — ie. names containing the element *Yah* (Yhwh) — Delayah and Shemayah. They had advised the satrap to permit use of the altar except for burnt offerings. The interesting point here is that

An example of a "Yehud" coin, so named because it bears the inscription YHD (in the archaic Hebrew script). These coins were minted in the closing years of the Persian empire (350–332 BCE) by the Persian and Judean religious authorities. The obverse shows a hunting falcon, whose symbolism is still unclear. The reverse bears the common motif of the lily, which was probably interpreted as an emblem of the land of Israel.

control of Jewish religious practice in the entire satrapy was apparently
vested in Jerusalem (a situation which perhaps makes a little more sense
of Ezra's commission). Another papyrus regulates observance of the Feast
of Unleavened Bread, claiming that the "Great King" had ordered the
satrap in Egypt concerning the observance of this feast. The interest
shown by the Persian king in matters of Jewish cult is confirmed.

ALEXANDER AND THE PTOLEMIES

In 333 BCE Syria-Palestine fell into the hands of Alexander, who, taking
Tyre and Gaza en route, marched to Egypt, back through Palestine, and
on to Mesopotamia. A story of Josephus (Antiquities xi 336–9) relating
that Alexander visited Jerusalem is improbable. However, although the
Samaritans were permitted to build a temple on their sacred mountain,
Gerizim, because of a rebellion against their local governor Samaria was
converted into a military colony. With this episode, most probably, are
connected the Wadi Daliyeh papyri: legal texts found in a cave in the
Jordan Valley along with several skeletons, and referring to the family
of a certain Sanballat, quite probably descended from the Sanballat who
opposed Nehemiah.

The sudden death of Alexander in 323 BCE threw the entire empire
into confusion, as his generals fought for their territories. Ptolemy,
governor of Egypt, seized Syria and Palestine, which he retained, after
losing it twice, from shortly after 301. From this period onwards Judean
loyalties were to be divided between the Hellenistic kingdoms of Egypt
and North Syria/Mesopotamia. Also, during the struggle for control of
Palestine, many Jews were, according to Josephus, taken to Egypt,
probably forming the nucleus of the large Egyptian community that
developed there.

In accordance with ancient Egyptian tradition, the Ptolemaic kingdom
was tightly organized under the exalted king, with considerable power
in the hands of his chief minister of finance. Syria and Palestine were
integrated into the Egyptian system of land allotment, in which the king
nominally owned all, requiring leases and taxes. However, this
administration did not restrict, but promoted trade. From the Zenon
papyri we learn of a visit, undertaken at the instruction of the Egyptian
finance minister, Apollonius, by Zenon, to Palestine, as far as the military
colony of Tobias (Tobiah) in Transjordan, and to the vineyard owned
by Apollonius himself in Galilee. The papyri also contain letters to
Apollonius from Tobias, which attest the pro-Ptolemaic attitude, and
the enterprise, of Tobias's family — one that was destined to play a
major role in the politics of Judea. In Jerusalem, however, there were
pro-Seleucid sympathies, fuelled by Seleucid attempts to regain control
of Palestine. The high priest Onias II withheld taxes. His nephew,
Tobias's son Joseph, now moved to Jerusalem, successfully opposed this
anti-Ptolemaic stand, and in return replaced the high priest as the people's

A coin showing the head of
Alexander the Great
(336–323 BCE), whose
military victories from
Greece to the borders of
India inaugurated the
Hellenistic period in the
ancient Near East.

political representative before the Egyptian king. He used this position to secure the rights to collect the taxes in Syria and Palestine, a lucrative sinecure which he held for a long while. Non-payment of taxes led to forfeiture of lands, and the personal wealth thus accumulated by the tax gatherer no doubt stimulated the economy of Jerusalem, a process which would also have widened the gap between rich and poor.

As the possibility of Seleucid takeover increased, Joseph's sympathies wavered. The Seleucid Antiochus III took twenty years to replace Ptolemaic rule in Palestine, and the tension split the Tobiad family. Joseph's youngest son Hyrcanus was sent to Egypt, where he tried to usurp his father as official representative (*prostates*). But he ended up, opposed by his family, in the family estate in Transjordan at Araq el-Emir. Excavations here have uncovered not only a fortress but, within it, a Jewish temple, perhaps, like that at Elephantine, a substitute for the one at Jerusalem rather than a local supplement. Judea passed under the Seleucids, and Hyrcanus finally committed suicide during the beginning of the "reform" in Jerusalem. Antiochus III, in an inscription found at Hephzibah near Bethshan, granted generous benefits and religious freedom to the Jerusalem community. Seleucid sympathies in Jerusalem presumably intensified, led by both the Tobiad family and the high-priestly family, the Oniads. However, tensions built up. The high priest Onias III and the Tobiads were vying for influence at the Seleucid court. Onias and his brother Jeshua (Jason) disagreed about the adaptation of the Jewish state economically and religiously to its Hellenistic environment.

The defeat of Antiochus III in Asia Minor by the Romans in 190 BCE was a serious setback to the Seleucid kingdom. The resulting loss of ambition, of territory in Asia Minor (hence also loss of revenue), and of cash payments to Rome initiated a process of financial crisis and gradual political instability. This development, coupled with struggles in Jerusalem, led to an unprecedented assault, both external and internal, on the character of the Jewish community. The opposition this engendered led in turn to a revival of Jewish independence, even imperialism. The scale of Jewish fortunes in the period following was far to exceed anything previously experienced.

A coin from the second century BCE, showing Seleucid and Ptolemaic rulers. Antiochus III captured Palestine from the Egyptian kingdom of the Ptolemies in 199 BCE, maintaining and substantiating all Jewish religious and political rights.

CHAPTER 7

FROM THE MACCABEES TO HEROD THE GREAT

Only one biblical book has an evident background in the period covered by this chapter. This is the book of Daniel, which was apparently written during the three-year period in which the Jewish religion was banned, probably around 165 BCE (see also chapters 9 and 14). But two accounts of these events are found in the deutero-canonical (or Apocryphal) books of 1 and 2 Maccabees. The first-century CE Jewish historian Josephus gives a history of this period, too (partly using 1 Maccabees), while other Greek sources, both Jewish and non-Jewish, afford us a much better knowledge of this period than exists for the preceding three centuries. Our information, however, relates mostly to external, political events; about internal religious and social developments we have little direct information. We can, however, guess that important changes were taking place. The existence, in the first century CE, of religious groups such as the Pharisees, Sadducees, and Essenes; a number of apocalyptic writings from the Hellenistic, Hasmonean, and Herodian periods; and the discovery of the Dead Sea Scrolls suggest a religious pluralism within Palestine (let alone in the Diaspora, or Jewish communities abroad), which, however ancient its roots, must have accelerated under the impact of the political and religious crises that succeeded each other from 175 onwards with hardly a break. In this chapter we shall sketch the relatively well known (if less well understood) political events. The corresponding religious and social developments will be covered in chapter 15.

THE ''HELLENISTIC CRISIS'' C.175—140 BCE

''Hellenism'' is the term for that culture which was produced by the spread of Greek influence throughout the eastern Mediterranean, an area already politically and economically interlocked for several centuries. What emerged was a fusion, in which the Greek language, Greek institutions, and Greek customs predominated, but in which Oriental elements were also present, and, in turn, influenced even Greece and Rome (as Christianity was to do). The Greek empire, of which the

Time Chart

	Syria		Judea
223–187	Antiochus III (the Great)	198	Judea comes under Seleucid rule
187–175	Seleucus IV		
175–64	Antiochus IV (Epiphanes)	167	Edict and onset of revolt
		166–160	Judas Maccabee
162–150	Demetrius I Soter	160–142	Jonathan
150–145	Alexander Balas	152	Jonathan becomes high priest
		150	Jonathan made military and civil governor by Alexander Balas
145–138	Demetrius II		
[145–142	Antiochus VI]	c.145	Jonathan made governor of Syria by Antiochus
		143–134	Simon appointed high priest and ethnarch by Demetrius
138–129	Antiochus VII (Sidetes)	134–104	John Hyrcanus I
129–95	Demetrius II	104–103	Aristobulus I assumes title of king in addition to that of high priest
		103–76	Alexander Jannai
95–78	Demetrius III		
83	Syria conquered by the Armenian king Tigranes	76–67	Alexandra/Shelomzion queen, Hyrcanus II high priest
		67	Hyrcanus II king
	Rome	67–63	Aristobulus II
64	Syria becomes a Roman province	63	Pompey captures Jerusalem and enters the Temple
		63–40	Hyrcanus II high priest (again)
		47–43	Antipater procurator of Judea
		40–37	Antigonus
		40–38	Parthian invasion: Hyrcanus II captured
		37–4	Herod the Great appointed king (That Herod appears to have died before the birth of Jesus (1CE) is due to an error in traditional reckoning. It is probable that Jesus was born in 6 or 4 BCE.)
		30	Hyrcanus II killed

Romans were heirs, was above all a *cultural* empire. Politically it hardly survived the death of Alexander (323 BCE), but its effect on the subsequent history of the Western world, at least, was deep and permanent. (For a description of its main elements, see chapter 3, pp. 113–14.) The impact of Hellenism on Judea, however, is impossible to trace in detail or to describe simply. It occurred gradually and on many levels. The province found itself increasingly surrounded by Hellenistic cities; its priestly and scribal classes confronted by Hellenistic ideas; its administrators and traders challenged in their affairs by the Greek language; and the whole society affected by the Hellenistic rulers under whom it lived.

The confrontation between Hellenism and traditional Jewish customs was not, on the whole, violent. Judaism was able to survive in fairly profoundly Hellenized forms, as we know very well from the Jewish literature from Alexandria and from archaeological evidence over a wide area. But in Judea, during the reign of the Seleucid king Antiochus IV (''Epiphanes''), a bitter conflict erupted, which is often referred to as the ''Hellenistic crisis''. This, however, is a simplification of a rather complicated web of issues.

Let us begin with the political context. The Ptolemaic kingdom was — as Egypt had always been — a united, relatively homogeneous, and organized realm. The Seleucid kingdom, by contrast, covered an area that had never been united and that consisted of several different nations and religions, being held together to some extent by the person of the king. However, there was no policy (at least until the reign of Antiochus IV) of interfering in the autonomy of the local cults — including that of Judea. The administration was essentially economic, with the king authorizing the minting of coins, the control of trade (especially the collection of taxes), and the granting of charters to cities.

It was not the Seleucid monarchy but Hellenism, as embodied in the institution of the Greek city or *polis*, that was to have a profound impact on Jewish culture. Alexander himself had founded a number of cities in Palestine, and many existing cities were Hellenized. These were concentrated along the Mediterranean coast and in Transjordan, with the important exception of Samaria (renamed Sebaste) in the highlands, not too distant from Jerusalem itself. The Greek city, with its semi-autonomous economy, its (limited) democracy, its gymnasium, arena, hippodrome, and schools (teaching Greek philosophy), implanted a radically different culture into the conservative, religion-centred society of Palestine. Within this context, the Greek and Macedonian soldiers and traders who settled in these cities met and mingled with the indigenous population. Gradually the two populations became integrated — at least at the levels of the artisan, merchant and aristocratic classes. Palestinian citizens even tended to dress according to Greek fashion. The ethos was somewhat hedonistic, tolerant, not particularly religious, and certainly condescending towards rigidly traditional cults such as that of Judea, where customs like circumcision, abstinence from pork, and adherence to ancient rituals would be seen as quaint, amusing, or annoying. Conversely, and predictably, many of the native population viewed the introduction of Greek attitudes with alarm and hostility; and this cultural-religious difference was to be a central factor in the conflict in Judea.

But there were several more immediate causes of the crisis. On the Seleucid side, one factor was the financial crisis of the Seleucid kingdom, brought on by Antiochus III's expulsion from Asia Minor in 190 BCE, and exacerbated by the inherent lack of political unity. Seleucus IV inherited this problem, which obliged him, among other things, to try to ransack the Jerusalem Temple treasury. It also prompted his successor, Antiochus IV, to invade Egypt. The humilating rebuff he received there from the Roman legate may have provoked him to deal more harshly with unrest in Jerusalem than he might have otherwise. This brings us to another oft-cited Seleucid factor, the character of Antiochus IV. Even in contemporary reports he is sometimes described as arrogant and greedy, even insane. He is also said to have wanted to unify his kingdom under a single cult. These explanations for the crisis are now generally held to be at best partial, and perhaps even based on a politically biased view of the king's personality.

Antiochus IV revoked the rights bestowed by Antiochus III (p. 173) and provoked the Maccabean rebellion. These events are briefly alluded to in Daniel 11: 9–39.

On the Judean side, we may note two causes, which are nevertheless closely related. One was the rivalry between the traditional high-priestly family of the Oniads and the non-priestly Tobiads, outlined in the previous chapter. Under the Seleucids, as previously under the Ptolemies, the political leadership of Judea was vested in the office of the high priest. Following the death of the high priest Simon II, the struggle between the two families centred on Onias III, his successor. Onias's sympathies with the Ptolemies allowed his Tobiad rivals to undermine his influence at the Seleucid court, while his conservative stance brought him into conflict with his brother Jason (Jeshua). Jason belonged to a large body of priestly and aristocratic Judeans who desired greater official recognition, if not adoption, of certain Hellenistic fashions which were already popular within the province.

This Hellenizing trend among the Judean aristocracy is the other, related, cause. The motives of the "Hellenizers" are widely overlooked or misunderstood. Jewish sources tend to regard the "Hellenizers" as traitors. But these men were *Jews* and not — at least in their own eyes — traitors to their religion. One suggestion for their motives is that they wished both to increase the economic wealth of their city and province and to make common cause with the many Jews in Syro-Palestine who had gone further in embracing the Hellenistic way of life than had the Judeans. Whatever the truth, we must at least accept that these "Hellenizers" had a vision of a "liberated" Judaism. Moreover, we might as well recognize that outside Palestine, forms of "Hellenized" Judaism, such as were perhaps envisaged by Jason and his allies, survived and flourished. However, the proposal to make a Hellenistic city in *Jerusalem*, the seat of the cult of the Jewish God, focus of political aspirations, and spiritual home of Jews everywhere, and to exclude from citizenship most of the populace was both religiously and socially provocative. We do not know exactly how this new *polis* was intended to relate to the Temple itself, and the proponents of the plan presumably did not intend to interfere with the traditional cult. They may, of course, have believed that ordinary Jews did not need to participate in it. Most Jews, after all, living far from Jerusalem, did not. But a person imbued with Hellenistic ideals might genuinely fail to understand the social as well as psychological and religious importance of ancestral forms of worship and its contribution to political stability and national identity. The proposal for a *polis* in Jerusalem was at the very least a serious mistake.

The "Hellenistic crisis" thus had both internal and external causes. It seems to have begun as a mainly internal struggle between two alternative views of how Judea should develop. Antiochus's intervention forced the issue dramatically, but did not in the end, perhaps, make a great deal of difference to the outcome. The Syrian kingdom was in decline, the traditional high-priesthood had become an office to be bought, and compromise with Hellenism was inevitable. What can be said is that Antiochus's extreme actions provided the Hasmonean family with the opportunity for political leadership.

Development of the crisis

Seleucus IV's shortage of funds and the Oniad-Tobiad rivalry conspired to start the chain of events. The king needed money, and whoever could provide it in Judea could buy power. Access to the Temple treasury, a key to this power, was controlled by Onias; but the Tobiad Simon, head of the Temple administration, tried to gain some financial leverage of his own. First he tried to get control of the Temple markets, a major source of revenue. Then he informed Seleucid officials that Onias was hoarding vast sums in the Temple. Consequently, Seleucus sent an official, named Heliodorus, to raid the Temple. Somehow Onias dissuaded him. The only account of this episode, in the Apocryphal book 2 Maccabees 3: 10ff., describes how Heliodorus was scared off by an angelic apparition. Simon then accused Onias of sedition, and the high priest went to Antioch to face the king.

But Seleucus was then assassinated by Heliodorus and succeeded by his brother, Antiochus IV. At this moment, the Tobiads rallied behind Jason, who offered to "buy" the high-priesthood by offering Antiochus a higher tax return and a policy of greater toleration of Hellenistic culture. Antiochus accepted the offer. His appointment of Jason constituted what must have been seen by many Judeans not only as a serious intrusion into whatever political autonomy they had previously enjoyed, but more seriously as a challenge to their law. From their point of view the whole crisis might be seen as religious from the outset, and both of our main sources, 1 and 2 Maccabees, interpret it so, if in different ways.

Jason, the lay aristocracy led by the Tobiads, and no doubt some of the priests also, then proposed to Antiochus, previously sweetened with a bribe, to make Jerusalem — or more strictly perhaps, an area within

Jerusalem — a Hellenistic city. This city would have an enrolment of citizens, ''Antiocheans in Jerusalem'', and would be provided with a gymnasium (in which athletics were practised naked) and an *ephebeion*, a sort of Greek ''youth club''. Yet this achievement does not appear to have satisfied the impulses that had secured it. Jason became himself a victim of the momentum of reforming Hellenism; he was outbid by a certain Menelaus (Menahem), who, unlike Jason, was not Oniad, or even a member of the family of Zadok, from whom the high priest had, in former times, been appointed. War between the rivals broke out, in the course of which Menelaus plundered the Temple and had Onias III, still in Antioch, murdered.

Returning from his first Egyptian campaign (169 BCE), Antiochus visited Jerusalem, now in revolt against Menelaus, and restored order, after killing many people and plundering the Temple. A year later, after his second and abortive Egyptian campaign, he sent his general Apollonius to repeat the exercise. On this occasion, according to the sources, many of the inhabitants were massacred on the sabbath or taken as slaves, the city was burned, and the walls were torn down. Apollonius then fortified the citadel, which stood on the western hill of the city (near the present Jaffa gate) and placed in it some of his troops and some sympathetic Judeans. This citadel (*Akra*) became a city within a city, a non-Jewish stronghold in the midst of a defenceless Jewish Temple city. Its inhabitants — the Syrian troops at least — went so far as to use the Temple for the worship of their own deities.

Shortly afterwards, in the winter of 167 BCE, Antiochus issued a decree forbidding the practice of traditional Judean religion, including festivals, circumcision, and the possession of copies of the Law. The

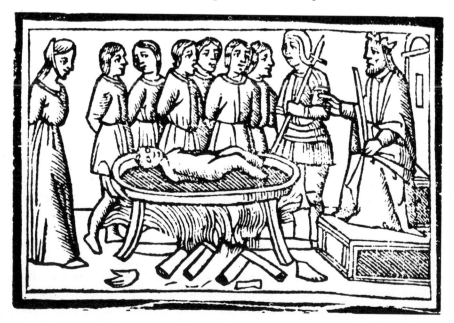

Second Maccabees provides graphic descriptions of the martyrdom of pious Jews by the Seleucid king Antiochus IV, and in particular of seven brothers, one of whom was ''fried alive in a pan'' (7: 5). The story, which illustrates a fervent belief in bodily resurrection and the efficacy of righteous suffering for the salvation of the nation, was popular in Christian rather than Jewish tradition, since Second Maccabees was written in Greek and included in the Apocrypha. This illustration is from an Italian bible of 1525.

crowning act, according to the book of Daniel, whose author was almost certainly an eye-witness, was the setting up in the Temple of an abomination that was "desolating" (*šōmēm*, a pun on *Baal Shamen*, the Syrian "lord of heaven"). We are uncertain what or where exactly this was, but it comprised at least an altar (see Bickermann, 1979; p. 61ff.). The cult of the God of Israel, whose chief feature was the twice-daily sacrifice, was terminated. Other festivals, such as the king's birthday, were imposed in its place. At this point the issue obviously ceased to be how far Jewish religion should be "modernized"; the struggle became essentially between a traditional religion or none at all. Reformers, however tenaciously they continued to hold their convictions, had no ground on which to stand in this phase of the struggle. Initiative passed to the "conservatives", who included most of the populace.

The Maccabean revolt

The story of the beginnings of the armed resistance is told in 1 Maccabees 2: 1–26. This story, often accepted as true, relates how, in the village of Modiᶜin, 17 miles (27 kilometres) northwest of Jerusalem, an aged priest named Mattathias, of the family of Hashmon, killed a Jew who was about to offer a pagan sacrifice. He then slew a Syrian soldier and destroyed the altar. With his five sons, he then withdrew to the countryside to wage a guerilla war against any Jews who capitulated to the Syrians. This account, though it may contain some truth, is not only intrinsically improbable (an aged priest doing all that?), but smacks of the influence of Numbers 25, where Phinehas, whom Mattathias commends to his sons as a model of the "zealot" priest, slays an idolatrous Israelite. Finally, 1 Maccabees itself is obviously written in order to enhance the reputation of the Hasmonean dynasty which sprang from the family of Mattathias, and to justify its leadership of the nation by giving it virtually exclusive credit for liberating the people from persecution and winning political independence. The story is undoubtedly a legend, and is not corroborated elsewhere. What is true is that Mattathias's son Judas was the first great leader of armed resistance to the Syrians. His nickname "Maccabee" ("Hammer") has come to be applied to the entire family.

Under Judas, the guerilla struggle progressed from campaigns against compliant fellow-Judeans to attacks on Syrian troops. It seems to have had widespread support, and those who fought in support of their traditional religion called themselves the "pious" (*Ḥasîdîm*). The terrain of the Judean highlands is ideal for guerilla warfare, and the Judean fighters were able to melt away into their villages and regroup at short notice. (The War Scroll from Qumran contains descriptions of military manoeuvres appropriate to guerilla warfare, which may well have originated in the early Maccabean days.) Judas inflicted four defeats on four different Syrian generals who had tried four different routes into Judea. Since these routes all followed valleys, the opportunities for ambush were excellent. The Syrian regent, Lysias, in control while

The *War Scroll* from Qumran Cave 1 describes the final battle between Israel and the "Kittim" (almost certainly intended to refer to the Romans). Written in the late first century BCE or first century CE, it depicts this battle as the outcome of a struggle between the forces of light and darkness, which will lead, after a further forty years of fighting, to the world-wide dominion of the God of Israel.

Antiochus campaigned against Parthia in the east, brought an army by a roundabout route from the south. He was defeated at Judea's southern border, near Beth-Zur.

At this point, war gave way to negotiation. Three years after the decree had been issued, Antiochus rescinded it, and the Temple was rededicated in December 164, an event now commemorated in the Feast of Hanukkah. The *polis* disappeared, but not the *Akra*. Most *Ḥasîdîm* presumably saw the conflict as won. But the impetus generated over three years drove Judas and his brother Simon to more ambitious ventures, in the direction of political independence, even regional power, and perhaps already in the direction of establishing a dynasty. Military campaigns were conducted outside Judea, and Jewish populations in Galilee and Transjordan were brought safely to Judea.

Judas went on to capture the historic city of Hebron, and destroyed its pagan altars. Hebron had not been Judean territory since the Babylonian exile, and Judas seems already to have been embarked on religio-political imperialism (assuming the facts to be correct, he was no more tolerant of pagan altars in his "realm" than Antiochus had been of the Jewish one in his!) But, of course, the evolution of successful self-defence into imperialism is the rule rather than the exception. The modern concept of "peace within secure borders" never applied to that part — or any part — of the ancient world, in which a nation had either to be a ruler of others or ruled by others. Judas, like David before him, was testing his power, and the Syrians were uncertain of theirs.

Judas's luck held for a while; besieging the *Akra*, he was attached by the Seleucid general Lysias, who then had to withdraw because of internal rebellion, leaving the *Ḥasîdîm* in a strong position. Menelaus was executed and Alcimus installed as high priest. At this point (if not several years earlier) the "legitimate" high priest, Onias IV, fled to Egypt and built in Leontopolis another temple.

Judas was not satisfied. He quarreled with Alcimus, who fled to Antioch, and the fight against Syria continued. The Seleucid king Demetrius sent Nicanor with an army, which was defeated. Later that year he sent Bacchides, who was more successful; Judas was at last defeated, and he died in battle. The result was that the upper-class reformers began to reassert themselves: Alcimus seems to have taken some pro-Hellenizing measures.

From here onwards, political developments in Judea were governed by the gradual collapse of the Seleucid kingdom, which manifested itself in a series of struggles for the throne. The ability of the Seleucids to retain control over Palestine fluctuated, and with it the opportunities for Judea to assert a degree not only of independence but of control over neighbouring territories. Opportunities thus remained for a family ambitious for political power, and with a good military record. The Hasmoneans' success in revolt gave a springboard for greater achievements. Impotent in the face of a determined and powerful Syria, they could exploit its periods of instability. The issues of Hellenism and religious freedom were quickly overtaken by political independence and dynastic ambition.

THE HASMONEAN DYNASTY

Jonathan and Simon

Resistance by the Hasmonean family to the state of affairs in Jerusalem began to build up very slowly under Judas's brother Jonathan, and the struggle reached a climax again when Bacchides, intervening against Jonathan, was defeated. As Syria was still unstable, Jonathan continued to build his power, playing off contenders to the Syrian throne while

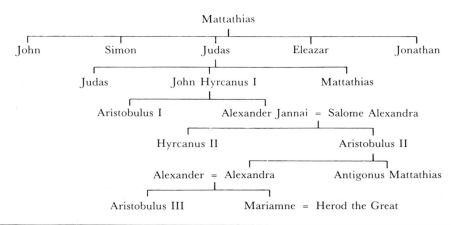

The Hasmonean Family Tree

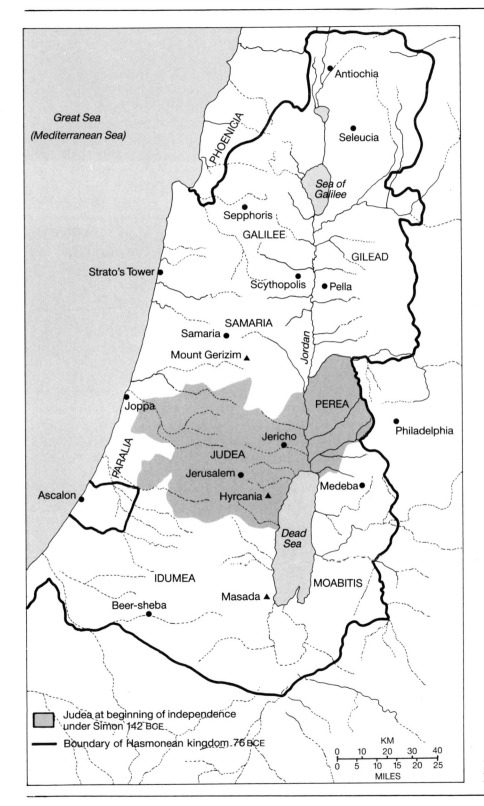

Great Sea
(Mediterranean Sea)

PHOENICIA

Antiochia

Seleucia

Sea of
Galilee

Sepphoris

GALILEE

GILEAD

Strato's Tower

Scythopolis   Pella

SAMARIA

Samaria

Mount Gerizim ▲

Joppa

PEREA

Jericho

JUDEA

Philadelphia

PARALIA

Jerusalem

Ascalon

Hyrcania ▲

Medeba

Dead
Sea

IDUMEA

MOABITIS

Beer-sheba

Masada ▲

Jordan

Judea at beginning of independence
under Simon 142 BCE

Boundary of Hasmonean kingdom 76 BCE

KM
0   10   20   30   40
0   5   10   15   20   25
MILES

Map 13 The Hasmonean
kingdom.

fortifying Jerusalem, securing Syrian nomination first as high priest, then as governor of Judea, and then as governor of Syria, and extending his territorial control to include parts of the coastal plain and the district of Samaria — and, according to Jewish sources, destroying non-Jewish altars. His blatant usurpation of the high-priesthood in 152 BCE may very well have created widespread resentment, for although the family was priestly, it had no close links with the traditional high-priestly family who traced descent from David's priest, Zadok. But no reaction is explicitly recorded. Jonathan's astute dealings with the Syrians finally got the better of him, and he was killed treacherously by a pretender named Trypho. His brother Simon succeeded him as high priest. Simon continued to extend the borders of his realm, and finally captured the Akra. He and two of his sons died at the instigation of his son-in-law Ptolemy, with whom they were feasting near Jericho.

John Hyrcanus

John Hyrcanus (Yohanan I), Simon's third son, survived Ptolemy's assault and established himself as his father's successor in Jerusalem, but only to face a siege by the Syrian king Antiochus VII. He had to surrender and disarm, relinquish all territories outside Judea, provide hostages, and pay a large sum of money. Effectively all this re-established Syrian sovereignty. But in the severe disruption into which Syrian affairs promptly fell, Judea could once again assert political independence. Hyrcanus set out to gain control of an area, which was to correspond closely to that ascribed to David. Like David, he also employed foreign mercenaries. But, with that characteristically Hasmonean mixture of religious zeal, political ambition, and expediency, he also enforced circumcision on the conquered Edomites, destroyed the Samaritan temple on Gerizim, obliterated the city of Samaria, and plundered the tomb of David. Hence, before his death in 104 BCE Hyrcanus had seen Judea triumph over most of (Hellenized) Palestine, though it was hardly a triumph of traditional Judaism.

Aristobulus I and Alexander

OPPOSITE The Herodium was built on a largely artificial mound, containing a residence at the summit, further rooms inside the mound, and extensive baths and gardens at the foot. It was also intended as a mausoleum for Herod himself, although his tomb has not yet been found. In this picture, looking north, Bethlehem can be seen on the horizon, left of centre.

Hyrcanus's son Aristobulus was high priest for one year only but accomplished three significant things: he took the title of king; he added Galilee to the Hasmonean teritories; and in the interest of his own security, he turned against members of his family, an expedient that Herod was later to adopt. The assumption of kingship and high-priesthood by one individual is just another symptom of the aspiration of the Hasmoneans to equality with their Hellenistic royal counterparts and of their insensitivity to the religious sentiments of many of their subjects. His successor, Alexander Jannaeus (Yannai), took the further step of minting — with the permission of the Syrian king — his own coins.

Alexander's reign was characterized by external and internal conflicts, as he sought, with some limited success, to extend the kingdom further, while encountering opposition within. He had narrow escapes in

Masada, on the western shore of the Dead Sea, was a site chosen by Herod the Great for one of his many fortress-palaces. This picture shows the three-tiered northern palace, perched on the edge of the rock, above which is a complex of baths, villas and stores. Water was supplied by a huge cistern carved inside the rock, but an aqueduct also brought a supply which had to be carried to the top on foot. The fortress is most famous for being the site of the final resistance and defeat by the Jewish Zealots in the war against Rome (74 CE).

confrontations with both the Egyptian king Ptolemy Lathyros and the Nabatean king Obodas, while at home he was, according to Josephus, pelted with lemons while officiating as high priest during the Feast of Tabernacles. Josephus, in fact, reports open rebellion against Alexander, resulting in the loss of thousands of lives; and both Josephus and rabbinic sources claim that the Pharisees took an active part in opposition to Alexander, culminating in the superbly ironic gesture of appealing to the Seleucid king to rescue them from the Hasmoneans! But Alexander survived the rebellion, and celebrated his victory by crucifying 800 of his opponents. The resulting calm enabled him to annex some more territory in Transjordan, so as to bring the Hasmonean kingdom to the largest extent it, or any Israelite kingdom, ever attained. The Seleucid dynasty had by now virtually vanished, giving way (88 BCE) to the Armenian king Tigranes.

Salome Alexandra (Shelomzion) and her sons

Alexander's widow, Salome, tried to achieve internal tranquillity by appeasing the Pharisees and appointing her son Hyrcanus (II), one of their supporters, as high priest. His brother Aristobulus (also II) did not approve. The struggle between them was still unresolved at their mother's death, and although Aristobulus subsequently emerged victorious as king and high priest, the cause of Hyrcanus was taken up by Antipater, the governor of Idumea. Antipater arranged for Hyrcanus to be supported by the Nabatean king Aretas, who laid siege to Aristobulus in Jerusalem.

No sooner was one foreign power established in Judea than another stepped forward. The Romans had already replaced the Armenians as the rulers of Syria, and now their general Pompey intervened. His motives are fairly transparent, of course, but he had a pretext. Several sources recount letters of treaty between the Hasmoneans and Rome, going back to Judas Maccabee. Such treaties perhaps constituted, for the Judeans, a plausible, if distant, threat to the Syrians, who had twice come off worse in a confrontation with Rome; to the Romans they had provided, at any rate, a "legitimate interest" in the region and a pretext for future intervention, which now offered itself. Pompey adjudicated in favour of Aristobulus; but a few years later he was faced with three delegations from Judea, one from each of the rival Hasmonean brothers plus a third group, possibly Pharisees, asking for the Hasmonean monarchy to be abolished. When Aristobulus pre-empted Pompey's decision and installed himself in Jerusalem, the Roman general lost patience, besieged and captured the city, and even entered the holy of holies. He also took away all the Hasmonean territory in Palestine except Judea, Idumea, Galilee, and Peraea, and appointed Hyrcanus as a vassal ruler with the title of "ethnarch" ("chief of the people"), a powerful title but not as fine as "king". Aristobulus and three of his children were taken hostage to Rome. Judea's independence had effectively come to an end after less than a century.

OPPOSITE, ABOVE The fortress-palace at Masada, built by Herod and used by Jewish terrorists during the war against Rome (66–74 CE), contains what has been identified as one of the earliest-known synagogues in Palestine.

OPPOSITE, BELOW The port of Caesarea Maritima was built by Herod between 22–10 BCE, and became the official residence of both Herodian kings and Roman procurators. Among the remains from that period to be seen there are an amphitheatre, a hippodrome, and this magnificent high-level aqueduct. Like many others built under Herod, its carefully controlled gradient enabled water to be conveyed over remarkably long distances.

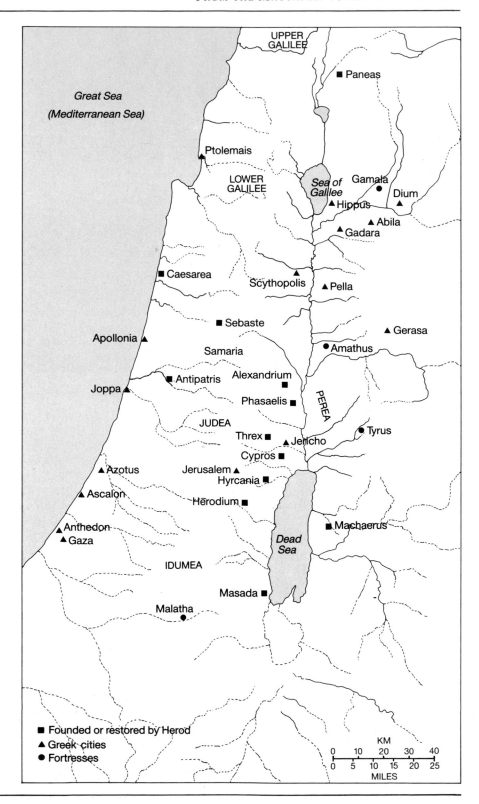

MAP 14 The conquests of
Herod the Great.

HEROD THE GREAT

The rise of Herod was prepared by his father Antipater and secured by his own powerful combination of charm, astuteness, and ruthlessness. It was also promoted by the behaviour of his rivals. The Hasmoneans did not acknowledge that Rome was there to stay whereas they were not; Herod did, and acted consistently on both points. Aristobulus's son Alexander escaped custody and went back to Judea to campaign. He was defeated by the Romans, aided by a Jewish army — led by Antipater, still investing in the future (including making friends with Mark Antony who was among the Roman commanders). Then Aristobulus attempted the same escapade as his son, with similar lack of success. The challenge to Rome presented by Parthians — now in control in Transjordan and threatening Syria and Palestine — made the tranquillity of Judea of some importance to Rome, which was now treating Judea as a Roman possession. (The Roman general Crassus plundered the Temple to pay his troops.) However, what might have been a dismal prospect for Judea was redeemed by the ever-opportunistic Antipater, who seized a chance to help Caesar when the latter was in Egypt pursuing Pompey. The grateful Caesar bestowed on the Jews, inside and outside Judea, a number of exemptions from obligations to Rome, and in Judea itself appointed the Jewish Idumean as procurator of Judea. Antipater promptly appointed his son Phasael governor of Jerusalem and his son Herod governor of Galilee. The whole family made itself disliked by the Judeans by its extreme complicity in any Roman measures, however unpopular. Not surprisingly, Antipater was assassinated — poisoned by a popular leader named Malichus. But Phasael and Herod remained in firm control, with the support of the new Roman ruler of Syria, Mark Antony, repaying one of Antipater's previous investments.

The Herodian Family Tree

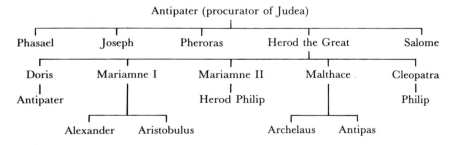

Even so, the Hasmonean line, and its hopes were not extinguished. One survivor was Hyrcanus II, high priest, though powerless. Antigonus, the remaining son of Aristobulus II, still awaited an opportunity to reassert his claims — an opportunity that presented itself when Antony's dalliance with Cleopatra invited the Parthians to invade Palestine. They installed Antigonus as high priest and king, giving him the Jewish name

On this model of Herodian Jerusalem can be seen in the foreground the three towers named (left to right) Phasael, Hippicus and Mariamne. Built by Herod the Great (37–4 BCE) and named respectively after his brother, a friend, and his wife, they formed part of his palace on the western hill of Jerusalem (near the present Jaffa gate).

of Mattathias. Hyrcanus and Phasael were captured: Hyrcanus's ears were cut off, invalidating him for the priesthood (see chapter 11, p. 243), while Phasael committed suicide. Herod fled, eventually to Rome, when he somehow won Roman appointment as king of Judea. With Roman military support (the Parthians having been driven back), Herod eventually forced his way to Jerusalem and had Antigonus beheaded. With the last Hasmonean pretender dead, and Hyrcanus out of the picture, Herod could now play the true successor by marrying the Hasmonean princess Mariamne.

In the year 37 BCE Herod thus became king of Judea — and also of Idumea, Perea, Galilee, and Jaffa. His subjects included both Jews and non-Jews and thus to some extent, irreconcilable interests, given the history of the previous 150 years. As an Idumean he was disliked by Judeans; as the usurper of the Hasmoneans he was resented by the aristocracy. During his reign he succeeded in creating his own ''aristocracy'' from those loyal to Rome and appointed by himself. But he apparently favoured those traditional religious groups who did not oppose him, such as Pharisees and Essenes. His own loyalty to Judaism was probably genuine; at all events, he did nothing that indicated the contrary. Even in his private residences there was nothing to offend Jewish religious scruples. But perhaps the nost widespread attitude towards Herod is represented in the *Psalms of Solomon*, a collection of poems written during his reign. One of these poems (number 17) calls for a king of David's line who will reprove the Gentiles and reign justly. No Idumeans, no Hellenizers . . . but no priests, either!

Apart from pleasing such a mixture of subjects, Herod also had to obey Rome, to whom he was entirely answerable. His kingdom was part of Rome's bulwark against Parthia. At first, ''Rome'' meant Antony, an old friend. Antony's defeat by Octavian in 31 BCE threatened to topple Herod. To secure his position, Herod had to meet Octavian, and before he left Jerusalem he took the precaution of having the last Hasmonean figurehead, the earless Hyrcanus, executed on some probably false charge, and of placing his own Hasmonean wife and mother-in-law under guard. Only a few years later he had both women killed; later still, the remaining members of the Hasonean family. Perhaps Herod was genuinely suspicious, or perhaps he was being callously pragmatic. We shall not know, possibly Herod did not know — at any rate, he mourned the death of Mariamne for the rest of his life. But Herod went on to dispose of more members of his family, prompting the comment from Octavian that he would sooner be Herod's pig than his son. (Remember that Jews did not eat pork.) Herod's kingdom was divided into regions ruled by the trusted surviving members of his family.

Despite Herod's homicidal tendencies, Octavian decided that he was nevertheless the best option for Rome, and not long afterwards gave him large tracts of territory in Palestine and Transjordan. During his reign the inhabitants of his kingdom, and indeed many non-subjects, enjoyed his generosity. Everywhere he built: he was arguably the greatest architectural patron in the entire Greco-Roman period, in terms of both quantity and quality. He built temples, baths, aqueducts, and other public works throughout the Hellenistic world. The motive behind this was probably personal esteem, though it is arguable that Herod was attempting to project a favourable attitude towards Judea and its religion among its Hellenistic neighbours. No doubt Jewish communities in cities blessed by Herod's generosity attracted a good deal of esteem also, whether or not they wished it — though they probably did. At home, he built for himself several well fortified, lavishly provided, and near-inaccessible residences, such as Herodion and Masada; he rebuilt the tower of the port of Strato and renamed the city Caesarea. In Jerusalem

View across the citadel of Jerusalem today, looking southwest.

he built two fortified palaces, the Antonia fortress, on the northwest corner of the Temple mound, and another on the western hill of the city, dominated by three towers named after his wife Mariamne, his brother Phasael, and his friend Hippicus. But his most famous building was, of course, the new Temple, which was begun in 20 BCE and whose finishing touches were completed only a few years before it was destroyed in 70 CE. Its precincts were twice the area of the previous Temple, being situated on an artificial platform. (The present "western wall", formerly the "wailing wall", is part of that platform.) The visitor to modern Jerusalem can easily identify Herodian masonry by its smooth-hewn, regularly-shaped, and well fitting stones. Herod built a lot; he also built well, and beautifully.

Herod also spent on other projects. Outside Palestine he subsidized games and festivals. And everywhere he provided water; his palaces were supplied by aqueducts, as were Caesarea and Jerusalem (impressive remains are still visible at both). Not only cities, but also the countryside benefitted from improved water supplies; thanks to improved irrigation, the kingdom became much more productive agriculturally. And when famine struck at home, Herod supplied grain from his own funds.

But how was this massive expenditure funded? Some of the funds were personal: income from estates and revenue from commercial concessions; but much of it came from taxes. The overall prosperity of the land certainly increased through better agriculture (helped by irrigation) and increased trade, thanks to peace secured by Octavian's treaty with Parthia in 20 BCE. But prosperity did not necessarily guarantee popularity.

Herod is widely depicted as despotic, cruel, and even insane ruler. But an equally good case can be made for his sensitivity to his Jewish subjects and their religion, his concern for Jews outside Palestine, and his determination to preserve as much independence as possible within the protection of Rome. Because Herod's private life was more interesting to ancient writers — as it is to many modern ones — and because of the unsubstantiated and improbable story in Matthew 2 that he slaughtered male children, he has tended to be judged not as a ruler but as a human, on personality rather than policy. As a human he was arguably not much worse than the Hasmoneans. His realm was unstable; he was unpopular, walking a tightrope, In his later years a painful disease may have deranged him. He was also ostentatious. But if one considers what was achieved and what might have otherwise occurred, he does not deserve to be a byword for tyranny. To assess his rule fairly, one needs only to contrast the state of affairs before and after his reign. The chaos in which the Hasmonean dynasty ended was due to the Roman presence but equally to internal, even fratricidal, rivalry. Herod appeased Rome and brutally suppressed even the possibility of rivalry. After his death the enormous tensions were released, and in 74 CE the final conflict between Jewish fanaticism and Roman intransigence was to be played out in one of Herod's own fortress-palaces, Masada.

PART III

LITERATURE AND LIFE

Gilgamesh was king of Erech, a city some 50 miles (80 kilometres) north of Ur, around 2600 BCE. Within a hundred years of his death he had been deified; he also became the hero *par-excellence* in the ancient world, figuring in many legends of adventure, bravery and the quest for immortality.

CHAPTER 8

CREATION AND ORIGIN STORIES

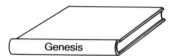

Genesis

No section of the Old Testament has been more fiercely argued about than Genesis 1–11. Because the Bible was held to be inspired by God, Jews and Christians believed for many centuries that the content of Genesis 1–11 was accurate science, history, and geography. This did not, however, prevent thinkers from discussing some of the difficulties raised by the narratives. For example, the creation of light before the creation of the sun (Genesis 1: 3, 16) worried interpreters from at least the fifth to the nineteenth century. The fact that the moon is not a light-emitting but a light-reflecting body was accepted by Calvin in the sixteenth century. Calvin also acknowledged that — against Genesis 1: 16, where the moon is identified as one of the ''two great lights'' — there are in fact planets much larger than the moon. His solution was that Genesis 1 described the world as it would have been seen with the naked eye by Moses and his contemporaries, not as it was seen through the telescopes of his own time. Despite such concessions however, Genesis 1–11 continued to be regarded as the prime authority regarding the origins of the world and mankind until the end of the eighteenth century.

In the 1820s, Old Testament interpreters were challenged by the findings of geologists, who argued that the world was thousands (*sic*) of years older than was implied by the Old Testament dates. (According to Archbishop Ussher's very influential interpretation of these dates, the world had been created in 4004 BCE.) The response of orthodox interpreters to the geologists was that the Flood had destroyed and distorted the original layers of the earth. The geologists were therefore being misled by their findings. The next challenge came from the publication of Darwin's *Origin of Species* in 1859. This was a challenge to Genesis 2–3, for if it was true that mankind had gradually evolved from elementary life forms, what was one to make of the biblical story that a once perfect human couple had ''fallen''?

The most interesting challenge to the interpretation of Genesis 1–11, however — and the one that will concern us here — came towards the end of the nineteenth century, with the discovery of ancient Babylonian and Assyrian texts, that contained material similar to that in Genesis

1–11. On 3 December 1872 a young scholar on the staff of the British Museum, George Smith, gave a lecture entitled "The Chaldean Account of the Deluge". It dealt with what is now known to be part of Tablet XI of the *Epic of Gilgamesh*. In 1875 Smith announced, in a letter to a London newspaper, the discovery of a Babylonian account of creation, part of the text now known as *Enuma Elish*. These discoveries aroused a great deal of interest, and within a few years Old Testament scholars began to argue that the material in Genesis was in fact dependent upon Babylonian material.

An important point was reached with the publication in 1895 of H. Gunkel's *Creation and Chaos at the Beginning and End of Time*. Gunkel argued that the Genesis creation story was dependent upon the Babylonian text *Enuma Elish*; but he also went further than this. In *Enuma Elish* the world is created by the god Marduk, after he has met and killed in battle the goddess Tiamat; he creates it from parts of her dismembered carcass. Now there is no hint in Genesis 1 that God created the world after having vanquished another god; but there are hints elsewhere in the Old Testament of a conflict between Yhwh and some kind of monster, which preceded the creation. A good example is in Psalm 89: 9–12:

> Thou dost rule the raging of the sea;
>> when its waves rise, thou stillest them.
> Thou didst crush Rahab like a carcass,
>> thou didst scatter thy enemies with thy mighty arm.
> The heavens are thine, the earth also is thine;
>> the world and all that is in it, thou hast founded them.

Other examples are Isaiah 51: 9–13 and Job 26: 12, where God is said to have defeated not only Rahab but also a "fleeing serpent". It will be noticed that, as well as, or as part of, defeating Rahab, God overcame the raging of the sea; and this is an immediate reminder that according to Genesis 1: 2 there was a watery chaos present before God began to create an ordered world. Gunkel argued that passages such as Psalm 89: 10–12 showed that a myth of God's defeat of the forces of chaos was known in ancient Israel, and that the Genesis creation story was directly or indirectly dependent on *Emuna Elish*.

For a long time after the appearance of Gunkel's book, it was commonly accepted that *Enuma Elish* was the source behind Genesis 1. When, for example, the order in which things were made was extracted from *Enuma Elish* and compared with Genesis 1, the correspondences were striking:

Enuma Elish	**Genesis 1: 1–2: 3**
Divine spirit and cosmic matter are coexistent and coeternal	Divine matter creates cosmic matter and exists independently of it
Primeval chaos: Tiamat enveloped in darkness	The earth a desolate waste with darkness covering the deep (*tehom*)

Light emanating from the gods	Light created
The creation of the firmament	The creation of the firmament
The creation of dry land	The creation of dry land
The creation of the luminaries	The creation of the luminaries
The creation of man	The creation of man
The gods rest and celebrate	God rests and sanctifies the seventh day

This table is taken from Heidel (1963 p. 129), who in fact was doubtful whether Genesis was dependent on *Enuma Elish*; and it is vital that readers should examine *Enuma Elish* for themselves in order to see to what extent it is similar to Genesis 1. With regard to the Flood, there can be no argument. The biblical account is only one of a number of flood stories, most of which are much older than Genesis.

SUMERIAN AND AKKADIAN TEXTS

The situation today with regard to Genesis 1–11 and other texts from the ancient Near East is much more diverse and complicated than it was in Gunkel's day. The object of the summary that now follows is not to try to prove or disprove the dependence of Genesis on other traditions. It is, rather, to indicate what themes are treated in the texts that have been discovered. This will give a range of possibilities in the light of which Genesis 1–11 can then be read.

First of all, a distinction must be made between the (older) Sumerian texts, and the Akkadian texts of the Semites who took over Mesopotamia from the Sumerians and who founded the later empires of Assyria and Babylon. In the Sumerian texts about creation there is no reference to a battle between gods preceding the creation. In fact, creation by division of things into classes, as we also find it in Genesis 1, seems to be indicated by the admittedly partly fragmentary evidence (Pettinato 1971, p. 31; ANET p. 43). It is only in Akkadian texts that a conflict precedes creation; but there are also Akkadian texts in which the conflict is absent (Heidel 1963, pp. 62–66).

Regarding the creation of man, there is again a difference between Sumerian and Akkadian texts. Some of the former allow that man may have grown spontaneously from the ground, rather in the way that the earth generates plants and trees in Genesis 1: 11–12 (Pettinato p. 31). At this stage, mankind was like a wild beast, eating grass and going on all fours, and it was necessary for the gods to introduce civilization in order to complete the creation of mankind. Akkadian texts, together with other Sumerian compositions, know only of the forming of mankind from clay, in some cases, mixed with the blood of a god, or, in the case of *Enuma Elish*, from the blood of a traitor god (ANET p. 68). Both Sumerian and Akkadian texts are agreed that the reason why the gods created mankind was so that the human race could perform manual labour for the gods, such as building canals or cities. However, there is apparently a difference between Sumerian and Akkadian texts about the dignity or otherwise of this work (Pettinato, pp. 25–30). Sumerian texts have a high view of the value of civilization, and therefore regard it as a privilege for mankind to be allowed by the gods to share its benefits. Akkadian texts, on the other hand, regard the work imposed by the gods as a heavy burden, and there is a rebellion of mankind that then brings about the Flood (Pettinato pp. 28–9). These differing outlooks may well reflect differing social and economic conditions under the Sumerians and their Semitic successors.

On the question of the destiny of mankind there is also a difference between Sumerian and Akkadian texts, a difference pointed up by the existence of Sumerian and Akkadian stories about Gilgamesh. In the Sumerian story *The Death of Gilgamesh* (ANET pp. 50–1), Gilgamesh is told to be content with the fact that he is to die. After all, he has enjoyed great privileges in his life and has been a mighty and victorious king. His reputation will live on after him. The Akkadian *Epic of Gilgamesh*, which is based upon some of the Sumerian stories (Tigay 1982), is far more pessimistic. The death of Gilgamesh's companion Enkidu (ANET pp. 87–8) plunges Gilgamesh into despair, and into a quest for immortality that remains unsatisfied.

Gilgamesh, king of Erech in the third millennium BCE, became the subject of many legends. On the left he is slaying the bull of heaven, and on the right, he is fighting a lion. In the middle is Enkidu, the wild man who became Gilgamesh's companion.

THE PROBLEM OF SOURCES

These, and other themes, will be picked up as Genesis 1–11 is examined in more detail. Before this is done, however, we must briefly consider two questions: the use of sources in the biblical material and the term "myth". The opening chapters of Genesis were the first parts of the Old Testament to be subjected to source criticism. This was because in Genesis 1: 1–2: 4a, the divine name *'elohim* (God) is used throughout, whereas in Genesis 2: 4b — 3: 24 the divine name is consistently *Yhwh 'elohim*, rendered in the standard English translations as "the LORD God". Already in the eighteenth century it was suggested that Moses (the presumed author according to eighteenth-century opinion) had used two different documents in compiling chapters 1–3. The search for sources was then extended further, and it was argued (still in the eighteenth century) that the Flood narrative could be attributed to two sources, one of which uses the divine name *'elohim*, and the other of which uses Yhwh (Rogerson 1984, p. 19).

However, this is not the end of the matter of sources. Genesis 1: 1–2: 4a and Genesis 2: 4b–3: 24 have both been further broken down into possible components used by their authors. It has long been recognized, for example, that Genesis 1 combines eight creative actions into six days of creation, necessitating two acts of creation on two days, the third and the sixth (Genesis 1: 9–13; 24–31). It has also been suggested that Genesis 1 combines two versions of creation, one in which God created by uttering commands and another in which he created by working like a craftsman. The stories of the creation of mankind in Genesis 2: 4b–25 and of the Fall in Genesis 3 have been held to be originally separate stories that were later joined together to produce a unified narrative.

In the following detailed comments on Genesis 1–11, sources and sources within the sources will be largely ignored. This is not because we reject the validity of source criticism; in fact, we accept its validity. At the same time it is not clear to us that the best way to understand what Genesis 1–11 is trying to convey is to divide it into sources. We are much more interested in identifying the motifs and questions contained in the final form of Genesis 1–11 and in seeing how the text wrestles with these ideas. In this connection, it is interesting to compare the Genesis material with Sumerian and Akkadian texts, as already mentioned. We know, from the history of the composition of the *Epic of Gilgamesh*, that ancient writers did indeed adapt and re-use older stories, and that once a new, lengthy composition had been established, it could still be revised and added to (Tigay 1982). This is, indeed, the justification for investigating the sources behind Genesis 1–11. But because we cannot identify the basic units used by the biblical writers, it is safer to content ourselves with comparing the motifs of themes of Genesis 1–11 with those of other ancient Near Eastern texts. In this way we acknowledge our belief that the biblical writers took over and adapted popular existing stories, while we confess our ignorance about the form and content of the actual stories that the biblical writers used.

THE MEANING OF ''MYTH''

This leads us to the problem of "myth". Genesis 1–11 is often described as myth; what does this mean? If we define a myth as a story about the gods, Genesis 1–11 is not myth. It is true that these chapters tell of the involvement of the God of Israel with the origin and earliest history of the world and mankind, but there is nothing comparable here to what we find in Sumerian, Akkadian, and Greek myths, where many gods are present, often in conflict and disagreement, and struggling for ascendancy. If, however, we mean by myth a story set in the beginning of time — a time different from that of the storyteller but one in which the conditions of the storyteller's own time were established once and for all — then Genesis 1–11 can be described as myth. There are clear indications in the text that the time of the stories is different from that of the storyteller. Take, for example, Genesis 6:4:

There were giants in the earth *in those days*.

The promise of God to mankind, in Genesis 8: 22, that he will never again destroy all that lives marks off the storyteller's time from a time when such destruction was nearly accomplished. Also, the storyteller of Genesis was quite aware that in his time the nations did *not* have a common language, and that the presumed existence of a universal tongue, before the attempt to build the tower of Babel, therefore took place in a different era. The same would be true of the claim that before the Flood people lived to be hundreds of years old.

If we accept that Genesis 1–11 is myth in the sense just defined, we must also say that we reject the popular understanding of myth as something that is not true. The stories of all the peoples of the ancient world that wrestled with questions of life, death, and origins were true for at least some of those who wrote and heard them. This was not so much an intellectual truth as a truth that enabled the world to be coped with and lived in. Faced with overwhelming manifestations of power in the natural world in storms, floods, droughts, and burning heat, and faced also with death, the inhabitants of the ancient world had to domesticate the world of nature in order somehow to feel at home in it. This was done by giving things names, by classifying them into groups, by devising strategies that might cope with floods and droughts, and by telling stories that set mankind within some sort of cosmic framework. The truth of these stories was their effectiveness in enabling those who heard and told them to cope with the world.

And so it is with Genesis 1–11. The truth of these stories is not to be measured by their agreement with modern astronomy, biology, geography, history, and linguistics. Their truth is bound up with their effectiveness in explaining for ancient Israel the origin and destiny of the world and humanity in the light of Israelite belief in God.

GENESIS 1:1–2:4a

The key to understanding creation in the Old Testament is the word "order". To say that the world is created is to say that it is ordered: divided into various sectors to each of which belong appropriate life forms. This can be seen from the following diagram:

Sector	Life forms
Heavens	luminaries (i.e. sun and moon); birds
Earth	humans
	animals
	plants and trees
Waters	fishes and sea creatures

This may look at first sight to be so obvious that it is hardly worth mentioning. However, in the light of other world-views of antiquity it is quite striking. There is no place in this scheme for the gods that we find in Sumerian and Akkadian stories. The nearest we get to the heavenly beings of those texts is the luminaries, but their role is strictly limited to that of giving light. Nor do we find any place for chaos monsters of the seas: the seas and their life forms in Genesis 1 belong entirely to this world and have no supernatural powers. Thus the rather obvious (to us) order implied in Genesis 1 is significant in what it omits. It portrays an order of things entirely subordinate to one God.

Genesis 1 not only speaks of order but exemplifies it, in the construction of its narrative. The first three days balance days four to six:

Day 1	Creation of light	**Day 4**	Creation of lights
Day 2	Creation of the firmament separates waters from waters, resulting in the heavens and the seas	**Day 5**	Creation of the sea creatures and birds
Day 3	Creation of dry land and plants and trees	**Day 6**	Creation of animals and humans

But this carefully constructed narrative has a further aim: to order time as well as life-forms and their sectors. The ordering of time into blocks of seven days, of which one is a day of rest, while so familiar to us, was unique in the ancient world, so far as we know. Even if it was not unique, it was an important way of organizing time into manageable blocks, and it was a further way of asserting God's sovereignty over the created world. By observing the Sabbath commandment, Israelites would both imitate God and remember that he was the author of time.

The climax of the creation story in Genesis 1 is the creation of male and female. The meaning of the statement that humanity is made in the image and likeness of God (Genesis 1: 26–7) has caused more discussion and disagreement than any other passage in the chapter. Whatever it means, it at least indicates that the relationship between God and humanity is one of dignity, responsibility, and intimacy. Compared with Sumerian and Akkadian texts, which agree that mankind was created to perform manual tasks for the gods, Genesis 1: 26–7 is breathtaking in the way it accords dignity to the human race. It is true that the command to multiply and to subdue the earth (1: 28ff.) is a command that will entail work; and the text implies that this work will be carried out by mankind as God's representative. But there is a great difference between the gods' making humans to serve as their lackeys and God entrusting to humanity a world that has been carefully ordered.

Another interesting point of contrast is that Akkadian texts such as *Atrahasis* (the story of the Flood) and the *Epic of Gilgamesh* contain no mention of the creation of woman (Von Soden 1985, p. 179). Genesis 1 implies that it is not males that are made in God's image and likeness, but that males and females together constitute the humanity that is made in God's image and likeness. To that extent we can say that there is a female side to God, whether or not this idea was intended by the biblical writer. It has often been pointed out that prior to the Flood, only vegetables, not meat, are allowed to humanity. This "vegetarianism" is reminiscent of the Sumerian story that mankind originally went on all fours and ate grass.

The idea of creation as order is not special either to Genesis 1 or to the Old Testament. Heidel (1963, pp. 68–9) records the following text from Ashur:

When heaven had been separated from the earth, the distant
    trusty twin,
[And] the mother of the goddesses had been brought into being;
When the earth had been brought forth [and] the earth had been
    fashioned;
When the destinies of heaven and earth had been fixed;
When trench and canal had been given [their] right courses,
[And] the banks of the Tigris and the Euphrates had been established,
[Then] Anu, Enlil, Shamash, [and] Ea, the great gods,
[And] the Anunnaki, the great gods,
Seated themselves in the exalted sanctuary
And recounted among themselves what had been created.

Although not as comprehensive as Genesis 1, this text is concerned with order, particularly with regard to channelling the great rivers and the canals that received their waters. In Job 38, an important creation passage, the sea is spoken of as being shut in by doors, of having been set limits, of having been told by God,

Thus far you can come, but no farther . . . . (Job 38: 8–11)

Genesis 1, then, has taken the idea of creation as ordering the world and setting limits to its powers and has given us a comprehensive and artistic statement of how mankind is to conceive of its place and duties in the world. One further aspect must be mentioned. In passages such as Leviticus 26 creation is linked to morality and obedience. Israel is promised that if it obeys the commandments God will give the rain at its proper times, and the earth will be fruitful and abundant. If Israel is disobedient the opposite will happen. The earth will produce no food, and the trees will be bare of fruit. It is legitimate to take this theme back to Genesis 1. If we do not, we may be left with the idea that God has entrusted an ordered world to mankind, but will not be bothered about how humanity discharges this trust. Nothing could be further from the truth. Genesis 1 bestows upon mankind a dignity that comes from God's graciousness. The world is not, or should not be thought of, as a place of interplay between overwhelming forces in whose presence mankind is merely a plaything. The world is subject to the will of a power who deals personally and graciously with mankind. This is a moral view of the world and carries moral consequences. However strange it may sound to us today that natural disasters have moral causes, this was certainly an integral part of the Old Testament understanding of creation.

GENESIS 2:4b–25

The second chapter of Genesis is often called the second or alternative account of creation. In fact, it says little about creation compared to Genesis 1. It says nothing about the creation of the sun and the moon, or the seas or sea creatures. The setting is a part of the earth rather than the whole universe, and the dominant figure is the first male. The theme of his creation out of the dust invites comparison with other ancient Near Eastern texts. In a text recorded by Heidel (1963 p. 67), man is created from a mixture of clay and blood:

> Let them slay a god,
> And let the gods . . .
> With his flesh and his blood
> Let Ninhursag mix clay.
> God and man
> . . . united (?) in the clay.

In the *Enuma Elish* man is created from the blood of a slain traitor god.

> Kingu it was who created the strife,
> And caused Tiamat to revolt and prepare for battle
> They bound him and held him before Ea;
> Punishment they inflicted upon him
>   by cutting [the arteries of] his blood.
> With his blood they created mankind.
>   (Heidel 1963, p. 47)

What is interesting about both of these passages is that they imply that man somehow shares something of the life of the gods. The blood that is necessary to sustain human life once belonged to a god. In the case of *Enuma Elish* it is tempting to conclude from the creation of man from the blood of a god executed for treachery that man has ''bad'' blood and is likely to go astray. On the other hand, there are texts in which man is created from clay alone. In the *Epic of Gilgamesh*, Enkidu is created as follows:

> [A]ruru washed her hands, pinched off clay, [and] threw [it]
>   on the steppe:
> ( ) valiant Enkidu she created, the offspring . . . of Ninurta.
>   (Heidel 1963a p. 19)

The Genesis account (2: 7) allows for no possibility that man could have originated from a divine being. He comes from the earth and is enlivened not by divine blood but by divine breath. (The Hebrew word here, *neshamah* [breath], does not mean spirit [*ruah*], as is sometimes asserted in student essays.) Life is given by God but is not a part of him.

The reason why man is created is in order to tend the earth (Genesis 2: 15). We are again reminded of the Sumerian and Akkadian texts which say that man is created in order to work for the gods, but again we find that Genesis stresses the graciousness of this arrangement. God goes out of his way to find companionship for the man. The naming of the animals recalls the theme of creation as order. If things are to be classified, they must have names. In this case, the order is imposed by the man upon the natural world, as he gives names to the animals and living things as he sees them (2: 19–20).

The creation of woman (2: 21–3) indicates, as does 1: 27, that complete humanity consists of male and female. But Genesis 2 goes further by stressing the social dimension of the male–female relationship. They are to become as one person (Hebrew: *basar*, ''flesh'') by setting up home together. That this is not to be understood in a physical sexual sense is indicated by the statement that they knew no shame in spite of being naked.

GENESIS 3

Of all the chapters of Genesis 1–11, chapter 3, which relates the events surrounding the Fall, is the most difficult to understand. First, it has played such an important role in Christian theology that it is difficult to read it as though this use had never taken place. The point is not whether Christian theology has validly used Genesis 3; it is simply what was the writer trying to convey? Second, there are no direct parallels with Genesis 3 in ancient Near Eastern literature which might shed light on it (although individual motifs occur also in other writings). Third, there is the puzzling fact that Genesis 3 is not alluded to anywhere else in the Old Testament. This may, of course, be simply an accident; or it may be that Genesis 3 serves to symbolize and dramatize ideas that *are* common in the Old Testament.

The closest parallel to Genesis 3 in other ancient Near Eastern writings is also found in the Old Testament, in the poem about the prince of Tyre in Ezekiel 28: 11–19. Here, the king of Tyre, presumably personifying the rich trading city itself, is described as having been in Eden, the garden of God, and of having been perfect until the day that he committed evil and was expelled to the earth from the mountain of God by a protecting cherub. The cause of his downfall was pride at his great beauty and riches. Although we must not overlook the differences between Ezekiel 28 and Genesis 3 — the former has no serpent, no woman, no tree of good and evil or of life — there are sufficient similarities (Eden, expulsion, guardian cherub) to suggest that both chapters are based upon some other, yet undiscovered story.

When we turn to ancient Near Eastern literature, we find a number

Depicted on this seal dated 2300 BCE is Utu, the sun god. He can be seen at the bottom of the picture, visible from the waist upwards, rising from the mountain. On his left is a goddess of vegetation and on his right is Enki, the god of water and wisdom. On the far left is a hunter, and on the far right, Isimud, Enki's minister.

of distant parallels. The Sumerian *Enki and Ninhursag* (ANET pp. 37–41) is set in the land of Dilmun, which is "pure, clean and bright" and where

> The lion kills not,
> The wolf snatches not the lamb,
> Unknown is the kid-devouring *wild dog*,
> . . . Its old woman [says] not "I am an old woman";
> Its old man [says] not "I am an old man."

This situation seems to be disturbed when Enki, the divine ruler of Dilmun, cuts down and eats eight plants created by the goddess Ninhursag. Ninhursag now curses Enki, saying that she will not look upon him until he dies. He presumably (though the text does not say this explicitly) begins to experience pains. The Sumerian gods, the Anunnaki, assemble; a fox brings Ninhursag to the assembly, and she creates eight deities from eight parts of Enki's body where he experiences pain. We are not told that Enki is now cured or that he does not die, although these things might be inferred from the text. The motifs in common with Genesis 3 are, first, the existence of a place where the animals are tame and there is no death (cp. also Isaiah 11: 6–9); second, the coming of sickness and death as a result of the cutting down and eating of plants; and, third, the birth of offspring as a result of bodily pains — albeit male, and not female.

A central role in Genesis 3 is that played by the serpent. The closest parallel found in other ancient Near Eastern literature comes from the flood story in the *Epic of Gilgamesh* (Heidel 1963a, pp. 91–2). Gilgamesh has travelled to visit Utnapishtim, the hero of the flood in this text, who gained immortality by building a ship and surviving the flood. Utnapishtim tells Gilgamesh of a plant that restores people's youth. Gilgamesh gets it by diving to the bottom of the sea. He means to keep it until he is an old man and then to eat it. Unfortunately on the return journey from visiting Utnapishtim,

Gilgamesh saw a pool with cold water;
He descended into it and bathed in the water.
A serpent perceived the fragrance of the plant;
It came up [from the water] and snatched the plant,
Sloughing [its] skin on its return.

As we can see, this text shares with Genesis 3 the theme of a serpent depriving man of immortality. Von Soden (1985 p. 181) has suggested an Egyptian source for the serpent in Genesis 3, referring to a story of an island paradise guarded by a divine serpent.

Genesis 3 itself is best understood in terms of a "before" and "after" The "after" is the world familiar to the writer. Men and women die, and the human race is continued by the painful female experience of childbirth. Serpents slither on their bellies and arouse revulsion in human beings. The earth is not wholly benign, but produces thorns and thistles as well as food. Tending the land is hard work. This "after", the world known to the writer, is the result of what was done in the "before", a world no longer available to human experience. That earlier world

The expulsion of Adam and Eve from the Garden of Eden, depicted in a monastery on Mount Athos, Greece. The Greek inscription in the centre reads "the story of Adam and Eve". Note that the human figures are clothed following their disobedience, and that Adam is carrying an agricultural tool, symbolizing his toil in cultivating the ground. On the right of the picture, Adam and Eve look back longingly to the Paradise from which they have been expelled.

is envisaged as full of wonders — epitomized by a serpent that can speak and go upright, and that arouses no revulsion. Contact between God and the man and woman was immediate. All this changed because the man and woman proved to be unworthy of the trust that was placed in their hands. Thus, in contrast to the Sumerian and Akkadian texts, mankind's hard lot in the world is the result not of a decree of lazy gods, but of the violation by humans themselves of a trust that was part of a favoured, blessed situation in which God had placed them.

But we must go a little further than this. We have already noted that passages such as Isaiah 11: 6–9 envisage a world restored by God to what we have called the "before"; and it is legitimate to ask whether such a restoration was envisaged by the writer of Genesis 3. If it was not, then man, not God, would have the final word about the destiny of the world and mankind. A comment is also necessary about the serpent. It is worthwhile noting that the idea of doing wrong does not originate with mankind but comes from another creature — even though mankind is fully responsible for actually doing what is wrong. This means that we should not read Genesis 3 to mean that wrong is simply something within human beings. In the real world it is much more complex than that. Wrongdoing is socially transmitted from generation to generation, and becomes almost demonic when a situation presents someone who is trying to do what is right only with a choice of wrongs. We do not know, of course, whether these thoughts were in the mind of the writer of Genesis 3; but they are certainly explored elsewhere in the Old Testament. The story of Moses, for example, shows the dilemmas faced by someone responsible both to God and to an unwilling and reluctant people. Jeremiah, in advocating submission to Babylon, as penance for the erring Judeans, was branded a traitor. Whatever the writer of Genesis 3 had in mind we may legitimately interpret this chapter as an embodiment of the idea that the present world is not what God intended, and that this is somehow bound up with human betrayal of a divine trust.

GENESIS 4

The motif of quarrelling brothers is found in the literature of many nations (Gaster 1969, pp. 51–5). In the Old Testament such conflicts occur between Jacob and Esau (Genesis 25: 29–34; 27: 1–41) and between Amnon and Absalom (2 Samuel 13: 22–33). Such stories may, of course, reflect the facts of life in some families; however, they also have a symbolic dimension. The quarrel between a shepherd and a farmer is contained in the Sumerian text *Dumuzi and Enkimdu* (ANET, 41–2). Here, the shepherd-god Dumuzi is rejected by the goddess Inanna. She favours the farmer-god Enkimdu and intends to marry him. Dumuzi argues his superiority in what he can produce as a shepherd, compared to that offered by a farmer, and begins a quarrel with Enkimdu, in which he appears to be victorious and to win over Inanna. We can detect behind this story the competing strategies of using land for agriculture, as against

This portrayal of the murder of Abel by his brother Cain, from Salisbury Cathedral, attempts to capture some of the details of the story in Genesis 4. Cain, the elder brother is bearded, whereas Abel looks more youthful. Also, the instrument of murder (not mentioned in the Bible) is something like a hoe, a reminder that Cain was a tiller of the ground.

using it to graze animals.

In the story of Cain and Abel it is the shepherd Abel who has the initial advantage, when God favours his offerings. The farmer, Cain, seems to have the last word when he kills Abel. However, this is not the end of the matter, because the blood of the murdered Abel cries out for justice, and God declares that because of this blood, Cain will get no return from the land if he tries to work it. There may be a hint here of the moral interpretation of the reason for agricultural failures. More striking, however, is what we might call an anti-civilization theme. Cain is the founder of the first city to be mentioned in Genesis (4: 17); and the development of civilized skills seems to bring more strife and killing in its train (4: 19–24). If this reading is correct, then Genesis views the rise of civilization more negatively than do the Sumerian texts.

GENESIS 5

The list of the long-lived men (and presumably women) who lived prior to the Flood invites comparison with the Sumerian king lists, although the men named in Genesis were not kings. The Sumerian list (ANET, pp. 265–6) gives figures for lengths of reigns compared to which the Genesis longevity figures of 900-plus years seem insignificant! The first two kings, for example; are claimed to have ruled (between them) for 64,800 years! After the flood, reigns were shorter. Twenty-three kings reigned for 24,510 years, three months and three-and-a-half days. We can assume that the Sumerian lists and the Genesis material shared the same function: to mark off present time from the time before the Flood. What is being said is that the world of the time of the writers is not the same as the world as it once was, when life expectancy was far greater.

GENESIS 6–9

The story of a universal flood is well attested in ancient Near Eastern literature. As we have seen, it is alluded to in the Sumerian king lists. There is also a Sumerian flood story, in which the hero, Ziasudra, survives by building a boat after being warned by a god of the impending flood. The flood lasts seven days and nights, after which Ziasudra leaves the ark, prostrates himself before the sun-god Utu, and is finally granted life "like that of a god" (ANET 42–4). The reason for the flood, however, is not clear from this fragmentary text.

In Akkadian texts there is a flood story preserved in various versions, whose hero is Atra-hasis. The reason for the flood, according to this story, is that humans have become numerous, and their noise (that of their work) has become more than the gods can bear. The hero is again informed, as in the Sumerian story, by one of the gods, that a flood is to occur. Atra-hasis is instructed not only to build a ship, but to take into it:

This tablet, discovered between 1845 and 1851 at Kuyunjik (ancient Nineveh) contains part of the story of the Flood. It is part of a late Assyrian version which was added to the *Epic of Gilgamesh* as part of Tablet XI.

Thy [wife], thy family, thy relations, and the raftsmen,
Beasts of the field, creatures of the field, as many as eat herbs.

(ANET p. 105)

This, then, is a rescue operation not only for mankind, but for other
living creatures also, as in the case of Genesis 6–9.

In Tablet XI of the *Epic of Gilgamesh* we find probably the closest
parallel to the biblical story (Heidel 1963a, pp. 80–88). The gods decide
to destroy mankind, although no reason is given for this at the beginning of the account. The hero, Utnapishtim, learns of this via one of
the gods, and proceeds to build a ship and to make preparations, which
are described in some detail. When the time comes to enter the ship,
he takes animals and craftsmen on board, as well as his family. The flood
turns out to be so violent that it frightens even the gods. Later they are
to say to Enlil:

Instead of sending a deluge, would that a lion had come and
    diminished mankind,
[Or] instead of thy sending a deluge, would that a wolf had
    come and diminished mankind. . . .

The gods seem to imply that whatever the offence that occasioned the
flood, the punishment was far too severe.

When the ship grounds as the flood subsides, Utnapishtim releases
a dove and then a swallow, both of which return. A raven, however,
does not return — an implication that the earth is once again fruitful.
The party leaves the ship and offers sacrifices, which, when the gods
smell them, causes them to gather ''like flies over the sacrificer''. As
a reward for saving mankind and human civilization, Utnapistim and
his wife are made to be like gods and to live in a far district.

In the Genesis Flood story there is no suggestion that the punishment
to be inflicted is too severe. The thoughts and intentions of human hearts
are, or have become, evil (Genesis 6: 5), and humans (and possibly
animals) have corrupted the earth (6: 11–22). Moreover, because Genesis
has one God, as opposed to many, the biblical account necessarily lacks
the motifs that one of the gods secretly informed a human about what
was to happen, that the gods were themselves terrified when the flood
came, and that the hero was rewarded for thwarting the original plan
of the gods to destroy mankind completely. In Genesis, God intends
that a righteous man (6: 9) and his family should enable a new start
to be made. Noah is, to be sure, rewarded, but not with immortality.
The Genesis story is concerned with God's justice and with his mercy.

After the waters have subsided, and Noah has discovered, by sending
out birds, that the land is dry, and has also offered a pleasing sacrifice
to God, there is what might be called a renewal of creation. The language
of Genesis 9: 1–7 refers to Genesis 1: 28–30, with the addition that
humans can now eat meat. This is preceded by a puzzling, perhaps
significant, statement that God will never again curse the earth; and
the reason why he will not do so is that the inclination of mankind is

evil from his youth (8: 21–2). But this was why the Flood happened in the first place! We may therefore have, after all, a hint of the motif that the effect of the flood was terrifying to the gods themselves — and that it was this, and not any softening of Yhwh's feelings towards humanity, that caused him to relent. At any rate, in Genesis God has deliberately discarded one way of punishing mankind, and seed-time and harvest, summer and winter continue, not because of, but perhaps in spite of, human nature. The natural world has been blessed. What happens to humans depends to some extent on what they do; and as if to point this up, Genesis 9 ends with the incident in which Noah gets drunk and Ham, the father of Canaan, sees his father naked. Noah's cursing of Canaan because of this is no doubt an Israelite justification for driving out the Canaanites from their land, or enslaving them within it. In the context of Genesis 6–9 it is a sign that, although the earth will never again be punished, the same is not necessarily true of mankind.

GENESIS 11: 1–9

The first nine verses of Genesis 11 (Genesis 10 was discussed in chapter 2) tell the story of the Tower of Babel. No other ancient Near Eastern text offers a parallel to this narrative, although it may be possible to link the story with the Etemenanki Temple in Babylon, an enormous ziggurat which may have stayed in an unfinished condition for some centuries (Von Soden pp. 134–47). The implication of Genesis 11: 4, that the city later to be called Babylon (verse 9) was the first great city to be built, does not correspond with history, but depends on the propaganda of the priests of Babylon. Other Mesopotamian cities, including Ur and Kish, were much older than Babylon. However, it is implied — for example in *Enuma Elish* — that Babylon was the first city to be built after the creation of the world and mankind (Tablet VI line 57, ANET p. 68). Incidentally, this passage does correspond to Genesis 11: 4 in that it relates the building of a mighty temple in Babylon:

> For one whole year they moulded bricks.
> When the second year arrived,
> They raised high the head of Esagila equalling Apsu,
> Having built a stage-tower as high as Apsu,
> They set up in it an abode for Marduk, Enlil, (and) Ea . . . .
> (ANET pp. 68–9).

This passage means that the height of the Esagila temple was equal to the depth below the ground of the primeval waters of Apsu. The Esagila was built not by men but by the Anunnaki gods.

It has been suggested by Von Soden that the separate Etemenanki Temple in Babylon, whose height when finally built by Nebuchadrezzar II (605–562 BCE) was about 280 feet (85 metres), was begun by Nebuchadrezzar I (1123–1101), and not completed. According to this view, stories about an uncompleted massive ziggurat in Babylon could

OPPOSITE Jericho of the Roman period lies a mile (1½ kilometres) to the south of the site of Old Testament Jericho (Tell es-Sultan), unoccupied since the time of Nebuchadrezzar. (Modern Jericho lies further east.) A Hasmonean winter palace was first built here, and Herod the Great built another, with extensive gardens and groves, watered by means of an aqueduct, parts of which can still be seen along the Wadi Qelt.

OVERLEAF This sixteenth-century window in St. Neot's Church, Cornwall, depicts Noah and his family and some of the animals leaving the ark, which looks more like a contemporary sailing vessel than the ark described in Genesis.

be the origin of the Genesis account of a tower in Babylon whose unfinished state suggested divine intervention — in this case to confuse the speech of mankind. Genesis 11: 9 contains a word-play on "Babylon" (Hebrew *babel*) and "confuse" (speech) (Hebrew *balal*).

As a story in itself, Genesis 11: 1–9 is about the attempt of mankind to preserve its unity and perhaps gain everlasting reputation by building a mighty tower. The meaning of verse 4 is not altogether clear:

Let us build a city, and a tower with its top in the heavens; and let us make a name for ourselves unless we are (? so that we are not) scattered on the face of all the world.

This action is seen, however, as a challenge to God. Humanity wishes to define itself in terms of its own achievements, and to this extent wants to do without God. We may also detect here the anti-civilization theme noted in chapter 4. The divine punishment in this case is the division of mankind into groups separated by the barrier of language. Mankind,

ABOVE An artist's impression of the Persian conquest of the city of Babylon. The view is drawn from the west bank of the Euphrates looking southeast. On the opposite bank can be seen the ziggurat (stepped tower) known as Etemenanki, the "foundation of heaven and earth building". Beyond it, what appears to be a representation of the Tower of Babel — inspired by the painting of Peter Bruegel the Elder — is most certainly unhistorical; it is more likely that the biblical description had a ziggurat in mind.

as a unified whole, has rejected God. From now on in Genesis the story will concern God's dealings not with mankind but with one people. These dealings will, however, have as their goal the blessing of all the nations (Genesis 12: 3).

Conclusions

Nothing has been said above about the date of composition of Genesis 1–11. This is because there is uncertainty about when these chapters were written, and because to know their date is not necessarily to be able to understand them better. Opinions about their date vary from those who believe that the J passages (2: 4b–4: 26, parts of chapters 5 and 6–10, and 11: 1–9) were written in the time of Solomon, to those who hold that the similarities between Genesis 1–11 and Babylonian stories point to the Babylonian exile as the date of composition. These questions, however, lie outside the scope of the present work.

Our aim has been to show how motifs common in ancient literature were used by the biblical writers to describe the realities of their times in terms of their belief in the God of Israel. They wanted to show that the world in which they lived was an ordered reality dependent on the power of God, who had placed mankind in a position of great trust. That there were divisions and hostilities between human beings, that some of them enslaved others, that producing food to eat was hard and precarious work, that mankind was faced with the final uncertainty of death — none of these facts counted against the belief of the writers that God had bestowed dignity and trust upon humanity. The story of Israel, to which Genesis 1–11 was the prelude, was the story of God's attempt, through Israel's cooperation, to realize something of the creation as it had once been. The fact that Israel was unwilling to cooperate only showed that it understood God's gracious purposes as little as did the humans that God had first created. He had embarked upon an enterprise which would cause him, looking at it from a human angle, disappointment, frustration, regret, anger, and pain.

CHAPTER 9

NARRATIVES

W hat is a narrative? It is a story, whether long or short, in poetry or in prose. A great deal of the Old Testament is narrative, and it would be true to say that it is through telling stories that the writers of ancient Israel generally conveyed their ideas about God and the world. In this chapter we shall examine the more important kinds of narrative to be found in the Old Testament and consider where they have their roots and how they functioned in Israelite society.

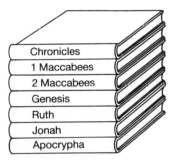

| Chronicles |
| 1 Maccabees |
| 2 Maccabees |
| Genesis |
| Ruth |
| Jonah |
| Apocrypha |

"FACTUAL" VERSUS "FICTIONAL" NARRATIVE

Scholars have long been fond of dividing biblical narratives into two kinds: those which in the words of Otto Eissfeldt, are "shaped with an imaginative or a purposeful attitude to the world and to life" and those which "adhere in a more scientific manner to what has happened, and set out to tell how things actually took place" (Eissfeldt 1966, p. 32). The former are often dubbed "poetic" (in the artistic, not the metrical sense of the word), and the latter "historical". The word "story" is generally reserved for the former.

Such a distinction is, in our opinion, a difficult and dubious one. Indeed, it is doubtful how far such a distinction was made in the ancient world. All narratives are what we can, and will, call "stories". What biblical stories do not have artistic merit, or employ the recognizable marks of the teller of tales? Think of Jonah's lucky escape from the great fish; or of the dramatic contest between Elijah and the worshippers of Baal on Mt. Carmel (1 Kings 18); of Daniel in the furnace; of the Tower of Babel; or of the deeds of Samson. Most biblical stories concern supposedly real people, and often the exploits are reasonably credible. But there is scarcely a biblical narrative in which "fact" can be neatly separated from "fiction"; sober reporting, from embellishment. For storytelling in ancient Israel was part of the culture and was mainly oral. Stories were originally *told*, not written, and they were not told in exactly the same way twice. A story is a telling, not a text.

Historiography

What were stories told *for*? First of all, to entertain; secondly, to instruct or instil certain feelings or stir the hearers to action. The idea of a story that sets out purely to give information about the past does not belong in the world of the Old Testament. This is not to say that the Old Testament contains no historiography. Much of its content — from Genesis to Kings, and Chronicles, Ezra, and Nehemiah — is historiographical: it concerns events in Israel's remote or recent past. "Historiography" is a better term for such narratives than "history"; the latter consists of the events of the past as a *continuum*, whereas the former is the selective telling of those events. But within these extended historiographical narratives we find such dramatic, epic stories as the Samson tales, the Flood, the plagues on Egypt. It is unlikely that the writers invented such stories. They must, rather, have used existing ones; but, obviously, stringing them together into an ostensibly historical narrative does not make them reliable historiography. How, then, can we make a meaningful distinction between "historiography" and "art" in the Old Testament? The quality that distinguishes historiography from other forms of narrative is not so much its veracity but its scope and subject. Whether historiographies are factually reliable depends on their sources, their proximity to the events, their audience, and many other things. Many biblical historiographies speak of matters that cannot be checked against other sources. We may or may not choose to believe them, but we can and must recognize their artistic features; only in this way can we come to understand what they are saying, how they are saying it and perhaps even why.

In short, then, we can often recognize a particular genre of narrative as historiography, but this is not the same as separating "true" from "fictional". Even ancient forms of prosaic "historical" writing such as annals, campaign reports, and dedication inscriptions, found among Israel's neighbours, are shaped by aesthetic or at least non-factual considerations, and sometimes take conscious liberties with the facts by telescoping, rearranging, omitting, and exaggerating. Nor is the presence or absence of miraculous or supernatural elements a relevant criterion. Sennacherib's siege of Jerusalem (2 Kings 19: 35ff.) is recounted as a miracle, but the siege and its end are historical facts. In the book of Esther, God is not even mentioned, but even so, the story is hardly historical. The distinction between "artistic" and "factual" is not only useless but frequently misleading as a criterion for classifying biblical narrative.

SIMPLE AND COMPLEX NARRATIVES

The book of Chronicles and the Samson cycle, to give two markedly different examples of biblical narrative, differ not in their factuality but in their length and complexity. The Samson cycle contains individual short tales, whereas the Chronicler strings episodes together into an extended and coherent narrative involving many persons over a long period. There is also an important difference in background; the Samson stories are popular, folk tales in form, and probably originated in oral storytelling. The book of Chronicles, a single narrative, was composed as a literary text by a scribe or scribes. The distinctions between simple and complex, folk and learned, oral and written, are basic, and they usually correspond to each other.

Here is a helpful analogy. Classical music includes many forms of varying complexity, from the song, or the dance at one extreme to the opera or symphony at the other. The first two are ''simple'', in the same of being (a) for a single performer or a small group, (b) generally shorter, and (c) having an atomic form (i.e. non-divisible into sub-units). They also have their roots in everyday life. The last two are complex in being (a) for larger groups of performers, requiring a conductor or director, (b) generally longer, and (c) composed of smaller units, often containing several of the ''simple'' forms — a symphony having a minuet, for example, or an opera songs. They are also the product of professional musicians working within a guild tradition and for patrons. Another important distinction is that although simple musical forms tend to appeal on a purely sensuous or emotional level, complex ones tend to have an intellectual dimension as well.

In the case of narratives we find similar distinctions. A complex narrative may appeal by virtue of its story line, but it will also usually have a serious dimension: a theme or didactic purpose. Although simple forms like the fable can also be didactic, they manage a lighter touch and aim to teach through delight rather than erudition. Finally, simple forms originate and remain alive orally — that is, in performance — whereas more complex forms are written compositions.

Complex forms, whether in music or narrative, are created by professional composers/authors. Simple forms, however, may be either folk or professional in origin; a Schubert song is a good example of a simple form used by a professional composer. Narrative can be classified in a similar way. Relatively simple stories, like those of Ruth or Jonah or Joseph, are by no means necessarily oral or popular in origin, but quite possibly literary compositions by professional authors. The patriarchal cycle (Genesis 12–36) is a chain of probably originally oral, popular tales, which may even have been linked together into a cycle at the same oral, popular level. But in their present form they show signs of having been edited by a professional.

Let us, then, imagine folk storytellers, reciting many times and with many variations, tales or cycles of tales, and also scribes, writing down more complex narratives such as histories or shorter polished pieces which imitate folk forms. One kind of story is not written, but performed, the other is written, and is intended to be read, not performed. Today, of course, all biblical stories are read, but they are often performed, too, in one form or another, from a simple Scripture reading in church to a fully staged mystery play.

Complex Narratives

Historiography

The Old Testament contains only one form of complex narrative, namely historiography. This form, which dates to the sixth century BCE in Israel, is not found among other extant contemporary Near Eastern literature; it makes its first appearance outside Israel in fifth-century BCE Greece, with Herodotus (c. 480–425). With the spread of Greek culture from this time onwards the form becomes more common throughout the ancient world. Those complex narrative forms that are found in other Near Eastern cultures include extended mythic or epic cycles, such as the Baal Epic from Ugarit or the Gilgamesh Epic. Although the individual myth may be originally a simple folk form, such literature has been preserved and developed in two ways: myths have become shaped into more aesthetic narratives, and they have been expanded and combined into cycles. It is for this latter reason that they can be called "complex". Another complex form is Ahiqar (see below), a text widely known in its day and best preserved in a fifth-century BCE papyrus. It contains a first-person narrative followed by proverbial sayings. Folk elements can be identified in this work also. But complex narratives of this type are not found in the Old Testament.

Historiography in the ancient world may either go back to origins, compiled on the basis of existing ancient records, together with whatever imagination or deduction the historian may employ; or it may recount recent events in which the writer seeks to explain the current state of affairs and in which greater emphasis will be placed on recent memory. Both types can be combined, and even the former is usually prompted by some recent event or chain of events which the "universal" history seeks to include and even explain.

Herodotus's history weaves legend, personal observation, causal connections (inherited and invented), and recent memory into an account of how Persia and Greece came into conflict. Behind this (see Van Seters 1983), lie other quasi-historiographical writings in the form of rationalized myths and genealogies. In the Greco-Roman period we also find writers from the ancient Near East writing, in Greek, national histories of their own nations. Of these historiographers we may mention Manetho (Egypt), Berossus (Babylonia), and Philo (Phoenicia). They wrote at least partly, it seems, to assert their own national identity and history against the claims of Greece and of Hellenistic culture (although they wrote in Greek!) and to demonstrate the antiquity of their respective nations, which they traced back to the very beginnings. Among the sources they used in compiling their histories are myths about the origins of the gods, the world, and society; other kinds of legend, annals; king-lists; and earlier histories, where they existed. The Jewish historian Josephus wrote similarly for his own people in his *Antiquities of the Jews*, using non-Jewish writers such as Manetho and Nicolaus of Damascus, but chiefly the Bible, where much of his work had been done for him.

QVOD VATES BELLVM CREVIT NON ESSE DVELLVM ·
EDIDIT & MVLTIS · VOBIS QVI CERNERE VVLTIS ·
EST IOSEPHVS DICTVS FERT LIBRVM CORPORE PICTVS ·

The Jewish historian Josephus carrying a copy of his book *The Jewish War*, in which he describes the course of Jewish history from the Maccabean revolt (167–163 BCE) until the fall of the Temple in 70 CE. Josephus was treasured by Christians because he mentioned John the Baptist and, in a passage of disputed authenticity, Jesus.

It is in the light of these works that we have to consider the biblical historiographies, since there is nothing comparable from earlier periods.

Old Testament Historiography

Why is historiography the only form of complex narrative in the Old Testament; and where did the form itself originate? According to Van Seters, its origins lie in the ancient Near East, in various kinds of record which deal with monarchs: king-lists, which consist of continuous, if fictive, chronologies, often going back to the beginning of the world; royal inscriptions reporting contemporary events; and, most important of all, chronicles, which combined both chronology and reportage of recent or contemporary events and which reached their zenith in the

Neo-Babylonian period. This last genre probably existed in ancient Israel — for example, in the "Chronicles of the Kings of Israel/Judah" so often mentioned in the books of Kings.

The first Israelite historiography ends with the Babylonian exile, and thus was written during or after it. Perhaps an earlier draft existed, as some scholars believe, in the reign of Josiah (late seventh century BCE). It comprises the books of Genesis-Kings in the Hebrew Bible (that is, excluding Ruth), but is now divided into the Pentateuch and the Former Prophets (see chapter 12, p. 274). These two parts may have been composed separately; but the prehistory of this long narrative is a question we shall reserve for chapter 18. The narrative begins with the origins of the world, explains how a rift between God and mankind developed, and — once the possibility of ending creation has been disposed of — narrates the division of mankind, focusing upon one particular family. From this family derive a number of nations, all living in, or in the vicinity of, Palestine (Ammonites, Moabites, Edomites, Ishmaelites, Israelites). By the end of Genesis the story has become a story about Israel. Exodus — Deuteronomy creates a nation, its laws, and its cult before any land is given to it. This nation then displaces the inhabitants of the land originally promised to the ancestors, and the land is gained by conquest (in Joshua) and apportioned. From Judges to 2 Kings is the history of Israel in the land, ending with the removal of political independence, of many of the people, and, effectively, of possession of the land.

This narrative is a tragic one. A tragic narrative or drama conveys one or both of two ideas. One idea is that of fate: humans are at the mercy of forces which are either indifferent or hostile to them. The other is that of flaw: humans bring themselves to ruin through some defect in their character. These two ideas are not, of course, incompatible; many tragedies portray a hero who is brought to grief by a combination of his flaw and inexorable forces. The Old Testament narrative as a whole emphasizes flaw rather than fate. Although the movement of history is directed by God, it is humanities's decisions that govern their destiny. Hence Adam and Eve choose to make their own decision and are subsequently expelled from the Garden; later, Israel chooses to disobey Yhwh and is expelled from its own "land flowing with milk and honey".

The juxtaposition of the Eden story with the history of the kingdoms of Israel and Judah gives the latter a cosmic, mythic dimension. At the same time, however, it subsumes the destiny of Israel under the destiny of all humans. The Eden story internalizes the relationship of God and humanity, since toil and childbirth, ambition and death are personal, not social experiences. The exile to Babylon is, in a sense, a reversal of the Tower of Babel story, in which the peoples were dispersed from Mesopotamia; Abraham's ancestors return to his birthplace. From these examples we can see that the biblical history is no mere recital of a chain of events, but a narrative constructed to carry many meanings. In its much larger scale, it is as artfully constructed as many of the biblical

short stories and uses the devices of the ancient popular story-teller —
with one character or event foreshadowing another, explanations of the
causes of things, and concentric structures (in which the beginning of
an episode or story is balanced and reversed by the ending, with similar
contrasts in between). Seen in the broader perspective, the biblical
historiography from Genesis to Kings stands as a monument to the
intellectual power of the Jewish scribes in the Persian period, but no
less to the story-tellers of earlier times who provided the rich materials.

The Chronicler

Like Josephus in his *Antiquities*, the Chronicler relies predominantly on
one source (Samuel–Kings). He is nevertheless deserving of the title
"historian". Of what is he writing a history? The answer depends, of
course, on the extent of the work. Did it include Ezra and Nehemiah?
Opinion and evidence are divided. Because trouble has been taken to
link the two by recapitulating 2 Chronicles 36: 22ff. at the beginning
of Ezra, it may be that someone proposed that they should be read in
sequence: this does not imply common authorship. But let us confine
our remarks in any case to Chronicles. Its first eight chapters are
genealogical. After a genealogy running from Adam to Israel (Jacob)
(1: 1–2: 2), chapters 2–8 give genealogies of Judah (chapters 2–4), then
the remaining tribes (chapter 5–8). Chapter 9 mentions the exile, then
lists those who "were *first* to dwell again in their possessions". Thus
the newly reconstituted community in the Persian period is given continuity with all that precedes. Then the narrative proper commences
with the death of Saul and runs as far as the edict of Cyrus repatriating
the Jews.

This narrative is, of course, a retelling of a story already told. To
what end? One may guess that a history of a nation-state now
irretrievable, based on a now broken covenant, was a history of a people
unrecognizable to Judah in the Persian period. In order for it not to
contradict the contemporary Jewish view of history, the existing story
required re-presentation. Accordingly, new perspectives are introduced. For example, the history of the northern kingdom is not related;
the kingdom of Judah represents "all Israel". That other kingdom, after
all, had been a "dead end", and the history of "all Israel" lay in the
Davidic monarchy of Judah. At this point, that monarchy is defunct;
but it is symbolized by the Temple; David is represented as designing
not only the Temple but its worship — and, naturally, the dispositions
attributed to David are those of the second Temple, not the first.

The Chronicler uses Samuel–Kings to serve his purpose. There is
a good deal of verbatim repetition. There is rearrangement of events
and omission and addition of episodes. These are performed sometimes
for ideological reasons, but also in order to form a coherent narrative.
All of these devices were known to ancient historiographers. One
interesting feature of the narrative, however, is its use of sermons (e.g.
1 Chronicles 28: 1–10; 2 Chronicles 15: 1–7; 16: 7–10). Since the work

of Von Rad (1966) they have been known as "levitical sermons", which reflect preaching activity in the Chronicler's time. They serve the same sort of function as speeches do in many other histories — namely, commenting on the significance of history, though they are less obtrusive and less obviously programmatic than the Deuteronomistic speeches (see chapter 10). They do, however, quote from other parts of the Old Testament, leading many scholars to suggest that an authoritative status was already accorded to some writings and that the Chronicler was consciously appealing to authoritative religious tradition. One notable example is 1 Chronicles 16: 8–36 where excerpts from three of the biblical Psalms are run together and ascribed to David.

When and by whom was Chronicles written? It is generally suspected that the author was a levite; the text gives considerable prominence to these people, who were the administrators of the Temple and its worship. The date of the composition is probably in the fourth century BCE. It therefore does not predate by very much the emergence of a genre known as "rewritten Bible" (like the Genesis Apocryphon found at Qumran, Jubilees, the first-century CE Biblical Antiquities of Pseudo-Philo), which it can in many ways be said to anticipate. The essential difference between Chronicles and this genre is difficult to specify, but perhaps it lies in the intention of the work, whether to clarify an existing text, as in "rewritten Bible", or give an account of the past, as in Chronicles. This intention, of course, can only be deduced from the manner of treatment, and it is sometimes a very fine distinction indeed.

The first and second books of Maccabees

The Apocryphal books of 1 and 2 Maccabees are interesting in their contrast. First Maccabees was probably written at the end of the second century BCE, originally in Hebrew, though it is now preserved only in Greek. It reads like a sober account of events from the edict of the Seleucid king Antiochus IV against the Jews until the reign of John Hyrcanus. But, in fact, it is cast in such a way that it presents its story as a re-run of events of biblical history, especially those found in Judges and Kings. The Jewish renegades who build the Hellenistic gymnasium are said to want to make a league with the "nations round about" (1: 12) — an allusion to the warnings of Deuteronomy about associating with the Canaanites; according to 5: 1, these "nations round about" want to destroy Israel. The story of Mattathias's assault (see chapter 7, p. 180) alludes to the act of Phinehas in Numbers 25 in slaying an apostate and thus both removing the plague from Israel and winning for himself an "eternal priesthood". The assembly at Mizpah (3: 46ff.) is modelled as a biblical event, and Judas Maccabee executes a "ban" in 5: 51, killing the inhabitants in the manner of Joshua. Two military leaders meet defeat because they are not "from those to whom the deliverance of Israel was given" (i.e. the Maccabees, who are seen as the latter-day "judges"). To reinforce that parallel, the land of Judah "has peace" after the defeat of Nicanor (7: 50), as it did after the victory of the judges. At the end of 1 Maccabees, the words, ''The rest of John's acts . . . are found recorded in the chronicles of his high priesthood . . . '', recall the formula used of the kings of Israel and Judah in the books of Kings. The aim of the book, which was certainly written in Judea, is undoubtedly to glorify the ruling Maccabean (Hasmonean) family and to justify their right to rule over Israel by dint of military prowess, given by God.

Second Maccabees, on the other hand, was probably written in Alexandra, and its style is that of the Greek ''pathetic history'', a rhetorical use of the past designed to entertain, instruct, and move the reader — as the writer explicitly announces (2: 19ff.), where he also claims to have abridged the work from an earlier account. This claim may or may not be true; it is like the claim made, for example, by Philo of Byblus to have drawn his account from a more ancient writer named Sanchuniathon. The story aims to demonstrate that the afflictions of Israel were the result of sinfulness, and that only after due atonement on behalf of the people by righteous martyrs could military victory (still with the aid of God, of course) be achieved. This plot allows the author to depict harrowing scenes of torture alongside the daring exploits of military valour and permits a much more colourful narrative than that of the first book.

Historiography was a popular form of writing among both Jews and non-Jews in the Greco-Roman period. Although, we know of several Jewish historians of this time, we unfortunately have little of their work remaining beyond fragments in other writers (see Holladay, 1983).

SIMPLE NARRATIVES

Folk forms

Folk narratives, since they generally survive in oral form, are not widely preserved in literary remains, except as episodes or elements in larger narratives. Where they do exist they may be the product of scribes imitating such forms (e.g the fable of the ''Dispute between the Date Palm and the Tamarisk'' (ANET 410)). Folk literature can be identified by the use of comparative materials from contemporary cultures where this use can be observed; and from such observation one can identify folk narratives — or at least their forms — embedded in the Old Testament. The four types of ''poetic narrative'' defined by Hermann Gunkel, and still largely recognized, are myth, saga, legend, and folk tale. Myth having been considered in chapter 8, we shall concentrate on the other three here.

Saga

The category of the ''saga'' (or, in German, *Sage*) has been introduced into Old Testament studies from two directions. On the one hand, it became an issue with the work of Gunkel, who applied it to the patriarchal stories in Genesis. *Sagen*, according to Gunkel and many since, are originally oral; deal with personal and private matters rather than public or political ones; are part traditional but part conscious invention; contain miraculous or fantastic events; and have aesthetic qualities which inspire, move, or at least gratify the listener. According to Gunkel's approach the saga is an individual story, which at a secondary stage may be brought into a cycle. Another approach derives from the work of André Jolles — the pioneer of this kind of study of the biblical stories at the beginning of this century, who studied Icelandic sagas — the essential structure of which he described as the idea of family. The subject of saga is not the state or the society but the ongoing family, and the relationships between the characters in a saga are familial. The Icelandic saga is, unlike Gunkel's *Sage*, a sequence of family tales, given in chronological order, with several minor characters, most of whom are provided with a genealogy when they appear. The style is factual and the action swift, with a minimum of background description or digression. The characters are not fully drawn, being described mainly in terms of their actions. Two or more versions of the same story may appear.

The clearest examples of this latter type of saga, or family-story, in the Old Testament are the patriarchal narratives in Genesis 12–36. They make up a cycle — possibly more than one — which is in turn made up of individual narratives. The ancestry of Israel is traced back to a family, which remains the centre of interest. All the main characters are related, and there is scarcely any concern with events or characters outside the family circle. This is one reason why attempts to relate the patriarchal stories to ancient history are doomed; the stories simply are not interested in history, only in ancestry. The narratives in their present form, nonetheless, are held together, sometimes loosely, by the theme of Yhwh's promise of land, heirs, and other blessings to his people. This theme ought probably to be regarded as a feature of the complex narrative, not the simple one of the sage (which is properly regarded as not containing it). The theme of "promise", for instance, can be seen as part of a complex historiographical narrative which has incorporated and adapted the saga.

This saga cycle, incidentally, affords an interesting perspective on the varieties of telling one story. There are three accounts of a patriarch passing off his wife as his sister, in Genesis 12, 20, and 26. It is easy for us to imagine that all three are the same story; but a careful comparison will show meaningful differences. *Are* they the same story? All three play a different role in the larger complex narrative to which they now belong. All the same, we can surely presume that behind each of them is a story of how a wily old ancestor gained wealth by deceiving the king of a lustful foreign nation and exploiting the beauty of his bride. The bowdlerized version of chapter 26 suggests a scribal revision, while chapter 12 conceals little of the hero's lack of scruple and, no doubt, reveals a (male) folk attitude to foreigners and women.

Legend

The distinction between legend and saga has never been satisfactorily expressed. Gunkel believed that legend was a degenerate offspring of saga. In English, in any case, the German *Sage* is often rendered as "legend" (Gunkel's *Legends of Genesis* being really *Sagas of Genesis*). Among the many definitions offered, however, one can see a tendency to regard legends as stories about great individuals. Jolles's classification of "legend" was "a virtue embodied in a deed", offering an example for the reader/hearer to follow. If indeed the genre "legend" is to be distinguished from "saga" and "folk tale", it must be seen as focusing on an individual hero, rather than on a family, and as emphasizing and exaggerating those virtues of the hero even to the point of creating an archetype or a paragon.

A characteristic feature of legends is that originally anonymous stories tend to become associated with known figures. In many cases we have to infer the presence of this process; but in one case we have proof. In a fragment from Qumran (4QPrNab), Nabonidus, a king of Babylon, relates how an unnamed Jewish exorcist cured him of an ulcer. Almost certainly this is a version of the story in Daniel 4. In the latter case, however, the unknown Jew has become Daniel, and the virtually unknown Nabonidus has become the famous Babylonian king Nebuchadrezzar. Another legend that may have gravitated from a less-known to a better-known figure is the slaying of Goliath by David. In 2 Samuel 21: 19 this feat is ascribed to Elhanan — a discrepancy which the Chronicler has neatly resolved: Elhanan is described in 2 Samuel, as a *beth-halahmi* (probably "Bethlehemite"), and in 1 Chronicles 20: 5 Elhanan is said to have slain "Lahmi the *brother* of Goliath . . . ". The implication is that the more famous Bethlehemite David, has been given credit for another Bethlehemite's exploit!

At the other extreme, however, we find alongside religiously appropriate prophetic legends, like that of the Shunammite widow or Naaman (2 Kings 4–5), stories about floating axe-heads (2 Kings 6: 1–5) and bears killing cheeky children (2 Kings 2. 23f.) which appear to be legends in a fairly unadulterated state, and hardly exemplary. In the Samson cycle, too, one can see how the cycle has been worked into a complex narrative about divine deliverance for Israel, but the underlying folk narratives are not far below the surface.

Folk tale

The term "folk tale" (or sometimes "fairytale") is the approximate translation of Gunkel's category *Märchen*, which embraces a number of different kinds of relatively simple, poetical folk narrative. The *Märchen* is told by and for ordinary people, not by any religious or intellectual élite. Gunkel himself was unable to define the form of the *Märchen* very precisely, and subdivided it into many types. Its essential features as he saw them, were fantasy and credulity: magical events are treated as a matter of course, people of lowly stock rise to thrones, animals talk, and so on. The *Märchen* is not meant to be taken literally; it projects a world of imagination, where different rules apply. In modern literature the "romance" carries something of Gunkel's definition — a make-believe narrative. But *Märchen* are not necessarily only about humans; they can involve nature and animals, demons, fairies, giants, and every-day objects which acquire magical characteristics.

The classifications given above, though by now almost traditional in Old Testament narrative research are not necessarily the most appropriate ones. Certainly, social anthropology does not uniformly support such distinctions. The folk tale can, as we have seen, be sub-divided into many different types, such as fables, trickster tales, tall tales, and trove tales (finding treasure). Many of these classifications can throw light on biblical narratives by pointing out typical features which recur universally in popular literature. A look at the variety of folk tales in the Old Testament, however, would be a lengthy exercise; Gunkel's survey (ET 1987) remains invaluable.

Non-folk forms

To illustrate simple non-folk forms let us consider royal inscriptions and didactic narratives. The former include commemorative inscriptions, which recount royal deeds and are inscribed on statues, cylinders, or tablets and record building activities or campaigns. A particular class of these, known from Assyria and Hatti, are annals, which record individual campaigns or series and are inscribed on a stela or a rock. These generally conform to fairly strict conventions of style, language, and motif, and serve not simply to record events but to inspire confidence or (usually) fear in the readers. Another type is the king-list, which sets out the reigns of kings with the length of the reign given and occasionally details of major works or deeds. The Sumerian king-list, perhaps the most famous, and also rather exceptional, begins, "When kingship was first lowered from heaven", and gives reigns of thousands of years for the earliest rulers, including events associated with these kings. Chronicles from Assyria and Babylonia recount political (i.e. military) events, precisely dated, of the recent past. Other forms of narrating events of the (recent) past also exist. Their interest lies chiefly in the contribution to the development of the major complex form, the historiography (see above).

The relatively modern term "novella" has come to be applied by scholars to a type of long story found in the ancient Near East and in the Old Testament. According to Gunkel, the "novella" developed from the *Sage*. These novellas are artistic fictions, but all of them are given historical settings, and they sometimes include historically identifiable characters. Many of them are set in or around a royal court, and may be classified as "court-tales". A very early example is the Egyptian story of Sinuhe, which dates from at least as early as 1800 BCE (ANET 18ff.). It relates to the travels and adventures of a courtier before, at last, he returns to Egypt. From about the eleventh century BCE, another Egyptian novella tells of a certain Wen-Amon — not a courtier but a temple administrator — who goes to Phoenicia on business. Like Sinuhe's story, its appeal seems to lie very much in its "travelogue" quality. But later court tales tell also of rivalry between courtiers, of individual courtiers who achieve their ambitions by cunning, of disgraced courtiers who eventually achieve restoration. Ahîkar, whose story was known all over the ancient Near East and in Greece, was a courtier of Sennacherib. He adopted a son, who repaid him by denouncing him to the king. After many vicissitudes, the hero is restored and chastens his son by teaching him parables and proverbs. Many of the motifs contained in this story are echoed in Esther, where the courtier Mordecai is made the victim of a plot by a fellow courtier, a plot foiled by Queen Esther. Daniel and his friends are also the victims of plots by kings or courtiers. But Daniel has two other attributes: he is able to interpret dreams, and he is cunning. His cunning is demonstrated in the stories called "Susannah" and "Bel and the Dragon" (found in the Apocrypha) in which (respectively) Daniel vindicates Susannah's reputation, rescuing her from false accusation, and then exposes the sham of idolatry practised by the priests of Bel. Both these qualities are shared by Joseph, who uses his interpretative powers to elevate himself in the Egyptian court and his cunning to get even with his brothers.

Not all biblical novellas are court tales. One exception is the story of Ruth, a Moabite girl married to a Judahite, Boaz. The book of Ruth is very hard to date, and the search for a theological message in it seems futile. It is a happy little story, and the information that this couple are the ancestors of King David hardly adds much to it. Like all Hebrew novellas from the classical period (eighth–fifth centuries) it is economical, neat, and simple but also quite sophisticated in its characterization and construction (for an excellent commentary with folkloristic analysis, see Sasson, 1979). It is less obviously didactic than the Joseph story, a novella embedded in the Pentateuchal historiography. But the story of Joseph, like Ruth, has no supernatural dimension, yet conveys the notion that events are guided by a providential God. Indeed, the same can be said of the so-called "Succession Narrative" in 2 Samuel 9–20. The ethos of these three novellas is humanistic, and their heroes and heroines behave, not as paragons but as recipients of divine favour.

The book of Jonah, which dates probably from the Persian period, is different. It, too, is superficially simple — naive, even — but more openly didactic. In it we see the first sign of the obsession with Nineveh (alternatively, Babylon) that characterizes novellas from this period and onwards. Jonah is increasingly being recognized as a satire on Deuteronomistic prophecy, containing as it does a prophet who preaches repentance with astounding success, a God who "appoints" things to happen, a hypocritical psalm, and an element of incredibility in the form of a man-eating fish. It is entertaining not for its story line but for its flashes of wit: Jonah is commissioned to "arise" and he descends — into the sea; the king of Nineveh, in an excess of penitence, orders sackcloth for the animals; a plant springs up immediately and a worm

The Prophet Jonah, a detail from the Shrine of the Three Kings, Cologne Cathedral, c.1182–90.

eats it immediately; the prophet sulks because a city has repented.

From the third or second century BCE comes the Apocryphal story of Tobit, probably written in Egypt. It tells of an exceptionally pious exile in Nineveh who becomes blind, and falls from prosperity to destitution. In Ecbatana (the Median capital) lives a woman named Sarah who has been married seven times, but lost each husband on the wedding night to a jealous demon called Asmodeus. Both Tobit and Sarah pray, and Raphael is sent to cure them. Tobit's son Tobias goes to Media, meets Raphael in disguise, and is nearly eaten by a fish. Instead, he catches the fish and keeps parts of it. Then he meets Sarah and marries her; when Asmodeus appears, Tobit repels him with the magical remains of the fish. On their return to Nineveh, Tobias applies another part of the fish to his father's eyes and so cures his blindness. This novella is presumably full of folkloristic motifs, many of whose meanings have now been lost.

The story of Judith, also from the Apocrypha, shares with Esther a heroine and a Jewish massacre of enemies, but the resemblance ends there. Like many stories from the Greco-Roman period, it centres on Mesopotamia; here, Assyria and Babylon are conflated, with Nebuchadrezzar being king of Assyria! The Jews, lately returned from exile, are faced by Holofernes, sent by Nebuchadrezzar to conquer Syria and Palestine. The core of the story tells how Judith, a widow, insinuates herself into Holofernes's camp, is invited by him to a banquet, and when they are alone cuts off the drunken general's head. Originally written in Hebrew, and probably dating from the first century BCE, it has no obvious purpose, apart from appealing, no doubt, to popular sentiment.

Other forms of narrative, omitted from consideration here, include the autobiographical (Nehemiah and Daniel 4), the Job story, the biography of Jeremiah, and the sacred historical recital, as in, for example, Psalm 136. But it is right that no exhaustive account should be attempted — any more than any precise classification. Narrative is a form that knows no boundaries either of form or imagination, of length, scope, or style. Even within the Old Testament there exists a very wide range in all these dimensions. Narrative is, in fact, the predominant mode of Old Testament literature, and the vehicle for most of its philosophy, theology, and anthropology. Even today, narrative — from the joke to the novel — remains a favourite and distinctive mode of Jewish expression.

CHAPTER 10

LEGAL TEXTS

Is the study of Old Testament legal traditions a study of Israelite law; or is it a study of Israelite ethics, or wisdom, or even religion? This may seem to be a strange question to ask. Surely, the legal traditions of the Old Testament are, in fact, laws, deriving from legal practice and recorded in order to further their observance and enforcement. Surely, this view is confirmed by the parallels that can be drawn between Old Testament law and law codes from elsewhere in the ancient Near East, such as the Babylonian Code of Hammurabi.

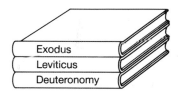

In fact, however, things are by no means as simple as this. In the first place, some experts in the study of ancient Near Eastern law have become reluctant to use the word "code" for collections of laws such as those of Hammurabi. The word "code" implies an official version of laws, made and promulgated with a view to its observance and enforcement in a given society. Although no scholar wishes to suggest that the laws in Hammurabi's collection have nothing to do with legal practice, it is certainly questioned whether they were gathered together on Hammurabi's instructions in order to be promulgated as a code. Rather, it is suggested that Hammurabi's collection is a text designed to commend the ruler to the gods as one who sought to uphold justice. Thus, the purpose of the *collection* was religious and political, rather than legal, even if that of the individual laws themselves was legal. If this is generally true of ancient Near Eastern collections of law, it may possibly be true also of Old Testament collections of law.

In the second place, the Old Testament collections bring together material that is quite disparate. Some of it is undoubtedly case law; but it is mixed up with cultic regulations and with injunctions of a categorical nature (i.e. applying to all situations and persons regardless of circumstances). For example in the so-called Book of the Covenant (Exodus 21: 1–23: 19) we find a law that distinguishes between intentional and accidental killing:

Whoever strikes a man so that he dies shall be put to death. But if he did not lie in wait for him, but God let him fall into his hand, then I will appoint for you a place to which he may flee. But if a man wilfully attacks

OPPOSITE Mount Sinai.

another to kill him treacherously, you shall take him from my altar, that he may die.

Exodus 21: 12–14

However, this is immediately followed by a categorical injunction:

Whoever strikes his father or his mother shall be put to death.

(Exodus 21: 15)

Nothing is said about the force of the blow, or about its results, and no allowance is made for the fact that a child or young adult might strike a blow in self-defence while being beaten by a parent. In the same collection we find cultic regulations such as the following:

You shall not offer the blood of my sacrifice with leavened bread, or let the fat of my feast remain until the morning. The first of the first fruits of your ground you shall bring into the house of the LORD your God.

(Exodus 23: 18–19)

To the disparate nature of the material in the Book of the Covenant we can add a third point, the fact that the actual case law in this collection deals with a very limited number of areas of human life: slavery, murder, damages to persons and property, and fornication. There is nothing about marriage, divorce, adoption, the rights of prisoners-of-war, redress against a physician for injuries received during medical treatment, or redress against the builder of a faulty house or defective boat — all of which are treated in the laws of Hammurabi. Although it would be wrong to insist that all of these matters must have been dealt with in Israelite laws in biblical times, it is reasonable to be surprised at the absence of laws about marriage, divorce, and adoption from the Book of the Covenant in view of the fact that marriage and divorce (but not adoption) are dealt with, albeit briefly, elsewhere in the Old Testament.

It is important that we approach the study of Old Testament legal traditions with a certain amount of caution. There is much that we do not know about them, and there are widely differing scholarly approaches and conclusions. This chapter will deal in turn with the development of administration of justice, the Book of the Covenant, the Holiness Code, Deuteronomy, and the Decalogue (Ten Commandments).

ADMINISTRATION OF JUSTICE

Michael Fishbane (1985, pp. 234–65) has suggested four categories of legal process: (1) the direct appeal to God, or the use of an oracle or ordeal procedure to decide a case; (2) making an ad-hoc decision in a particular case, perhaps with the help of an arbitrator; (3) laws collected, systematized, and administered by established legal authorities; and (4) law making and law drafting within a professional school of lawyers or scribes. Although these four categories suggest an historical development from the first through the fourth, it is likely that they also overlapped to some extent. The four categories will be briefly outlined here, to provide

ABOVE The stela of Hammurabi (king of Babylon in the eighteenth-seventeenth centuries BCE) containing his law code. The relief at the top (opposite) shows the enthroned sun god Shamash with rays or flames coming from his shoulders extending his rod to Hammurabi.

In this depiction of Moses telling the Ten Commandments to the Israelites in the wilderness (Exodus 19: 25 to 20: 17), Moses's successor Joshua is standing behind him. Aaron, the high priest stands immediately before Moses, at the head of the representatives of the people.

a framework against which the Old Testament legal traditions can then be discussed.

Direct appeal to God, or use of an oracle, or ordeal procedure

The direct appeal to a supernatural being or force was used in a variety of cases: to discover the law; to discover the culprit; and to determine guilt where there were no witnesses.

An example of the first situation can be found in Numbers 15: 32–36. A man is gathering sticks on the sabbath, presumably to light a fire. Does this action constitute ''work'', which is prohibited on the sabbath? As there is no way of knowing the answer to this, Moses seeks a ruling directly from Yhwh. The answer is that the man should be stoned to death. As we have the incident in Numbers, it conforms, of course, to the requirements of the narrative sequence. According to the narrative, Israel has already received the Ten Commandments, one of which forbids work on the sabbath (Exodus 20: 8–10), although nowhere is there a definition of ''work''. Moses therefore has to seek a ruling from God in this case. However, we do not have to accept the historicity of the incident in order to accept the procedure. The narrative, whatever its origins, indicates a method of deciding a case by seeking direct illumination from God. Since this concerns a cultic matter, we can guess that such rulings were delivered by priests.

The use of an oracle to discover a culprit is instanced in 1 Samuel 14: 40–42 (where the fuller Greek text is to be preferred, though it is not followed in most modern translations). Here the casting of a lot reveals that Jonathan had unwittingly broken the oath that Saul had administered to the people (1 Samuel 14: 24).

The establishment of guilt where no witnesses are present can be illustrated from Exodus 22: 7 and 10, in which a person entrusted with someone else's property, which has then been stolen, can take an oath that he is not guilty. Numbers 5: 11–31 describes an ordeal ceremony which a man can use if he suspects his wife of unfaithfulness.

Making an ad-hoc decision in a particular case

The most notable instance of this is in 1 Kings 3: 16–28, where Solomon decides the custody of a disputed baby. Fishbane (p. 239) suggests that judges such as Deborah and Samuel functioned in this manner, and to this suggestion we can add the judges listed in Judges 10: 1–5 and 12: 8–15. We have already seen above (p. 120) that these judges were people of substance and position, and we can further guess that, as local chieftains, they had the authority and skill to adjudicate cases. The same is probably true of David after he became king. One of the reasons why Absalom was able to win over the hearts of the people was that he spread the rumour (we are not told whether it was true or false) that David was neither hearing cases brought to him for arbitration (2 Samuel 15: 2–4) nor appointing a deputy to do so.

It is probable that before and during the early monarchy, a good deal of family law was decided locally, by heads of families or by locally-convened courts "in the gate" (of the city), as their meeting place is described in Ruth 4: 1–12, which gives an account of such a case. However, it would still be necessry to have to resort to higher authorities in instances where local self-help was insufficient to decide a case, and the refusal of the king (whether real or imagined) to arbitrate would have serious implications for the rule of law in the community.

Laws collected, systematized, and administered by established authorities

According to 2 Chronicles 19: 4–11, Jehoshaphat (c. 871–848 BCE) established judges in Judah in every fortified city and charged them to administer justice impartially. Deuteronomy 17: 8–13 presupposes a system of local justice, with appeal to a central court in the "place chosen by God" when local justice is unable to cope with a case.

With the establishment of recognized legal authorities in Israel and Judah, whenever that took place, laws were collected together, presumably from oral as well as from written local sources, and formed into official collections. Once this had been done, there began the practice of written interpretation of laws, a process that can be easily discerned within the Old Testament (see, most fully, Fishbane 1985). Examples of this written interpretation include Exodus 23: 11b, where the words "you shall do the same to . . ." indicate that the law of leaving a field fallow every seventh year is extended to vineyards and olive orchards, and Exodus 22: 9, in which the words "or a garment or any other case" have been added to a law dealing originally with entrusting animals to someone's care to look after them.

It is often assumed that the Book of the Covenant (Exodus 21: 1–23: 19) is a collection made after the formal establishment of legal administration, an assumption strengthened by evidence in the Hebrew that laws within this corpus have been expanded. However, the Book of the Covenant in its present form has, as we shall argue below, a religious rather than a legal function in its present context, although we do not deny that Exodus 21: 1–23: 19 may be based upon a collection of laws made during the monarchy.

Law making and drafting by professional lawyers or scribes

Within this process we may distinguish between the practice of law, where legal jurisdiction approaches cases by drawing out principles from particular laws, and what we might call theoretical reflection on the law, where laws or principles may be framed independently of actual practice. As an example of the second type of procedure, Weinfeld (1972) has argued that in its final form, Deuteronomy is the product of a wisdom school of scribes, whose aims lay more in the realm of ideology than of legal practice.

This typology of four legal processes has been freely adapted from Fishbane to provide a framework for our discussion of the main sections of legal tradition in the Old Testament.

THE BOOK OF THE COVENANT

The legal part of the Book of the Covenant begins with a law about the release of Hebrew slaves (Exodus 21: 2–11). Such slavery is restricted to six years for a male, unless he wishes to remain permanently in servitude, in which case a publicly attested ceremony is prescribed for this agreement. Female slaves have no such right of release, except that if they become the wife of a master or a member of his family, they assume some of the rights of wives. Some of these provisions can be paralleled from Babylonian cuneiform law (Paul 1970, pp. 45–61).

An important question is why the Book of the Covenant should begin with laws about slaves. It has been suggested (Phillips 1984) that since the laws are meant to apply to Israelites who are free, a law enabling slaves to regain their freedom is an appropriate opening for the collection. Another suggestion (not necessarily contradicting that of Phillips) is that in its final form, the Book of the Covenant looks back to God's freeing of his people from slavery. The enslavement of people who have been freed by God must thus be regulated at the outset of these laws.

Verses 12–17 deal with four cases: killing a man, striking one's parents, robbing a man of his freedom, and cursing one's parents (for the order see Jackson 1975, p. 144). We may assume that originally the four cases were simple categorical statements:

Whoever strikes a man mortally . . . .
Whoever strikes his father or mother . . . .
Whoever robs a man (of his freedom). . . .
Whoever curses his father or mother . . . .

As such, they may have been religious rather than legal exhortations, for although we know that murderers were proceeded against by the victim's next of kin, and that kidnapping was a capital offence in the laws of Hammurabi (Paul 1970, p. 65), we do not know whether children who cursed their parents were executed (Paul 1970, p. 66). The assumption here may be that judgement will be carried out ultimately by God, and that originally the laws dealing with the murder or forcible enslavement of a person were undetected offences, while those concerning parents were not punishable by humans. However, in their present form, precisely those two offences against a person (as opposed to the parents) have been brought into line with case law to some extent. Whether this represented actual legal practice or scribal activity for its own sake, we cannot say. However, even in their amended form, these verses have a moral and religious thrust rather than a purely legal one.

Verses 18–27 deal with injuries inflicted upon men, women, and slaves by human agency. They have been the subject of much discussion as they contain the law of talion (''an eye for an eye''), popularly and wrongly supposed to epitomize Old Testament morality, as well as the only passage in the Bible (verse 22) that can be pressed into the current debate about abortion. Verses 18–21 seem to be straightforward. A man who injures another in a fight is required to compensate for the loser's inability to work and to assist his recovery. These are important considerations in an agricultural society. A male or female slave who dies immediately after being beaten by the master can be avenged in the usual way. This is not so, however, if the slave lives for a day or two after being struck. Presumably, the master is given the benefit of the doubt that the beating was not the only cause of death.

With verses 22–4, we encounter difficulties, which may be the result of a complicated process of interpreting and addition (Jackson 1975, pp. 75–107). The case concerns injury done to a pregnant woman who intervenes in a brawl on behalf of her husband, as a result of which she gives birth prematurely. Verse 22 seems to imply that if the only harm is the (successful) premature birth, then the husband can fine the person who struck the blow. An addition at the end of the verse restricts damages to what is decided by arbitrators. Verse 23 then specifies what happens if there is further injury, without making it clear whether the injury is to the child or to the woman. In the case of such injury, the rule is ''life for life''. Jackson has argued that in the form of the law prior to the addition of verses 25–8 (''eye for an eye'', etc.), the law meant that a living child was to be substituted by the offender if the premature birth was a miscarriage. With the addition of verses 24–5, however, the remedy for the premature birth was overlooked in favour of providing compensation for the injured woman. Finally, there was added to the passage a provision awarding freedom to slaves who lost an eye or tooth when beaten by their master. Jackson's agument is based partly upon the Middle Assyrian Laws, from which it is clear (Table A line 50: ANET p. 184) that the penalty for causing a miscarriage by hitting a pregnant woman is the giving of a living child to replace the miscarried one.

Verses 28–32 deal with injury inflicted upon human beings by a goring ox. An ox that gores a man to death is stoned (to death), probably by the local community, to whom it constitutes a threat. Vicious bulls can inflict fatal injuries on farmers even today. If an animal is known to be potentially dangerous, is not restrained by its owner, and then causes fatal injuries, both the animal and the owner are to be killed (verse 29). The Hebrew words rendered ''not kept it in'' raise questions about how a vicious animal was to be restrained, and it has been suggested (see Jackson 1975, p. 123) that a very slight alteration to the Hebrew should be made, producing the meaning ''has not destroyed it'', thereby eliminating the danger. Verses 30–32 introduce the possibility of a fine instead of the death of the owner, and this is extended to include compensation if an ox kills a member of another man's family. The death of a slave is to be compensated for by a fine.

Verses 33–6 deal with injuries caused to other animals by a goring ox. We can assume that the passage began originally with verse 35, and that 33–4 were added later to cover injuries caused accidentally to animals by human activities, such as digging pits.

In 22: 1–4 (Hebrew 21: 37–22: 3) attention is switched to the theft of animals. On the face of it, 22: 1 belongs with 22: 4, since they both concern this subject, whereas 22: 2–3 may be an insertion. As 22: 1 and 22: 4 stand, two different penalties for theft seem to be envisaged, depending upon whether the thief has disposed of the stolen animal by selling or killing it (in either of which case he must pay compensation of four or five times its value) or whether he still possesses the animal (in which case compensation is to be double its value). However, it may be that 22: 4 represents a later stage in biblical law from 22: 1, when the penalty for theft became compensation of double the value of what was stolen. Verses 2–3 are usually held to distinguish between intended burglary during the night and during the day. The owner's right to self-defence is implicit in the provision that he can with impunity strike a burglar entering at night, even if the blow is fatal.

Verses 5–6 (Hebrew 4–5) presuppose the practice, well known in modern farming, of burning off a field or vineyard, prior to preparations for new planting. Where the property of another person is damaged, there must be compensation.

In verses 7–15 (Hebrew 6–14) there is a complicated passage dealing with compensation for property entrusted for safekeeping by one person to another, which is then lost or damaged. The main problem is for the person who has been entrusted with something to look after. How can he prove that he had not in some way used it for his own purposes? We notice the use of cultic oaths, lots, or oracles (verses 8 and 10) to help establish guilt or innocence.

With 22: 16–17 (Hebrew 15–16) we come to the end of the section dealing with damages. This passage concerns damage done to an unbetrothed virgin who is abducted and loses her virginity. The damage is considered to be done to her father, since he will not get the normal bride price for a daughter who is not a virgin. The man responsible must marry her and pay the normal bride price; even if he refuses the marriage, he must still pay it.

From 22: 18 to 23: 19 we have a mixture of social and cultic laws which have a different tone from the preceding section on damages. The injunctions cover witchcraft, bestiality, and idolatry (verses 18–20); support for foreigners, widows, orphans and the poor (verses 21–27); due respect to Yhwh and the ruler (verse 28 — note that the Hebrew word for ruler is *not* king); the dedication of first-born sons and animals to God; a prohibition against eating dead animals found in the open (verse 31); a call to fair dealing in matters of justice (23: 1–3); kindness to one's enemy's domestic animals (verses 4–5), and support for the rights of the poor and foreigners (verses 6–8). The Book of the Covenant ends with specific cultic rules about the sabbath, the sabbath (seventh, fallow) year, the three major festivals (note that Passover is not explicitly mentioned), and, finally, rules about sacrifice and first-fruits.

Is it possible to suggest a date and setting for the Book of the Covenant? Any answer to this question has to assume things that we do not know. For example, did the Book of the Covenant (Exodus 21: 1–23: 19) ever exist separately in substantially its present form? Did the instances of case law (e.g. Exodus 21: 18–22: 17) exist separately from the rest? If we assume the unity of Exodus 21: 1–23: 19), we can guess that it dates, at the earliest, from before the establishment of the monarchy, to, at the latest, the establishment of official local courts (possibly during the reign of Jehoshaphat: 871–848 BCE). Jackson (1972, p. 225 and *passim*) argues that those parts of the Book of the Covenant dealing with theft do not presuppose the existence of courts or the need for witnesses, but point, rather, to self-help. We notice, for example, at Exodus 21: 22, that the husband of the woman injured in a brawl can determine the size of the fine, and that this early provision is then modified by the addition of the role of arbitrators. Other clues that point to an early date for the Book are the fact that the ''ruler'' is not described as king and that in 23: 14–17, Passover is not included as one of the three major festivals. We could say, then, that the Book of the Covenant dates from the time when justice was still largely a matter of family and local self-help, with difficult cases being dealt with by special arbitrators such as Deborah and Samuel. There are still many unanswered questions, however. If the Book of the Convenant originated in this early, pre-monarchic period, what event or situation caused it to be written down? We can give plausible answers, but they may be quite wrong. One attractive suggestion, proposed by Otto is that it was necessary to record the laws of Israel as a free association of settlements for mutual defence against the injustices and abuses of power by centralized government.

Whether or not this is correct, it brings us to a conclusion. In its present setting Exodus 21: 1–23: 19 is as much religion and ethics as law. It presupposes the appointment of judges by Moses (Exodus 18), the divine revelation (Exodus 19), and the solemn acceptance of the covenant laws by the people (Exodus 24: 1–12). It sets out what it means to live as the people of Yhwh. It stresses the freedom of individual male Israelites: the loss of their liberty is a serious matter, as is the safeguarding of their persons and their property. Israel is also marked out as a people with a special relationship with Yhwh, with the duty to avoid pagan practices (Exodus 22: 18–20; 23: 18–19), to uphold justice (23: 6–8), and to support the weak (22: 21–27). The guarantor of the observance of the laws is Yhwh himself; for the categorical injunctions (e.g. 21: 15–17) indicate that he will punish those who fail to observe them.

LEVITICUS 17–26

Chapters 17–26 of Leviticus are usually called the Holiness Code because of their repeated insistence that Israel should be holy because God is holy (e.g. 19: 2). As in the case of Hammurabi — but for different reasons — the word ''code'' may be a misnomer. Several instances of repetition and overlap in these chapters (for example between 18: 2–18 and 20: 11–17, 19–21) argue against this being a formal codification of laws. However, in view of the currency of the term ''Holiness Code'', we shall use it here. In its present form the Code probably dates from the fifth century BCE but some of its material may be more ancient. For example, some writers trace the regulations about sexual offences (18: 6–18) back to the pre-monarchic period.

Probably the most valuable way to approach these chapters is in terms of their content and ideology. We notice at once a striking contrast with the Book of the Covenant. The central core of the Exodus chapters deals with damages; there is no mention of priests. In Leviticus 17–26, however, there are only six verses (24: 17–22) about damages, whereas several large sections deal with priests and the special regulations that govern their lives (e.g. 21: 1–22: 9). At several points, the Book of the Covenant and the Holiness Code overlap: they both deal with respect for parents, treatment of slaves, and observance of festivals. However, Leviticus 17–26 sets all its material into a view of the world in which the holiness of God requires a strict separation between priests and the people, and between Israel and other peoples. Within Israel itself, one of the main purposes of regulated order is to allow God's blessing to fall upon the land. The land can be made impure and thus barren by violating the divine order. Our brief discussion of Leviticus 17–26 will cover some of its most important themes.

Priestly families

Because priests stand between the ordinary people and God, a higher degree of purity is required of them and their families. All priests must, first of all, be free from physical defects (21: 16–23); their other special requirements can be shown as follows:

	high priest	**priest**
marriage	may marry only a virgin from his own tribe	may not marry a harlot or a divorced woman, but presumably may marry a widow.
corpses	may not prepare for burial (i.e. touch corpse of) anyone at all	may prepare for burial (i.e. touch corpse of) only a close relative, i.e. father, mother, son, daughter, brother, unmarried sister

	priest's daughter
sexual behaviour *eating ''holy'' food*	If she becomes a harlot, she de-consecrates her father. May eat the priestly portion of a sacrifice only if she is unmarried, or is divorced and childless and living with her father.

Sexual relations

Chapters 18 and 20 prescribe degrees of relatedness within which sexual intercourse is prohibited. We shall not discuss here whether one passage is earlier than the other, or whether the regulations deal with the quite different matters of marriage and incest. It will be assumed that, in its final form, Leviticus 18: 6–19 sets down boundaries in regard to both marriage and incest. From the standpoint of a given male (here called ''Ego''; there are no comparable female-oriented regulations) all the women are prohibited except Ego's wife and — apparently — his daughter, who is, for some reason, not mentioned.

The diagram overleaf assumes that the father of Ego will have more than one wife, and that Ego will then have half-sisters. If Ego himself were to have more than one wife, the diagram would be more complex. The nearest relative with whom marriage is allowed is a first cousin on either the father's or mother's side, and marriage with a first cousin was probably quite common in Israel, as it is today in many parts of the world. We should not draw conclusions from the fact that, in the narratives about them, Abraham, who married his half-sister (Genesis 20: 12) and Jacob, who married two sisters (Genesis 29: 16–30; cp. Leviticus 18: 18) transgressed these regulations. What we have here is

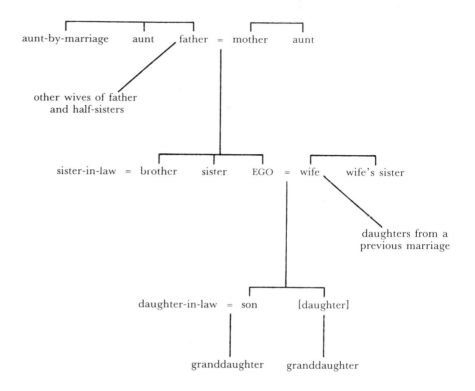

an ideal from a priestly point of view. We do not know to what extent these regulations were enforced or enforceable. The prohibitions against homosexual acts (18: 22; 20: 13) and against intercourse with an animal (18: 23, 20: 15–16) are to be seen in terms of preventing the violation of order in which men, women, and animals have specific functions which may not be confused.

Religious life

Where the Holiness Code deals with religious festivals it is, not surprisingly, far more detailed than the Book of the Covenant (cp. Exodus 23: 14–17 with Leviticus 23: 4–8, 15–22, 33–36). It includes the Passover (23: 5), and it specifies sacrifices that are to be offered at the major festivals: the New Year Festival (23: 23–5) and the Day of Atonement (23: 26–32). However, it is not so much in giving fuller details about festivals that the Holiness Code asserts its priestly interest, as in the attempt to bring secular aspects of life into the religious sphere.

Leviticus 17 is concerned with the proper disposal of blood. This is because blood has a religious function from the priestly point of view, that of purifying what has been stained by wrongdoing. Thus blood must be handled properly, even when it comes to the innocent business of killing an animal or bird hunted as food. The blood of the prey must be properly drained from its corpse, and then must be covered over with earth (17: 13). The blood of a menstruating woman makes her unclean (18: 19), requiring her to undergo purification rituals presumably because it belongs to the sphere of the sacred. A man may not have intercourse with his wife during her period.

A good example of the different outlook of the Book of the Covenant and the Holiness Code comes from the treatment of an animal corpse found in the open. Exodus 22: 31 (Hebrew 22: 30) simply says that the flesh of such an animal may not be eaten. Leviticus 17: 15–16 prescribes a ritual of cleansing for those who have eaten such flesh. This involves washing the body and the clothes, and waiting until sunset, after which the person becomes clean. This seems to be a clear example of extending to lay people the priestly regulations (22: 1–9) about becoming pure following contact with impurity, thus well illustrating the extension of religious ideas of purity into everyday life.

Social relationships

Regulations governing social matters are confined to two sections, chapters 19 and 25. The latter of these looks like a unified composition, whereas chapter 19 is more of a collection of oddments. The basis of the regulations in 19: 11–18 about fair dealing with one's neighbours is not so much social solidarity as mutual religious responsibility. This is even more sharply seen in chapter 25, where regulations about not charging interest on debts and about the freeing of slaves are integrated into the regulations for the jubilee year. The purpose of the jubilee year is to allow all debts to be cancelled, all Israelite slaves to be freed, and all sold land to revert to the traditional owners. Although we are here in the realm of religion, not law, this is a noble religious vision: one in which abuses and inequalities have been set aside so that the social order can reflect the will of a God who acts graciously towards his people and will have them do the same to each other.

The Holiness Code ends (chapter 26) with the stipulations that undergird the preceding laws. Their observance will ensure the fertility of the land; their neglect will result in the loss of it. Leviticus 26: 39–45 is clearly addressed to the situation of the exile. Israel has lost the land, and it will be restored only with the passing of a number of sabbath years equal to those that the people ignored. The restoration of the land will be achieved by virtue of God's covenant with Jacob, Isaac, and Abraham (26: 42).

DEUTERONOMY

In its present form, Deuteronomy dates from the exile. Chapter 30 presupposes that the Israelites are already in exile, but promises their restoration to the land if they return to God ''with all their heart and all their soul'' (Deuteronomy 30: 2). There is an apt parallel between the Israelites about to enter the land of Canaan for the first time (which is the literary setting of the book) and the Israelites about to return to the land where they once dwelt. In both cases, Deuteronomy sets out what God requires of his people.

It is clear, however, that Deuteronomy has had a long and complex literary history. Its core may go back to the time before the monarchy, and it may well have been preserved for centuries in the northern kingdom until its guardians came south to Judah after the fall of Samaria (c. 722 BCE). An important stage in its composition was its reworking, probably early in the reign of Josiah (640–609 BCE), after which it became the basis for Josiah's reforms in 622 (2 Kings 22: 8ff.). Many interesting suggestions about its purpose in the reign of Josiah have been made. According to Weinfeld (1972, p. 139), it may be the work of the scribal family of Shaphan, whose members supported Jeremiah. Weinfeld thus sees Deuteronomy as a product of a secular ''wisdom'' school of scribes. Frankena (1965) suggests that Deuteronomy took the form of a treaty between God and the people of Judah. Before the reign of Josiah, Judah had been a vassal of Assyria, and probably subject to a vassal treaty. With independence from Assyria, Judah now reaffirmed its allegiance to God by means of Deuteronomy, which uses the treaty structure of prologue (chapters 5–11), obligations (chapters 12–26), and blessings and curses (chapter 28).

These matters are dealt with fully in the commentaries (see Mayes 1979). The aim of what follows will be to discuss the central part of Deuteronomy (chapters 12–26) in the light of the Book of the Covenant and the Holiness Code.

The most striking thing about these chapters is that they deal with matters that are treated nowhere else in the Old Testament legal traditions. Rules for the conduct of wars, for example, take up chapter 20; parts of chapter 13 concern an individual or a town that has decided to follow false gods; and the setting up of courts and judges is dealt with in chapters 16 and 17. Chapter 24 contains the only explicit regulation in the Old Testament about divorce, although divorce is actually only incidental to the main point that is being made: namely, that a man may not receive back his divorced wife if she has remarried and redivorced. And this brief selection of what is peculiar to Deuteronomy leaves out what is best known about the book — the insistence that sacrifice may be offered to God only at a single and central sanctuary designated by him.

The main ideology that unites the regulations is the need for unity. There is to be one sanctuary, and individuals or groups who seek other gods must be punished severely. Similarly, false prophets who support other gods are to be eliminated. The decisions of judges are to be accepted unconditionally. Although exemptions from military service are envisaged, the rules about warfare imply the duty of Israelites to serve in the army. However, along with the stress on the unity of the people and their absolute loyalty to God, Deuteronomy contains some of the most humane regulations anywhere in the Old Testament and, as we shall

see, is remarkable for its positive attitude to women. If we bring these
twin themes of unity and humanitarianism together, we get the essence
of Deuteronomy. The former guarantees the latter. Only a people fully
united under the God of Israel can be obedient to the calls for fair-dealing
and compassion that characterize the book. Even the king himself is part
of this unity, and is subject to its regulations. These will now be
considered in more detail.

Religious practice

Weinfeld (1972) has made an interesting attempt to demonstrate the
"secular" nature of Deuteronomy compared with the Holiness Code
of Leviticus. Thus, there is little in Deuteronomy about priests; the section on festivals is comparatively short (16: 1–17); the animals that may
be eaten as food are no longer restricted to those that are hunted (12:
20–28); and there is no necessity for the blood of such animals to be
covered over by earth (12: 24). On the other hand, we must not overlook
the book's persistent, if not boldly stated, stress on purity. Deuteronomy
14: 3–21 distinguishes carefully between clean and unclean creatures,
and 17: 1 insists that animals that are to be sacrificed must be perfect.
At 21: 1–9 there is a description of a ritual to be carried out where there
is an unsolved murder. The elders of the town nearest to where the body
is found are to take a cow that has not yet been yoked to a cart or plough,
and are to bring it to a perpetual stream, where its neck is broken. The
elders wash their hands over the animal, asking that the effect of
unavenged blood will be set aside. The whole passage is a mixture of
the secular (the ceremony is carried out by elders, and although priests
appear in verse 5 they are not given a function) and the ritualistic. For
example, the precise details about the type of cow and the place where
it is to be killed, must be noted.

In Deuteronomy 21: 22–23 the regulation requiring the corpses of
those executed by hanging to be buried the same day is justified on the
grounds of not making the land impure, and avoidance of impurity in
the sense of the confusion of things that ought to be kept separate is
probably behind the prohibitions of men wearing women's clothes and
vice versa (22: 5), vineyards being additionally planted with non-vines
(22: 9), and wool and flax being woven together (22: 11). Deuteronomy
23: 10–15 indicates that the purity of the army camp can be violated
if a man ejects sperm during the night, while proper toilet arrangements
in the camp are grounded not in the need for hygiene, but for purity.
Finally, as mentioned earlier, the main thrust of the passage about divorce
in 24: 1–4 is that if a divorced woman has remarried, her sexual
intercourse with her second husband will have made her impure, and
thus forbidden to her first husband.

Deuteronomy's concern with purity may reflect the relatively early
date of some of its provisions; in its present form, the stress on human
purity is linked to maintaining the purity of the land. We may detect
a move towards theologizing purity: to observe it is not to observe an

irrational taboo (as would be the case in a primitive society) but to respond responsibly to a God who has given a special land to a special people, and has set down boundaries whose violation will result in the loss of the land.

Women

Of all the legal traditions in the Old Testament, those in Deuteronomy grant the greatest recognition to the rights of women. This is most clearly apparent at Deuteronomy 15: 12 and 17, where the right of release of female slaves (denied in Exodus 21: 7) is allowed. Women are also protected in 21: 10–14, regulations dealing with the treatment of female prisoners-of-war. We notice again the interest in ritual details: the prisoner undergoes a rite of passage from her own people to that of her captor. This involves shaving her hair, clipping short her nails, wearing different clothes, and mourning her previous family for a month. Only then can her captor have intercourse with her, and though he may later divorce her, he may not sell or enslave her.

In Deuteronomy 22: 13–19 safeguards are given to a newly-married woman against her husband trying to divorce her on the grounds that she was not a virgin at the time of the nuptials. As evidence of her virginity, she can deposit with her father her stained night-garments from the first night of her marriage. A man who is proved to have accused his wife falsely of not being a virgin may never subsequently divorce her. In another regulation, a man who forces an unbetrothed virgin must pay a fine to her father, must marry her, and may never subsequently divorce her (22: 28–29).

Regulations about war

In Deuteronomy 20 we are faced with material that is pure ideology. These regulations can hardly have been carried out in practice, and they exhibit clearly the themes of unity, purity, and humanitarianism that are characteristic of Deuteronomy. In 20: 1–9, the humanitarian provisions allow that the following may absent themselves from the field of battle: anyone who has just built a house but not yet dedicated it (verse 5), anyone who has newly laid out a vineyard but not tasted its first vintage (verse 6), and anyone who is betrothed but not yet married (verse 7). In addition, anyone who has the courage to say that he is afraid is excused the battle (verse 8). These concessions, astonishing to a modern reader, can be made because of the certainty of victory when Israel fights with Yhwh on its side (verses 2–4).

In verses 10–17, a distinction is made between conquered enemy cities within the land claimed by Israel and those outside it. Whereas the latter are to be treated relatively fairly, the former are to be utterly destroyed, together with their inhabitants. If we feel that this apparent heartlessness contrasts strangely with the humanitarian provisions for the betrothed, etc., we must appreciate that here, too, we are in the realm of ideology rather than actual military practice. Verse 18 makes it clear that the need to destroy entirely the non-Israelite inhabitants of the land is to prevent them from leading Israel astray to the worship of other gods. We are thus in the realm of the important themes of purity (no foreign gods) and unity (no foreign peoples). We can see, incidentally, this same ideology in those parts of Joshua that were edited by the Deuteronomic writers. For example, in Joshua 10: 40, Joshua is described as having killed all the inhabitants of the land, as God had commanded. This, too, is ideology rather than reality.

The regulations about attacking cities outside Israel return to the theme of humanitarian behaviour. The cities must be given the chance to surrender, and only if they do not will all the males be killed following the inevitable Israelite victory (verses 10–15). When cities are besieged, fruit trees may not be used to build siege works (verses 19–20).

The regulations about war probably give us the clearest clue about the date of chapters 12–26 of Deuteronomy. They can only have been put in their present form in a period of national euphoria, when a religious reform, with sincere and genuine attempts to show compassion to the weak, was coupled with the belief that this generosity would be rewarded by God in the form of military invincibility. This can only have been during the reign of Josiah (640–609 BCE), when Assyria was weak and Josiah was able to extend his power over parts of the former northern kingdom, and when he energetically carried out a reform designed to unify the people through their allegiance to a purified national religion.

Humanitarian provisions

In addition to those humanitarian measures already discussed, we can note the special tithes every third year for the benefit of levites and the poor (14: 28–29), the cancelling of debts every seven years (15: 1–2), the respecting of landmarks (19: 14), the protection of birds and the young in their nests (eggs or young may be taken, but not the mother (22: 6–7), the prohibition against ploughing with an ox and an ass yoked together, the prohibition against taking the tools of a person's livelihood as a pledge (24: 6), the payment of a day-labourer's wages on the same day (24: 14–15), the leaving in the field for the use of the poor a forgotten harvested sheaf (24: 19), and the harvesting of grapes in such a way that some will remain for the poor (24: 20–22).

To sum up: if the Holiness Code seeks to bring aspects of everyday life under the influence of priestly ideas of purity and separateness, Deuteronomy understands purity more in ethical terms, and sees its expression as a matter of right dealing and the compassionate treatment of the poor. There is, as we have pointed out, an emphasis in Deuteronomy on details of ritual insofar as they affect purity, but priestly language and ideas are entirely absent from such passages. It is as though the details about ritual are relics of older practices, still adhered to out of a superstitious fear of ignoring them. Whereas in the Holiness Code the land will be restored to Israel when the number of ignored sabbatical years has been made good (and then out of consideration for the covenant with the patriarchs), in Deuteronomy the land will be restored when Israel seeks God with all its heart and soul. There is thus a much closer causal link in Deuteronomy between obedience and blessing and disobedience and punishment. Yet Deuteronomy is realistic about human obstinacy, and constantly holds up before the Israelites the example of God himself, who showed his graciousness by freeing his people from slavery in Egypt. If, for the Holiness Code, the purpose of the Exodus was the creation of a people marked off from others by a religious purity, for Deuteronomy its purpose was to create a people marked off by ethical purity. Thus the religious element in Deuteronomy, though appearing to be dominant, is in fact subordinate. What is wrong with the worship of other gods is simply the fact that it was not they who brought Israel from slavery in Egypt; therefore they cannot command and inspire the type of society that truly reflects the nature of the God of Israel.

THE DECALOGUE (TEN COMMANDMENTS)

The discussion of the Decalogue has deliberately been left until last. Of all the texts that we have been considering it is the most difficult to date and to place. Its origins have been attributed to Moses, at one end of the time scale, and to the late monarchy, at the other end. Attempts have also been made to reconstruct its original form in terms of ten negative commandments; as we have it, two commandments are in the positive form: remember the sabbath, and honour your parents.

Extensive scholarship on the Decalogue enables us to be fairly confident about its evolution. First of all, the Decalogue consisted at an early stage, if not originally, of ten short statements (cp. Exodus 20: 3–17 with Deuteronomy 5: 7–21). The presumed original Hebrew version translates as follows:

1. You must have no other gods alongside me.
2. You must not make a *pesel*.
3. You must not misuse the name of Yhwh.
4. Remember the sabbath.
5. Honour your father and mother.
6. You must not murder.
7. You must not commit adultery.
8. You must not steal (?a person).
9. You must not give false evidence.
10. You must not covet.

In the Hebrew, statements six, seven, eight, and ten are each expressed in only two words.

These statements were later written down, at which point they began to be expanded in order to be clarified. Whether this activity was purely scribal, or whether it was done to enable offenders to be punished, we do not know. The most obvious, and interesting, expansion occurred in connection with statement two: you must not make a *pesel*. A definition of *pesel* was needed, and was given in the form:

> . . . the likeness of anything in the heaven above or in the earth beneath or in the waters under the earth . . . .

> (Exodus 20:4; Deuteronomy 5:8)

(Note that the Exodus version in its present form obscures the point by adding "or" before the statement quoted above. This, wrongly, makes the statement not a definition of *pesel* but a set of additional prohibitions.)

This definition, however, raised a further question: is art for its own sake excluded? This was answered by a further, qualifying clause:

> You must not bow down to them or worship them.

Other expansions were made to statements three, four, and ten.

By the time of the editing of Deuteronomy in the reign of Josiah, the Decalogue had evolved into more or less its present written form. Deuteronomy took this over and made the following changes:

(a) "observe the sabbath" is substituted for "remember the sabbath";
(b) a man's ox and ass are added to the list of those forbidden to work on the sabbath;
(c) either the sabbath commandment was expanded by the addition of a motive clause linking sabbath observance to Israel's deliverance from slavery in Egypt, or the motive clause found in Exodus 20: 11, linking the sabbath with the Creation, was omitted in favour of the motive clause about the freedom from slavery;
(d) the commandment about honour to parents is slightly expanded.

Exodus 20: 12	**Deuteronomy 5: 16**
Honour your father and your mother,	Honour your father and your mother, as the Lord your God commanded you,
that your days may be long	that your days may be long, and that it may go well with you, 'in the land which the
in the land which the Lord your God gives you	Lord your God gives you.

(e) the word "and" is prefixed to the last four commandments, giving the text greater literary continuity;
(f) the last commandment is rewritten so that not coveting one's neighbour's wife becomes the first item.

When we consider the content of the Decalogue in both its initial and final forms we see that it covers a number of areas. The absolute claim of Yhwh upon his people is backed up by the practical requirements that no other representatives of gods may be made or placed alongside Yhwh in the sanctuary, that the divine name will not be used for swearing or for magical purposes, and that Yhwh's lordship over time will be recognized by the observance of the sabbath. In the matter of social relationships, stress is put upon the sanctity of people and their property. Within the family group this entails honouring and supporting one's parents. Between families it upholds the sanctity of life by prohibiting premeditated murder, and in declaring against adultery and theft it protects a man's property from invasion by another. False evidence is prohibited because it undermines the entire workings of justice. The commandment against coveting, together with that against theft, shows that the Old Testament condemns those who *plan* mischief as much as those who carry it out.

What of the origin and purpose of the Decalogue? The only evidence that we have is its position in the books of Exodus and Deuteronomy. In both cases, the Decalogue occupies a key position. In Exodus 20 it is the opening statement of what God revealed to Moses on Mt. Sinai. In Deuteronomy, it is also the beginning of the "statutes and ordinances" declared by Moses. The tradition, then, gave to the Decalogue a place of prime importance in the setting out of God's requirements of his people. Although we cannot prove it, it is reasonable to assume that the original ten short statements were the possession of the group that came from Egypt, and that they set out in a simple form the nature of Yhwh's claim upon them. Perhaps it was around these words, and on their basis, that the villages that constituted Israel took as their own the faith in Yhwh brought by the group from Egypt.

If this is so, then the purpose of the Decalogue was initially religious: it expressed an exclusive claim of Yhwh and indicated how life was to be lived in the light of this claim. If the commandments were violated, then the party principally aggrieved was God, even if the offence involved wrongdoing against another Israelite. In the course of the development of the administration of justice, the injunctions of the Decalogue were incorporated into the system. We have noticed earlier in this chapter that the Old Testament also contains specifically legal injunctions regarding homicide, adultery, theft, false evidence, and apostasy. But, in spite of its amplifications, the Decalogue seems to have remained as a coherent text which served to express most definitively the exclusive demands of Yhwh upon his people.

We began by asking whether the legal traditions of the Old Testament are to do with law, ethics, wisdom, or religion. We have not really dealt with wisdom; we have hinted at it by suggesting that some material may reflect the activity of scribes rather than the actual practice of lawyers. Of the other categories we have given ample evidence. We have tried to show that it is certainly a mistake to regard the legal sections of the Old Testament simply as collections of laws. Their content is always a mixture of the legal, the ethical, and the religious, and they are certainly as much a source for knowledge of Israelite ethics and theology as they are a source for Israel's legal practice.

CHAPTER 11

SACRIFICES AND PSALMS

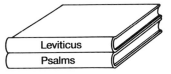

Leviticus
Psalms

This chapter will deal with Leviticus 1–16, plus other references to sacrifice, and with the book of Psalms. Sacrifices and psalms are two different ways of approaching God. The first involves offering to God something that is a gift, or a substitute for the offerer; this is usually an animal, but sometimes a bird or an offering of grain. The second is an activity in which worshippers offer themselves, using words of praise or petition, and sometimes joining in liturgical movements such as processions. We presume that sacrifices and psalms both had their setting in the Temple in Jerusalem; but this likely assumption is virtually unsupported by any evidence. Sacrifices are only occasionally mentioned in the psalms while we have no idea of what, if anything, was said when sacrifices were offered. In fact, the study of sacrifices and of the psalms presents difficult problems. First of all, there is hardly any evidence in the Old Testament outside of passages such as Leviticus 1–16 that the sacrifices as prescribed were ever offered. Secondly, whatever may have been the use of the psalms in the Temple service, the book of Psalms in its final form is intended to be a collection for private, individual meditation, and not for public use. The exploration of these two problems will be the main concern of this chapter.

SACRIFICES

Leviticus 1–16 assumes that the Israelites are in the wilderness. They obviously have no permanent place of worship. Instead, there is the Tent of Meeting, which is a portable shrine standing at the centre of the camp, with an altar of burnt offering at its entrance, an altar of incense within, and a holy of holies separated by a veil from the remainder of the tent. For this portable sanctuary there are regulations about burnt offerings (chapter 1), meal offerings (chapter 2), peace offerings (chapter 3), sin offerings — for involuntary transgression (chapter 4), and offerings for atonement for deliberate offences (chapter 5). Following rules for the consecration of priests and the offerings special to them (chapters 6–10), there follow rules about purity, including clean and unclean animals, and how one deals with 'leprosy' (chapters 11–15). Chapter 16 deals with the Day of Atonement.

Leviticus sets these regulations in the wilderness because they are represented as having been revealed by God to Moses on Mt. Sinai. However, if these regulations are as old as this, it is surprising that there is no reference to them in other parts of the Old Testament. The difficulties can be outlined as follows:

First of all, the very existence of the Tent of Meeting is problematical. The Tent is supposed to have contained the Ark of the Covenant. However, we know that the Ark was in a temple while it was at Shiloh (1 Samuel 1–3). Furthermore, when David eventually brought the Ark to Jerusalem, the king himself provided a tent for it (2 Samuel 6: 17). What happened to the Tent of Meeting? A widely held scholarly view is that the supposed instructions to Moses for making the tent and its appurtenances (Exodus 36: 8ff.) are based upon what was actually the case in the Temple at the time Exodus was written. In other words the description of the tent in Exodus 36 is a fiction.

Another problem is that the history of sacrifice, so far as we can reconstruct it from the narrative traditions of the Old Testament, seems to present a different picture from that in Leviticus 1–16. Manoah (Judges 13: 19), Samuel (1 Samuel 7: 9), Saul (1 Samuel 13: 9), David (2 Samuel 6: 17), Solomon (1 Kings 3: 4), and Elijah (1 Kings 30–38) all offered sacrifices, whereas none of them was a priest. These sacrifices were primarily burnt offerings. Of sin offerings there is no mention in these traditions. The narrative traditions give the impression that any head of a family could and did offer sacrifice, when occasion demanded it, on behalf of the household or lineage. Thus a widespread scholarly view holds that the sacrifices detailed in Leviticus 1–16 were introduced only after the exile, and that the stress in Leviticus on purity and atonement reflects the mood of the post-exilic community in Judah.

Also, there are prophetic criticisms of the abuse of sacrifices, which can be read to mean that sacrifice was never part of the original (Mosaic) religion of Israel. In Amos 5: 25 we read:

Did you bring to me sacrifices and offerings the forty years in the wilderness, O house of Israel?

Jeremiah 7: 22 is even more explicit.

For in the day that I brought them out of the land of Egypt, I did not speak to your fathers or command them concerning burnt offerings and sacrifices.

If we took these passages at their face value we could conclude that the religion of Israel was largely non-sacrificial, and that the custom of sacrifice was taken over from the Canaanites.

It is worthwhile noting that the book of Psalms also seems to have a low view of the value of sacrifice. Psalm 40: 6 reads:

Sacrifice and offering thou dost not desire;
but thou hast given me an open ear.
Burnt offering and sin offering thou hast not required.

Psalm 50: 13–14 seems to say that God prefers spiritual worship to the offering of animals:

> Do I eat the flesh of bulls,
> or drink the blood of goats?
> Offer to God a sacrifice of thanksgiving.
> and pay your vows to the Most High.

In Psalm 51: 16–17 are the well-known words:

> For thou hast no delight in sacrifice;
> were I to give a burnt offering, thou wouldst not be pleased.
> The sacrifice acceptable to God is a broken spirit;
> a broken and contrite heart, O God, thou wilt not despise.

Sentiments such as these suggest that although sacrifices and psalms both figured prominently in Temple worship, one of these forms of worship was sometimes used to express strong criticism of the other! In order to try to resolve this paradox, we must try to describe the history of sacrifice in the Old Testament.

SACRIFICE IN ANCIENT ISRAEL

Almost every people known to scholarly research engages in, or has engaged in, sacrifice. No doubt the need to sacrifice arises from the need for mankind to make the world intelligible. Where technology cannot help — for example, in situations of sickness, death, danger from enemies, or threats to the production of food because of droughts or floods — the attempt to please, to placate, or to persuade unseen powers believed to be able to help plays an important role in enabling humans to cope with everyday life. But belief in unseen powers that control the forces of nature and can influence life and death means that the world has to be divided into areas of the sacred and the ordinary. The sacred is where the unseen powers can be approached, and access may be dangerous. Thus, there often arises a professional class of those who alone can have the most immediate access to divinity, and this class determines how and with what offerings divinity may be approached. In particular, divinity may be approached only by what is perfect and pure physically; but the idea of purity can extend widely into the world of the ordinary, so that happenings or objects that are common in everyday life are perceived as potentially dangerous to ordinary people, because they belong to the realm of divinity, or because they blur the boundaries within which the life of a society is ordered.

Within the framework just described, various types of sacrifice can be made. There may be regular offerings of food and drink. It is not necessarily believed that the divinity needs them in order to survive, and they probably function primarily as a reassurance to the worshippers that because they continually remember the divinity, it will not forget them. There may also be regular offerings of what are regarded as the result of blessings from the divinity, for example, first-born sons and animals, and the first-fruits of crops. Second, there may be offerings to placate the divinity when its property has been damaged, or a prohibited boundary has been crossed. For example, eating the flesh of a forbidden animal would be the violating of such a boundary. Third, there may be sacrifices at times of individual or national crisis. As we shall see later, burnt offerings were sometimes made in ancient Israel prior to a battle. Offerings might also be made along with vows in the face of illness. Such offerings, and others, formed part of Old Testament sacrifice.

Regular and special offerings

We begin a survey of Old Testament sacrifice with regular offerings of food. Exodus 25: 30 commands:

> You shall set the bread of the Presence on the table before me always.

This practice of always having the bread of the Presence, or showbread, in the sanctuary is certainly a survival of an ancient custom of offering food to the gods. The same idea is also found in the phrase ''a pleasing odour to the Lord'' in Exodus 29: 18, where the ancient underlying custom is that of offering to the gods a pleasant smell of incense or burnt flesh. Furthermore, there is a command that there should be each day a morning and an evening sacrifice, consisting of a lamb, together with flour and oil.

> It shall be a continual burnt offering throughout your generations at the door of the tent of meeting before the Lord . . . .
>
> (Exodus 29: 42)

These are all regular offerings which are made by the priests, but they would have to get the necessary fuel (one tree to burn wholly an ox) and animals from the people.

The people themselves would be responsible for bringing offerings of what God had blessed them with: first-born sons and animals (Exodus 22: 28–9) and first-fruits of agricultural produce (Exodus 23: 19).

Offerings designed to help restore boundaries that have been violated are dealt with especially in Leviticus 4–6 and 12. To modern readers, these sacrifices seem especially irrational. For example, there is nothing irrational to us about women losing blood during their monthly periods, but for a society in which blood was held to be sacred, not least because it was used to purify sacred things (see below), its loss was regarded as a serious matter. For normal menstrual periods no actual sacrifices were required, but for prolonged menstrual periods, or for abnormal loss of blood, a sin offering and a burnt offering were required eight days after the discharge ceased (Leviticus 15: 25–30). Sin offerings will be discussed more fully shortly.

The offering of burnt sacrifices on occasions of national or personal crisis is reasonably well attested in the Old Testament. It has already been noticed that Samuel (1 Samuel 7: 9) and Saul (1 Samuel 13: 9) offered burnt sacrifices prior to taking part in battle, and that Manoah made a similar offering when confronted by an angel (Judges 13: 15–23).

The history of Old Testament sacrifice

Having briefly examined various types of sacrifice described in the Old Testament, we shall now try to discover something of their history. Earlier scholarship made the mistake of supposing that sacrifice had developed along a single line in ancient Israel, and that this could be divided into three periods. In the first period, there had been no established priesthood or rituals, and sacrifices were family or clan celebrations at which the male head of the group carried out the sacrifice and the participants shared the flesh of the animal. In the second period, Josiah's reform, and his centralization of the cult in Jerusalem, moved things decisively in favour of greater regulation. In the third period, after the exile, the religion of Israel became dominated by the sacrificial rituals of the second temple, with particular emphasis on sin and atonement.

Although this reconstruction is not without its merits, it is too rigid. When Israel existed as an association of villages c. 1230 BCE, it is quite likely that part of its religion was carried out locally without the need for priests, and that there were communal festivals, especially at harvest-time, and sacrifices offered by male heads of families. However, there were also many regional sanctuaries: Bethel, Shiloh, Shechem, Gilgal, Beer-sheba, Mizpah, Gibeon, Nob, to name only some. These were not, of course, necessarily Israelite sanctuaries, and the rituals performed in them were no doubt based upon superstitious notions of religion which were already very ancient. We can guess that at these sanctuaries food offerings were made to their gods (cp. perhaps 1 Samuel 21: 4 where David is given holy bread to eat from the sanctuary at Nob), and that they were the places to which offerings of first-born animals and first-fruits were taken. Also, since fears about uncleanness can be deeply rooted, we can assume that it was at these regional sanctuaries that offerings to restore purity were made. Such sanctuaries were also the places where disputes were decided by the swearing of oaths or the undergoing of ordeals (see below). In short, there was *not* an early period of Israelite religion in which priests and purification rituals played no part. Rather, in the early period, religion was based upon the local social group *and* on the regional sanctuaries.

The first important change came with the rise of the monarchy. We know that Saul, who was sympathetic to the prophetic groups, tried to suppress mediums and witchcraft (1 Samuel 28: 3). The beginning of the centralization of power had consequences for local religion. We also know that Saul eliminated the sanctuary at Nob because it assisted David (1 Samuel 22: 11–19). Under David's rule, a new cult was established in Jerusalem which combined existing rituals of Jebusite Jerusalem with the Israelite worship of Yhwh, centred upon the Ark of the Covenant; this was further consolidated by the building of the Temple by Solomon.

ABOVE, LEFT A model of the Second Temple as it may have been in the first century CE after its renovation and enlargement by Herod the Great. The sanctuary itself, facing east, is surrounded by the court of the priests. In the foreground is the court of the Israelites. The court of the women and the court of the Gentiles lie outside. The two pillars on either side of the entrance to the sanctuary, Jachin and Boaz, are a feature of Solomon's Temple (1 Kings 7: 15–22).

The Temple was essentially a royal shrine under the control of the king, and hardly affected the lives of ordinary Israelites; but it is almost certain that regional sanctuaries were also brought under the control of the king to some extent.

When the northern tribes rebelled under Jeroboam, it was the Israelite king himself who reorganized the sanctuaries of Bethel and Dan and appointed new priests (1 Kings 12: 28–31). Such royal patronage, however, brought doubtful benefits when some later kings of Israel became supporters of the religion of the fertility god Baal, and when some kings of Judah encouraged the pagan practices of their Assyrian overlords. How royal patronage of the local sanctuaries affected the lives of ordinary Israelites we do not know, but we cannot rule out a move towards the imposition upon these local sanctuaries of standardized rituals from the time of the monarchy onwards.

The reforms of Josiah (and possibly those of Hezekiah before him) involved closing down the regional sanctuaries and centralizing worship at Jerusalem. No doubt there were good political reasons for this. Such a move signalled the need for greater national unity; and if Josiah hoped to extend his territory to include the Bethel and Samaria hills, the pressing of the exclusive religious claims of Jerusalem would indicate the end of the division inaugurated by Jeroboam. But Josiah's reforms also implied that Jerusalem was no longer simply a royal sanctuary; it was now a national sanctuary, which the people were expected to patronize. Although the reform was short-lived, it paved the way for the situation after the exile, in which Judah became a community centred upon the Temple.

We must not suppose, however, that in this post-exilic period Judah was now a devoutly religious community dutifully carrying out the rituals prescribed in Leviticus. The evidence from Ezra and Nehemiah, and for the period before the Maccabean revolt show otherwise. It was now possible, however, for the priests to rewrite and to re-present ancient rituals in idealistic terms which assumed that the people of God was gathered around one sanctuary, as it had been gathered around the Tent of Meeting in the wilderness period.

The history of Israelite sacrifice is not, then, a movement from a ritual free-for-all to a total conformity to the rituals of Leviticus. At all periods there existed both freedom from and dependence upon the sanctuaries and their rituals. The changed circumstances of the post-exilic period, however, enabled the priestly writers to describe the rituals in such a way as to express a total world-view, in which Israel lived its life as the people of God by observing the levitical prescriptions. What this world-view was will be explored below.

What about the prophets' criticisms of sacrifice? If they are examined closely it will be seen that they are not so much criticisms of sacrifice as such, but criticisms of a form of religion in which outward behaviour (the offering of sacrifices) was not matched by a regard for truth and justice. Isaiah 1: 11–17 puts it well — verses 15–17 especially:

> When you spread forth your hands,
> I will hide my eyes from you . . .
> your hands are full of blood,
> wash yourselves; make yourselves clean . . .
> cease to do evil, learn to do good;
> seek justice, correct oppression.

We might say that, for the prophets, it was absurd to insist on offering only physically perfect animals to God if worshippers had stained themselves by acting in evil and corrupt ways. Not to condemn such worshippers would only strengthen their false sense of security. No prophet knew enough about the past to be able to mean that God had not instituted sacrifices in the wilderness period; and no movement in Israel, prophetic or otherwise, succeeded in abolishing sacrifices. They came to an end only because of the intervention of outside forces, when the Babylonians destroyed the first temple in 587 BCE and when the Romans destroyed the second one in 70 CE.

The World-view of Leviticus 1-16

So far we have tried to sketch the history of Israelite sacrifice in order to reject the idea that rituals such as those described in Leviticus were introduced only after the exile. In fact, many of these rituals are probably very ancient, although we do not know their origin. In their present form, however, they date from the post-exilic period, and are best read as articulating a distinct world-view that is to be dated in post-exilic times. We shall deal with three particular areas: defilement and purification

OPPOSITE This magnificently preserved gate to the city of Dan, dated around 1800 BCE, is an indication of the high level of culture in Canaan in the Middle Bronze Age. Genesis 14: 14 records that Abraham led an expedition to Dan and beyond in pursuit of the kidnappers of his nephew Lot. Although both the interpretation of Genesis 14 and the dating of Abraham around 1800 BCE are problematical, as well as the fact that, according to Judges 18: 29, the city was not called Dan until the twelfth century BCE, this discovery enables the story of Abraham to be read with greater sensitivity to the sort of conditions implied in narratives about him.

of the sanctuary; rites of passage; and atonement for the whole people.

Defilement and purification of the sanctuary

Leviticus 4 deals with the steps to be taken if divine regulations are broken unwittingly. The implication is that such offences defile the sanctuary, which must then be purified. The more senior or important the offender, the greater is the degree of defilement; and therefore more powerful methods of purification are called for. This can be illustrated as follows:

Offender	Animal	Blood	Fats, etc.	Remainder
Priest, or the whole congregation	bull	sprinkled seven times in front of veil of sanctuary; some put on altar of incense, rest poured out at foot of altar of burnt offering	burnt on altar of burnt offering	burnt outside the camp
ruler	male goat	put on horns of altar of burnt offering, rest poured out at foot of altar of burnt offering	burnt on altar of burnt offering	burnt on altar of burnt offering
ordinary Israelite	female goat	as for ruler	as for ruler	as for ruler

An offence by a priest or the whole congregation was held to defile the entrance of the sanctuary, and the altar of incense within it. These were therefore sprinkled with blood, and because the blood had been used for so holy a purpose, the flesh and skin of the animal had to be burnt outside the camp. A ruler or ordinary Israelite was held to have defiled only the altar of burnt offering, and after this had been purified, the fat parts and then the remainder could be burnt on the altar.

Rites of passage

The rites of passage specified in Leviticus 1–16 assume that there are three spheres: the sacred, the ordinary, and the abnormal; they are rituals designed to enable a person to pass from one sphere to the next and have similar features in quite differing circumstances.

The most striking similarities are in the anointing of the right earlobe, thumb, and big toe in the case of the priest and the leper. This ritual takes place at different points in the ceremony for obvious reasons. The priest is not unclean at the outset of his ceremony, whereas the leper

is considered to be so. A noticeable feature of each case is the period
of seven days of waiting, which permits the transition from one sphere
to the next. The washing or consecrating of clothes also helps to mark
the process of transition from one sphere to the next.

Atonement for the whole people

On the Day of Atonement, the most powerful of the rituals is performed,
in order to purify the holiest part of the sanctuary:

Person	Sphere	Destination	Initial	Clothes	Waiting	Final stage
priest (Lev. 8–9)	ordinary	sacred	bull and ram; blood put on right earlobe, thumb and big toe	consecrated with oil	seven days at door of tent of meeting	offers bull
leper (Lev. 14)	abnormal	ordinary	two birds; one released, the other killed and its blood mixed with water and sprinkled on leper seven times	washes clothes	seven days outside his tent; on 7th day shaves off all his hair	offers two male lambs; blood put on right earlobe thumb and toe; sprinkled seven times with oil, and oil put on right earlobe, thumb, and toe
male who has a discharge of fluid (other than semen)	abnormal	ordinary	none	washes clothes	counts seven days	offers two turtledoves or young pigeons
female who has unusual discharge (not menstruation)	abnormal	ordinary	none	not specified	count seven days	offers two turtledoves or young pigeons

> . . . because of the uncleanness of the people of Israel, and because of their transgressions . . . .
>
> (Leviticus 16: 16)

Here the divisions between the sacred, the ordinary, and the abnormal are at their sharpest. In order to enter the holiest part of the sanctuary, the priest has to make a sin offering, for himself and his house. Once he has entered the most holy place, he sprinkles the mercy seat (a piece of furniture symbolizing God's presence) seven times with the blood of a bullock. He then repeats this with the blood of a goat. When he has completed the purification of the sanctuary, he brings forward a live goat, lays his hands upon its head, and confesses (verse 21):

> All the iniquities of the people of Israel, and all their transgressions, all their sins . . . .

This is the one of the very few places in the Old Testament that indicates that there was a liturgy of things spoken which accompanied the ritual of things done. The goat (the original scapegoat) is now led from the sphere of the sacred, through the camp (the sphere of the ordinary), and released into the abnormal and chaotic world outside the camp. Its progress symbolizes and effects the removal of the defilement suffered by the sanctuary because of the people's transgressions.

Perhaps one surprising thing about all these ceremonies is that they are directed more towards ritual offences than towards moral ones. It is true that Leviticus 5–6 deals briefly with deliberate offences of a moral kind, such as fraud, robbery, oppressing one's neighbour, and lying; but there is no mention of sacrifice for what we today would call more serious offences such as murder. Yet this should not surprise us. Murder was dealt with by members of the victim's family, and the penalty was the death of the murderer. An *unsolved* murder raised the problem, dealt with in Deuteronomy 21: 1–9 (see chapter 10, p. 247) of freeing the land from impurity caused by the unavenged shed blood of the victim, but no sacrifice could atone for murder. The very fact that the ceremonies of Leviticus 1–16 and elsewhere concentrate upon ritual rather than moral offences is a testimony to their age; but we should not regard them as quaint or unnecessary. Insofar as they expressed a view of the world, they were an attempt to remind Israelites in many ways that their everyday lives were lived in the presence of God. This reminding was achieved by the marking out of boundaries or the defining of ''taboos'', together with offerings for the restoration of normality when there were violations.

If the rituals of Leviticus are looked at purely from an anthropological point of view, they appear to be survivals of primitive ideas about purity. In the context of Genesis to Leviticus, however, they take their meaning from the story as a whole. This story concerns the deliverance of Israelites from slavery in Egypt to freedom in the wilderness, and later in their own land. In the larger context, the rituals concerning purity are in effect theologized, so that they become part of Israel's response to a God who deals personally with his people. Thus, ancient ceremonies, whose origins and development are largely unknown to us, take their place in the whole story of Israel's witness to God, and express from a priestly point of view what it means to be a people having a special relationship with their God.

THE PSALMS

In the matter of their interpretation, the psalms present a similar problem to that of the ceremonies described in Leviticus. We know what the whole Psalter in its final form is meant to be: not a collection of pieces for use in public worship, but a manual of private devotion and meditation which encompasses confession (Psalm 51), lament (Psalm 3), adoration (Psalm 8), and praise (Psalm 150), to name only some of the contents. Yet some of the psalms must have been used in the worship of the Temple, and were surely the spoken or sung accompaniment to solemn and festive ceremonies. Even so, whatever these ceremonies were, they have receded so far into the background that they are virtually impossible to recover from the psalms in their present form (Wilson 1985, pp. 170–172 and *passim*). We shall try to deal with these matters in relation to three topics: the royal ceremonies of the psalms, the form-critical study of the psalms, and the collection and editing of the psalms.

The royal ceremonies of the psalms

The Jerusalem Temple was a royal foundation and a royal chapel. Probably until the time of Josiah (640–609 BCE) the ordinary people used other sanctuaries when they needed them. It would not be surprising, then, if some of the psalms reflect ceremonies that centred upon the king and his household.

The attempt to identify such psalms and to guess at the underlying ceremonies is quite old in biblical scholarship. The seventeenth-century Puritan commentator Matthew Poole, for all that he saw many references to Christ in the psalms, noted that Psalm 2 had been connected by some scholars with David's inauguration as king. He accepted that psalms 24, 47, and 68 were composed on the occasion of the bringing of the Ark by David to Jerusalem (2 Samuel 6). He also connected Psalm 132 with the same ceremony, although he believed that 132 was written by Solomon and was used by him as a prayer which reminded God of how David had given the Ark a resting place.

Scholarship in the twentieth century has enlarged the scope of so-called royal psalms to include those that may have been used by a king prior to a battle (e.g. Psalm 44) and those that may have been used at an annual ceremony, such as the anniversary of the king's coronation or a New Year Festival. Into this category have come psalms 93 and 96–99, which celebrate God's universal kingship over the world. There have also been variations upon the view that some of the psalms accompanied royal occasions. One variation suggests that some psalms were composed

ABOVE Part of the decoration of the fourth-century limestone synagogue at Capernaum is a building on wheels. Although the interpretation of the carving is disputed, it may well be an attempt to depict the return of the Ark of the Covenant to the Israelites by the Philistines (1 Samuel 6).

OPPOSITE Bethel (modern Beitin) was an important religious site in the northern kingdom of Israel. The sanctuary was closely linked in Israelite tradition with the Israelite ancestor Jacob (Genesis 28). When the Israelite (Jacob) traditions were joined with the Judahite (Abraham) traditions, Abraham was also credited with having dwelt and worshipped at Bethel (Genesis 12: 8).

before David captured Jerusalem, and were used by the northern tribes at a New Year celebration. These psalms were brought to Jerusalem by the attendants of the Ark of the Covenant. Another variation suggests that at the New Year Festival in Jerusalem, the king suffered ritual humiliation, death, and resurrection. We do not believe that either of these variations can be convincingly demonstrated, and we content ourselves with outlining the possible ceremonies that lay behind the so-called royal psalms.

Psalm 2 pictures the nations of the world conspiring together to overthrow the king in Jerusalem. The text asserts, however, that this is useless, because God says (verse 6):

I have set my king on Zion, my holy hill.

This is probably the point at which we should say something about "Zion ideology". When David incorporated Jerusalem into Israel, he also incorporated its Jebusite ideology into Israelite religion. We glimpse something of this ideology in other psalms, most notably Psalm 46. Here, the city of God is built above a river (46: 4), which was probably believed to be a river of paradise. As the place where God dwelt (46: 5), Jerusalem was safe from all its enemies, and this sense of security is expressed in the psalm by the refrain, twice repeated:

The Lord of hosts is with us;
The God of Jacob is our refuge.

This refrain, incidentally, indicates the fusion of northern and southern religious ideas. Jacob was the patriarch associated with the northern tribes and ''Lord of hosts'' was a title associated with the Ark (see below). These ideas of northern origin have here been located in Jerusalem and fused with the Jerusalem ideology that the city of God, situated above the river of paradise, will endure for ever.

Returning to Psalm 2, we can now see why the psalm expresses so much confidence. Zion is not just *any* city; it is the dwelling place of the one who (verse 4):

sits in the heavens . . . .

This is why human plotting against it can never succeed. But the king has a further ground for confidence. At his coronation he is given a scroll which sets out the mutual obligations between the king and God. This scroll contains (verse 7) the words:

You are my son,
today I have begotten you.

The king has thus been received on his coronation day into a special relationship with God by adoption. This is guarantee enough that he will withstand assaults upon his power; for such assaults will be against his ''father'' also. Thus, the kings of the earth are addressed (verses 10–11):

Now therefore, O kings, be wise:
be warned, O rulers of the earth.
Serve the Lord with fear,
with trembling kiss his feet.

Modern scholarship suggests that this psalm was used not only at a king's coronation, but thereafter on its anniversary.

Psalm 24 is widely held to have been used, if not on the occasion when David brought the Ark to Jerusalem, then at least annually thereafter. The psalm is thought to consist of two parts: a liturgy of confession for those who are to bear the Ark to its resting place after it has been carried in procession outside Jerusalem, and a question and answer ceremony (verses 7–10) at the city gates. In the latter, the bearers of the Ark demand admittance in the name of the king of glory:

Lift up your heads, O gates!
and be lifted up, O ancient doors!
that the king of glory may come in.

The gatekeepers ask:

Who is the king of glory!

The bearers of the Ark reply that it is the Lord, strong and mighty, mighty in battle. When the questions and answers are repeated the bearers answer:

OPPOSITE Old Testament tradition regarded David as the author of many of the psalms as well as the person responsible for establishing the musical arrangements in the Temple. His musical skill became a feature of Christian art, as depicted in this illustration from the Oscott Psalter, c. 1270.

> The Lord of Hosts,
> he is the king of glory!

We know from 1 Samuel 4: 4 that the full name of the Ark was the Ark of the Covenant of the Lord of Hosts (see also Numbers 10: 35–36). This is why the guess is made that Psalm 24 reflects a ceremony in which the Ark was carried in procession, and that the name ''Lord of hosts'', so closely associated with the Ark, was the final word of authority which caused the gatekeepers to admit the procession.

Psalm 44 is believed to have been used by the king prior to battle. This is partly because of the sudden switch from the first person plural to the first person singular in verses 5–6 (and in 14–16):

> Through thee we push down our foes;
> through thy name we tread down our assailants.
> For not in my bow do I trust,
> nor can my sword save me.

It is suggested that this surprising change can best be understood if the king is speaking for the people as a whole. He can use both ''we'' and ''I'' language. From its content, the psalm is clearly a prayer for success in battle.

In Psalm 47 the phrase (verse 5)

> God has gone up with a shout,
> the Lord with the sound of a trumpet

has suggested a sort of coronation festival for God, in which the Ark was carried up the hill of Zion (God has gone up . . .), and trumpets were blown to celebrate this enactment of his kingship. The subject-matter of the psalm celebrates the universal kingship of God.

In psalms 93 and 96–99 there are no references to anything like processions or removals of the Ark. It is the subject-matter of these psalms that has suggested that they were used at a ceremony to celebrate God's universal kingship. They share certain themes: that the seas or powers of nature roar in defiance of or obedience to God; that he has founded the world and ensures its stability; and that he has also established moral decrees. He is coming to execute judgement and justice, and this will be welcomed by the powers of nature. These psalms are called ''royal'' because it is presumed that the king would have taken an important part in the ceremonies.

Psalm 110 appears to be connected with David's or his successor's coronation in Jerusalem. It is addressed by a priest to the king, and the priest speaks the words of God (verse 1):

> The Lord [i.e. God] says to my Lord [i.e. the King],
> ''Sit at my right hand, till I make your enemies your footstool''.

We meet again the theme prominent in Psalm 2, that God will give victory to the Jerusalem king. There is here, however (verse 4), a new element:

The Lord has sworn
and will not change his mind,
"You are a priest for ever
after the order of Melchizedek".

It is generally supposed that the king is here being admitted to the rights
and privileges that the priest-kings of Jerusalem had before its capture
by David. Thus David and his successors are in a sense priests, although
not members of the priestly families of Israel.

Psalm 132 has been held to contain clear traces of a ceremony in which
the whole story of David bringing the Ark from Kiriath-jearim to
Jerusalem (2 Samuel 6) was re-enacted. Two verses, 6 and 8, are
especially pertinent:

Lo, we heard of it in Ephrathah,
we found it in the fields of Jaar . . . .
Arise, O Lord, into thy resting place,
thou and the ark of thy might.

These verses suggest a mock expedition to seek and find the Ark, followed
by its festal removal to Jerusalem, where it was lifted up and placed
upon the site prepared by David. However, as older commentators
(e.g. Poole p. 198) had already noticed, verse 10,

For thy servant David's sake
do not turn away the face of thy anointed one,

suggests that a successor of David is speaking. Moreover, the word
"there" in verse 17 is strange:

There I will make a horn to sprout for David . . . .

This implies that the setting of the psalm is not in Jerusalem, but
somewhere else (? in Babylon during the exile).

This section has not exhausted the royal psalms or the ceremonies
that have been detected behind them. Approaching the psalms in this
way has the merit of bringing the psalms to life as they are set in the
great ceremonial occasions of the Jerusalem Temple. Yet a word of
warning is needed. It is difficult to reconcile the suggestion that the Ark
was regularly carried around in processions with the ritual of Leviticus
16, which specifies that the high priest could only enter the holy of holies
(where the Ark was placed) once a year, and then only after elaborate
rituals. Moreover, there is no hint in Leviticus 16 that the Ark could
be removed from its place. It may be possible to overcome the difficulty
by saying that in its final form Leviticus dates from, and reflects a time
when, there was no king and thus no processions. It is not impossible
that when Leviticus 16 reached its final form, there no longer was an
Ark — it having been destroyed or carried off by the Babylonians. There
is much that we do not know.

Form-critical study of the psalms

The branch of psalm study known as form-critical is usually linked with
the name of the German scholar Gunkel. It has been a major aspect
of the psalms studies in the twentieth century; but its roots go back at
least to the beginning of the nineteenth. Briefly, it involves grouping
psalms together on the basis of content, and then trying to suggest the
situation in the life of the individual or the community to which a
particular psalm was appropriate.

A major group is known as individual laments, and a glance at Psalms
4–7 indicates that they have certain common features. Each begins with
a prayer to God either to hear or to be gracious to the psalmist. Each
implies that the psalmist is in some difficulty, chiefly from enemies; each
ends on a positive note, as though the psalmist has been reassured of
God's favour and can now face life once more in confidence.

Another major group is that of communal laments. Psalms 79 and
80 both imply that the people as a whole are in distress, and the speakers
use the "we" form of address to God, reminding him of how much they
are suffering. Both of these two psalms end with a prayer for deliverance,
not with a confident assertion that all is now right.

Parallel to individual and communal laments are individual and communal thanksgivings. Psalms 30 and 34 are examples of the former,
Psalm 34 beginning with the words

> I will bless the Lord at all times;
> his praise shall continually be in my mouth.

In both cases, the psalmist celebrates how God brought deliverance in
time of trouble. An example of a communal thanksgiving is Psalm 65.
Another class consists of the "wisdom" psalms, which reflect upon the
problem of the suffering of the innocent and the prosperity of the wicked
(e.g. Psalm 73). We have already mentioned royal psalms in the
preceding section.

The form-critical approach helps to bring the psalms to life, as texts
bound up with the problems of individuals and the community; but again,
the approach raises questions that are not easy to answer. Who are the
individuals who composed or used these psalms? Were they ordinary
Israelite worshippers? If the answer is yes, we must suppose that these
psalms were composed during or after the time of Josiah; for it has been
pointed out that Jerusalem was a royal sanctuary, and that ordinary
Israelites made use of local sanctuaries when they needed them. Perhaps
they were composed and used in regional sanctuaries, or the laments
were composed by or for members of the king's entourage. We must
be careful, in view of the limitations of our knowledge, not to read too
much into the situations at which the psalmists hint. The psalms are
vague, perhaps deliberately so, about their circumstances of composition. This may be because they were meant to be used in all sorts of
situations, in which case the search for greater precision would be
self-defeating.

The collection and editing of the psalms

We know very little about how the psalms were collected and edited; but what we can reasonably guess sheds some light which is quite instructive. The psalms are traditionally separated into five books: I, 1–41; II, 42–72; III, 73–89; IV, 90–106; and V, 107–150. There is some evidence that Book I, at the very least, was a separate collection, for beginning with Psalm 42 (the first psalm of Book II), editors changed the divine name Yhwh to the more general word for God, *'elohim*. This can be seen if you compare psalms 14 and 53, which are almost identical apart from the use of "God" instead of Yhwh in Psalm 53. The fact that this process began at the beginning of Book II indicates that Psalm 42 was the first psalm of a collection separate from psalms 1–41. It is also to be noted that whereas most of psalms 1–41 are headed "A Psalm of David", Psalms 42–49 are psalms of the "Sons of Korah", and Psalm 50 is "A Psalm of Asaph".

We do not know the length of the collection beginning at Psalm 42. The changing of the name Yhwh to *'elohim* went as far as Psalm 83, i.e. into Book III but not quite to its end. Support for the traditional view that psalms 42–72 were originally a separate collection can be found in the ending of Psalm 72, which takes the form of a doxology:

Blessed be the Lord, the God of Israel.
who alone does wondrous things.
Blessed be his glorious name for ever;
may his glory fill the whole earth! Amen and Amen.

To this are added the words

The prayers of David, the son of Jesse, are ended.

(It is worthwhile noting, however, that many psalms from 73 to 150 are also ascribed to David.)

Also supporting this division is the fact that psalms 73–83 are psalms "of Asaph", suggesting a new, or separate, collection. We may therefore guess that psalms 1 (or perhaps 2 — see later) through 41 and 42–72 and 73–(?)83 were originally separate collections. The name Asaph is known to us from Chronicles (e.g. 1 Chronicles 25: 2) as one of David's chief musicians; but how far this information is accurate we do not know.

For books IV and V we have evidence from manuscripts from Qumran that even as late as the first century CE the order of the psalms was by no means fixed. The scroll known as 11QPs a, and usually dated 30–50 CE, has a most irregular order between psalms 100 and 150, including ten pieces that do not appear in the final collection of the psalms in the Old Testament. The most spectacular deviations are as follows (see Wilson 1985, pp. 124–5, for an outline): Psalms 106–8 and 110–17 are omitted. Examples of deviant order are the following sequences: 103, 109, 118, 104, 147, 105, 146; and 132, 119, 135; and 93, 141, 133, 144, 155, 142–3, 149–50. It is possible to argue, of course, that the evidence from Qumran is not representative, because the Qumran community was outside mainstream Judaism (if there was such a thing). But there is another approach, which looks for reasons for the order of psalms in 11QPs a and uses these as a clue to the arrangement of the Psalter.

Wilson (pp. 124–31) points out that psalms 118, 104, 147, 105, and 146 in 11QPs a all contain in their superscripts or postscripts either the word *hodu* (''praise'') or *hallelujah* (''praise the Lord''). Furthermore, this block comes between psalms 101–3, 109 (ascribed to David), and 120–32, which are all ''Songs of Assents''. In other words, parts of 11PQsa are grouped together in blocks, depending on the superscripts and postscripts, with *hodu* and *hallelujah* psalms marking a transition from one group to the next. Wilson detects similar phenomena in the Psalter as we know it. For example, psalms 104–6, which end Book IV, are all *hodu* or *hallelujah* psalms, as are psalms 146–50 which end Book V.

There are many things that remain unexplained, but the following points can be made about the collecting and editing of the Psalter in the light of the section on the psalms as a whole.

First, if there *were* royal psalms which were used in the way suggested above, they form no collection in the Psalter. This is evident from their numbers: 2, 24, 47, 110, 132, and possibly 93 and 96–99. This is not to say that it is wrong to try to identify royal psalms and to reconstruct the ceremonies at which they were used; but it is to say that the compilers of the Psalter were probably unaware that there was a group of psalms that had been thus used.

Second, the form-critical division of psalms into communal and individual laments, etc., likewise represents an approach to the Psalter quite different from that of the collectors and editors. Again, it is not being suggested that the form-critical approach is wrong or useless.

Third, evidence from Qumran indicates that, by the second century BCE, the order of the psalms in Books I–III was more or less fixed, but that there was no fixed order, or even number, for Books IV–V. The principle of arrangement of Books I–III seems to have been that of presumed authorship. All but four of psalms 2–41 are ascribed to David; psalms 42–49 are ascribed to the sons of Korah; and then following the psalm of Asaph (50), there are seventeen more psalms of David (51–65 and 68–69). We have already pointed out that Book III begins with eleven psalms of Asaph (73–83), while of the remaining six in Book III, four are ascribed to the Sons of Korah (84–5 and 87–8). In Books IV and V the situation is different. The only recognizable block of psalms according to their titles are the Songs of Ascents (120–34) and a group of David psalms (138–45).

Fourth, it is possible that at one stage, the Psalter was completed by the addition of Psalm 1 at the beginning and Psalm 119 at what was, at that time, the end. Psalm 1 stresses the importance of delighting and mediating in the law (Torah) of God (Psalm 1: 2), while Psalm 119 is an elaborate meditation upon the law in all its aspects (see Rogerson and McKay 1977, vol. 3, pp. 90–1 for a plan of the psalm). This ''framing'' of the Psalter with two psalms concerned with meditating upon God's law indicates an important shift in the understanding of the psalms. So viewed, they become not so much the words of worshippers addressed to God, but the word of God to worshippers.

Finally, although the Psalter may once have ended with Psalm 119, the fact that it now ends with a block of David psalms (138–45), followed by five *hallelujah* psalms, indicates a further shift in intention on the part of the compiler(s). The Psalter can now be seen more or less as a whole in terms of the life of David (see Wilson, pp. 172–3 and 209–28). The prefacing of particular psalms with references to events in the life of David clearly suggests their intended use as texts to be read and meditated upon. The original cultic settings (if we are right about them) have receded so far into the background that not one single psalm title supports the cultic interpretation of psalms such as 2, 24, 47, 110, and 132. On the other hand, where there are psalm titles with cultic indications, they can surprise us. Psalm 30, for example, is described as "A Song at the dedication of the Temple", although nothing in the content of the psalm suggests that this is so; and form-criticism would classify it as an individual thanksgiving for deliverance.

Wilson (pp. 209–28) suggests that each book of the psalms can be seen in terms of God's covenant with David. Book I introduces the covenant (Psalm 2) whereas Book II concludes (Psalm 72) with a prayer that its benefits be passed to David's son. Book III concludes (Psalm 89) with the extension of the covenant to David's descendants, while giving the impression that the covenant has failed. Book IV explores the reasons for this failure (the frailty of mankind [Psalm 90] and the disobedience of Israel [Psalms 105–6]), while Book V outlines the way back from exile: observance of the law (Psalm 119), hope of blessing for Zion (Psalms 120–134), and a shift back to David's confidence in God in Psalms 138–145.

Conclusion

The sacrificial and psalms traditions share the difficulty for the modern interpreter that they have taken a long time to reach their final form. We can only guess about their origins, we know little about their history, and in their final form they seem to have an intention different from that which modern historical research would suggest. In this chapter we have only been able to hint at these problems and at the fascinating questions that they raise. Taken together, however, the sacrificial and the psalm traditions are necessary complements. If each seems to be hardly aware of the other's existence, in spite of their presumed common setting in the Temple, this does not prevent us from reading each in the light of the other. The elaborate ceremonies for dealing with ritual impurity are offset by the sincere requests for forgiveness and salvation, while the joy in the psalms that God is the lord of the whole earth and of all the nations is seen in the light of the practical ceremonies which mark out those areas of life that properly belong to God and must be approached with reverence and awe.

CHAPTER 12

PROPHETIC LITERATURE

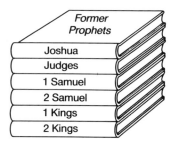

Former
Prophets

Joshua
Judges
1 Samuel
2 Samuel
1 Kings
2 Kings

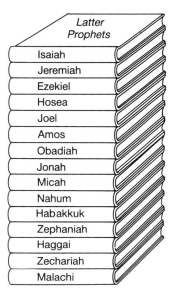

Latter
Prophets

Isaiah
Jeremiah
Ezekiel
Hosea
Joel
Amos
Obadiah
Jonah
Micah
Nahum
Habakkuk
Zephaniah
Haggai
Zechariah
Malachi

The second division of the Hebrew Bible is called "Prophets". It comprises the books of Joshua-Kings (excluding Ruth), which describe, among other things, the activities of prophetic figures such as Samuel, Elijah, and Elisha, together with three large and twelve small books consisting mostly of sayings attributed to "prophets". The books of Joshua–Kings are called the "Former Prophets", while Isaiah–Malachi are the "Latter Prophets". In contrast to the Hebrew Bible, the Old Testament arrangement separates these two sub-groups: the former Prophets, plus Ruth, are placed before Chronicles, Ezra, Nehemiah and Esther (plus 1 and 2 Maccabees in the fuller canon) and grouped with them to make a collection of historical books; and the Latter Prophets are placed at the end of the canon.

WHAT IS "PROPHECY"?

Most readers of the Bible will assume that they know what prophecy is. But prophecy in ancient Israel and prophecy as presented in the Old Testament are two different things. If we want to investigate prophecy in Israel we must first of all analyze the numerous roles and functions that "prophets" play, not only in the Old Testament records, but also in other ancient Near Eastern texts and, as is becoming more common nowadays, in other societies too. As we shall see, this line of investigation splits up the concept of "prophecy" to include the activities of several different kinds of person. In fact, Hebrew has several words for "prophet" — *hōzeh* and *rō'eh*, which mean literally "seers", and *nābî'*, which is the most common word by far.

If, on the other hand, we wish to understand what the Bible means by "prophecy", it is not the diversity which strikes us, but the presentation of a single institution and a single theory: persons called by God to deliver his word, in contrast, very often, to the kinds of "prophets" that sociology would recognize, i.e. professional intermediaries. Even in the Bible, however, we can see obvious differences between the "former" and "latter" prophets. As we shall discover, Elijah and Hosea have little in common apart from the title.

PROPHECY AS A SOCIAL INSTITUTION

Anthropology and sociology are increasingly being used to define ''prophecy'' as a social institution. For neither biblical nor non-biblical literature gives us a sufficiently precise indication of how prophets were viewed, or what their influence was. Efforts to define prophecy as an ''office'' or a prophet as a person with ''charisma'' do not work. Israel's prophets were presumably recognized as such because of patterns of social behaviour, and their function was understood in terms of fairly clear conventions, involving the interaction of individual, group, and society and fulfilling a social role.

Most anthropologists avoid the term ''prophecy'' because of its biblical connotations and because it does not apply in other societies. Robert Wilson (1980), for example, surveys alternative words such as ''shaman'', ''medium'', ''witch'', ''sorcerer'', and ''intermediary'', and opts for the last of these. Now, intermediation between the society and its gods can occur through possession, in which the god takes over the intermediary, or through ''soul migration'' or ''soul-loss'' where the intermediary's soul or spirit temporarily leaves the body. Intermediaries can be formed through mental or social predisposition, by mystical experience or divine election. The role of society in creating and supporting intermediaries also varies widely. In some places we find prophets chosen by ''peer evaluation'', in which a guild of intermediaries controls entrance into its profession, often through apprenticeship, or even by succession and inheritance. It is likely that such mystical and social factors influenced the role of prophecy in Israel also.

PROPHETS IN THE ANCIENT NEAR EAST

Like ''prophecy'', the word ''prophet'' is an impossibly broad term for activities which include ecstasy, the giving of messages to individuals (including the monarchy), and the pronouncement of oracles, whether public or private. One of the richest archives here are the Mari texts (see ANET 623–5, 629–32), which contain descriptions of several quite specific and named ''prophetic'' types, but also mention other, anonymous figures who give oracles. Texts from Assyria, Babylonia, and Syria give us the names of classes of prophets, divinatory texts, and letters to and from intermediaries requiring or giving messages. Prophecy in Egypt, however, is represented in predictive texts, which belong, rather, to apocalyptic categories (see chapter 14) and do not seem to be products of any ''prophetic'' office.

Among the types of ''prophet'' at Mari (eighteenth century BCE) were *Muḫḫū*, ecstatics whose trances, probably induced, were often accompanied by violent behaviour and would produce oracles. *Muḫḫūs* were found both at regional cult-centres and around the royal court. The Assyrian kings Esarhaddon and Ashurbanipal also employed such persons. Another type of prophet at Mari, known as *āpilu*, delivered oracles, often in standard stereotyped language, including ''messenger''-

language (see below). But these were apparently not influential with the monarch or in the royal cult. Yet another group, the *assinnu*, belonged to the cult of Ishtar. Their activities are unclear, but may have included female impersonation. In addition to all these, there were various individuals who uttered oracles, usually derived from dreams. But the most influential ''prophetic'' group was clearly the *bārŭs*, experts in divination and readers of omens; an account of them is given in chapter 14. Organized into guilds, they formed a major part of the religious and political establishment, and their practices were dictated strongly by tradition and convention. Finally, in seventh century Assyrian records, we find other prophetic types, such as the *raggimu* or ''shouter'', the *šabru* (probably a dreamer), and the female *šēlūtu*.

Two important texts from Syria-Palestine also have a bearing on prophecy. The Zakir inscription (ANET 655–6), probably from about 800 BCE, tells how Zakir, king of Hamath, prayed to Baal Shamen, who answered him through seers (*ḥzyn*) and *ᶜddyn*. However, we cannot tell by what methods intermediation was actually obtained. The Deir ᶜAlla inscription from Transjordan, dating from about 700 BCE, contains a text ascribed to Balaam, son of Beor, who appears in the Bible in Numbers 22–24. He is called a ''seer (*ḥzh*) of the gods'', and according to this text the gods visited him at night. The text is obviously of immense interest to biblical scholars; so far as our understanding of prophecy is concerned, it tells us, like the Zakir inscription, that the biblical word *ḥōzeh* is also the name of a prophetic office in Syria-Palestine from the time of Israel's origins.

PROPHETS IN ANCIENT ISRAEL

This rather sketchy review of ancient Near Eastern materials confirms that ''prophecy'' is a term for several different forms of divine-human mediation. But in the Old Testament not all mediation is regarded as prophecy: ''And when Saul enquired of the Lord, the Lord did not answer him, either by dreams, or by Urim [the drawing of a lot by the priest], or by prophets'' (1 Samuel 28: 6). Why does the Old Testament exclude dreams and Urim from prophecy? Dream-interpretation it assigns to wise men like Joseph and Daniel, while the manipulation of the lot — whether Urim and Thummim or ephod (Exodus 28: 30; 1 Samuel 30: 7) is always entrusted to priests. But prophetic activity in the Old Testment, though narrowly defined, still includes several different techniques. Like the *Muḫḫū*, Elisha, in 2 Kings 3: 15ff, goes into a trance, induced by music, upon which he is touched by ''hand of the Lord'', and utters an oracle. Saul's behaviour, described in 1 Samuel 10: 10ff. as ''prophesying'', when the ''spirit of God came mightily upon him'', seems to have been an ecstatic but inarticulate experience. At least, if he uttered any valuable words, they were not thought fit to be recorded. Instances of violent behaviour associated with ecstasy, however, are attributed only to non-Israelite prophets, such as

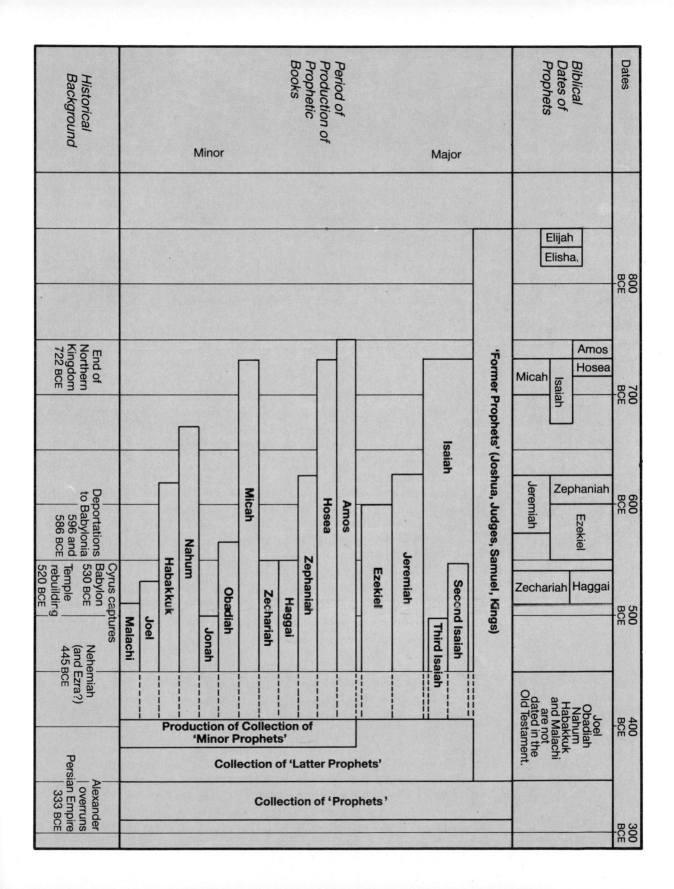

the prophets of Baal, who, in the Elijah story, "cried aloud, and cut themselves after their custom with swords and lances, until the blood gushed out upon them" (1 Kings 18: 28).

Other features of prophecy include its assocation with a cult-centre (e.g. Gilgal, 2 Kings 2: 1) as well as with the royal court. Prophetic "guilds", the "sons of the prophets" (e.g. 2 Kings 2: 3ff.) are depicted, (as in 1 Samuel 19: 20ff., where three groups of men sent by Saul to capture David are seized, like Samuel and his company, with fits of prophesying. The "messenger"-language, as used by the *āpilu*, is the most pronounced feature of Old Testament prophetic speech. In Genesis 32: 3 Jacob sends messengers to Esau with the words, "Thus you shall say to my lord Esau: Thus says your servant Jacob, 'I have sojourned . . . .' " Compare Jeremiah 21: 3: "Then Jeremiah said to them 'Thus you shall say to Zedekiah, "Thus says the Lord, the God of Israel: 'Behold, I will turn back . . . .' " ' " — a message within a message! Here, perhaps, a word of caution is needed. Messenger-speech in the Old Testament may be associated with a theory of "prophecy" subsequently developed by the Deuteronomists, in which the "prophet" conveyed the "word of the Lord". Hence, the use of such speech — although it has parallels in the Mari texts (see above) — may not have been so distinctive a feature of the behaviour of the prophets themselves.

What of female prophets? Although it is usual to think of Israelite prophets as male, we must, of course, not forget Miriam, Deborah, or Huldah. Although the first two are called "prophets ", nothing is actually said of their prophetic activity. Huldah, on the other hand, gives an oracle, exactly as many male prophets do (1 Kings 22: 14ff.). Has the number of female prophets in ancient Israel been concealed in the Old Testament, together with their range of activities? We can suspect that this may be so. Should we also suspect that other types of prophecy besides the officially approved kind were concealed? Although divination is condemned, there is evidence that it might have been practiced (see chapter 14). Finally, we should remember the possibility of prophetic activity independent of any particular prophetic type or group — the individual "holy man" — which is what "man of God" probably means.

PROPHECY IN THE OLD TESTAMENT

A largely literary product

The Old Testament prophetic literature is not directly the product of prophets, but of scribes who have compiled books of "prophecy" under the names of individuals. The contribution of any particular individual to the book ascribed to him varies considerably; in the case of Jeremiah or Isaiah we have a good deal that is certainly not. And what is not from these individuals is not necessarily all from other "prophets" either. Inserting "prophecies" into existing collections is often the work of a commentator, who (as we shall see) interprets by amplification. Israelite prophecy has come down to us as an essentially literary phenomenon, in which prophetic words and descriptions are written in books.

We should recognize first a basic difference between the prophetic figures in the two parts of the ''prophetic'' canon. First of all, only two of the Latter Prophets appear in the books of the Former Prophets: Isaiah appears in 2 Kings 18–20 and Jonah in 2 Kings 14: 25. Another difference is that while the Former Prophets contain stories, with prophetic speeches occasionally inserted, the Latter Prophets are mostly words attributed to prophets, with occasional narrative as a framework for the words. Isaiah 36–39 and Jonah, together with Jeremiah 36–43, are the only extended narratives in the Latter Prophets. So what do all these characters have in common?

Isaiah is named as ''the prophet'' only three times in his book, all in chapters 36–39, a section that is actually copied from the Former Prophets (2 Kings 18–20). Jeremiah is called a prophet twenty-one times, but in his own speech the term is used only of those sent in the past and of contemporaries who are also alleged to be liars. Twice Ezekiel is indirectly referred to as a prophet (2: 5; 33: 33); otherwise ''prophet'' is also used of figures of the past or of contemporary liars. Nowhere is Hosea or Micah or Malachi called a prophet; and Amos denies being one in 7: 14. Zechariah is only the ''son of a prophet''. Only Habakkuk and Haggai are called prophets; and in the remaining books of the Latter Prophets the word is not even used. To be fair, Jeremiah and Ezekiel are often said to ''prophesy''; Amos is forbidden to ''prophesy'' by Amaziah the priest (before his denial of being a prophet). The verb occurs in Zechariah three times, but is nowhere applied to Zechariah himself, and nowhere else is it found in the Latter Prophets.

What all this means is that the farther we go back from the finished Old Testament, the more elusive becomes an institution of ''prophecy''. The producers of the prophetic books, including the books of the Former Prophets, used the term ''prophet'' (*nābî'*) in a way that the prophets themselves did not! Why is this so? Those who produced the prophetic books worked for the most part in a period (see chapter 16) when there was no king, no local cults, and only a small society gathered round a single sanctuary and city. Pre-exilic ''prophetic'' institutions were a thing of the past. Biblical prophecy, and in many cases individual prophets, were re-created through these writers' books. As the Jewish society of the Second Temple looked back on their depleted fortunes, they ''recognized'' in their past a series of God-sent persons who had warned the nation of its impending punishment but had also promised a brighter future in the end. Why had the nation not heeded? One reason offered was that Israel had been misled by ''false prophets'' giving wrong messages. If only the ''true'' prophets had been taken seriously!

''True'' and ''false'' prophecy
Inaccurate or unreliable prophecy is a universal problem. In Babylon, it was common for the respected *barû* to be consulted as a ''second opinion''. But in the Jewish religion, the problem raised questions of

theology. What did the fact of wrong prophecy mean? Why did Yhwh allow it? A brief look at some Old Testament texts on this problem will show us a good deal about the *theological* dimension of prophecy, as it emerged in retrospect.

Deuteronomy 18: 20 considers the case of a prophet who has not been "sent by Yhwh". But how will such a prophet be known? "When a prophet speaks in the name of the Lord, if the word does not come to pass or come true, that is a word which the Lord has not spoken . . . ." But people will know only when it is too late; no allowance is made for divine change of mind (as in the case of Jonah), and, of course, prophets can often predict what will happen without help from heaven. Deuteronomy 13: 1 recognizes a further difficulty: a "false" prophet may be able to offer a "sign" which people believe. So further help is given: if a prophet (or a dreamer) tells you to "serve other gods", then Yhwh is testing you. But this undermines even "true" prophecy by subordinating it to an unalterable divine law; the principle here is that the people can judge prophecy by what they know to be right and wrong! And how can Yhwh "test" Israel by false prophets if he has not sent them?

In 1 Kings 22, despite the unanimous agreement of all the prophets to go to war, Jehoshaphat, king of Judah, insists on a final opinion from Micaiah. This prophet is unpopular with the king of Israel because "he never prophesies good concerning me, but evil". Micaiah first confirms the advice of the prophets; then, when challenged, he reverses his message. He explains that he had seen Yhwh instructing one of his spirits to trick the king of Israel by becoming a "lying spirit in the mouth of all his prophets". Micaiah is then put into prison, and the Deuteronomy 18 test of false vs. true prophets is applied; the kings go to war and the king of Israel is killed. Now, here the reliable prophet is apparently distinguished by speaking evil against the Israelite king. But the other prophets are not accused of being fake, since they have heard from the divine spirit. The "true" prophet (in this case, anyway) had access to the heavenly court, and was not tricked by a "lying spirit". But by speaking the truth Micaiah betrayed a deceiving Yhwh, although only on the second occasion, when he spoke the "truth".

Finally, 1 Kings 13 tells of a "man of God" from Judah, who completes a mission in Bethel and declines an invitation to stay because, he says, Yhwh has forbidden him to eat or drink in the northern kingdom, or to return the way he had come. However an old prophet in Bethel invites the Judahite to his home, pretending that he has also received a divine word to do this. Persuaded that Yhwh's original instructions have now been superseded, the "man of God" goes with him. During the meal the host receives a genuine word from Yhwh condemning the "man of God" for disobeying his original instructions and sentencing him to death. On the way home he is indeed killed. Upon hearing this, the old prophet penitently fetches the body and buries it, asking that when he dies he be buried in the same sepulchre. Perhaps this story is meant as a warning to "men of God" not to believe each other but to adhere to what they themselves have been told. But who is "true" and who "false"?

In the Latter Prophets a different problem arises. The "prophets" of these books actually condemn prophecy. Isaiah speaks of the "prophet who teaches lies"; Micah accuses prophets of prophesying for money (3: 11); they "cry 'Peace' when they have something to eat, but declare war against him who puts nothing into their mouths". Zephaniah (3: 4) calls the prophets "wanton, faithless men". According to Jeremiah 14: 14, God declares that "The prophets are prophesying lies in my name; I did not send them, nor did I command them or speak to them. They are prophesying to you a lying vision, worthless divination". Jeremiah 28: 8, while condemning the prophets, offers a developed version of the Deuteronomic criterion: the prophets of old had prophesied "war, famine and pestilence amongst many countries and great kingdoms. As for the prophet who prophesies peace, when the word of that prophet comes to pass, then it will be known that the Lord has truly sent that prophet".

The purpose of Old Testament prophecy

The books of the Latter Prophets are generally thought to have been formed in some cases, and certainly collected, under the influence of Deuteronomistic thought (see chapter 16). For the Deuteronomist writer, history demonstrates how the prophetic message is fulfilled. It serves in its final form to explain why disaster struck (the Babylonian invasion), and uses prophecy as vindication. Likewise, the formation of many of the books of "Latter Prophets" seems to have grown initially from the need to explain the past disaster and thus to avoid future disaster. Equally, these books display a message of hope (see chapter 17), for the "prophets" remain authoritative mouthpieces for times later than their own, for whom a different future was to be offered than to those awaiting exile for their sins.

We may as well note one other treatment of prophecy, which absorbs it into the Temple cult. Chronicles emphasizes the prophetic warning which precedes disaster by means of sermons (e.g. 2 Chronicles 12: 5ff. and 16: 7–10) which have often been thought of as levitical in origin; and the Chronicler does indeed describe certain levites as "prophets". This seems to fit with his presentation of the chief task of levites as Temple singers who should ". . . prophesy with lyres, with harps, and with cymbals" (1 Chronicles 25: 1). In 2 Chronicles 20, a "holy war" story has been devised in such a way as to replace all the military aspects with liturgical ones. The king calls a fast, and the people gather to fast, sing hymns, and march to battle with a band in a sort of Old Testament "Salvation Army". They have previously been addressed by a levite, who gives the kind of encouragement prophets often give in the Former Prophets: "Fear not, be not dismayed" and assures them that God will give them the victory without fighting.

No attempt should be made here to trace the development of the historical institution of "prophecy" in the Persian period; we have here an attempt to transform an already idealized notion of "prophecy" into something of contemporary relevance. The move can be seen — though this would be a large oversimplification — as part of the longer process by which individuals critical of the "establishment" became seen retrospectively as bastions of it; the final irony of vesting this prophetic "office" in the Temple, of all places, is indeed magnificent. But that is how ideology works. Successful rebels, protesters, or revolutionaries become the new "establishment".

INDIVIDUAL PROPHETS AND PROPHETIC BOOKS

In this last section we shall look at the individuals — so far as we can see them — whose personalities and words lie at the beginnings of the books bearing their names in the Latter Prophets. Even in the case of Jeremiah, who is given the fullest description, little can be certainly known. These people are not, on the whole, authors or initiators of a prophetic "tradition" represented by "disciples". But such individuals — with maybe one or two exceptions — did exist, and their words are contained (somewhere) in the books credited to them. What, then, shall we call these persons, if "prophet" is a title they would not have claimed? Wilfred Owen once said, "All a poet can do today is warn", and the word "Poet" is not an inappropriate term for these individuals (Carroll 1983). Indeed, in the case of Deutero-Isaiah, few scholars would offer a better title, and even the contents of Ezekiel, though in prose, are not naturalistic prose, but more like non-metrical poetry. Now, poetry does not communicate in a literal vein; nor does it communicate simply by sense. It communicates by sound, by word-association, word-play, rhythm; it plays on emotion, it evokes images, it is memorable. The turning of "poets" into "prophets" can create a distortion: their language is read prosaically, literally, while their denunciations and descriptions become objective comment, their dreams predictions, their visions real psychological experiences. Most of these persons were oral poets, no doubt, though their books contain much poetry that is anonymous, pseudonymous and literary.

Prophetic speech

The analysis of "prophetic" speech has been very widely used to try to recover the historical profile of prophets and their social context, since so little information is otherwise given. Genres such as the oracle of judgement, the salvation oracle, the *rîb* or lawsuit, the woe-saying, the proverb, the account of a vision, the prayer of intercession, and the oracle against foreign nations can frequently be identified, and some of these are paralleled outside Israel. But the use of these and other genres implies really very little, except that poets borrow forms of speech from their society, using the form as part of the impact of the poetry. For us to use these forms in order to identify the author with a particular role

OPPOSITE The prophetic image: this portrait of the prophet Elijah, and that of Elisha overleaf, are two of twelve from the dome of a twelfth-century monastery in Cyprus. The creation of an image of a series of prophets, all ultimately proclaiming the same basic message (here written, of course, in Greek!), had already begun in the Old Testament itself. The total of twelve prophets (not to be confused with the biblical twelve minor prophets) is a post-biblical Christian development intended to provide a counterpart to the twelve apostles.

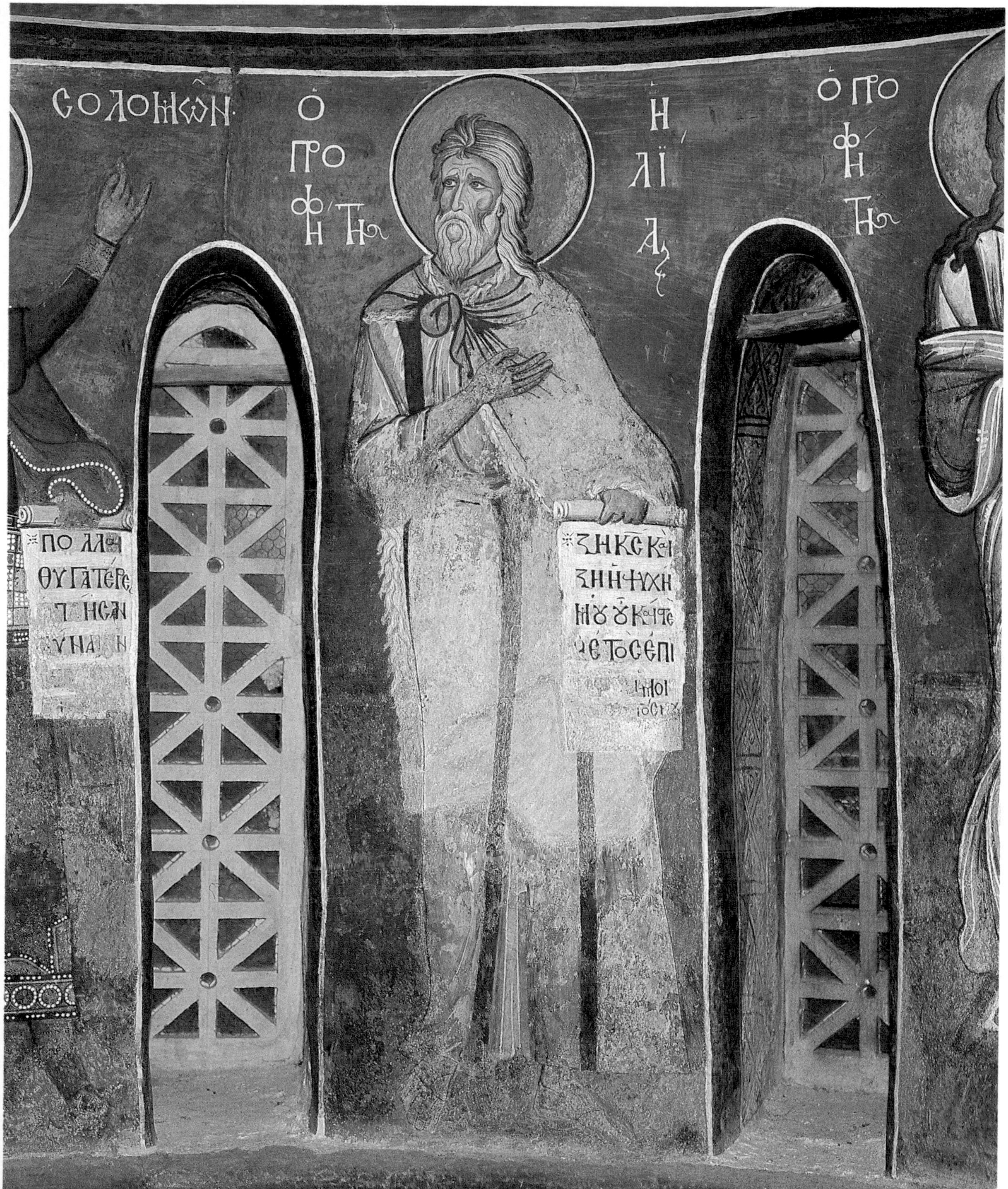
ΣΟΛΟΜΩΝ
Ο ΠΡΟΦΗΤΗΣ
ΗΛΙΑΣ
Ο ΠΡΟΦΗΤΗΣ

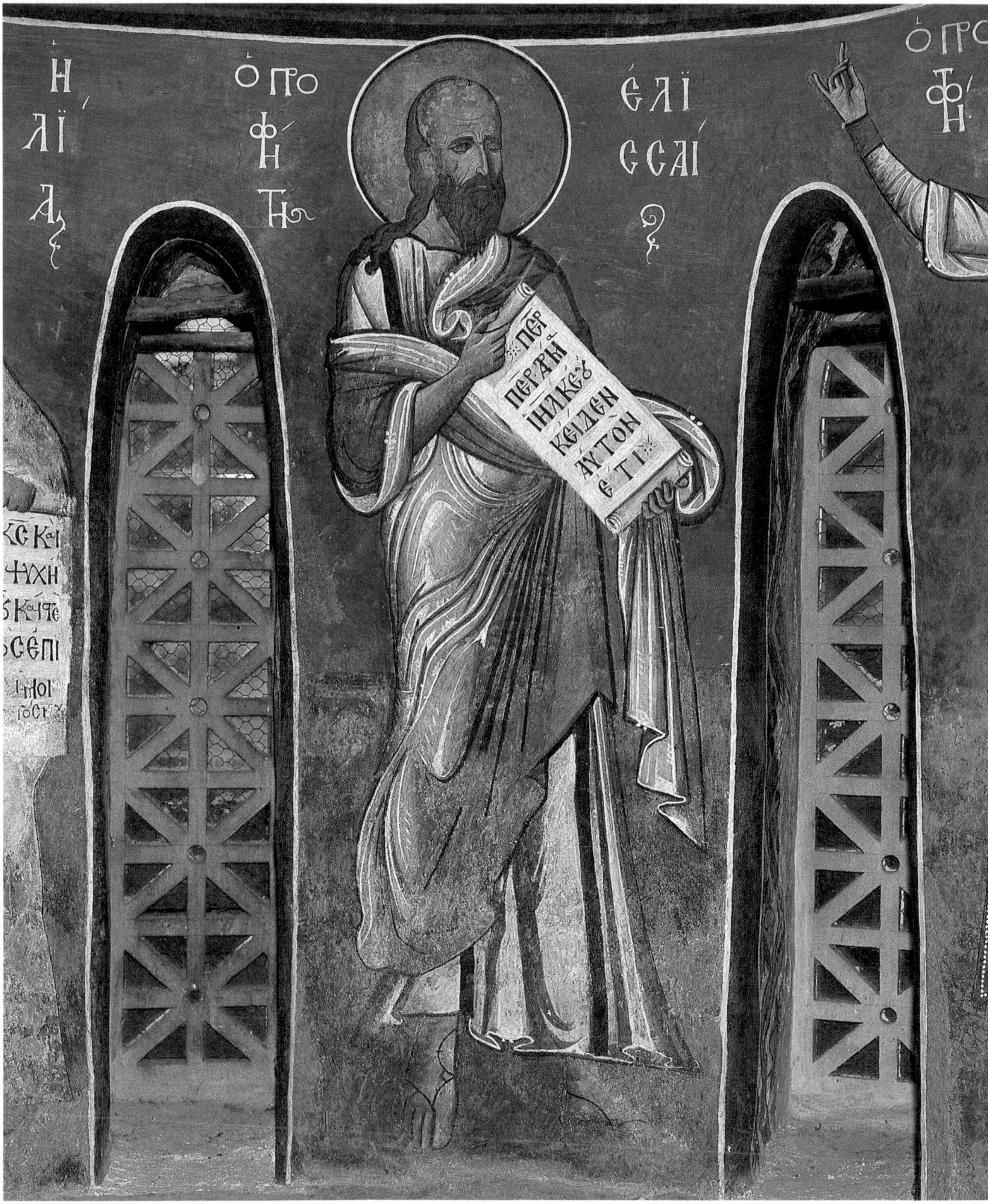
Ο ΠΡΟ ΦΗ ΤΗ
ΕΛΙ ΣΣΑΙ Ο
Ο ΠΡΟ ΦΗ

is hardly justifiable. Perhaps the notion of a prophetic ''office'', if abandoned, can be replaced by that of ''public poet''. Not that prophetic functionaries of different kinds did not exist. But perhaps the poets represented in the Latter Prophets used ''prophet'' as a term of abuse — implying that their rival poets were mere oracle-mongers, in the pay of the court or Temple.

ISAIAH

The book of Isaiah is the largest of the Latter Prophets. Moreover, this book offers the best opportunity for explaining how the words of an individual grow into a complex literary product over a long period.

Scholarship has long recognized three different, related sets of writings, which it refers to as First, Second (or Deutero-), and Third (or Trito-) Isaiah. The First, in chapters 1–39, is the Isaiah who is identified in the book. The Second, in chapters 40–55, is anonymous (or pseudonymous) but is generally thought to be a single poet. Finally, in Third Isaiah, chapters 55–66 are widely thought to be not one individual, but many different poets. The historical, as opposed to the literary, relationship between the three Isaiahs is an intriguing problem. The contributors to Third Isaiah are often thought to be disciples of Second Isaiah. But Second Isaiah has never been supposed to have met First Isaiah, since the Second was living in Babylon a century later than his predecessor. So Isaiah gives us a nice sample of the kinds of relationship between author and book which the Latter Prophets as a whole gives us — a named and dated historical figure at one end; an anonymous and only vaguely datable collection at the other.

The ''original'' Isaiah — ''Isaiah of Jerusalem'', according to the book — must have been born about 760 BCE and lived at least till 701, when Sennacherib besieged Jerusalem. There is no evidence for his often-assumed connections with the court and the Temple. The major political events of his life were the Syro-Ephraimite war, in which King Ahaz, opposed by Damascus and the northern kingdom of Israel called on Assyria to assist him; then later the unsuccessful gesture of revolt by Hezekiah against Assyria, which was averted at great price but by a means that remains obscure. This Isaiah seems to have spoken of the power of Yhwh in history and the social ills of Judean society, which he portrayed as rebellion against Yhwh's sovereignty. He viewed Judah as a remnant of the ''chosen people'' surviving after the end of the northern kingdom, confirming Yhwh's attachment to his Temple and city of Zion. Later editors of First Isaiah developed these themes further, enlarging his poems and adding new ones.

An example of the former process is Isaiah's speech to Ahaz (7: 3ff.) In response to an alliance between Israel and Syria which is threatening Judah, and to which Ahaz proposes to respond (and did) by summoning the help of Assyria, Isaiah calls for trust in Yhwh and predicts that Judah will be safe. Ahaz asks for a sign, which Isaiah offers (verses

OPPOSITE The prophet Elisha, a portrait from the dome of a twelfth-century monastery in Cyprus.

14ff.): a young woman will have a son, named Immanuel (''God with us''), and before this son reaches a certain age (presumably only a few years) there will come ''such days as have not come since the day that Ephraim departed from Judah'' (i.e. since the kingdom was divided). The promise must obviously have been in its original context a favourable one, or the entire conversation makes no sense. But what seems a promise is then turned into a threat by the addition of the sinister words ''the king of Assyria!'' The ''sign'' is now a prediction that Assyria will afflict Judah (Ahaz's ''father's house''). But immediately afterwards (verses 21–22), the threat is turned into a promise of peace and prosperity. Finally, in verses 23–25, that promise is reversed: where there used to be a thousand vines, there will be briers and thorns; men will come with bows and arrows. The ''original'' speech encouraged Ahaz to rely on Yhwh. As it happened he did not, and the result was Assyrian control of Judah. This is reflected in the first addition to the speech. But later Assyria was defeated, so that the Assyrian threat given by Isaiah was now understood as having been meant to apply to the fall of Samaria in 721 BCE — i.e. that part had been fulfilled. A better future could be read from the *original* oracle: everyone would, like Immanual (7: 15) eat ''curds and honey''. But after that, the land of Judah was partly depopulated by exile. So again, the prophecy was extended.

A different process by which the eighth-century prophet is made to speak to later days is illustrated in 39: 5–7, where he warns King Hezekiah of the Babylonian exile while Hezekiah is entertaining the king of Babylon! The inappropriateness and uselessness of such a prediction in that particular historical context, more than a century before it took place is underlined by Hezekiah's understandably placid reaction: ''The word of the Lord is good'', he says, realizing that it would all happen long after he was dead! We know that these words were written after the exile had occurred, since they are copied from the Deuteronomistic history that records the exile (2 Kings 20: 16–18).

As an example of straight insertion let us take chapters 24–27. It is a poem (possibly a group of poems) dealing with the question of Yhwh's ultimate purposes in history. They are generally agreed to be late insertions (possibly as late as the third century BCE); but whatever their structure or date, their position at the end of a series of poems dealing with foreign nations (chapters 13–23) shows that their function is to put such poems into a perspective, that of a new age about to dawn. They can thus be seen as independent compositions, as glosses on the Isaianic collection, and as part of the ''prophecy of Isaiah'', depending on the stance of the critic.

The processes just described make sense of any number of similarly obscure and contradictory passages in the Latter Prophets, and they demonstrate a concern with the continuing relevance of ''prophetic'' speeches as predictions of the future or even criticisms of social practice. But in what sort of context has this process taken place? Was there, as most scholars maintain, an ''Isaianic tradition'', preserved by "disciples"? The answer is probably no. The idea of a "prophet" having "disciples" who preserve his words is a product of modern imagination. The word translated "disciples" in Isaiah 8: 16–17 — to which appeal is often made — is better translated, "those I have instructed", i.e. the two witnesses to the tablet in 8: 1ff., and the "testimony" or "deposition" to be "bound up" is that tablet and not a prophecy.

Jeremiah is also said to have dictated a scroll to his scribe, Baruch (Jeremiah 36), but as the story makes clear this is to circumvent his lack of access to the Temple, where it is to be read out. There is no basis for supposing — as later tradition did — that Baruch was a disciple, or that he founded a Jeremianic school, or wrote the first draft of the book of Jeremiah. There are, in Isaiah 1–39, some prominent themes, but hardly of such distinctiveness or coherence as to characterize a "tradition". As for the development of the Isaianic collection itself, some scholars propose a major edition in the time of Josiah while others argue that the bulk of chapters 13–39 is post-exilic. At the other extreme, Hayes (1986) attributes most of the contents to Isaiah himself. Such disagreement about the extent of the original prophet's contribution is not unusual in the prophetic books of the Old Testament.

Second Isaiah

Chapters 40–55 of Isaiah originated in a different time and place from those of Isaiah of Jerusalem and contain a number of poems in which the Babylon invasion has already occurred. Cyrus is mentioned twice as Yhwh's appointed liberator, and, specifically, as the restorer of Jerusalem and its Temple. The imminent downfall of Babylon is repeatedly and gleefully anticipated. The exiles will be led back across the desert in a repeat of their first entry in Canaan, this time to a future which will be radically different from the past. The best known and most studied poems concern a "servant" (42: 1–9; 49: 1–6; 50: 4–9; 52: 13–53, 12), whom the poems describe as a recipient of Yhwh's spirit — gentle, just, the victim of human reproach. The last song dwells on his abasement and humiliation, his suffering for others, his intercession for rebels, and his vindication. The identity of the "servant" is much disputed. The poems were taken messianically by many Jews in the Second Temple period, as indeed they have been taken since by Christians. The poet himself, or even other heroes of Israel's past, have also been proposed as candidates. The now-traditional Jewish interpretation, and most biblical scholars, see in the "servant" the people of Israel collectively. Poetry, we should remember, thrives on such multiple interpretation; theology does not.

The poet presumably wrote in Babylon in the 540s. His view is that Yhwh, as the creator of the world, controls history. Yhwh is thus, as the only God, also the God of non-Judeans, though where exactly they fit into God's plans is not made clear. Babylonian gods, the poet declares, are human artefacts of wood, metal, or stone. He writes, at all events, to stir up in his fellow-exiles the hope and desire of returning soon to

Judah, with Babylon destroyed and Yhwh's sovereignty over the world acknowledged. The poetry is certainly of very high quality and, like all good poetry, transcends its particular historical context.

Third Isaiah

In Isaiah 56–66 we are mainly in the world of the Palestinian community soon after the "return", though the various poems come from different times: a rebuilt Temple is mentioned in 60: 13, but still awaited in 63: 18, while 66: 1–2a seems to reject such a temple, whether rebuilt or not. There are signs of division within the community between those who represent themselves as loyal to Yhwh and others who, being called "watchmen" and "shepherds" in 59: 9ff., may be community leaders. Similarities of style with Second Isaiah have been detected alongside sharp differences of subject matter. For example, 61: 1–3 reads very much like a deliberate development of 42: 1–4. But much of the content appears to be trying to come to terms with the fact that the eloquent promises in Second Isaiah of the restored Zion and Israel have not been fulfilled. One reason given (especially in chapter 59) is human injustice. Some scholars (e.g. Hanson, 1975) find in this collection indications of a basic rift in ideology in late sixth-century BCE Palestine, between returned exiles and those who had remained. But many of the poems may be later still. And it is always worthwhile remembering that one poet's view may be peculiar to him. Extracting social and religious history from poetry is precarious — even out of Isaiah of Jerusalem or Amos or Micah.

The separate consideration of the three Isaiahs does not, of course, address the question of the shape, intention, and date of the book as a whole. Answering these questions is not easy. Clements (1987) has suggested that Second Isaiah makes direct allusions to First Isaiah, and that the two collections were combined through their common concern with the fate of Zion and the Davidic dynasty. Third Isaiah is thought by many to be a deliberate development of ideas in Second Isaiah; it is possible that these two were combined even before being attached to First Isaiah. These considerations apart, the arrangement of the book into three sequential "sources" is instructive in confirming that under the rubric of one prophet the words of other prophets can be included, however different their style, historical context, or views. That these sources have been kept separate has allowed us to comment on them individually. But we have also seen that sources in the Latter Prophets are not usually separated, and are not intended to be.

The Latter Prophets as historical figures

Why certain individuals gave their names to books, and why there should be a distinction between the three major and twelve minor prophets we cannot easily answer. Generally speaking, it is significant that the earliest of the Latter Prophets date from just before the end of the northern kingdom. Perhaps the shock waves of this event created, first, a need for an explanation. Such an explanation, based on social abuses and the anger of the national god, is not by any means unique, but rather a norm among ancient Near Eastern cultures. In Judah these explanations would also be used as advance warnings of a similar fate to befall that kingdom.

Hosea

The book of Hosea dated by its superscription to the final decades of the kingdom of Israel. In chapter 1 Hosea is told by Yhwh to marry a whore; he does so, and she bears him three children, whose names proclaim Yhwh's rejection of Israel. Chapter 2 consists of a poem in which Yhwh reproaches Israel for her whorish behaviour in following other gods/lovers. In chapter 3 Hosea is told to take another woman. So far there is a certain coherence which may indicate the work of a single writer. After chapter 3 the structure falls apart, though there is a continuity of imagery and theme. The poetry attacks the transformation of the worship of Yhwh into a fertility religion, but it uses the language of fertility, characterizing Yhwh as Israel's true *baal* (which means husband and lord). The thrust of the poems is that after numerous betrayals by Israel, Yhwh is finally going to punish it.

Much of this, too, may have been written by Hosea, though we cannot be too certain. Interspersed with threats, however, are moments of hope and promise, whose authenticity remains disputed. Favourable references to Judah are generally thought to have been added later by Judahite writers to give reassurance that Judah would not necessarily go the way of Israel. Certainly, the book of Hosea, like all the prophetic books, has been produced in Judah, as the superscription, which dates primarily to Judean kings, shows. Perhaps, as many scholars think, the book's production was linked to the Deuteronomistic movement, whose language and themes it widely shares. But if Hosea the man addressed the kingdom of Israel, the book of Hosea addressed Judah at a later period.

Amos

A contemporary of Hosea, Amos is said (1: 1) to have been "among the *nōqedîm* from Tekoa", usually taken to be a village near Bethlehem, in Judah. A *nōqēd* is probably a sheep-rearer; the word occurs elsewhere only in 2 Kings 3: 4, where it is applied to Mesha, king of Moab! A popular image of Amos is that of a simple shepherd, but the text gives no evidence for this, apart from the writer's evident dislike of city-dwellers. A single biographical passage locates him at Bethel, where he is told to go to Judah and earn his living there. Amos denies being a prophet and claims that he was summoned by Yhwh "behind the flock". The book consists mainly of short sayings, but there are two long sections in 1: 3–2: 2, 16 (denouncements of nations, culminating in Israel) and a series of visions in chapters 7–9 which must have been originally in this extended form. The book has been edited in Judah — as witness the superscription, the insertion of an atypically mild oracle against Judah in 2: 5ff., and a promise of restoration for the "falling booth of David" in chapter 9. It also has some hymnic interpolations. Altogether, there is plentiful evidence of careful editing, together with a basic coherence of speech, which suggests that much of the material derives from one individual. Like Hosea's prophecy, the original warning to Israel has been reapplied in the wake of the fall of Samaria to Judah (Amos 9: 11ff.); however, it may suggest that the destruction of Jerusalem has taken place. Hosea and Amos, the earliest of the Latter Prophets, are quite different in every respect except their prediction of doom. Attempts to locate behind them a common "tradition" of prophecy remain largely unsuccessful.

Micah

According to the superscription, Micah was a contemporary of Isaiah from Moresheth, in Judah. His words, however, are addressed to both kingdoms. The poems in the book are arranged into two sets of threats (chapters 1–3 and 6: 1–7: 6) and two of promises (chapters 4–5 and 7: 7–20). The threats concern both Israel and Judah, and the complaints are directed at social abuses — greedy landowners, deceitful prophets, corrupt judges, avaricious priests. These negative passages can fit quite easily into the historical context of Micah, but the promises often presuppose the exile, especially the final section, which has a marked liturgical character. The contents would thus seem to reflect a rather longer period of growth. A number of linguistic and editorial similarities link Micah with Isaiah, and it is entirely possible that the books ascribed to these two seventh-century Judean figures were assembled by similar processes and perhaps within the same editorial circles (see Childs, 1979, p. 434ff.).

Jeremiah

We are told more of the individual Jeremiah and his background than of any other of the Latter Prophets, both in narrative and in first-person speech. He is said (1: 1–3) to have been a priest from Anathoth, in the land of Benjamin (but only 5 miles [8 kilometres] from Jerusalem), and was active, according to 1: 1–3 from 626 BCE until 586 (though many scholars now place the beginning of his activity after Josiah's death in 609). Although most of the book is set against the background of the last kings of Judah (Jehoiakim and Zedekiah), there are several speeches warning about an enemy from the north which do not seem to refer to Babylon and thus are placed earlier, in the reign of Josiah. The advice consistently given by Jeremiah is that because the impending fall of the city is, he says, a judgement from Yhwh, the Babylonians should not be resisted. Not surprisingly, Jeremiah met with popular and official displeasure.

Of how much of this profile can we be certain? Little information comes from material most plausibly ascribed to Jeremiah, and although many scholars feel confident in reconstructing quite precisely his life and

thc words that belong to each period in it, good reasons have also been
given for viewing Jeremiah as a shadowy figure, and as substantially
a creation of later groups, who between them brought the present
collection (or collections, for the Septuagint, the early Greek version
of the Old Testament (3rd-2nd century BCE) has a different selection
and arrangement) into being. Of all the prophets, Jeremiah, as an
individual human being who suffers from his call, has attracted the most
interest, although his so-called "confessions" may not be authentic. Like
Isaiah and Micah, the book contains material that relates to the Jerusalem
community of the Persian period.

Ezekiel

The problem of the book of Ezekiel, as B.S. Childs has pointed out (1979,
p. 357), is the difficulty of reconciling it with thc main features of Hebrew
prophecy as modern critical scholarship recognizes it. According to the
book, Exekiel was taken to Babylon with the first group of captives in
597/6 and settled in Tel Abib. He was a priest, and his ministry is dated
from 593 (1: 2). The major historical problem connected with the person
of Ezekiel himself arises from the fact that many of the speeches are
apparently addressed to the Palestinian community, rather than to the
exiles. The book claims that he visited Jerusalem in visions (e.g. 8: 1f.;
11: 1); and it has sometimes been asserted that his exile was a fiction
and that he remained in Jerusalem. The styles of speech familiar from
other prophetic books are also missing; instead we find a great deal of
allegory, vision, and symbolic acts. From his weird behaviour, a mental illness, such as schizophrenia, has more than once been suggested.
Once thought to be largely the work of Ezekiel, the book is now widely
regarded as a product of an Exekielian "school" following the work of
the German scholar W. Zimmerli (see chapter 17).

Haggai

Haggai is mentioned in Ezra 5: 1 and 6: 14, along with Zechariah, as
having "prophesied to the Jews who were in Judah and Jerusalem in
the name of the God of Israel who was over them", with the aim of
building the Temple. The book contains four "oracles" dated to the
second year of Darius (521–520 BCE). These are not in poetry. The first
two oracles indeed urge the building of the Temple: a third offers
more encouragement in the work; and the fourth hails Zerubbabel's
leadership in highly extravagant political terms. Chapter 1: 12–15 records
the consequences of the first oracle. But of the person or role of Haggai
we know no more. The editors of this book seem to have tried to
present Haggai as a direct successor of pre-exilic and exilic prophets by
using formulas such as "the word of the Lord came to"; but the
profile of Haggai emerges as a quite different one from an Amos or a
Jeremiah. He is a champion of the Temple and supporter of the
priesthood, a restorer of those institutions so often condemned in other
prophetic books.

Zechariah

Associated in Ezra with his contemporary Haggai, Zechariah is mentioned also in Nehemiah 12: 16, but only in a list of priests. It is common to separate chapters 9–14 from the rest as "Deutero-Zechariah," since they are believed to be unconnected with Zechariah himself. This leaves us with eight chapters consisting of a series of visions, followed by a loose collection of sayings, apparently originally prompted by a discussion about fasting. The visions, too, have been expanded. The principal topic in chapters 1–8 is, as in Haggai, the building of the Temple, but the form and tone are quite different from those of Haggai. The visions contain some weird images, interpreted by an angel, and they convey the expectation of great political upheaval. Other nations will be punished; Jerusalem will be preserved. If these visions come from Zechariah, we can say that he was not a speaker but a writer, whose medium was prose, rather than poetry. The tradition here seems to be closer to that of Ezekiel in both these respects.

About the remaining books of the minor prophets, we can say very little. Nahum, Joel, Habakkuk, Zephaniah, Obadiah and Malachi are entirely unknown figures; possibly some of the names are pseudonyms. Of the dates and circumstances of their composition, we can guess only from allusions to events like the fall of Nineveh in 612 (Nahum) or the advent of the Babylonians (Habakkuk). The book of Jonah, which describes the activities of a rebellious prophet, is best considered as a narrative (see Chapter 9).

On the whole, as this chapter has tried to show, prophecy can more fruitfully be studied as a literary corpus containing the accumulated words of many generations, which have in their continual re-forming of poems, narratives and oracles, overlaid whatever original 'prophetic' contribution may have existed. If this conclusion seems less straightforward and less satisfying than the biblical pictures of a sequence of inspired individuals, it reminds us that the Old Testament is not the work of a few great individuals but the work of a host of mostly unknown and entirely forgotten Israelites and Judeans who, generation after generation, kept the religious tradition alive by preserving, arranging and commenting upon what they had received from the past.

CHAPTER 13

WISDOM LITERATURE

T his chapter deals with a significant portion of Old Testament literature which — since it represents, in large measure, the ethos of the scribal classes to whom we owe the final shaping of the Bible — takes us to the heart of the character of the Old Testament itself. But the category of "wisdom" also embraces popular lore, such as "old wives' tales" and proverbs. In what follows, we shall try to define "wisdom", search for its adherents, explore its literary forms, and look at some of the wisdom books in the Old Testament and Apocrypha.

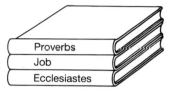

What is "Wisdom"?

One is often led to think of the Old Testament as a testimony to Israel's unique experience of God, conveyed in its own historical traditions and inspired by the doctrine of a covenant; however, there are large parts of Israel's scripture, namely the "wisdom literature", that take a quite different approach. The major books of this category are Proverbs, Job, and Ecclesiastes, and in the Apocrypha, Ben Sira and the Wisdom of Solomon. They share certain literary forms, such as the proverb, the parable, and the discourse, and also a stock of vocabulary — "understanding", "wisdom", "justice", "way" — much of it shared with other forms of literature, but used here either more frequently or in a more technical sense. Finally, they are bound together by a similar understanding of the meaning of life, or at least a disposition to approach the problem in a certain way. The leading principle of these writings is "wisdom", and even when this is not made explicit, a piece of wisdom writing can usually be identified by the implicit acknowledgement of this principle.

However, as with many of the categories with which biblical scholars work (we have already seen the problem with "prophecy" and will meet it again with "apocalyptic" in chapter 14), there are different ways of using the word "wisdom". The primary sense is — or should be, in a scholarly context — the literary one. We can classify wisdom literature on the basis of the criteria given above. But it is also common for biblical scholars to assume that behind any literary corpus lies a "tradition" which implies a particular set of conventions or, we might say, a common interest pointing to a concrete social group as authors and transmitters. This gives us a second usage: the tradition of such writing. Thirdly, ''wisdom'' has been understood as a set of ideas, an attitude; hence ''wisdom thinking''. In this sense it can be abstracted from its concrete social setting and analyzed as a system of thought.

As to the social setting of wisdom within Israel, there are several views. The narrowest sees it as the product of a certain class, the ''wise'', usually identified with scribes. A broader view sees wisdom as the product of intellectuals in Israelite society. An even broader view recognizes that there is also a popular element in wisdom, since proverbs and fables are common forms of folk literature. Of course it is not necessary to adopt any one of these views to the exclusion of the others. The wisdom literature that we have in the Old Testament may well be a product of the deliberate collection and cultivation of wisdom sayings and the development of a certain coherent attitude to the world and to humanity which such sayings support. This way of thinking, however, need not have been confined to a particular class but may have been of interest to a wider circle. And although folk sayings do not necessarily add up to a ''way of thinking'' in the same coherent sense as the ideas emanating from the ''wise'', folk wisdom is not a phenomenon to be disregarded. In view of what has just been said, it may seem that the term ''wisdom'' is far too broad and unwieldy. If we proceed carefully, however, we may still find it useful, especially if we concentrate our attention on the biblical wisdom literature itself.

TYPES OF WISDOM LITERATURE

''Instructions''

The last few decades have seen a number of different approaches to the definition of wisdom. On the one hand, attention to the linguistic and literary features has tended to lead to the assumption of a precise tradition linked with a precise social class, the ''wise'' or ''scribes'', as the creators and transmitters of wisdom. A major reason for this is the evidence of parallels to biblical wisdom literature in Egypt and Mesopotamia particularly. From Egypt we have many examples of what are called ''Instructions'', which date from much earlier than the biblical period. These contain practical advice for successful living, and they are largely written by or for pharaohs or their senior administrators. Hence the inference that this particular literary form derives from the court, an inference strengthened by the probable dependence of Proverbs 22: 17–24: 22 (the ''Words of the Wise'') on the *Instruction of Amen-em-ope*, dating from perhaps 1100 BCE. Moreover, the whole book of Proverbs is ascribed to ''Solomon, son of David, king of Israel'' (1: 1., cp. 10: 1), while 25: 1 contains the heading, ''These are also the proverbs of Solomon which the men of Hezekiah king of Judah copied''.

One may ask why this instruction should belong to the royal court? The reason may be — in Egypt anyway — that the king was regarded

Assyrian scribes depicted on a relief from Nineveh (seventh century BCE). The scribe in the foreground has a tablet of wet clay in his left hand and a stylus for inscribing the wedge-shaped syllables in his right hand. The other scribe appears to be holding a scroll. The depiction of one bearded and one shaven scribe, each with a different form of writing material, is found elsewhere and is probably conventional.

as the upholder of cosmic order, being himself a divine or quasi-divine being. The Egyptians also venerated a goddess called Maat, who represented such order, which included the proper administration of justice. Thus the concepts of royalty, divinity, and wisdom in various forms were interconnected.

A text from Mesopotamia known as the *Counsels of Wisdom* provides an instance of moral teaching given by a ruler to his son. In Israel, too, justice was the prerogative of the king, and wisdom the attribute that inspired justice and made it possible. The biblical story of Solomon's acquisition of wisdom (1 Kings 3: 5–15) is followed by the two major applications of that wisdom: wise judgement in a particular lawsuit (1 Kings 3: 16ff.) and administrative organization of his kingdom — bringing order to his realm. Social order was exercised through bureaucrats, whom Solomon is said to have appointed in large numbers (1 Kings 4: 1ff.). Such bureaucrats, it is claimed, were specially trained; their education, their ethos, and their view of life are enshrined in the Egyptian ''Instructions'' and in the Hebrew book of Proverbs.

Argument

Among the wisdom books of the Old Testament are Job and Ecclesiastes (Hebrew *Qoheleth*; see below), which certainly appear to question the confidence in natural justice and the ability to understand the world rationally which Proverbs entails. There were similar kinds of writing in Mesopotamia and Egypt. A work often referred to as the "Babylonian Job" (and sometimes as the "Babylonian *Qoheleth*") consists of a dialogue between a sufferer and a friend from whom he unsuccessfully seeks comfort; another text, "I will praise the Lord of Wisdom" (ANET 434–437), is the monologue of a person of high rank; he describes misfortunes that have beset him and blames the "lord of wisdom", Marduk, for these. He claims to have been righteous and finally records his deliverance, first through a dream and then in reality.

Narrative

A third form of wisdom literature, also connected with scribal and court circles, is the wisdom tale. The foremost example of this is the story of Aḥîqar, which seems to have been very well known throughout the ancient Near East (see chapter 9, p. 229). The earliest text we have is from the late fifth century BCE. It is certainly much quoted in the Apocryphal book of Tobit, and quotations or allusions have also been discerned in other biblical books, both Old and New Testament. It is the tale of a wise courtier (a "scribe") who, after misfortunes in life, is restored to an honoured place. The narrative is interspersed with wisdom sentences. There are several other examples in the Bible and Apocrypha of stories whose heroes are also honourable men of the scribe/sage class and who, by various stratagems and despite setbacks, achieve the place they deserve. We may include among these the story of Tobit himself, the contents of Daniel 1–6, perhaps Esther, and certainly the Joseph story (see chapter 9). These stories, though in the guise of folk tales, appear to be didactic, aiming to persuade the reader that virtue will, in the end, always achieve its due reward.

Manticism

In Mesopotamia, "wisdom" was predominantly associated with quite a different form of practice and the accumulation of quite a different kind of knowledge. The court and the temples were ministered to by several groups of practitioners of what we can call "mantic wisdom". This worked on the principle that understanding earthly things meant understanding the secrets of the heavens, and that these could be known by the interpretation of "signs" such as entrails, heavenly bodies, and unusual phenomena of various kinds. It produced a vast amount of literature based on the observation of such signs, on the basis of which not only could the future be predicted but also, by means of appropriate forms of preventive action, its negative aspects could be avoided. In the next chapter we shall describe this form of wisdom in some detail as the background to apocalyptic literature. In the Old Testament, mantics appear in Exodus 7: 11–12, where Moses' brother Aaron surpasses them in skill. And, of course, Joseph possesses mantic wisdom in his ability to interpret dreams.

WHO WERE THE "WISE"?

Wisdom and the scribal class

It is generally acknowledged that the profession of scribe existed, and that it is denoted in the Old Testament by the literal Hebrew translation, *sōfēr*. The scribes draw up contracts (Jeremiah 32: 12) and take dictation (Jeremiah 36: 26); there are royal administrators, the "king's scribes" (2 Chronicles 24: 11); and some scribes are attached to the army and the Temple, in which some had their own offices (Jeremiah 36: 10). In a word, they are civil and public servants, privileged members of a largely illiterate society. One view of wisdom literature is that it represents substantially the values of such a class (McKane 1965). Trained in political and diplomatic skills, they advised the monarch on policy (as does Ahithophel, David's "counsellor") and were pragmatic, worldly, and committed to order in human affairs and the enjoyment of life's benefits to the privileged. Scribal schools apparently existed in Mesopotamia and Egypt, where in addition to reading and writing, such values might also have been instilled into aspiring bureaucrats. If such schools existed also in Israel, presumably in Jerusalem, some of the wisdom literature in the Bible may have originated there.

Wisdom as an intellectual tradition

Another view (Whybray, 1974) of the milieu of "wisdom" is that it reflects the values of the intelligentsia. In every place and every time intellectuals bring their ideas to bear on life, and in particular on the problems of life on a personal, rather than a national, level. Modern intellectuals tend to use a particular kind of vocabulary and to read the same sort of books. But they are not a professional scribal class or caste, and the word "wise" does not seem entirely the right word to apply to a particular profession. "Wisdom" in the Old Testament (argues Whybray) was not peculiar to a certain profession, but was an attitude of mind found among people from different walks of life. Yet clearly the intellectual tradition must have been associated with certain professions, even as it is in modern society; one can easily name the professions in which one might expect to find intellectuals, and those in which one would not.

Folk wisdom

Another likely source of wisdom in ancient Israel is the extended family, which prevailed especially in rural areas. In the Israelite extended family circle, ethical instruction was conducted within the family, the moral code was defined by the social group, and justice was administered by the elders (see chapter 10). Other research into folk elements within the wisdom literature has strengthened and broadened this perspective. Fontaine (1982) has detected in the diplomatic correspondence of the Amarna letters associated with Pharaoh Akhenaten (and elsewhere), references to the custom of using proverbs as a means of settling disputes among and between tribes. In comparative studies of folklore, the existence of "folk wisdom" or "traditional wisdom" is firmly established, and the growing scholarly attention to biblical folklore is showing particular interest in the wisdom literature.

It is thus apparent that we must acknowledge that "wisdom" is a concept that covers a large number of related environments, functions, and traditions. We are justified in focusing attention on the formal preservation of wisdom in literary forms only because it is through this medium that the biblical literature has come to us. A discussion of wisdom from a social-scientific point of view, for example, would necessarily emphasize different aspects of the subject. But the essence of wisdom is its content, and our interest now lies in articulating the kinds of ideas that the Old Testament contains.

THE BOOK OF PROVERBS

Whether the proverb by itself implies a philosophy of life is a moot point. It does, however, carry the kernel of one. Its authority does not rest on any divine revelation, but is self-contained, drawing on human experience and inviting the listener or reader to test its truth against his or her own experience. The proverb often, though not always, carries some practical, even ethical element, being not simply a statement of act, but an implied recommendation to behave in a certain way. The same is true of those closely related popular forms, the parable and the fable. These are all forms of *instruction*. Moreover, one would hardly contest the claim that they belong to no single class or profession, but are universally employed and coined.

The book of Proverbs is not merely a ragbag of wise sayings; it is a collection including other collections. It also contains passages that are not proverbs but more extended discourses. Among the proverb collections are the "Proverbs of Solomon" (1: 1; 10: 1; and 25: 1). The "Sayings of the Wise" (22: 17 and 24: 23), the "Words of Agur" (30: 1), and the "Words of Lemuel" (31: 1). Within these units are extended passages such as the female personifications of wisdom and folly in chapters 7 and 8.

Types of proverb

The simple proverb, of which the book is mainly composed, comes in several different forms. It nearly always consists of two parts, but the types can be analyzed according to different criteria. For example, we can contrast the linguistic forms:

Statements of fact:

"'It is bad, it is bad', says the buyer, but when he goes away, he boasts." (20: 14)

Statements in which the consequence is also pointed out, so that they are exhortations rather than observations:

"Fear the Lord and the king, and do not disobey either of them; for disaster from them will arise suddenly." (24: 21–2)

Condemnations:

"The evil man has no future; the lamp of the wicked will be put out." (24: 20)

Antithetical comparisons:

"A wicked man earns deceptive wages, but one who sows righteousness gets a sure reward." (11: 18)

Commands:

"Leave the presence of a fool, for there you do not meet words of knowledge." (14: 7)

Antithethical commands:

"Do not reprove a scoffer, or he will hate you; reprove a wise man and he will love you." (9: 8)

Similes:

"As a door turns on its hinges, so does the lazy person in his bed." (26: 14)

Numerical sayings:

"Three things are too wonderful for me; four I do not understand . . . (30: 16ff.)

Some proverbs are combinations of these forms. Such formal classifications, although shedding little light on the content of proverbs, at least give an idea of the variety of approach.

As we have already noted, the book is not just a collection of individual sayings. The cumulative effect of a series of proverbs, even chosen at random, is not to be ignored. First, such a series produces reinforcement; the repetition of similar sorts of truth, especially if the external forms vary, tends, while it reduces the impact of any single proverb, to create a kind of awareness of the system of values being advocated. Second, the frequent contrast between types of behaviour or types of person — the "wicked" and the "righteous" or the "foolish" and the "wise" — conveys the perception that there are no shades of grey in these matters. There is a right thing to do and a wrong thing; a person is either wise or foolish.

Another type of analysis aims at distinctions of quality or character, rather than form. Some proverbs seem to be of popular origin. An example is "He who digs a pit will fall into it, and a stone will come back upon him who starts it rolling" (26: 27). Other proverbs seem more cultivated, and have perhaps been composed as an exercise in literary skill; for example, "Three things are too wonderful for me; four I do not understand; the way of an eagle in the sky, the way of a serpent on a rock, the way of a ship on the high seas, and the way of a man with a maiden" (30: 18–19). This is not so much a proverb as a riddle, so clever that one is constantly drawn back to it, each time with a new answer. One of the best interpretations is that it refers to different patterns of movement: the eagle circles, the snake zig-zags, the ship rolls and pitches . . . A third kind of proverb includes those that do not convey empirical wisdom but dictate what is or is not pleasing to God, or simply command obedience to his will, without stating what that will is. Of these there are numerous examples. From this kind of classification it is possible to posit a history of proverb collection; proverbs that belong originally to folklore become a popular sport of intellectuals, who try to coin their own; then, when wisdom becomes a servant of the orthodox religion, it is identified with obeying the will of God.

If the origins of proverbs (and the contents of the book of Proverbs) are so diverse, can we extrapolate from the contents anything like a "wisdom theology", or perhaps a wisdom "way of thinking"? The justification for looking for some kind of "meaning" in proverbs is twofold. First, it is part of the Bible, and was probably at some time thought to convey, as a whole, some coherent statement. Second, there are signs that parts of Proverbs have been assembled thematically, and perhaps even the entire book has been organized in some coherent manner. Two important features of a "theology" of Proverbs can be derived. One is the concept of order, particularly moral order; the other, which follows from the first, is that of retribution. The simplest way to expound this theory is to start with the statement of "Wisdom" herself in 8: 22ff.. She declares:

> Yhwh created me at the beginning of his work,
> the first of his acts of old,
> Ages ago I was set up,
> at the first, before the beginning of the earth . . .
> When he established the heavens
> I was there
> when he drew a circle on the face of the deep,
> when he made firm the skies above . . .
> then I was beside him, like a master workman
> and I was daily his delight.

This poem we can reasonably take as a cultivated literary composition, in which the nature of wisdom in the abstract is being discussed; it is a kind of meditation, or even a thesis, on what wisdom is, though expressed in poetry through an extended metaphor. What light does this throw on the collection of assorted sayings and exhortations in which it is embedded? What is the poem saying? It is saying that wisdom was the criterion or blueprint by which the earth was created. The world operates according to the principles of wisdom. It can also be seen as a comment on the proverbs contained in the book, identifying them, individually and collectively, as "wisdom" — that is, a description of how the world is. In other words, the world is rational and just.

This claim brings together the natural and the human, the individual and the social elements in proverbs. It also reconciles the tension between the empirical basis of some of the proverbs and the religious claims that wisdom comes from God. Since wisdom was built into the world by God, observation of the world delivers to the wise person the knowledge of God's will.

The book of Proverbs also expresses conviction in retribution. That is to say, when a proverb states the consequence of an action, the consequence emerges as a natural outcome, a just result of the deed. Wisdom literature as a whole does not as a rule deal in miraculous events, but confines its observations and deductions to the operations of the laws of nature, and it is in accordance with these laws that human behaviour receives its due recompense. The lack of any appeal to Israelite history or to covenant in Proverbs is quite understandable, since all people are equally subject to the laws of the natural world. The wisdom of Proverbs is personal, universal, and also implicitly monotheistic; its only God is the creator of the world in physical and moral order. Or, at the very least, perhaps, Proverbs tries to *impose* that order, believing that people should act as if it did exist.

We must not leave this topic without pointing out that even the wisdom ethic of Proverbs allows for limits to human understanding, and does not pretend to comprehend entirely the order of things. Wisdom cannot consist merely of knowing the proverbs. Wisdom must be a gift of knowing how and when to apply which proverb, of seeing order by instinct. Is this instinct what wisdom means by "knowledge" of God? Arguments continue to seethe as to whether the wisdom of Proverbs was originally, or is essentially, anthropocentric, even non-religious. The argument evaporates if we allow Proverbs its own formulation of what religion is, rather than trying to impose upon it a modern concept of religion or one we think represented the biblical "norm".

THE BOOK OF JOB

In the Hebrew Bible Job immediately precedes Proverbs. In the English Bible Job precedes Proverbs but is separated from it by Psalms. Christian and secular scholarship often treats Job as if it were a retort to Proverbs, whereas Jewish tradition tends to see matters the other way! The two books certainly represent different viewpoints, although both are wisdom literature. Job sarcastically rebukes his companions — "Truly you are men of knowledge, and wisdom will die with you!" (12: 2–3) — for his own predicament is that of one who does not understand, for whom the natural order makes no sense. The reader, who has the whole story (unlike Job), comprehends all. But, comprehending all, on whose side does the reader belong in the end? With or without the notion of a God who created order and remains just? The central challenge of the book of Job is to decide whether, in the end, order is re-established; whether justice rules.

The argument against the notion of a moral universe is nowhere more economically or cogently put than it is by the Satan to God: "Does Job serve God for nothing?" A philosopher might have devoted volumes to debating whether or not disinterested goodness is possible. If God is known to be just and thus to reward goodness, goodness can hardly be distinguished, even by the good person, from self-interest. If God does *not* reward goodness, he is unjust and has no right to demand goodness from humans. There is, of course, no answer. If wisdom is a way of thinking that employs observation and reasoning, it will inevitably stumble upon the unanswerable question, and here is a big one.

Apart from this large philosophical conundrum, Job also poses a structural problem: the story is contained in two and a half prose chapters, separated by nearly forty chapters of poetry, in which nothing happens but talk. For many scholars a solution can be found to both problems by supposing that the poem was originally separate from its framework. Considered by itself, the poem is open to a different interpretation. In these lines, only Job's faith is evident, not his righteousness; he ends not by being given back his goods in double measure but by meeting God. Job (as seen only in the poem) may then be either a righteous person, to whose legitimate challenge God responds with a personal reply, or, as some would assert, a self-righteous prig whom only a divine rebuke can puncture. The meaning of the poem itself surely lies in God's final speech (chapters 40–41), which, indeed, reads like a rebuke (unlike the mollifying divine words in chapter 42). God's answer to Job is that he has been trying to understand things which he cannot. To illustrate what Job is up against, God invokes his creative power. This, as we have seen in Proverbs, is an argument especially dear to wisdom literature. But here it is used differently. God does not point to the orderliness of nature, to the hills, rivers, and clouds; he does not present himself as a grand designer of a magnificent, orderly system. Instead he speaks of himself as one who created monstrous animals like the crocodile and the hippopotamus (Leviathan and Behemoth). Let man understand *these* creatures, mightier than men. If one cannot understand even these, how can one understand God? Job has been challenging God as a God of order and of justice. God responds as one whose ways do not make sense. One cannot "draw out" a crocodile, and one cannot "draw out" God in debate, either. One can only accept and fear these terrible beasts, and one can only accept and fear God.

So Job accepts, and so the poem undermines any complacency that wisdom might induce, any security in the ultimate *reasonableness* of life, or indeed of God. The poem, if anything, affirms God as a free agent, answerable to no-one, nor even to any principle such as justice. But God's speech to Job and Job's submissive acceptance is not the end of the book of Job. Job knows nothing of God's motives, and God does not speak of them. But the reader of the book knows more than Job does, or than God admits. For God has previously (1: 8–12; 2: 3–6) been challenged by the Satan to a test. God has accepted, and Job's sufferings will determine whether righteousness really exists or not. What a daring picture is being painted: the Satan is tempting God, and God is powerless to affect the outcome. That outcome lies in the hands of a human, the only one who can vindicate God. In the story the test is a test not of

Job but of God. And Job, not God, is the free agent.

How, then, does the ending of Job (chapter 42) strike the reader? After his powerful speech rebuking Job, God (who in the prose passages is called Yhwh) turns his anger on Job's companions (who have assumed that Job was guilty because of his afflictions), endorses everything that Job has said, and restores Job's fortunes. A complete reversal has occurred. Yhwh has changed his mind. Job had insisted that he was in the right and that God ought to vindicate him. God now agrees and vindicates him. The reader knows, too, that God has, through Job, surmounted the Satan's challenge. But the ending poses many problems. By restoring the fortunes of Job twofold, God is giving the game away; the old wisdom belief in God's justice and the prosperity of the righteous is reasserted. Job's companions, though rebuked, were basically right.

The ending of the book — and with it the meaning that the reader extracts from it — is not as simple as this. Job presumably knows that his good fortune is a blessing which God gives and can withhold: it is not — if it ever was — to be taken for granted. Moreover, now that disinterested righteousness has been demonstrated, God can feel free to reward it. But the book remains subversive. In explaining that material rewards are blessings of God and are not to be taken for granted, it still undermines the view represented in Proverbs that the reward of wise behaviour is security. And yet the book does not solve the problem of the suffering of the righteous. For if Job proved the existence of disinterested righteousness, for what divine motive can righteous people still suffer? The problem is not resolved by this book; indeed, it becomes more acute. The tensions in the book of Job are intrinsic to all wisdom: between the intellectual search for order and the experience of disorder, and between the knowability of God and the unknowability of God — or, put another way, the limitations of the intellect.

THE BOOK OF QOHELETH

The name *Qoheleth* (Greek translation, Ecclesiastes) is the author's own designation of himself. *Qāhāl* means "congregation", and the usual English rendering is, therefore, "preacher". But both *qāhāl and ekklēsia* can also mean "assembly", and in a non-religious context "orator" might be an appropriate translation. The contents of the book of Qoheleth offer an even more direct challenge than that of Job to the competence of wisdom. The author, in ironic vein, uses traditional methods to destroy traditional teachings. He appeals to experience but his own experience contradicts traditional experience. He appeals to the order of nature, but only to compare its permanence with the transience of human life. He recognizes the difference between the righteous and the wicked — and finds that they meet the same fate. He looks for success in life, and finds that it is an empty thing. Ironical too — if not intentionally so — is the traditional ascription of the book to Solomon, the personification of everything that this book denies! (This identification of Solomon as the author may derive from the Egyptian genre of collected sayings of royal individuals.)

The book is not a random collection of statements, but presents a series of topics. It opens with a demonstration of the ''vanity'' (better, ''emptiness'' or ''futility'') of human effort, which it characterizes as ''toil'' or ''labour'' (1: 12–2: 26). Then it shows the futility of attempting to find what lies in the past or the future. Things happen in their appointed time, and although this can be observed, it cannot be understood or predicted (3: 1–5). Justice is a vain pursuit (32: 16–22), as is wealth (5: 9–19). This is followed by observations on unpunished wickedness (8: 10–15), on the fact that all men share the same fate (9: 1–10) and, finally, on the brevity of life (11:7–12: 7), which is a continuing motif in the whole book. According to Qoheleth, there is a God, and there is a certain order which he has imposed. But humans cannot comprehend it and so cannot achieve any security, either material or spiritual. Reason and observation demonstrate no sense in human life.

Where Qoheleth stands apart from the wisdom of Proverbs is that he assumes an intensely personal perspective. Proverbs is essentially collective in its ethic, being an anthology of sayings from many sources and taking as its yardstick social values: respect, honour, wealth, posterity. It thus accords a certain authority both to society as a whole and to the tradition of wisdom sayings. Qoheleth does not. He observes on his own authority, and he is overwhelmed by the fact of death, presumably his own most of all. Does he, then, have any practical advice to offer? Despite the fact that he regards it as preferable not to have been born, he does not adovcate suicide, or even despair. He is more of a realist than a pessimist, and he is not without practical advice. Seven times he makes a specific recommendation, to be happy, enjoy life, eat and drink, have a cheerful heart (see Whybray, 1982). But he does not suggest that this can be done by abandoning oneself to a life of dissipation. Joy is to be found in eating and drinking, to be sure, but as regular human activities, not in the sense of revelry. He enjoins pleasure in work also. The proper response to life, according to Qoheleth, is to accept it, and while one has the opportunity, make the most of it.

From the evidence of both Job and Qoheleth, we can see that wisdom is not a body of doctrine, but a way of looking at the world which can produce quite different answers. Qoheleth was undoubtedly a controversial book, and later copiers or editors interlaced it with more conventional and pious comments (e.g. 2: 26; 7: 18; 8: 12–13). The end of the book provides evidence of lively reaction. After Qoheleth has ended with one of his recurrent slogans, ''All is vanity'', an appended note states that ''besides being wise, Qoheleth also taught the people knowledge . . . [He] sought to find pleasing words, and uprightly he wrote words of truth''. There follows another comment: ''The sayings of the wise are like goads . . . my son, beware of anything beyond these''. Then, finally, ''All has been heard. Fear God and keep his commandments; for this is the whole duty of man''. For some readers, evidently,

Qoheleth's words needed to have a health warning attached to them. The pursuit of wisdom does not necessarily, then, lead to knowledge of God, and certainly not to a consensus. In Qoheleth we have seen the limits, at least within the Bible, of an independent and critical use of wisdom. The attentive reader may even have realized that Proverbs, Job, and — with the exception of its pious additions — Ecclesiastes might have been preserved in cuneiform or hieroglyphs and found in Mesopotamia or Egypt. What is there in the contents of these books which would enable us to identify them as Israelite? The answer is that, frankly, these books have little or nothing distinctively "Israelite" about them — a point to which few biblical theologians address themselves. But the problem was certainly acknowledged within Israel. In the remaining wisdom books we shall find an attempt to integrate wisdom with other religious traditions and perspectives, such as the national historical traditions and the law.

Wisdom Psalms

Within the Psalter are psalms that reflect the wisdom of Proverbs and of Qoheleth and others that identify wisdom with obedience to the law in the manner we shall presently find in Ben Sira. Psalm 37 reads like a chapter from Proverbs. However, there are signs of an integration of these sentiments with other religious attitudes. There is increased emphasis on the promise that Yhwh himself will punish the wicked. He will look after the righteous in many ways and give them the "desires of their heart". Also — it is said several times — they will "live in the land", perhaps an allusion to the central promise of the Deuteronomic writings. Also, the righteous person has the "law of God in his heart" (verse 31). Rather than take refuge in the worlds of the wise, the psalmist urges refuge in God (verse 40).

Psalm 39 is closer to Qoheleth. Verses 4–6 dwell on the brevity of life, even its uncertainty: "Man heaps up, and knows not who will gather" (verse 6). There are also similarities with Job: the psalmist claims that he has committed no sin, but kept his mouth firmly closed, yet God has afflicted him. He asks God to "look away from me, that I may know gladness" (verse 13). Here the musings of the wise are brought to bear in an appeal to God to remove whatever distress he is believed to have brought — which Job did not ask for, and which Qoheleth would have regarded as futile.

The very first psalm is concerned with wisdom. It compares the righteous and the wicked; likens the righteous man to a tree planted by a stream, who prospers (an important term in wisdom vocabulary). Other wisdom words such as "way", "counsel", and "meditate", are also used: the psalm's language, tone, and structure are very like the "Instruction" (see above). But it does not use the word "wise", and it makes clear what the "blessed man" should do: meditate on God's law day and night.

The wisdom of Psalm 119 is less obvious, but a careful reading will show that it derives much of its style from wisdom literature. It is also saturated with the language of law — ''commandments'', ''testimonies'', ''precepts'', ''ordinances''. In the Second Temple Period the scribes, transferring their allegiance from the defunct court to the religious establishment, became, as Ezra was, more and more involved with the interpretation of the religious law, and with the transmission of other religious literature. We have seen scribal appendices to Qoheleth; there is another equally famous wisdom epilogue to Hosea; ''Whoever is wise, let him understand these things, whoever is discerning, let him know them, for the ways of the Lord are right . . . '' (14: 9). But as the influence and authority of the scribe waxed, so waned the independence of wisdom, which increasingly had to accommodate itself to the interpretation of authoritative texts. Speculation and the search for the meaning of things was to survive in the vein of mantic wisdom (see chapter 14), but there was to be limited scope for ''wisdom'' as a means of religious knowledge independent of both the law and Israel's own sacred traditions.

BEN SIRA

Yeshu ben Sirach (or Sira) lived at the end of the third century BCE, and his book (included in the Apocrypha and known as Ecclesiasticus) is a collection of his own sayings, presented in the well known form of the Instruction. However, the book also includes some extended essays and hymns of his own composition. The topics range widely, but his central theme is the ''fear of the Lord''. What does this mean? ''Fear of the Lord'' is an attitude of reverence which will prompt the righteous man to seek to do the divine will and to seek divine guidance in fulfilling it. But as to Ben Sira's understanding of the relationship between ''wisdom'' and ''torah'', (understood as the revealed will of God, primarily in scripture, often translated as ''law'') there remains some uncertainty. Some find him convinced that true wisdom is enshrined in the law of Moses; others claim that his allegiance was primarily to wisdom, and that he sought to explain the law as wisdom, rather than wisdom as the law. The most probable explanation is that Ben Sira regarded both wisdom and the law as leading to the ''fear of the Lord'', and as ideally in harmony. But if they came into conflict, he had no doubt:

> Better is the man who fears God without understanding
> than a man of prudence who transgresses the law. (19: 24)

> How great is one who has gained wisdom
> But there is none above him who fears the Lord. (25: 10)

> All wisdom is the fear of the Lord
> And in all wisdom fulfilment of the law. (19: 20)

On the other hand, Ben Sira utters a great hymn to wisdom in chapter 24, and he advises the study of sages and of elders. His allegiance to the priesthood is also manifest. His greatest heroes are priests, and his description of the contemporary high priest is magnificent (50: 6–8).

The way to understand Ben Sira is not as a great thinker, or even a very consistent one, but as a practical man. The overwhelming impression one gets from reading his words is of a great compromiser. On almost every question, he fudges. On the relationship between wisdom and the law he wants to approve both. On giving to the poor he advises giving, but not too much. He advises a sick person to call the doctor but also to pray for healing. He says that sin came into the world through a woman, and also that sin is every person's responsibility. He says that wisdom can be obtained but also that it is beyond man. Does retribution overtake the wicked man? The answer is either "wait and see" or the suggestion that it does in the last moments of his life. Ben Sira certainly does not believe in being dogmatic, but in treating each case on its merits, using common sense and divine guidance. It is perhaps not appropriate, then, to search too strenuously for a clear point of view.

It has been thought that Ben Sira can best be understood against a background of cultural conflict, when Hellenism was making a serious impact on religious belief within Judaism (see chapter 7). It is quite possible that his work is an attempt to tread a middle ground between two ideologies and their adherents. The extensive treatment of the topic of God's justice suggests that some Jews were abandoning their religion because they did not accept the idea of this justice. On the other hand, there were those attracted by wisdom but preferring the Hellenistic kind. It is indeed possible to see in Ben Sira attempts to accommodate varying viewpoints and to define a fairly catholic form of Judaism. Certainly, wisdom plays a central part in this, but quite clearly it is expected to supplement and to support the distinctive religious traditions of his own people. Ben Sira looks forward to national independence; his book is also littered with references to the Scriptures (for a list see Crenshaw 1981, p. 150f.). The scribe, or wise man, is now a pillar of the religious establishment, an affirmer, and an optimist — not a critic or questioner like Job or Qoheleth.

THE WISDOM OF SOLOMON

This work, written probably in the first century CE in Alexandria, represents an attempt to adapt the wisdom tradition for a people living in a non-Jewish city —indeed, an Egyptian city and one of the cultural centres of the Mediterranean world. The Solomonic ascription is a convention: the book employs both the Greek language and a Greek literary style. A prominent theme of the book is the election and protection of Israel by God — the nationalistic sentiment we also noticed in Ben Sira. But whereas Ben Sira did not wish, or perhaps need, to defend this claim, the Wisdom of Solomon appeals to divine sovereignty. God has chosen, and upon his chosen people (though not upon others) he exercises compassion. Thus election precedes justice. This position, however, is qualified by introducing foreknowledge: God knew that Gentiles would not abandon their folly, so he did not consider choosing them! Much of the polemic of the book concentrates on idol-worship, which makes it clear that the danger being confronted was non-Jewish religion. On the other hand, the book retains the universal dimension of wisdom, in the form of a predicted battle in which cosmic elements join forces against the power of wickedness.

The concept of wisdom itself is highly developed here. It becomes a projection of God, an advance on the personification in Proverbs. Whereas in Proverbs Wisdom claims to have attended God in the creation of the world. Wisdom here becomes the agent that guided Israel's early history, starting with Adam and culminating with Moses. In the final ten chapters the author uses the Exodus story to develop a contrast between Israel and Egypt. Wisdom is Solomon's bride; an emanation directly from God; the source of all knowledge, including all the sciences and arts learned in the Hellenistic schools.

Despite its hostility to Egyptians in particular and to Hellenistic culture in general, the Wisdom of Solomon assimilates many ideas from its environment. In particular it believes in the immortality of the soul, which it describes as a mind imprisoned in a body. This permits the belief that long life is not necessarily a great reward and that retribution and recompense can take place after death.

Conversely, the connections between the Wisdom of Solomon and traditional Hebrew wisdom appear tenuous. The appeal to human experience is absent, and the universal dimension of human experience is obliterated by a concern to contrast God's treatment of Israel with his treatment of Gentiles. Concern with material well-being in this life, with death, and with individual suffering are absent. And there is, like Ben Sira, no place for doubt or questioning.

We can explain the attitudes of Ben Sira and the Wisdom of Solomon in terms of social and religious identity, so long as we realize that such an explanation is only partial and that individual authors do not necessarily represent their society in every respect. Where identity is not at risk, speculation, free-thinking, toleration of differing viewpoints can exist. In the face of a threat to identity, however, different emphases must come to the fore. Ben Sira wrote in Palestine and in Hebrew, in a milieu that was open to other cultural influences and yet wary of them. His attitude of compromise together with his dedication to the national institutions, addresses a society uncertain of how far to accommodate its beliefs to alien ways of thinking. Compromise, which Ben Sira advocated, was to be ruled out within a few decades of his death by the force of events.

By contrast, the Wisdom of Solomon is an extreme case of a community seeking to define and assert its identity. It does this by reinterpreting its own traditions, but *in the presence and forms of its new environment*, because this is where the community feels at home.

Wisdom, then, has travelled from the court, the extended family, through the individual protester, to the Jewish community in an alien environment. It has expressed scepticism and has upheld religious dogma. It is indeed an elusive quality. But for all its variety, it remains an important aspect of the religious orientation of the Old Testament, and enables the traditional tenets of the religion of Israel to be accommodated within the cosmopolitan culture into which Israel found itself increasingly drawn.

CHAPTER 14

APOCALYPTIC LITERATURE

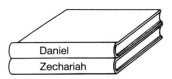

Daniel
Zechariah

THE MEANING OF ''APOCALYPTIC''

The word ''apocalyptic'' nowadays is used to describe a scenario that heralds the end of the world, or at least the end of life, or civilization, as we know it. This meaning lies some distance from the original meaning of the word. The Greek word *apokalypsis* means ''revelation'' and is the Greek name (and the first word) of the New Testament book of Revelation. That book contains many descriptions of future events, particularly a time of great distress and persecution, followed by one of judgement and of bliss for the faithful. A number of books of this kind were written during the Greco-Roman period, not only by Jews and Christians, but also by Greeks, Romans, Egyptians, and Persians. These, too, have come to be known as ''apocalypses''. An apocalypse is thus a genre of literature which, using certain devices and conventions to be explained presently, conveys what are claimed as direct revelations from heaven, given usually in a vision or by angelic dictation, and often ascribed to a venerated figure of antiquity; in the latter case celestial journeys to heaven may be the author's means of discovering the heavenly secrets. We should be careful to remember that although many such books sought to disclose the future, others had additional — or completely different aims. They might offer revelations about the law, or about the movements of the star, or the meaning of history, or the geography of heaven, the names of angels, or even the appearance of God.

Besides referring to a literary genre, the adjective ''apocalyptic'' has acquired, among biblical scholars and theologians, wider uses, which are not altogether helpful, but which the reader may encounter in other texts. ''Apocalyptic'' or ''apocalypticism'' is sometimes used to describe a way of thinking, even a kind of religion, which is other-wordly and focused on some imminent moment which will bring the world-order to an end. On other occasions, ''apocalyptic'' may be used to mean ''eschatology'', or ''eschatological'', which means belonging to the end of things, concerned with the end or goal of history or the cosmos. Finally, ''apocalyptic'' is occasionally used of communities that are created or sustained by hope or belief that the order will soon change; and hence literary apocalypses have tended to be understood in some quarters as being the product of millenarian sects. One can see how these meanings bring us to the contemporary usage of the term ''apocalyptic''. But they are really not very helpful in the examination of ancient apocalypses, which were generally not produced by sects, often not concerned with the future, and, so far as their world-view is concerned, not very different from popular beliefs, which included the existence of demons and angels, astrology, incantations, magic and exorcism. Apocalypses are really a refined expression of a religion that believes in the overwhelming reality of the transcendental world and its effects on everyday life. Such a religion also believes, together with popular superstition, that the heavenly world can be interpreted and understood by various means.

In the Old Testament, apocalyptic literature (or simply''apocalyptic'', as the genre is often called) might not seem to occupy a prominent place. There is only one book that falls into this category, namely Daniel. But if we are interested in the world that the Bible reflects — and not just the physical world but the world of ideas as well — we must take account of the fact that there is a fairly large body of Jewish apocalyptic literature outside the Scriptures, some of it as old as later parts of the Old Testament itself. In this chapter we shall first try to discover what kind of religious and social background this kind of writing might reflect. We shall find ourselves dealing with a class of scribes who, apart from being responsible for writing apocalypses, were as much the religious leaders of Second Temple Jewish society as were the priests, and certainly as influential. These men were the copiers and compilers of prophetic and wisdom books; they were students of the law; they were teachers. They were the theologians, and also part of the ''establishment''. Despite its poor representation in the Bible, apocalyptic literature is not a fringe activity, nor are its contents peripheral to an understanding of Judaism (or Christianity, for that matter). It represents the essence of both popular and élite Jewish religion in the Greco-Roman period.

It would be impossible even to begin to cover the range of apocalyptic writings now known to us that date from between 300 BCE and 100 CE; for this the reader can consult *The Old Testament Pseudepigrapha I* (Charlesworth 1983). Instead, we shall, in the last part of this chapter, focus attention on the book of Daniel and the book of 1 Enoch, which, in the form we now have it, contains the earliest and in many respects most important Palestinian Jewish apocalypses (Enoch himself is referred to in the New Testament, in Jude verses 14–15. The material in this collection known as 1 Enoch dates from the third century BCE onwards and is often simply referred to as the 'book of Enoch'.

APOCALYPTIC SUBJECT MATTER

The apocalypse, as we have said, is a literary genre that claims to impart knowledge of heavenly secrets. In what way does an apocalypse differ from wisdom or prophecy, or law? The contents of these, too, are often explicitly or implicitly "revealed". The differences lie, basically, in the words "knowledge" and "secrets". Prophecy is a public announcement of a message that God wishes the recipient to hear.Instruction is worldly wisdom derived from observation and experience by a sage and passed on in his name to his disciples or a wider audience. The apocalypse pretends to offer what cannot be normally known and what is not supposed to be known, or at least widely known. And, unlike prophecy and instruction, it is not an exhortation to behave in a certain way. It is essentially "privileged information" which enables the recipient to know what is "going on". This knowledge is the key to salvation.

Naturally, since this knowledge is presumed to be confidential, the apocalypse employs devices to explain how it has been acquired. The name of the recipient of the knowledge and (pretended) author of the book is given, along with details of the experience by which his (or her) knowledge was obtained. More often than not, the "author" is a great figure of the past — Daniel, Enoch, Moses, even Adam — hence many apocalypses are "pseudepigrapha" — given a specious authorship. The "knowledge" they contain is acquired by dream, vision, angelic tip-off, or even (as with Enoch) a guided tour of heaven itself. Sometimes the knowledge is encoded in the natural world — the movements of the stars, the calendar, events of history; sometimes in holy books, such as ancient prophecies, in which case the author of the apocalypse derives from heaven the true meaning (as we shall see in Daniel 9). The "author' is often claimed to have passed his knowledge on to his children, or to have written it down in a book which the reader is to assume has never been published, or only recently. In this respect, the book of Revelation, paradoxical as this may seem, is not like other apocalypses; and actually does not call itself an apocalypse. The "revelation" of its opening verse refers to what is described, not the book itself — and the author actually dubs his words "prophecy" (1: 3).

We may finally note that apocalypses represent the world as governed from heaven, and thus can imply, where they do not make it clear, that everything is predetermined. Were it not so, the universe would not be orderly, and nothing could be learned about it which would enable humans to understand. In a way, apocalyptic literature is trying to grasp the sense that lies beneath the nonsense of the present world — or, more graphically, the sense which lies *above* it!

What sort of culture produces works that speculate on what happens behind the scenes? What sort of culture is concerned with the hidden, the mysterious, the unknown? Not prophets, or the authors of proverbs. For these, what God revealed was sufficient, and what lay beyond was not for humans to penetrate. For the origins of apocalyptic writing we must go outside the orbit of Israelite prophecy and wisdom and look at an aspect of religion that was prevalent throughout the ancient Near East, including ancient Israel: divination.

DIVINATION

Babylonian mantics

Manticism is a name for a system of belief and practice in the discovery of heavenly secrets from earthly signs. The signs may be encoded in animal entrails, in anomalous births, in the movements of the heavenly bodies and in dreams. These are collectively called "omens", and each of these kinds of omen requires learning the decipherment appropriate to it. Guilds of mantic priests/diviners existed in Mesopotamia from well before the biblical period.

Interpretation of omens presupposes a belief in the possibility of communication with supernatural forces — forces that encode their secrets in signs on earth. Interpreting such signs reveals the intentions of the gods and can help to avert what is projected for the future, be it for the nation or the individual. Two-way communication could be conducted through pouring oil on water or making smoke. We have from Babylonia extensive lists of omens and their meanings, typically in the form "if . . . then . . . ", listing the consequences expected to derive from certain phenomena. If the presupposition was not scientific, the procedures were, and, in the case of observing the heavenly bodies, led to astronomy as well as astrology. To sum up: manticism was based on the interpretation of signs as a means of determining the will of the gods, especially for the future.

The omen literature seems to have played a role in the development of other literary types, such as the so-called "Akkadian prophecies" or "Akkadian apocalypses". These are essentially "predictions" of past events, which usually conclude with a genuine prediction. The statements about historical events past and present are markedly similar to the interpretation of an omen on an omen-list. The point here is not that these are also based on omens, but that the presuppositions of manticism and the language of the omen literature could be taken over into other literary forms. And all this was the product of a central cultic institution, the mantic priests/prophets or bārû.

Divination in Israel

The extensive records of Babylonian manticism raise a question: Did this sort of thing occur also in ancient Israel? Now, divination (which is what manticism deals in) was practised, but condemned in the Old Testament:

> There shall not be found among you . . . any one who practises divination, a soothsayer, or an augur, or a sorcerer, or a charmer, or a medium, or a wizard, or a necromancer.
>
> (Deuteronomy, 18: 10–11)

Jeremiah condemns prophets and diviners in the same breath:

> The prophets . . . are prophesying to you a lying vision, worthless divination . . .
>
> (Jeremiah 14: 14; cp. 27: 9–10 and 29: 8–9)

During their exile in Babylonia the Jews were exposed to a religious culture dominated by manticism. Isaiah 47:9–15 gives an eloquent condemnation of this practice:

> In spite of your many sorceries and the great power of your enchantments . . . Evil shall come upon you for which you cannot atone; disaster shall rain upon you which you will not be able to expiate; and ruin shall come on you suddenly, of which you know nothing. Stand fast in your enchantments and your many sorceries with which you have laboured from your youth; perhaps you may be able to succeed, perhaps you may inspire terror. You are wearied with your many counsels; let them stand forth and save you, those who divide the heavens, who gaze at the stars, who at the new moons predict what shall befall you . . . .

The passion of this nationalistic and fervent Yahwist contrasts with the patient and faithful service of the "wise man" Daniel, who learnt the wisdom of the Babylonians, surpassed them in his mastery of it, and rescued them from extermination (Daniel 2). He is superior to them because his God, the Most High, is the true source of all knowledge and can reveal secrets to whom he chooses. Nevertheless, deciphering writing on the wall is manticism, and the writing of pseudo-predictions of history (Daniel 11) a by-product of mantic literature. Daniel is a *true* mantic, that is all — a *Jewish* mantic. How has this come about?

Mantic wisdom

In the Neo-Babylonian and Persian periods Babylonian mantic traditions were known as far west as Greece; eventually they reached Rome. By the time of the first Jewish apocalypses, in the Greco-Roman period, manticism formed part of a culture in which Judea was inevitably immersed. In Babylonia the mantic class, who increasingly focused on astrology, came to be called "Chaldean" (as in Daniel); the mantic priestly class of the Persians were the Magi whose religion was Zoroastrianism and whose speciality was the interpreting of dreams. But the Magi gradually became identified with the Chaldean astrologers. Thus Matthew's "wise men from the East" (*magoi*) are guided to Bethlehem by a star, and are warned in a dream to return home without seeing Herod. Other Magian beliefs and practices included the worship of Zurvan, a time-deity, and with him the notion of world-epochs. Ahura-Mazda, the creator, was their chief god, and they also believed in the pre-natal and post-mortem existence of the soul in the realm of light. Such beliefs, in fact, profoundly influenced Judaism in the Greco-Roman period.

In the Persian and Greco-Roman periods we are examining, however, manticism is no longer tied to a cult. We are talking less about priests practising manticism and more about scribes using and developing its lore. The word "scribe" in this period refers, broadly to the writing classes, including readers and writers of ancient texts, administrators and bureaucrats, teachers, linguists, historians and scientists. Is this a single profession? Hardly; but it certainly is a *class*, and perhaps a sufficiently coherent one to share several cultural assumptions. Among the famous scribes, real or fictitious, who figure in this period are Ezra, Daniel, Enoch, and Ben Sira. Here is how the latter, who lived a few decades before the book of Daniel was produced, picked the scribal activity:

> . . . he who applies himself to the fear of God
> And to set his mind to the law of the Most High
> Who searches out the wisdom of all the ancients
> And occupies himself with the prophets of old
> Who attends to what eminent men say
> And investigates the deep meaning of parables
> Searches out the hidden meaning of proverbs
> And is acquainted with the obscurities of parables . . .
>
> He shall be filled with the spirit of understanding
> He himself pour out wise sayings in double measure . . .
> He himself direct counsel and knowledge
> And set his mind on their secrets
> He himself declare wise instruction . . . .

(Ben Sira 39; 1–8)

Note here the preoccupation with understanding secrets, which includes parables and proverbs (as we might expect of a wise man), but also prophetic sayings. And what is the "wisdom of the ancients"? We find a clue in Ben Sira's litany of great figures from the past (chapters 44 – 49), which begins and ends with Enoch. Now, there is hardly any more "establishment" figure than Ben Sira. He reveres the priesthood, the Temple, and the cult. His greatest concern is the law. He is knowledgeable in the Scriptures. At the same time, he studies prophecies and proverbs, the meanings of hidden things, and ancient sayings. He shows us that he is quite at home with typical apocalyptic topics — myths, historical reviews, eschatology and heavenly secrets, and profound old sayings.

JEWISH APOCALYPSES

It is now time to turn to the earliest Jewish apocalypses, which those familiar with Old Testament literature often find hard to understand. The language and even the *point* of a lot of apocalyptic writing can seem elusive. But, after the rather lengthy introduction, perhaps what follows will not seem so strange. At all events, it would not have seemed strange to any ancient reader.

Enoch

We must look at 1 Enoch first, because, although not part of the Old Testament, it contains the earliest known Jewish apocalypses. In fact, the book is a collection of writings attributed to Enoch. Thanks to the discovery of literary fragments at Qumran, we can now confidently date the collection (except for chapters 37–71) to the pre-Christian era, and the earliest parts to the third century BCE. The four early Enoch books in this collection are the Astronomical book (chapters 72–92), the book of the Watchers (chapters 1–36), the epistle of Enoch (chapters 91–105) and the book of Dreams (chapters 83–90). They represent a body of traditions, rather than a single tradition, and we shall concentrate on some of those features that bear on the Old Testament and on the literary forms and ideas that lie behind the creation of apocalypses.

How did Enoch become a patron of apocalyptic literature? The biblical notice about him (Genesis 5: 18–24) is brief: he was the son of Jared and father of Methuselah; he lived 365 years and then "walked with God". Then "he was not, for God took him". It is usual to consider this tantalizing hint of something special as the origin of the Jewish Enoch tradition; his lifespan suggests a connection with the solar calendar, and his manner of departure suggests that he did not die. As for "walking with God", this suggests a fairly intimate acquaintance. But this assumption is probably the reverse of the truth. There are good reasons for seeing Enoch as derived from an old Sumerian prototype, in which case the biblical mention perhaps refers to an existing Enoch tradition, which it declines to relate. This, after all, would be consistent with the tendency of biblical literature to allude to myths and legends which it did not desire to expound. For the reference to Enoch in Genesis 5 departs from the norm (in the curious "walking with God") and 365 years is a far lower figure than found elsewhere in the chapter. Genesis 5, then, does not give us the starting point for the Enoch legend.

The legend begins rather, with the Sumerian King List. This is a list of rulers of Sumer before the Flood, and is preserved in several forms, including Berossus (see ANET, p. 265). Here one of the kings, often given as the seventh (as Enoch is in his list), is called Enmeduranki or Enmeduranna. He is generally associated with the city of Sippar, which was the home of the cult of the sun god Shamash. Moreover, in other texts (see VanderKam 1984, p. 39ff.) this Enmeduranki was the first to be shown, by Adad and Shamash, three techniques of divination: pouring oil on water, inspecting a liver, and the use of a cedar (rod), whose function is still unclear. These were to be transmitted from generation to generation, and in fact became the property of the guild of *bārû*, the major group of diviners in Babylon.

These details show how the biblical portrait of Enoch may have been compiled from Enmeduranki: each is seventh in the antediluvian list; the biblical 365 preserves the affinity to the sun, rather than the sun god; walking with God (or perhaps, "angels"?) suggests the intimacy between god(s) and man. The final connection links not with Enmeduranki, but with a fish-man (*apkallū*), with which each of the first seven kings associated and from whom they learnt all kinds of knowledge. Enmeduranki's *apkallū*, called Utu'abzu, is mentioned in another cuneiform text, where he is said to have ascended to heaven. This last link remains provisional; but at all events, the writer of Genesis 5: 21–24 appears either to have created Enoch as a counterpart of Enmeduranki or, equally probably, to have alluded to an already existing Jewish tradition about Enoch, already modelled on the earlier figure.

In the Astronomical book, possibly from the third century BCE, Enoch reveals to his son Methuselah what the angel Uriel had shown him of the workings of the sun, moon, and stars. Most of this book is entirely scientific, being a description of the movements of the heavenly bodies, ostensibly revealed in heaven, but obviously the result of many generations of sky-watching. However, there is a brief section (chapters 80–81) which is especially important. Here Enoch also tells of the deeds of righteous and unrighteous men, forecasting a disruption in the natural order. It is very likely that this passage is not original, and its presence shows us how a text of purely astronomical observations was used in the service of ethical exhortation and eschatological prediction — something closer to what have traditionally been regarded as apocalyptic concerns. One way in which ''apocalypses'' emerge is by the application of ethical concerns and warnings about the future to what are otherwise not much more than lists of things revealed (see Stone 1976).

In the book of the Watchers, perhaps compiled in the late third century BCE, the interests in natural (and supernatural) phenomena acquire a more ethical dimension (as in the additional chapters of the Astronomical book), and in connection with these ethical concerns, we find speculation about the beginning and the end of the present order, particularly the origin of sinfulness and its ultimate solution. These ethical concerns can be seen, perhaps, as a broadening of the traditional emphases of wisdom — from a concern with right behaviour and with harmony with the natural order, through the mantic-scribal involvement with ancient lore, including myths; to speculation about the transcendent world. This development brings the Enoch tradition even closer to what are generally recognized as ''apocalyptic'' concerns.

The book of the Watchers opens (chapters 1–5) with a warning which applies the orderliness of the natural world in obeying the laws set for it by God to an ethical and eschatological argument. Those who adhere to these natural laws are righteous; those who do not are sinners. Note that righteousness and wickedness are seen as a function of *knowledge* and *understanding*, rather than of simple obedience, a pervasive theme of both wisdom and apocalyptic writings, with their emphasis on the created order, and not on a set of covenant laws. Although the Enoch corpus does not contain very much direct or indirect interpretation of Scripture, chapters 1–5 seem quite clearly modelled on Balaam (Numbers 22–24) — though we now know that this tradition was not confined to Israel. Chapters 6–11 describe how it was that sin first came into the world, with the descent of heavenly beings called the Watchers. Once again we encounter in Enoch a fuller version of an episode that is only briefly related in the Old Testament; and once again we have to ask whether this fuller version is an imaginative expansion of the biblical text or the biblical text a highly condensed version of the fuller story.

The biblical episode is in Genesis 6: 1–6, where the "children of God" come down and have intercourse with women producing a race of *Nephilim*, "mighty men that were of old, men of renown". First Enoch 6–11 has woven together two versions of a fuller account in which a group of Watchers descend, "defile themselves with women" and then teach the women about spells, root-cutting and plants, astrology, weapons of war, and cosmetics. The women give birth to giants, who turn to cannibalism and drinking blood. The earth cries out to heaven for help, and God orders the execution of the giants, the binding of the Watchers beneath the hills until the day of judgement; thereafter in a fiery chasm. The leader according to one version, Azazel/Asa'el, is buried under a rock, until, after judgement, he is hurled into the fire.

Many scholars take the view that this story, in its various forms, is inspired by the Greek legend of Prometheus, the Titan who brought heavenly secrets to men, and that it has developed the Genesis story. But the biblical story itself makes little sense except as an allusion to some fuller version. The parallels between the story of the Watchers and the story of Cain are also intriguing: bloodshed on the earth, the earth crying out, the villain cast into the desert, the acquisition of technology, and the increase of violence among descendants. Furthermore, the Enoch story explains the ritual of the scapegoat of Leviticus 16, where a goat is sent into the wilderness "for Azazel". The biblical account of the ritual makes sense in the light of the fate of Azazel in Enoch. It is thus difficult to explain the Enoch story simply as an expansion of Genesis 6: 1–4. More probably it is a version of an older myth about the origin of sin, which held sin to have originated in heaven and been brought to earth together with illicit knowledge which enabled mankind to progress in arts and sciences. Isaiah 14: 12 possibly echoes a story about a fallen rebellious angel whom it names as the morning star (note the later identification of Satan with Lucifer ["light-bearer"] in Christian mythology). Even Psalm 82 may refer to a form of this myth, if we translate verse 7, "Yet you shall die like Adam, and fall like one of the angels".

Later in the book of the Watchers Enoch enters the divine presence, and learns in more detail about the future. Here he is called a "scribe of righteousness", who records the divine sentence on the Watchers. But in this capacity he also intercedes for them with God. In the rest of this book, Enoch travels twice, to the west and around the world, including visits to Jerusalem, Eden, and Sheol, thus adding a knowledge of geography to his understanding of astronomy. In all this, we can see Enoch as a type of scribe whose goal is universal knowledge, gained by experience but also by revelation, and who hands it on to his "children" (the disciples of the wise man). But Enoch is also more and more a heavenly figure, becoming not only the patron "angel" of the wise man, but the "recording angel", a heavenly intercessor. Perhaps we may regard him as the scribal version of the "messiah" (see chapter 15).

In terms of *literary* development, we may also notice the introduction of a more narrative form in this book. This, as well as the change in subject-matter, might suggest a chance of audience. Perhaps an essentially esoteric tradition (as represented in the Astronomical book) is being adapted for wider consumption?

In the remaining two books of 1 Enoch we find two substantial apocalypses (there is also a brief third one in 83: 3–5) both dating from the first half of the second century BCE. The earlier of these, the Apocalypse of Weeks (93: 1–10 and 91: 11–17) divides Israelite history into ten periods ("weeks"), the time of the author being the seventh. There is a probable allusion here to the political-religious crisis beginning around 175 BCE (see chapter 7). The form of this apocalypse is of the pseudo-prediction of past events and a genuine prediction of the future, a form we already know in the "Akkadian apocalypses" (see above). But the context is Jewish, and the eschatological emphasis is distinctive, as is the attention drawn towards religious-social matters, rather than political ones, in the closing weeks. The periodizing of history and the eschatological culmination may be inspired by Persian ideas, and seems to have been a common practice among the scribal classes. The apocalypse sees a restoration of order and righteousness, first in Israel, then in the world, and finally in the whole cosmos, when a new heaven and a new earth will appear.

The other apocalypse is the "Animal Apocalypse" (chapters 85–90), which is also an example of periodized history and prediction and acquires its name from its depiction of individuals and nations in the guise of animals. Unlike the Apocalypse of Weeks, it commences only with the exile, and it enumerates seventy shepherds who have ruled Israel; here it is almost certainly inspired by Jeremiah 25 (especially verses 32ff.) This relationship introduces us to another prominent feature of scribalism and of apocalyptic, mentioned in the passage from Ben Sira (see above): the interpretation of scriptural books as if they, too, were encoded messages to be deciphered, especially in terms of what will happen in the future. We shall meet the same phenomenon in Daniel 9 (see below). The Animal Apocalypse is also more specific in its historical description (like Daniel 10–11), enabling us to discern an account of the career of Judas Maccabee, whose successes inaugurate the eschatological section.

Neither of these apocalypses is concerned merely with periodizing history for the sake of the exercise. Both are responding to problems raised by their own time, problems that raise the question of the orderliness and purpose of history as a whole. In Jewish apocalypses we find the scribes turning their attention to these immediate issues and offering an account of history that makes sense of what is going on in their own time. Ben Sira had done the same; in particular, he lamented the inequalities of his society; but he did not perceive in these inequalities any kind of crisis or any challenge to his belief in the orderliness and permanence of the world and his society. The apocalypses, by contrast, convey a radical account of the world order which assumes its imminent surrender to a new state of things.

From this overview of the Enoch corpus as a whole we have been able to see how the content, form, and world-view of the apocalypse develops from a more general concern with things unseen, with ancient secrets and their inspired revealers. But we can offer here only a sketch of apocalyptic; for it is the product of a very rich and varied culture — not an esoteric and intra-Jewish development but a cosmopolitan, variegated, many-sided, cross-cultural phenomenon. And far from being sectarian, it carries the authority of the scribal establishment, the intellectual leaders of society. We can observe the same processes at work in the formation of the book of Daniel.

Daniel

Like Enoch, the book of Daniel is a composite collection, not all of which have the form of an apocalypse, but which allows us to see how the apocalypse form emerges. The stories that form the first part of the book (see chapter 9) portray the adventures of a Jewish wise man initiated from his youth into Babylonian manticism. His gifts are those of interpreting dreams and (at least on one occasion) mysterious writing on a wall. But the stories also tell of persecution and how the righteous escape it. In these deliverance stories Daniel's profession is important in that it has placed him in a prominent position and this very prominence renders him vulnerable as a victim of anti-Jewish manoeuvres. Daniel is required under these circumstances to show exemplary behaviour, to teach by his deeds rather than by his words.

At the close of the book of Daniel, the authors reveal their own identity:

Those among the people who are wise shall make many understand, though they shall fall by sword and flame, by captivity and plunder, for some days, but when they understand, they shall be helped a little . . . some of those who are wise shall fall, to refine and to cleanse them, and to make them white, until the time of the end, for the time appointed is yet to be.   (Daniel 11: 33–35)

Those who are wise shall shine like the brightness of the firmament; and those who turn many to righteousness like the stars for ever and ever.

(Daniel 12:3)

This description must surely apply to the authors of the book. The "wise" are *maskîlîm*, as is Daniel himself (1:4). Their task is to suffer and to reach righteousness, as did Daniel (though only, in the stories, to the foreign kings). The profile of Daniel as an educated "wise man", serving at court, a political administrator, an interpreter of the future for the king, is a profile of the scribe, learned in mantic lore, but also practical. The book of Daniel is indeed the product of "Daniels". The stories they used were traditional, and we shall find their own distinctive stamp more in the second half of the book, where we find, of course, the "apocalyptic" material. Three techniques in particular are prominent there: the vision, the inspired interpretation of scripture, and the historical review with its genuine prediction. All of these are present also in 1 Enoch.

Daniel 7–12 is an account of his visions, though from chapter 9 onwards the emphasis shifts from visions to Daniel's penitence and prophecy, the vision itself being only a vehicle for a sketch of future history. But in the first two chapters we find a form familiar from biblical prophetic literature, the "symbolic vision". It has even been suggested that such symbolic visions as those in Zechariah constitute the origin of apocalyptic.

In the simplest form of this literary device, as found in the visions of Amos or in Jeremiah 1: 11–19, 24, the objects seen in the vision belong to everyday life (e.g. a linen girdle, bottles of wine) and yield their meaning by metaphor or word-play. The accounts of the vision use a simple question-and-answer pattern. Jeremiah 24 represents an important innovation in being dated (approximately). In a second phase, represented by visions Zechariah 1–6, the form of the symbolic vision develops into a more elaborate narrative, with rather more unusual objects seen, and an extended dialogue between the prophet and an interpreting angel in place of God. The third stage, found in Daniel, has a more "anthological" style, including poetic interludes, conscious borrowing from earlier examples, and even more weird objects of perception. But a straightforward line of development, at least into Daniel, is improbable. The vision of judgement in Daniel 7 borrows from many sources. From Zechariah 1: 18 it gets four horns, and perhaps from Zechariah or from Ezekiel 40 (where the prophet is shown the future Jerusalem), it gets an interpreting angel. The heavenly scene itself is reminiscent of scenes in Enoch, although no precise parallel can be cited. From the earlier story of Daniel 2 the author borrows not only in the theme of four empires but the phrase "visions of his head as he lay upon his bed" (7: 1, cp. 2: 28). The origin of the description of the beasts remains disputed, but among the possibilities are zodiacal representations and conglomerations of physical anomalies, such as are catalogued in omen-lists — in either case subjects of particular interest to scribes. The scribes who wrote Daniel, like other scribes as we have portrayed them, are encyclopaedic in their interests.

Interpretation of scripture is more significant in Daniel than in Enoch. We have seen one example of possible interpretation of a prophetic text in the case of Zechariah 1: 18. A more explicit one is Daniel 9, where we find the hero preparing for an inspired interpretation of a biblical passage in Jeremiah which he cannot understand. He is given the meaning — seventy years means seventy weeks of years, i.e. 490 years — and the events of those weeks are enumerated in a manner similar to the Enochic "Apocalypse of Weeks". Yet another example of the use of biblical prophetic texts is in Daniel 12: 3, quoted earlier; this is probably a paraphrase of Isaiah 53: 11 (Daniel 11: 17 quotes Isaiah 7:7). More so than in Enoch (where chapters 1–6 are clearly influenced by the Balaam story in Numbers), Daniel draws on biblical language. But the biblical allusions are used regardless of their historical or even literary context; they are either reapplied in another way, or tossed off almost carelessly — perhaps sometimes even unwittingly — from the pen of one steeped in the study of the scriptures, as was Ben Sira. Apocalyptic was, after all written by Jewish scholars, foremost among whose interests were surely their national scriptures.

As in the case of the Enochic apocalypses, the Danielic historical summaries are designed to account for a present crisis in terms of the meaning of history as a whole. The crisis, first appearing in Daniel 8, is the cessation of the twice-daily offering (''the evenings and the mornings'') under Antiochus IV (see chapter 7) and the solution to this problem is not given immediately or clearly. The message is simply that it will come, for God has so ordained it. This is essentially what the stories also imply: be faithful, and God will protect you when crisis attends. Only in chapter 12 do we find a statement of what actually is predicted to happen, and even here it is not described in much detail. There will be trouble; some will be raised from the dead to be punished or rewarded. The wise who set the example to the people will truly reach the pre-eminence which their exemplary behaviour in this present life merits.

The religious crisis, which in the case of both Daniel and Enoch led to the application of scribal lore to the production of ethical and eschatological writings, and the apocalypse form, occurred elsewhere, too. There is evidence in other Hellenistic apocalypses of a reaction against the Hellenistic kingdoms on the part of nationalists. Examples of this evidence in Egypt are the ''Demotic Chronicle'' and the ''Potter's Oracle'' (Collins 1984, p. 94). In the case of Palestine, political reaction took the form of religious reaction. The Enochic and Danielic apocalypses are inspired by the events of the reign of Antiochus IV, when Hellenistic culture posed a concrete threat to the character of the religion of the Jewish people. However, this threat was probably not a necessary cause: one might have expected apocalypses in any event. They were part of the *Zeitgeist*. With the exception of Daniel's visions, they are not represented in the Old Testament, largely because of their late date. Nevertheless, they represent the literary output, and with it a world of ideas, which we should not ignore in describing the background of the Old Testament. Far from separating apocalyptic into a literary and theological ghetto we ought to recognize it as representative of a mainstream movement, indeed, as articulating the world-view of the Jews and their neighbours in the Hellenistic Near East.

CHAPTER 15

BEYOND THE
OLD TESTAMENT

By the end of the second century BCE all the Old Testament books had been written. By 100 CE, or soon after, two religions, Christianity and modern Judaism, were in the process of formation, each a product of these books and of the political events of the preceding two centuries. In this chapter we shall look at this transitional period (as it turned out to be), in particular at the religious developments, and especially those that concerned what became in one religion "Scripture" or "Tenak" (*Torah, Nebi'im, Ketubim*) and in the other "the Old Testament". The period is a fascinating and controversial one, not only because of the complexity of the picture it offers, but also because of the often intense involvement with which Christians, in particular, deal with it. Before we can look at a few of its important aspects, however, we ought to address some misconceptions about the period.

"JUDAISM"

For scholars of the last century and the early part of this century, the word "Judaism" (as distinguished from "Modern Judaism") was used for the religion of post-exilic Judea, which was widely seen as a legalistic and hierocratic cult, bereft of the inspiration and ethical fervour of the prophets and represented by the "scribes and Pharisees", who were rightly condemned in the New Testament for their hypocrisy. This Judaism could be more or less defined in terms of doctrines such as resurrection of the dead, messianism, sacrifice, law, covenant, and so on. It was seen as a foil to "Christianity" which was understood to have inherited or "fulfilled" some of these doctrines (such as messianism) and superseded others (such as Jewish law). Modern Judaism was regarded as a continuation of Pharisaism.

Ironically, Jewish scholarship concurred in the description, though not the evaluation, regarding Judaism from the time of Ezra (fifth century BCE) to modern times as essentially unchanged and indeed Pharisaic in a benign sense — that is, enshrining the legal and ethical values of these 'rabbis'. The judgement on both sides owed much to religious dogma. But even at the end of the last century and the early part of this one, the influence of these traditional attitudes was weakening. Critical scholarship on Judaism came from Jewish scholars in Germany especially and from Christian scholars who attempted to study Judaism both critically and sympathetically (e.g. Travers Herford and G.F. Moore). The success of such scholars was limited in many ways, but it marked an important step forward. The reasons for this development are many. One factor was the emergence of critical historiography as a science; another was the publication, from the middle of the nineteenth century onwards, of Jewish and Christian apocalypses, which revealed quite different aspects of Judaism and a new dimension to the contrast (as then seen) between Judaism and Christianity. Since the Second World War, more intense dialogue between Judaism and Christianity has prompted a more objective look at the historical relationship between the two religions, and new discoveries, especially the texts from Qumran, have altered the picture radically.

"EARLY" JUDAISM

The name "early Judaism", is now often applied to the religion of the post-exilic period. Although more precise than "Judaism", it is misleading in that it implied a continuity with what is strictly rabbinic Judaism which began to develop after the destruction of the Temple by the Romans in 70 CE. By "rabbinic Judaism" is meant the form of Judaism which, accepting first the loss of the Temple and its priests, and later (in 135 CE) expulsion from Jerusalem, devoted itself, under the leadership of rabbis, to the carrying out of divine will as revealed in scripture, expressed in terms of everyday laws governing personal and social life (*halakhah*) and moral lessons taught by scripture (*haggadah*). These laws and other teachings discussed and developed in the rabbinic academies in Palestine and then in Babylonia, were collected in the Talmud (sixth century CE). By then, rabbinic Judaism and Christian Judaism had diverged into two distinct religions. Both rightly claim parentage in "early Judaism", which therefore must be defined in such a way as to embrace both equally. This is not a theological point but an historical one.

The idea of a "normative" Judaism

G.F. Moore, one of this century's greatest non-Jewish students of Judaism, although fully aware of different forms of Judaism, proposed Pharisaic Judaism as the "norm", on the grounds that it did indeed *become* the norm in rabbinic Judaism. But, however Moore intended this to be understood, it is historically a deceptive usage. In the period we are examining, there were many other subgroups and trends within Judaism (and even among the Pharisees), and some of these movements were highly influential.

"Apocalyptic" versus "Rabbinic" Judaism

During this century many New Testament scholars have worked with a distinction between the literature of "mainstream' or "official' Judaism and "apocalyptic" Judaism — the latter represented by books not preserved in the Jewish canon, rejected by the rabbis, and preserved by Christians. The claim is often made that "apocalyptic" Judaism was the forerunner or "matrix" of Christianity. But the notion of a *kind* of Judaism which was "apocalyptic" is fanciful. Nevertheless, an important distinction can be made here. The literature of the period includes few if any elements of popular religion. It is in any case customary to regard the religion of the sacred books and the authorities — not popular variations of it — as defining a religion. But we now know that many Jews accepted astrology, magical spells, and mystical ascents to heaven as natural ingredients of their religion.

"Palestinian" versus "Hellenistic" Judaism

The distinction between "Hellenistic" and "Palestinian" Judaism is attractive to many Jewish and Christian scholars. The former regard "Hellenistic Judaism" as degenerate; the latter regard "Palestinian" as Pharisaic. Alas, this convenient dichotomy is largely false. Palestine in this period was certainly "Hellenized" to a considerable degree (see chapter 7). The concept of a "traditional" Judaism, at this time free of Hellenism, has had to go; but so has the notion that Greek ideas in Christianity must have been non-"Jewish" or alien to "Judaism". It is more useful to draw a distinction between Diaspora Judaism and Palestinian Judaism, since the social and political conditions inside and outside Palestine were different. In Palestine the unavoidable facts of life were the economic and political power of the priesthood, of the Temple, and of the Roman occupation. In the Diaspora (though it is, of course, simplistic to generalize) the emphasis was on identity and survival as social and religious groups, with the role of the Temple being largely symbolic. One kind of Judaism belonged to a majority, the other to a minority. Broadly speaking, the Old Testament is a product of Palestine, whereas the New Testament (despite the Palestinian setting of the Gospels) was written for a non-Palestinian audience.

Four Jewish "parties"

One favourite scheme for analyzing early Judaism has been to start from the description of the Jewish "parties" given by Josephus at the end of the first century CE in Book 2 of his *Jewish War* (revised in Book 18 of his *Jewish Antiquities*). His four parties are Essenes, Pharisees, Sadducees, and a "fourth philosophy", which some scholars identify as being the party of the Zealots but which is actually much older, since the Zealots did not arise until the middle of the 1st century CE. The problems with following Josephus's account too closely are that it is addressed to non-Jewish readers and couched in terms of Greek philosophical schools. He wishes to project a suitable image of Judaism, and, for example, in his

OPPOSITE, ABOVE Only a small group of Israelites may actually have experienced the deliverance from slavery in Egypt. However, this did not prevent the story becoming the property of the whole people, a story that powerfully expressed their belief in God. Here, the destruction of the Egyptians is contrasted with the deliverance of the Israelites. Divine hands hold back the waters of the Red Sea allowing the Israelites to pass over, while, on the right hand side, the Egyptians are engulfed by the waters.

OPPOSITE, BELOW The prophet Ezekiel: the upward gaze perhaps reflects the strong visionary element in the book of Ezekiel, which includes a description of the throne of God and of the future city and Temple of Jerusalem.

Antiquities he promotes the Pharisees as the representatives of the Jewish people, as they were perhaps bidding to become after the destruction of the Temple. Josephus does not explain the origin of these parties, or their interrelationship. Nor does he tell us about the vast majority of Jews who did not belong to any of these. We cannot therefore divide early Judaism into four little segments in this way, though we ought to *include* these ''parties'' in any description of the whole picture.

''Early'' Judaism was not, then, a uniform theological or doctrinal system. As a purely descriptive term, it includes any belief or practice which one who called himself or herself a ''Jew'' might construe as ''Jewish'' in the period between 150 BCE and c. 70 CE, i.e. after the Maccabeans revolt until the fall of Jerusalem. As we have seen, the world in which ''early'' Judaism existed was culturally complex, and Jews absorbed a tremendous amount from their Hellenistic environment. One matter that is often overlooked is the extent to which Judaism, or at least some of its practices and ideas, attracted non-Jews, many of whom regarded it as a philosophy rather than a cult. (Many Jews also favoured this definition.) One startling example of such adoption of Jewish customs is that (according to the Roman historian and gossip Suetonius) the Emperor Augustus observed the sabbath! At the other extreme we find the ultra-legalistic sect at Qumran organized like a typical Hellenistic religious association, holding a doctrine of dualism which is almost certainly Persian in origin and writing horoscopes. How can one classify such a sect? Indeed, if there is no mainstream, how is a ''sect'' defined? In the remainder of this chapter we shall try to describe some of the main institutions and ideological models of early Judaism.

OUTWARD CHARACTERISTICS OF EARLY JUDAISM

The measures taken against the Jews by Antiochus IV included the abolition of Temple sacrifice, the profanation of the sabbath, worship of other gods, eating of ''unclean'' food, suppression of the books of the Law, and a ban on circumcision. Assuming the reports to be correct, we have here a convenient list of matters that might be taken to constitute Jewish practice at that time. Practice is a good place to begin; religion is as much to do with behaviour as with belief. But these practices also relate to ideological components of early Judaism, such as law and holiness. The practices of circumcision, avoidance of idolatry, observance of the sabbath, and certain dietary restrictions emerged as religious issues most probably during the exile and shortly afterwards, with the challenge of defining a religious affiliation without any political entity. Later, with the irresistible encroachment of Hellenism, these outward practices again became tokens of identity. From the most conservative and xenophobic forms of Judaism to the most flexible and universalistic, these practices were accepted. They form the foundation, then, of any description of early Judaism beyond the Old Testament.

Circumcision

The practice of circumcision, the ban on idolatry, and the strict observance of the sabbath probably all acquired their high religious significance at the same time, during the Babylonian exile. All Jewish males were circumcised eight days after birth. Although not exclusive to the Jews, this practice was always represented by Jews as the sign *par excellence* of membership of the Jewish people, and was understood to be a mark of the covenant (see the story of its institution in Genesis 17). Some Jews were accused, during the time of Antiochus, of concealing their circumcision, presumably in order to perform in the gymnasium. According to Josephus, John Hyrcanus obliged the Idumeans to be circumcised in order to remain in their homeland, and Aristobulus, his successor, did the same to the Itureans. In this connection it is worthwhile remembering that Judaism during this period was by no means racially exclusive. But circumcision, so far as we can tell, was always required for membership.

Anti-Idolatry

The first two of the Ten Commandments forbid the placing of other gods before Yhwh and the making of images or pictures. These two provide the basis for the Jewish attitude towards other religions, and were combined in that other gods were usually ridiculed as the "work of men's hands". In the Greco-Roman period the importance of this principle lay in resisting the tendency, characteristic of Hellenism, to see every religion as a form of one universal religion and thus to pair deities — Thoth and Hermes, Baal and Zeus, Astarte and Aphrodite. Yhwh was identified by some non-Jews with Jupiter or Dionysus.

There were two strategies for coping with the conflict between universalism and adherence to the national deity. One was to refer to "The Most High", "Heaven", "Lord", or "God". The disappearance of "Yhwh" from Jewish literature in this period is usually explained in terms of the ineffability of the name, which is doubtless true; but was it the only reason? Another device was to consider other deities as heavenly beings inferior to the one supreme God worshipped by Jews. In Deuteronomy 32. 8 (probably a post-exilic text), God is said to have created the nations and their territories "according to the number of the sons of God", with Jacob as his own charge. Other nations were thus under the patronage of subordinate deities, or, as we now like to say, "angels". In Daniel, the "princes" (that is, patron angels) of Greece and Persia are mentioned, as is Michael, the "prince" of Israel (Daniel 10: 20f.; 12: 1). It is also worthwhile noting (since many people assert the contrary), that Jewish literature of the post-exilic period does not attest a growing gulf between humanity and deity. On the contrary, it can suppose humans going to heaven without dying (Enoch, Moses, Elijah), or perhaps becoming heavenly beings after their death (Daniel 12: 3), or visiting heaven during their lifetime (Enoch), and can accept that humans may have the heavenly parentage we find attributed to Cain, for example, or Noah in Jewish texts. The principle of early Judaism, then, is not accurately defined as *monotheism* but as *monarchical theism*: the insistence that however many divine beings there were, there was one supreme God.

Diet

Jewish dietary laws, as more fully developed in rabbinic Judaism, are complex. The main biblical injunctions are not to drink blood and not to eat animals that are unclean (these are listed in Leviticus 11; the pig is the best known, but also excluded are the camel and the hare). The law forbidding "boiling a kid in its mother's milk" (Exodus 23: 19; 34: 26; and Deuteronomy 14: 21) came to be understood as a ban on mixing meat and dairy produce, but at what time we do not know. Now the ban on drinking blood was given to Noah and was regarded by the rabbis as forming part of the "Noachic covenant" binding on all humans. Meat that might have been slaughtered without removing the blood, or that might have been sacrificed to a god before being sold would not be acceptable to Jews. Dining with non-Jews was undoubtedly practiced, but to those with a conscience, a delicate situation.

TIMES AND SEASONS

The importance of time in early Judaism cannot be overstressed. The Jewish calendar was (and still is) a major factor distinguishing Judaism from other religions. Time was perceived both cyclically and linearly; that is to say, there was both an annual cycle and a seven-year cycle. The Temple cult itself depended on both holy time and holy space. The Temple was in the correct place, and all sacrifices had to be performed there. But they also had to be performed at the right *time*. The account of Creation in Genesis 1 states not only what God created but when. Or, to put it another way, God created time when he created the world. For this reason, sacred occasions were of great importance to Judaism, and differences over how to reckon time of considerable religious significance. We also find in writings from this period an interest in a world-calendar in which the number of basic cycles is predetermined and the end of history is foreseen.

Two different ways of reckoning the year were proposed in early Judaism. In one, the month is tied to the phases of the moon, and the year has to be adjusted by intercalating additional months periodically; in the other, the year is tied to the sun, and the months are set at thirty days regardless of the behaviour of the moon. The lunar calendar had its new year in autumn; the solar calendar in spring. During the period we are studying the former system was officially observed and used to control the Temple worship, but some Jews believed that the other system was correct, and that therefore most of the Temple festivals were wrongly conducted, because at the wrong time. Their views are found in the books of 1 Enoch and Jubilees, and were adopted by the Essenes, including the community at Qumran. How or even whether these views were put into practical effect we have no idea. But the calendar issue is far from a trivial one. It was one of the few matters on which a Jew could later be regarded as heretic.

The Jewish calendar also gave an important perspective on a much-debated question; the origin and nature of sin and evil. The fundamental problem is this: is the sun right or the moon? Further: if God made both, why are they not in step? According to the book of Enoch, which adopts a solar calendar, the moon is out of phase. But if the heavens could go wrong . . . ? Speculation that evil originated in heaven with a revolt of angelic beings had a basis in such astronomical disorder.

The day is the smallest unit in the calendar. For religious purposes, in Judaism it was considered to begin in the evening (since darkness preceded light; see Genesis 1). There were two prescribed regular sacrifices in the Temple, evening and morning (the *Tamid*), and perhaps prayers were said at these times by pious Jews. However, in the solar calendar it is possible that the day began at sunrise.

The next unit is the week, marked by the sabbath. The biblical legislation concerning sabbath observance is extremely brief; however, by the first century CE, the sabbath had become an important issue, and some Jews had elaborated detailed rules for its observance. The Temple had a special service for the sabbath, and it is probable that gatherings for prayer were taking place, with possibly the reading of Scripture (see Luke 4: 16ff.). There is a text from Qumran (the ''Songs of the Sabbath Sacrifice'') which provides a liturgy for the sabbath, consisting mostly of descriptions of worship in heaven. During the resistance to Antiochus IV in the second century BCE, the issue of whether to fight on the sabbath seems to have been debated; and the book of Jubilees, later in that century, avoids having the patriarchs undertake any journey on the sabbath.

The new moon, which had been a religious festival in earlier times, was now relatively insignificant. The next liturgical unit is the year, which contained the major feasts occurring annually. There were three major festivals: in spring (Passover plus Unleavened Bread, now merged), summer (Weeks, or Pentecost), and autumn (Booths or Ingathering). A system of reading through the law every year in synagogues may have operated, before the present three-year cycle was introduced into rabbinic Judaism. According to both Deuteronomy and Leviticus, there was a sabbatical year, during which fields were not to be sown and debts were to be remitted. Although it is difficult to see how such a system could really operate, we have the evidence of a decree from the rabbi Hillel (first century CE) which implies such a practice. There was even a sabbath of sabbaths, a jubilee year (see chapter 1, p. 42), either the forty-ninth or fiftieth. The ''book of Jubilees'' derives its name from the system of dating years by jubilees. Since the sabbath symbolized both rest (this is the explanation in Exodus 20) and deliverance (as in Deuteronomy 5), in some texts from this period, there are assertions and suggestions that history would be fulfilled in the final jubilee or sabbatical cycle of years. The sabbath and its system thus offered a framework for the important *temporal* dimension of early Judaism.

THE HOLY PLACE: TEMPLE AND PRIESTHOOD

Temple

Politically and economically, as well as religiously, the Temple was the focus of life in Judea. So far as we know, it was the only Jewish sanctuary in the land, and all religious activity was conducted with reference to it. In addition to making various offerings, private sacrifices, tithes, and first-fruits, all males over twenty paid a Temple tax of half a shekel. Thus the upkeep of the Temple affected all Jews in Palestine, at least in theory. Three times a year there were the pilgrim festivals of Passover, Weeks, and Booths, while Hanukkah celebrated the rededication of the Temple by Judas Maccabee. The Temple cult, at least in priestly theory, mediated between God and Israel in all important respects.

There is little evidence of resentment against the Temple as such, or rejection of its significance. But several writings are critical of its practices, and either condemn those priests running it or anticipate a new Temple to be built in the future, or both. We may assume that these writings (e.g. Jubilees, the Temple Scroll from Qumran Cave 11, and parts of Enoch) came from disaffected priests, or at least from those who still believed firmly in the centrality of the Temple. Even the Qumran community, which seems to have boycotted the Temple, regarded this as an interim measure. Even after its destruction, the rabbis, in describing their vision of a Jewish people governed by the law, retained the Temple at the centre of their system and took the ideology associated with it into all areas of life.

The Temple was important to Palestinian Judaism in other ways. It brought in wealth from visitors and overseas pilgrims, and it was a major consumer of produce. Moreover, it was a political symbol, representing a degree of Jewish independence. Even so, the Temple did not necessarily play any part in daily Jewish religion, and both rabbinic Judaism and Christianity developed without it. However, the synagogue — about which we know practically nothing in this period — eventually assumed a degree of Temple symbolism (the ''ark'' — a substitute for the original — which housed the scrolls of law, for example); and Christianity retained a doctrine of atonement by sacrifice and, in time, reinstated both priesthood and altar.

Priesthood

According to Leviticus (the priestly code *par excellence* of the Bible), Israel's destiny was to be holy, since God was holy. And the priests were responsible for not only maintaining but defining holiness: Aaron is ''to distinguish between the holy and the common, and between the clean and the unclean'' (Leviticus 10: 10). ''Holiness'' was definable in cultic terms. Anything given to, or belonging to, God (such as sacrifices and priests) was to be ''holy''. What was not holy was ''common''. What was common, furthermore, could be clean or unclean. Many things, from moral offences to accidental contact with unclean objects (such as corpses) could render one ''unclean''. In priestly theory, priests ministering before God had to be holy, while Israelites were expected to be clean. Transition between these states is legislated for in Leviticus, and involves, generally speaking, washing for bodily impurities and sacrifice for ''sins''; sometimes both are needed (see chapter 11, p. 261).

The priesthood was hereditary and comprised two levels: levites (all members of the tribe of Levi) and, within this group, priests, who were descended from Aaron. Within the priesthood, moreover, were those who traced their descent from Zadok, and who, according to Ezekiel, should enjoy exclusive rights of sacrifice. At the head was the High Priest and a deputy, possibly the ''captain of the Temple''; these were permanently at the Temple. Otherwise, priests and levites were divided into twenty-four shifts, each serving for one week twice in the year. Within the shift each priest might expect to be on service one or two days. For the remainder of the year, they presumably lived outside as well as inside Jerusalem. The priests' livelihood came from prescribed portions of the sacrifices, but also from other contributions like first-fruits and tithes. With some over-simplification, it may be said that a priestly view of early Judaism would assert that the Temple and its cult guaranteed the holiness of the entire nation and earned God's favour. Without the Temple, no holiness, no forgiveness, no Israel, could be envisaged. Narrow though this view may sound, it was probably accepted, at least on the whole, by many laymen as well as priests.

SCRIPTURE, LAW, AND SCRIBES

Scriptures

As explained in chapter 17, by the end of the second century BCE the Jews had a body of Scriptures consisting of ''law'' and ''prophets'', with some other writings also. These provided a history of the Jewish people, showing how they had been chosen by the God who created the world, promised a land, rescued from Egypt, and given a law to live by. That story defined who Jews were: chosen, promised, given a law. Jews who were priests or scribes read these Scriptures in other ways too: priests understood the Law to mean that Israel was commanded above all to be holy (see below). Scribes could read in the Scriptures hidden meanings, could find either hints about the present time or moral truths. Writings from the period reveal such activity. The book of Jubilees, written in the second half of the second century BCE, combines many of these concerns. It is a retelling of the biblical story from Adam to Moses. It explains how even the patriarchs obeyed the law and instituted

An important genre among the Dead Sea scrolls is the *pesher*, a commentary on a biblical book which interprets each verse as a reference to events in the interpreter's own time (first century CE), believed to be the last days. This explanation is referred to as its *pesher* ("interpretation"). The most important of these manuscripts, shown here, is the *Habakkuk pesher* from Cave 1.

the festivals and stresses the need for the separation of Jews from other nations. Other retellings of the story are also known. Examples of reading esoteric meanings into Scriptural texts can be found in Daniel 9, where a prophecy of Jeremiah is re-interpreted, or in the Habakkuk commentary from Qumran, in which every verse of the first two chapters is taken to speak of events in the recent past or near future.

The Scriptures appear to have been read aloud in synagogues, and were probably accompanied by translations into Aramaic. These translations, or "targums", may have been literal (like the targum of Job found at Qumran) or free, like the targums written later, which may nevertheless be of quite ancient origin. Additionally, the Scriptures were probably studied privately by those who could read.

The Law

Since the "return" from Babylon, the religion of the Jews in Palestine had been centred almost as much on the law as on the Temple. Ezra was credited with having brought back the "law of Moses" and had the people instructed in it. Thereafter, the task of developing and applying Jewish law was presumably set in hand. But, as we have seen, the law, enshrined in the five books of Moses, deals mostly with cultic matters; on civil matters it is vague. For instance, Deuteronomy 24: 1–4 is the only piece of legislation on divorce: it requires a "bill of divorce" to be written in the case of "some indecency", permits the woman to remarry, even to re-divorce, but forbids the first husband to remarry that woman. On the manner of marriage nothing is said; the custom is merely implied. Jewish law on these matters proceeded on the whole from Scripture, but in many cases quite independently.

The law consisted of more than was contained in the books of Moses. It was expanded in three ways: by legal exegesis, by tradition or custom, and by decree. Legal exegesis developed a number of principles by which laws could be inferred from Scripture. Tradition and custom are self-explanatory, as is decree. Eventually, in rabbinic Judaism, these were to become also Mosaic law. A fourth possible means of lawmaking was by direct revelation. Certain legal texts (like the Temple Scroll from Qumran Cave 11) seem to fall into this category; but in fact upon examination their contents can be explained as the outcome of exegesis. Such lawmaking was rejected by the priests and Sadducees (see below), but was practised by Pharisees and Essenes. However, while some groups sought to encourage adherence to these "revealed" laws throughout

Israel, others turned their back on the larger Jewish community and formed themselves into associations for the purpose of strict adherence to these laws — as they understood them. The Essene communities appear to have done just this, and we also know of religious associations called *haburoth* (composed of Pharisees) which attempted to apply to themselves conditions of purity required of priests.

In the Hellenistic world, the notion of law was both politically and philosophically central. Cities were established with written constitutions. Those philosophers, then, who taught that the world was a single *polis* and that all were its citizens, taught that the world also had its constitution, its laws. Those who had written constitutions and laws for cities (e.g. Draco, Solon) were venerated. It was not difficult, therefore, for the Jewish law and its great lawgiver Moses to be understood and presented in this way. Within the Old Testament, wisdom had been understood as a kind of natural law; its equation with Torah was not merely an inner pietistic development, but was appropriate to Hellenistic ideas and probably inspired by them.

Scribes

What the Temple was to priests, literature (in this case, Scripture) was to the scribes. As a class they belonged to no one religious group, though predominantly they seem to have been Pharisees, who were keenly interested in the development of legal theory. They assumed responsibility for making Jewish law, and, as with so many developments in this period, we can see both internal and external factors at work. The first great scribe of the Old Testament is Ezra, who, according to tradition, brought a lawbook and had it read out and explained to the assembled people. However, the Greco-Roman period saw the preservation and study of national literatures and the growth of the scribal class everywhere. The introduction of schools for educating young Jews in their national literature was probably prompted by Hellenism. But the influence and the responsibility of scribes in Judaism was no doubt enhanced by the indifference of priests to instructing Jewish people in the law and the extent of priestly participation in Hellenistic customs, which was seen by non-priests as destructive of Judaism.

The business of the scribes, then, was manifold. They gave rulings on matters of Jewish law. They ran schools for children and for apprentice scribes. They also studied Scriptures and wrote about them. They were judges, teachers, theorists, and authors. From their study of Scripture they extracted legal, ethical, and sometimes mystical interpretations.

The Identity of ''Israel'' in Early Judaism

In turning to a consideration of the ideological trends and particular religious groups or movements within early Judaism, we must address ourselves to the question: who and what, according to the views of these groups, constituted Israel?

According to the book of 4 Ezra (2 Esdras in the Apocrypha), Ezra dictated from memory ninety-four books of scripture which had been lost at the Captivity, the twenty-four of the Old Testament and a further seventy secret books, to be given only to the wise. In this eighth-century CE illustration Ezra is shown copying out the books (represented as codices, not scrolls); a number of completed books lie on the shelves beside him.

The Jews of the early post-exilic Judea of Ezra and Nehemiah committed to Israel as a religious community, separated from other nations and obedient to the law. Holiness was in their midst, in the Temple, priesthood, and the cultic objects. By the first century BCE partly as a result of the crises of the preceding century (see chapter 7), this basic view of an Israel separated from outsiders and committed to the idea of holiness actualized in its cult had been developed in different ways. But holiness and separation remained fundamental.

Sadducees

The Sadducean party mentioned by the Jewish historian Josephus (end of first century CE) and in the New Testament appears to have adhered most closely to the traditional view, as stated above. Howwever, their viewpoint was dictated by their economic and social interests, and it is doubtful whether they constituted a religious party in any meaningful sense. The Sadducees were composed of priests and aristocrats who adhered to the Torah but to nothing else. They were, according to Josephus, wealthy and unpopular. We have no writings from them that we can identify, and thus they remain shadowy, described only vaguely by opponents. Obviously, the preservation of the lucrative Temple and of a peaceful cooperation with Rome were their aims. ''Holiness'' meant the conduct of the cult, over which they seem to have had stringent and conservative views. Separation to them meant not only separation of priests from non-priests, but also of rich Jews from poor Jews, of the privileged from the unprivileged. Separation from non-Jews must have been less important for them than for Ezra or Nehemiah; these were the Jews whose status was not at stake by such contact and who presumably benefited from their association with non-Jews, including the Romans, with whom cooperation meant the preservation of privilege.

Pharisees

The Pharisees, who in Herod's time numbered, according to Josephus, more than 6,000 families (not a large minority), were both influential and concerned with the strict observance of the law, which was made possible by ''traditions of the elders'' or ''the law of the fathers''. These were accumulated interpretations and rulings made by their scribes (see above) which defined the law in such a way as to make obedience possible. They claimed authority for these rules equal of those written down in Scripture, and regarded them as applicable to all Israel. Their belief in resurrection underlines their personal commitment to piety; every Israelite was responsible for taking the ''yoke of the law'' upon himself. Such views were hardly sufficient in themselves to constitute a distinct party. Taking ''Pharisee' to mean ''separated', then, we should probably imagine that they carried their own observance of the law to the point of restricting contact with Israelites who did not observe the Pharisaic definitions of law, and whom they referred to as ʿam ha'arez. They formed themselves into societies (called haburoth, ''fellowships''), the chief communal activity of which was dining. This explains their emphasis on laws relating to the cleanliness of vessels and the necessity of tithing (untithed food was unclean). It is widely understood that the Pharisees aspired to the level of cleanliness required of a priest ministering in the Temple, and desired this status for all Jews. Such an ideology is fully worked out in the Mishnah, the programme of rabbinic Judaism.

What was the political attitude of the Pharisees? The party enjoyed political power in the first century BCE, and regained it after the destruction of the Temple in 70 CE. In between, they apparently eschewed politics. Being drawn from many different classes, including priests and scribes but probably also lower classes, they did not represent any single economic or social interest. There is enough evidence that on political matters, including "messianic" beliefs, Pharisees held a variety of beliefs (see below).

Essenes

The Essenes, of whom Josephus gives a fuller description than he does of either Pharisees or Sadducees, are mentioned by other ancient writers but absent from the New Testament, a puzzle yet to be solved. They were constituted in communities throughout Palestine — possibly with

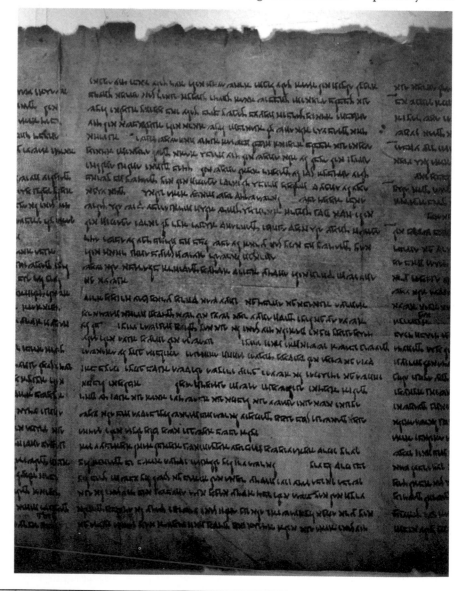

Among the Dead Sea Scrolls were found many biblical manuscripts, which are now the oldest in our possession. These show clearly that before the first century CE there was no single authoritative wording of the biblical books, but a considerable variety. This Isaiah scroll, one of the first manuscripts from Qumran to be published, is unusual in that it differs very little from the so-called Masoretic text which was finally fixed as the unalterable form.

related communities in Egypt and Syria. The discoveries at Qumran, on the northwest shore of the Dead Sea, in 1947, prompted renewed interest in this group, since the contents of the *Community Rule*, found in Cave 1, and the remains of a settlement nearby corresponded remarkably to the details given about the Essenes by ancient authors.

Why and how the Essenes were formed, and what their ideology was, remains, even forty years after the discovery of the Dead Sea Scrolls, unclear. The Qumran settlement was occupied somewhere around 100 BCE and was abandoned during the war with Rome, in 68 CE. But was Qumran a typical Essene community or a splinter group? Josephus notes that there were two "orders" of Essenes, one of which did not marry (as at Qumran). The documents found in the caves contain, in addition to scriptural books and documents about the Qumran community itself, other writings which appear to point to a kind of Judaism from which the Qumran community can plausibly have derived, but which was not exactly identical to it. We can distinguish, in fact, between what may have been "Essene" ideology and practices and what obtained at Qumran, without becoming involved in the controversial question of the exact relationship between Qumran and other Essene settlements.

The Essenes believed that God had revealed to their founder the true law now lost to the rest of the nation Israel, and had made a covenant with the "remnant" of Israel who survived capture by Nebuchadrezzar. During the period of divine anger which followed that capture, and which would one day end with the arrival of "one who would teach righteousness", this true Israel, possessors of the true covenant and law, would live strictly according to the law revealed to them by God. They rejected both the (lunar) calendar and many of the laws followed elsewhere in Israel, and although they appear to have used the Jerusalem Temple, their participation may have been quite restricted. Their law was generally very strict with regard to holiness, and association with outsiders was severely regulated. (This description is drawn mainly from the *Damascus Document*, fragments of which have been found at Qumran, and from two texts from the tenth and twelfth centuries found in a Cairo synagogue and published in 1910.)

Another Essene work, the *Temple Scroll* contains instructions for a temple service, but may be part of a longer Torah scroll. The scroll envisages a huge temple covering most of the city of Jerusalem and of the Kidron Valley, its cult regulated by Essene laws, which included some otherwise unknown feasts (such as New Wine and New Oil). The impression one gains from this is that the Essenes had a fairly detailed definition of what Judaism should be. Did they imagine that one day it would be fulfilled? Despite their segregated existence, they apparently proselytized (as did the Pharisees). Where they came from remains unclear, and none of their ideas point to any specific moment in Jewish history. The crises of the second century BCE are not reflected in their texts, and they might have started at any time from the Babylonian exile to the third century BCE.

The Qumran community's own texts claim that it was founded by a "teacher of righteousness", which implies that it believed that the awaited Essene "messiah", had arrived. The group did not marry, abandoned the Temple cult, and adopted the notion that they were participants in the worship of a presumed heavenly Temple. The clues all point to a group formed in anticipation of the "end of days", the last times. The non-fulfilment of such hopes makes the ideology of such a group unstable and erratic. And this is what we find in their writings, which contain, for example, descriptions of a war between the forces of light and darkness in terms drawn from Persian dualism, and elaborate efforts to prove from Scripture that their experiences, including those of their founder, were really foretold. It would not be surprising to find that they participated in the war against Rome, as may have occurred. They obviously regarded themselves as the only true Israel, and, like other Essenes, regarded the rest of Israel as doomed.

Israel, according to the Essenes, was therefore based on obedience to the law, but to a law which, like the Pharisees, they defined more and more exactly. Their separation from other Jews was more extreme than that practised by the Pharisees, and their detailed laws were different from those of the Pharisees (so far as we know); but they, too, cultivated the degree of cleanliness required of priests. From a sociological point of view they were "sectarian', but their basic religious ideology conformed basically to that of many other Jews.

The "fourth philosophy"

As we noted above, Josephus mentions, in addition to the three "philosophies" of Judaism just described, a fourth, which was founded by Judas of Gamala and Zadok the Pharisee at the time of Quirinius's census (6 CE). This group, he said, called upon Jews to rebel against Roman "slavery". Some have identified this "philosophy" with the Zealots, which is improbable. But perhaps it underlay a number of revolutionary movements which all believed that Roman domination was intolerable and that Judaism could be practised only under the sovereignty of God.

Other Jews

Still other Jews — among them Philo and the writer of the Wisdom of Solomon — defined their religion in terms of Greek philosophies. Diaspora Judaism is simply too vast and varied to be considered here; we cannot be sure that holiness and strict obedience to the law were its common denominators, whereas it incorporated many features of local culture and religion. Of the Judaism of the eastern Diaspora we know little. Another little-known group is that dubbed the "people of the land" (Hebrew 'am ha-arez) by the Pharisees. How religious they were and in what ways, we do not know. How many other religious movements existed? We have names such as Boethusians and Zadokites, (Essenes? Sadducees?). Similarly, we know little of other religious leaders who started movements. What kind of Judaism, for example, did John the Baptist represent? Or those itinerant miracle workers who healed and made rain, such as Honi the Circle-Drawer and Hanina ben Dosa, remembered in the Talmud. Or Jesus of Nazareth, for that matter?

Samaritans

Were Samaritans Jews or not? According to the famous New Testament parable (Luke 10: 25–37) they were: the hero is a member of the most peripheral branch of the Jewish race. Until recently scholarly opinion had suggested that the rift between Judeans and Samaritans began in the time of Nehemiah, but it now seems to have developed gradually and somewhat later. Its causes were apparently not political, but concerned the Temple and the priestly line. In the early Greek period, the Jewish inhabitants of the city of Samaria were displaced by Macedonians and moved to Shechem, where they built a temple on Mt. Gerizim, one of two hills overlooking Shechem, where a Mosaic covenant ceremony has been recorded (Deuteronomy 27, especially verse 11). Serious antagonism between Samarian and Judean Jews probably dates from the establishment of this temple and from the production of a Samaritan version of the Pentateuch, edited so as to justify it. Obviously, if by the time of Hyrcanus the two communities were not already completely divided, his destruction of their temple ensured this.

The Samaritans themselves would have claimed they were not Jews, but Israelites, retaining the religion of the ancient kingdom. However, this view is questionable. It is wrong, too, to think of Samaritans as a Jewish splinter group, since they did not exactly break away from the Judean community. Rather, we have to see the Samaritans, in this period at least, as another variety of early Judaism. This variety was, of course, to develop in quite different directions of its own, and to form a religion distinct from rabbinic Judaism, with its own complexities and its own sects.

MESSIANISM

This unfortunate and inappropriate term is nevertheless commonly used to convey the various and widespread Jewish belief during this period that the course of history, which had recently turned against Jews in Palestine, would soon be brought to an end. "Messianism" is worth discussing, even briefly, since it has two different but important aspects. One is the political, social, and economic frustration which appears to have existed in Palestine after the collapse of the Hasmonean monarchy and the arrival of the Romans. "Messianic expectation" is essentially not a religious doctrine but a political reflex. There is no evidence for it until the middle of the first century BCE. But allied to this reflex are opinions about the ideal political structure of Israel: should it be ruled by priests? kings? both? or directly from heaven? Specific formulations of messianic beliefs were informed by such political philosophy.

The other aspect of messianism is its religious or scriptural dimension. The variety of messianic beliefs found in the literature of the period betrays differing allegiances. "Messiah" by this time meant effectively the ruler of the people chosen by God, and had been applied in the Scriptures to kings or priests (and rarely to individual prophets). We have the hope of a king in the *Psalms of Solomon* (a collection of religious-political protest poetry, which called for a king like David to restore justice), making its author a critic of the high-priesthood (as he certainly was); we have the idea of two messiahs, one royal, one priestly, in the Dead Sea Scrolls and elsewhere — with priority given to the high priest. We have the notion of direct heavenly rule, too. In one of the texts from Qumran, we have a description of a heavenly high-priestly messiah. There was no "messianic Judaism" and no "messianic doctrine", but the *notion* of a "messiah" was widely spread. Among Sadducees, of course, messianic ideas of any kind were rejected. And they reached Hellenistic Judaism only in the form of Christianity.

PART IV

THE FORMATION OF THE OLD TESTAMENT

Abraham visited by the angels, sixth-century mosaic, Ravenna.

CHAPTER 16

ORAL TRADITION AND PRE-EXILIC COLLECTIONS

The present chapter has two aims. One aim is a straightforward attempt to describe how much of the Old Testament existed, and in what form, before the exile in 587 BCE. The simplicity of this aim should not, however, give the impression that we know all the answers; in fact, there are many uncertainties. The other aim is more complex: to determine how — and whether — the study of oral tradition should be used in interpreting the Old Testament. Before we tackle this complex matter, a little background explanation is required.

The story of the Hebrews begins, in the Old Testament, with Abraham (Genesis 12). According to the biblical chronology, Abraham lived round about 2100 BCE. This estimate is based upon 1 Kings 6: 1, which says that the Temple was begun in Solomon's fourth year (c. 957), and 480 years after the Exodus; upon Exodus 12: 40, which says that the Israelites sojourned in Egypt for 430 years; upon Genesis 47: 28, which says that Jacob lived 130 years before he went down into Egypt; and upon Genesis 25: 26, which says that Isaac was 60 when Jacob was born. Adding up these figures, we get 2057 as the year of Isaac's birth, during Abraham's lifetime. Using these same figures, we can estimate that Moses, who was traditionally held to be the author of Genesis, lived around 1400 BCE — that is, some 600 years later than Abraham.

The question as to how Moses knew about events that happened 600 years before his lifetime did not worry those who believed that God had divulged the information to Moses; but in the eighteenth century, serious attempts began to be made to bridge the gap between Moses and the time of the patriarchs. Without denying that Moses was inspired by God, scholars assumed that he had used written sources, from which he compiled the account of events that long pre-dated him. In the nineteenth century, there was a significant shift towards an interest in oral traditions as the source for information about the patriarchs (cp. Rogerson 1978, p. 68). This was accompanied by the belief that the stories about Abraham and Jacob (there is little in Genesis about Isaac) were really stories about groups of people whom Abraham and Jacob personified. Around the turn of the century there was another shift, especially apparent in the work of Gunkel (Rogerson p. 69ff.). This new approach was less interested in history and more concerned with literature. Gunkel believed that the stories in Genesis had been oral tradition circulating among the people, and that they were mostly based upon folk-tales which could have parallels among many peoples of the world.

In the present century, the date for Abraham has been brought forward to round about 1750 BCE, but the belief that Moses wrote the Pentateuch has been generally rejected. The earliest date at which anything was written down, according to modern scholars, was during the reigns of David and Solomon. This widens the gap between the presumed time of Abraham and the writing down of traditions about him by 800 years. The issue here is not whether or not the Israelites *could* have written down traditions about Abraham prior to the time of Solomon. Obviously they *could* have done so, since writing was used in the ancient Near East from about 3500 BCE. The question is whether they *did* write anything down.

The writing and preservation of documents implies a technology which is taken for granted by us today, but which has to be thought about in relation to the ancient world. It implies the existence of people who can read and write, who have access to writing materials, and who are supported by an institution or by arrangments that enable writings to be handed on from one generation to the next. Israel, as an association of villages existing round about 1230 BCE, almost certainly lacked the necessary social conditions to support a class of professional scribes. It was not until the time of David that such conditions existed, and it was probably not until the time of Solomon that they flourished. We thus come back to the question of the gap between the presumed time of Abraham and the time when social conditions made it possible for traditions to be written down. Can that gap be bridged, and if so how?

The simple answer is no, it cannot be bridged, if what one is looking for is the preservation by oral tradition of specific and accurate details over a period of 800 years. All the evidence from folklore studies shows that this is barely possible for 100 years or so, and not even conservative critical scholars would claim that details about the patriarchs have been accurately orally transmitted for the very much longer period in question. This being admitted, can the gap be bridged partially? Here, Old Testament scholars are divided between those who would say that the patriarchal narratives are late, literary compositions (Von Seters, 1975) and those, especially German scholars, who would hold that the narratives do in fact contain authentic scraps of material that date from the pre-1200 BCE period (cp. Otto 1976). Other experts (e.g. Westermann 1964) point to the social setting and preoccupations of the patriarchal narratives: they are concerned with acquiring land (e.g. Genesis 12: 7; 26: 22) and ensuring that there are descendants (Genesis 16, 18, 24). There are quarrels between brothers (Genesis 25: 27–34; 27: 1–45), while the wives of the patriarchs find themselves in danger, so that the continued existence of the family is put at risk (Genesis 12: 10–19; 20: 1–18; 26: 1–11). These stories, it can be argued, reflect the social conditions of migrant families, and are thus to be dated in the pre-settlement period, from which they have been preserved orally.

Having looked at some of the chronological and technological factors bearing upon the dating of the Old Testament, we can now turn our attention to the more complex of our two questions: how can, and should, the study of oral tradition be used in Old Testament interpretation? At the outset, it must be bluntly stated that oral tradition cannot help us to bridge gaps between the time of writing down of traditions and the alleged earlier times or events which oral traditions portray. The view that we can do this rests upon a false assumption, the belief that society develops along a straight line from being pre-literate to being literate. If we take the example of the patriarchal stories we can explain this more fully. The fact that the patriarchal stories are concerned with promises about land, with family rivalries, and with the need to protect the patriarch's wife, may show that they come from a particular social background; but it tells us nothing about the date of these stories. If it is argued that these stories must pre-date the monarchy, because in those times, Israel's ancestors were migrants concerned with land and family matters, it can be replied that there must have been family groups during the period of the monarchy that had just the same concerns. The fact that a centralized monarchy introduced scribes and scribal schools into the court did not mean that oral storytelling immediately ceased among the people, so that anything that looks as though it was originally oral must pre-date the introduction of scribal schools. In fact, an oral and a literate culture must have existed side-by-side in Israel for many centuries.

This is not to say that the patriarchal stories could not have pre-dated the monarchy. The point is that there is no way of knowing whether they do or not. "Oral" does not equal "early" if a society is both oral and literate. The greatest probability is that the characters of the patriarchal story, Abraham and Jacob, were real ancestors of Judah and Israel respectively and that they pre-dated the monarchy. Oral traditions told about them, however, would change over the generations, as the storytellers adapted the tales to the needs or the situation of the hearers.

The same uncertainty exists with regard to the use of oral tradition to reconstruct tribal movements from the patriarchal stories. The classic instance is the interpretation of the Jacob cycle. In the story, Jacob flees from his brother Esau and goes to Haran, where he marries his cousin's daughters, and later returns to his home in Canaan as a wealthy man. It is widely held that the episode of Jacob fleeing and returning is a device to link together traditions about two different groups of people, one of which was settled in Canaan, the other of which came from Haran, in northeast Mesopotamia. But there is a possible alternative interpretation. The motif of the hero being forced to leave home and later returning as a rich and powerful person is a common one in folk literature (Propp 1968, pp. 39, 55). We get a variation on it in the story of Joseph: the banished brother becomes powerful, and his family have to come

The stories of Jacob and Esau, from which Isaac's blessing of Esau is depicted here, probably reflect the political realities of the time when the stories were written down. This was probably the time of David or Solomon, when Edom (where Esau's ancestral roots lay) was subject to Israel and Judah.

to him and acknowledge his power. We cannot be certain, then, whether the Jacob cycle does contain memories about social migrations, or whether it merely conforms to a typical folk-tale plot structure. We must not overlook the fact that, in the Jacob story, Jacob represents Israel, and his brother Esau represents Edom. The Edomites were subject to Israel during the ninth century (2 Kings 3: 9). Thus, one could argue that the story of Jacob used a folk-tale plot in order to express Israel's superiority over Edom in the ninth century. We are not suggesting that this is the most likely explanation of the origin of the Jacob story in its present form; our point is that there are many possibilities.

Although oral tradition is of little use in reconstructing Israel's earliest history, we can certainly use it to trace the development of the Old Testament, and to understand why some of its material is patterned as it is.

A VARIETY OF ORAL TRADITIONS

The book of Judges

The book of Judges contains no fewer than three stories that deal with the tragic hero; and these are the only instances of this theme in the whole of the Old Testament. The simplest is the story of Jephthah (Judges 11–12). He is an example of the brother who is rejected by his brothers (Judges 11: 2) and who becomes more powerful than they (cp. Joseph). Jephthah is a tragic hero in that his vow to sacrifice the first person he meets if God grants his victory, eventually forces him to sacrifice his only child, a daughter (Judges 11: 34–40); cp. Gaster 1969, p. 430–1). He ends up victorious but without an heir. The story of Samson is more complex, but ends with him destroying his enemies and himself (Judges 16: 30) after his weakness for women has led to his downfall. The story of Abimelech (Judges 9) transforms some themes found in the Jephthah and Samson stories; Abimelech eliminates his brothers instead of being rejected by them, and ends his life in defeat. His demise, too, is caused by a woman — one who throws a millstone onto his head from the top of a tower.

The three stories are not only about tragic heroes; they contain religious sentiments that are surprising when considered in the light of the Old Testament as whole. Jephthah's vow to sacrifice a human being to God if he is granted victory is unparalleled in the Old Testament, and hardly represents its religion at its best. Samson, who is a Nazirite — that is, someone specially dedicated to God — hardly acts in a way that is creditable to God. He kills thirty men of Ashkelon in order to pay for a lost wager and seems to have a special liking for Philistine women. Abimelech also acts in an arbitrary and bloodthirsty manner. It is not unreasonable to conclude from these facts that the stories of Jephthah, Samson, and Abimelech were popular stories about local heroes, which, in the retelling, came to stress the tragic element, and which embodied popular superstition and crude morality. They were most probably collected and written down in Judah (see below) during the period of David or Solomon, because Jephthah and Abimelech are northern heroes, and it is unlikely that their stories would have been collected in Judah after the division of the kingdom on Solomon's death.

The books of Samuel

Even casual readers are likely to notice the great differences in style within the two books of Samuel. The first six chapters of 1 Samuel, apart from one short passage, are a coherent story, recounting the birth and dedication of Samuel; the wickedness of the priests, Eli's sons; the special message to Samuel from God, which, with great artistry, is only vaguely hinted at (1 Samuel 3: 18); and the sequel, in which Eli's sons are killed in battle, and the Ark is lost and then returned. First Samuel 2: 27–36 is a later addition, which both supplies the word of judgement, which is deliberately only hinted at in 3: 18, and spoils the artistry of the section. From 1 Samuel 7 to 24 the material becomes episodic, and sometimes chaotic. There is no clear picture, for example, of how and when Saul becomes king. At 10:.1 he is privately anointed by Samuel; at 10: 20–24 he is chosen by the casting of lots; and in 11: 1–15 his kingship is "renewed" after he defeats Nahash the Ammonite king. From chapter 18 to 24 we have a poorly-integrated series of episodes about David and Jonathan and about Saul's pursuit of David. It is very difficult to get the sense of a consecutive narrative. Then things begin to change from chapter 25, and from here until 2 Samuel 20, with only very occasional unevennesses, we get a highly artistic and connected narrative.

But from 2 Samuel 21–24 we are back with episodes that do not form a connected narrative.

The most likely explanation for the variations in style and coherence in the books of Samuel is that we have a mixture of original narratives, composed in a royal scribal school, and episodes that are written versions of oral stories. Because, during the reign of Saul and the beginning of that of David, there were no official chroniclers in Israel, it is not surprising that information about these periods could be obtained only from oral sources. Thus it is not surprising that there are differing accounts of how and when Saul became king, and that it is difficult, if not impossible, to trace the actual course of events once David appeared on the scene. Some points are clear from the episodes: David and Jonathan loved each other in spite of Saul's hostility to David, and Saul's daughter Michal was also faithful to David. Saul pursued David relentlessly once the latter had left the court. But these points are gleaned from originally unconnected stories rather than from a coherent narrative.

If some of the episodes in 1 Samuel 9–24 are written accounts of oral stories, then it is likely that they were written down fairly soon after the period with which they deal, and no later than the reign of Solomon. The conclusion that prevents us from supposing that authentic stories about Abraham could have circulated unchanged for hundreds of years, also commits us to accepting that oral stories about Saul, Jonathan, and David must have been written down within a generation when we come to work out how much of the Old Testament existed before the exile.

In this section on the books of Samuel, no attempt has been made to indicate the origins of the opening six chapters of the first book, which, as we noted, form a coherent narrative. Their source could well be oral stories about the Ark and about Samuel himself, but in their present form they seem to have been worked together into an artistic whole. This does not necessarily mean that this was done at the writing stage. Oral storytelling is quite capable of producing coherent and dramatic narratives, as we shall see later. Thus the form of 1 Samuel 1–6 could be the product of either oral performance or written composition. By contrast, the short, episodic parts of 1 Samuel have the earmarks of being originally oral units which have not been integrated at either the oral or written stage.

Genesis

Having considered Judges and Samuel, we can return to the stories about the patriarchs in Genesis. The Abraham cycle runs from Genesis 12 to 24: 10. In its present form it is a combination of a priestly and a non-priestly version of the story, of which the former was probably not added until the exile. If, for the moment, we exclude the priestly material (Genesis 12: 4b–5b, 16: 15–17: 27, 23: 1, and 25: 7–11), we are left with what is probably a mixture of oral-based traditions combined with literary compositions. The oral-based material probably consists of the Abraham–Lot cycle (13: 2–5, 8–13, 18: 1–15, and 19: 1–38) and the

Events from the life of Abraham in Genesis 18 and 22 are illustrated in this sixth-century mosaic from the basilica of St. Vitale in Ravenna. Beneath a tree in the centre are the three visitors who are given a meal of cakes and a calf by Abraham and his wife on the left. On the right, Abraham is prevented from killing Isaac by the voice of God, symbolized here by a four-fingered hand so that a representation of God in completely human terms is avoided. The substituted ram is at Abraham's feet.

story of Abraham purchasing a burial cave at Mamre (23: 1–20). In the Abraham–Lot stories there are a number of folk motifs: the visit of unrecognized angelic guests (18: 1–8), the promise of a child to a barren woman (18: 9–15), the superior powers of angelic visitors (19: 11), the dangers of looking back (19: 17–26), and the incest of a man with his daughters (19: 30–38). The account of the destruction of the Sodom area (19: 24–5) is probably a folk explanation for the weird landscape in the Dead Sea basin.

If parts of Genesis 18–19 and 23 are correctly identified as oral-based traditions, it is possible to make suggestions about their origin. All have as their main setting the oaks of Mamre, near Hebron. They legitimate Abraham's settlement there, and they stress that Abraham's descendants came as a result of divine promise, whereas the neighbouring and related peoples of Ammon and Moab are descendants of a man who committed incest with his daughters. If these stories reflect the circumstances of the times when their spoken form was written down, this is most likely to have been the time of David and Solomon. In this period, Ammon and Moab were subject to Judah, and Judah would be represented in in the story by Abraham, whose residence of Hebron was the Judahite capital. We are not denying that Abraham was an historical figure, who may well have been part of a migration of peoples from northeast Mesopotamia to Judah. Our point is that these oral traditions about him reflect the circumstances of the time of their telling. These circumstances fit the time of David or Solomon better than any other, and give us a clue as to when they were written down.

The Dead Sea and Judean desert.

The Jacob cycle is much more extensive, stretching from Genesis 27 to 33. It shows every sign of being an expanded oral narrative on the theme of a hero leaving home because of danger, and returning a powerful man. It abounds with folk motifs: Jacob and Esau are twins and rival cultural heroes; the blessing intended for the elder is diverted by trickery; in Haran a false bride (Leah) is substituted for the intended one (Rachel); while the basis for Jacob's outwitting of Laban is the folk belief that what animals look at affects the colour of their offspring (30: 5–43). The wrestling at the river Jabbok with a heavenly messenger that cannot endure the arrival of the dawn contains several well known motifs.

It may be possible to detect behind the Jacob cycle the reality that his descendants had come to Canaan from the northeast and had established themselves in the Bethel and Samaria hills with some difficulty. In its present form, however, the cycle celebrates the superiority of Jacob over the inhabitants of the northeast and over the people of Edom, personified by Esau. Again, the reign of David or Solomon is the most likely period for the writing down of the situation reflected in the Jacob cycle. Both Edom and northern Syrian kingdoms were subject to Israel in the latter part of David's reign and the early part of Solomon's.

Exodus

With the account of the Exodus in Exodus 1–15, we are in a different situation. The stories of Abraham and Jacob were traditions preserved respectively in Judah and Israel, centring upon ancestors of those peoples; the story of the Exodus is the story of a corporate deliverance, and as such probably owes its existence to an annual celebration. In its present form it consists of priestly and non-priestly material; but it also has many folk motifs.

In Exodus 1: 15–22 the pharaoh speaks to the two (!) midwives who deliver all the Hebrew babies. This extreme simplifying of matters is typical of oral narratives. When one considers what an exalted person the pharaoh was, and what an extensive bureaucracy he possessed, it is ludicrous to suppose that he talked personally to two midwives; but folk narrative necessarily simplifies these things. In Exodus 2, the birth of the hero in circumstances of danger is a well-instanced folk motif, while the flight of Moses to Midian and his subsequent return parallel the flight and return of Jacob.

In chapters 5–11 the narrative is shaped into a series of episodes in which Moses (accompanied by his brother Aaron) has interviews with the pharaoh. Each interview ends with Pharaoh agreeing to let the Israelites go if the particular plague that is afflicting the people is ended. As soon as there is respite from the plague, however, the cycle begins again. The pharaoh goes back on his word, he is threatened with a new plague, and then temporarily relents when the plague comes. Behind this shaping is probably the art of the oral storyteller, holding the attention of the listeners, and building the story to a climax. Chapters 12–14 contain priestly regulations about the Passover and an evidently written literary account of the Exodus. Chapter 15, however, is probably based upon an old hymn which celebrated the deliverance at the Red Sea.

There are no clues within Exodus 1–15 about the date of recording of the oral elements. If we could be sure that Exodus 15 was recorded at the same time as the other oral-based traditions, we would have an indication of the date. The hymn ends with the words

> Thou wilt bring them in, and plant them on thy own mountain,
> the place, O Lord, which thou hast made for thy abode,
> the sanctuary, O Lord, which thy hands have established.
>
> (Exodus 15: 17)

This is clearly an attempt to link the Exodus deliverance with the establishment of Jerusalem as God's abode. This could point, again, to the time of David or Solomon. However, we must also accept that the hymn could have been written down, or that verse 17 could have been added later, at any period after the establishment of Jerusalem as Israel's religious capital.

With the Exodus traditions, we come to the end of those parts of the Old Testament in which it may be possible to detect the presence of originally oral traditions. This is not to say that material such as Numbers 12–24 or Joshua 2–12 are not based upon oral tradition; it is just that we cannot be sure of this. Also, we must add that Judges probably contains more oral-based material than we discussed above. Further examples would be the traditions about the local heroes Ehud (Judges 3: 15–25), Deborah and Jael (Judges 4), and Gideon (Judges 6–8).

WRITTEN FORMS OF THE OLD TESTAMENT

So far, we have tried to identify material that is derived from oral traditions. We now try to outline how that material was used in the process of the growth of the Old Testament. Our starting point is the view that Israel was initially an association of villages in the Bethel and Samaria hills from about 1230 BCE. This group of people possessed oral traditions about a common ancestor, Jacob, and stories about the struggles of tribal leaders with Canaanite cities (cp. Genesis 34, Judges 4–5 and 9, and possibly Joshua 9 and 12). The villages may also have been united by faith in Yhwh, who had delivered the ancestors of some of those now settled in Canaan from slavery in Egypt. Among these people there was probably a group who were custodians of the stories about the Exodus and who observed the Passover. Judah was a separate entity with traditions about an ancestor, Abraham, who had settled in the Hebron area, and traditions about tribal leaders who had fought against Canaanite cities (cp. Judges 1: 11–17, and possibly Joshua 10). We are not suggesting that the traditions as now written down in the Old Testament are identical with their oral form or content in the period 1230 to 1050 BCE.

Political considerations

With the triumph of David over the Philistines, the establishment of his rule over Judah and Israel, and the designation of Jerusalem as the political and religious capital of the united kingdom, there arose two important needs. First of all the kingdom needed a "story" that would explain its existence. In particular, the Judahite Abraham traditions needed to be integrated with the Israelite Jacob traditions, and Judah itself had to be seen as a member of the Israelite association of villages and their "tribes". Secondly, an "apology" for David was needed. He had, after all, been a Philistine vassal, and was arguably related to the royal house of the Ammonites (see chapter 4, p. 123). These needs led to the creation, during the reign of Solomon, of what we might call a first draft of parts of Genesis, Exodus, Numbers, Joshua, Judges, the books of Samuel, and 1 Kings 1–10.

This composition produced a continuous story from Abraham to the time of Solomon. In integrating together the traditions that needed to be included, a number of choices, some of them unavoidable, were made.

First of all, the Judahite ancestor, Abraham, was placed prior to the Israelite ancestor, Jacob, by the device of making them respectively grandfather and grandson, via the probably Judahite ancestor Isaac (see chapter 2, p. 53). This produced the oddity that the most prominent of the patriarchs, namely Abraham, is not the immediate ancestor of Israel; but the compilers had no choice, given the prominence of Jacob within the traditions possessed by the Israel group, i.e. the villagers in the Bethel and Samaria hills. In any case, the order Abraham → Jacob expressed Judah's dominance.

Moreover, the wish to make the deliverance from Egypt the religious event that founded Israel necessitated constructing the story in such a way that the ancestors of all the tribes journeyed to Egypt, and that all their descendants experienced the Exodus, travelled through the wilderness, and forcefully occupied the land of Canaan.

It was also necessary to demonstrate the loyalty of David to Saul and to his own people. No opportunity was lost in this respect; for example, it is stressed that David spared Saul's life (1 Samuel 24: 1–22; 26: 6–25) and punished with death someone who claimed to have killed Saul (2 Samuel 1: 1–16). We are not concerned here with the historicity or otherwise of these passages; their purpose is clearly to exonerate David.

Finally, it was necessary to portray David and Solomon, and their capital, Jerusalem, as the true successors and fulfillers of promises made to Abraham about the possession of the land.

Given these choices, the literary work telling the story from the time of Abraham to that of Solomon integrated the recorded versions of oral traditions about Abraham, Jacob, the Exodus, the "Judges", and the period of Samuel and Saul with exquisite literary compositions, such as the Joseph story (Genesis 37, 39–45) and the story of David's rise and the succession to his throne (parts of 1 Samuel 16–24, and substantially 1 Samuel 25–31, 2 Samuel 1–6, 9–20, 1 Kings 1–2).

The edition of the reign of Josiah

The next stage in the growth of these traditions was their adaptation to a new history of Israel and Judah during the reign of Josiah (640–609 BCE). At its simplest, this involved bringing the history up to date. The first draft had concluded with the reign of Solomon. Josiah lived 300 years later, and the intervening events could be described on the basis of royal archives, referred to as the books of the Chronicles of the kings of Judah and Israel. But the events following the reign of Solomon raised enormous problems for a people that believed in the power of Yhwh. The kingdom had split after his death; both Judah and Israel had at times lost their independence to Syria, Egypt, or Assyria; and the northern kingdom had disappeared in 722/1 BCE.

The purpose of the new edition of Israel's history that was produced in Josiah's reign was not only to record but also to explain the many setbacks that had been experienced. This explanation not only affected how the events following Solomon's death to Josiah's day were presented; it also affected the form and content of earlier books.

This can be seen most clearly in Judges. In its first draft, the book of Judges was intended to show that Israel needed permanent leadership, but leadership of God's choosing (i.e. David's). The heroes who might have set up dynasties were unsuitable; Gideon produced a son who indeed tried to set up a dynasty (Judges 9), but with disastrous results; Jephthah's vow compelled him to sacrifice his only offspring; Samson seems to have died childless. The so-called epilogue to Judges (chapters 17–21; there is no reason to exclude these from the first draft) shows the increasing chaos resulting from the fact that "there was no king in Israel" (Judges 17: 6).

The second edition of Judges puts the material into a totally different scheme: the scheme of the constant rebellion of Israel, which led God to punish the nation through the agency of neighbouring peoples and to deliver the nation by means of the "judges". The perspective of the book has shifted so that it has become an object lesson pointing up the perils of disobeying God by serving the gods of Canaan. This same theme is also present in 1 Kings from chapter 12 onwards, with the difference that here it is not the people but the kings who are judged for compromising total allegiance to Yhwh.

A further device used in the second edition of Joshua, Judges, and the books of Samuel is the address by a leader, or a theological meditation. Joshua 1 begins with an address by God to Joshua (Joshua 1: 2–9) and ends with an address of Joshua to the people (Joshua 23; part of Joshua 24 already existed in the first draft). In 1 Samuel 12 there is a speech by Samuel; and 2 Kings 17: 7–23 contains a meditation upon the reasons for the loss of the northern kingdom, Israel, in 722/1 BCE. These key passages contain two main themes: that the diasters that befell Israel and Judah were the fault of the people, because they turned from the God of Israel to other gods, and that they were the fault of the kings, because they did not obey the law of God given through Moses. There is a framework that contains the second edition of the history. It begins with Joshua 1: 9

> Only be strong and very courageous, being careful to do according to all the law which Moses my servant commanded you; turn not to the right hand or to the left . . .,

and ends with 2 Kings 23: 25:

> Before him [Josiah] there was no king like him, who turned to the Lord . . . according to all the laws of Moses. . . .

The twin themes of the disobedience of the people and the need for kings to obey the law produce a curious contradiction in the books of Joshua and Judges. In Judges, it is necessary that there should be Canaanites remaining after the conquest, because it is their gods who lead Israel astray, resulting in the divine punishment. In Joshua, the picture of Joshua as the one who totally obeys the law results in his totally destroying all the Canaanites (Joshua 10: 40). Thus, in one view there are no Canaanites left, and in the other their presence is the snare that leads to Israel's downfall.

To summarize therefore, we can say that before the exile there existed in written form parts of Genesis, Exodus, Numbers, Deuteronomy, Joshua, Judges, 1 and 2 Samuel, and 1 and 2 Kings to 2 Kings 23: 25a. Originally, the material from Genesis to 1 Kings 10 had told the story of Israel from Abraham to David and Solomon. The second version had added 1 Kings 11 to 23: 25a, and had also edited Joshua to 2 Kings to make this, in fact, a separate work with a distinctive viewpoint: disobedience brings disaster, and kings must be faithful to the law of Moses. In the next chapter we shall describe how Genesis to 2 Kings reached its final form.

What of the remainder of the Old Testament? Of some parts we can definitely say that they were composed during or after the exile, and therefore did not exist before 587 BCE. These would include Chronicles, Ezra, Nehemiah, Esther, Isaiah 40–66, Jeremiah, Ezekiel, Daniel, Joel, Jonah, Haggai, Zechariah, and Malachi. About the remainder we are uncertain. It is quite likely that parts of the book of Proverbs existed, as indicated by Proverbs 25: 1:

> These also are proverbs of Solomon which the men of Hezekiah king of Judah copied.

Whether or not these proverbs were really spoken by Solomon, it is likely that proverbs believed to be by him were copied in the royal scribal school of Hezekiah's time (late eighth century BCE).

Some of the oracles attributed to Isaiah, Hosea, Amos, Micah, Nahum, and Zephaniah were probably written down and were preserved among prophetic groups. There were probably collections of laws and of psalms, while details of priestly rituals, if not written down, were carefully passed from generation to generation. Whether any of these materials at this stage were regarded as Scripture is unlikely. For the collecting together of books that began to be regarded as authoritative for Israel's faith, certain social conditions were necessary. A beginning had been made, of course, in the reigns of David and Solomon, although the motivation had probably been as much political as religious. The reign of Josiah, however, was probably a watershed. Political considerations were not absent, but Josiah's reform seems to have been a sustained attempt to unite the people by means of a single national cult based upon obedience to divine law and set in the context of an enlarged story about the identity and responsibilities of Israel. It would be the exile and its aftermath, however, that would provide the circumstances in which the tendencies apparent in Josiah's reign would become movements, and the idea of an authoritative collection of sacred books would become an actuality.

CHAPTER 17

POST-EXILIC COLLECTIONS AND THE FORMATION OF THE CANON

In this concluding chapter we shall consider the final editing (or writing) of the Pentateuch and the Former Prophets, the creation of the books of the Latter Prophets, and the collection of Prophets as a whole; the composition of the Writings (the blanket term for the remaining Old Testament books), and the creation of the canon. We shall also consider that part of the text of the Hebrew Bible which is now canonical, and the evidence of other non-canonical texts which have been preserved or are attested in ancient translations.

THE PENTATEUCH

The process by which the Pentateuch was formed is highly disputed. Until recently it was widely accepted as a fact that it had been put together from four major literary "sources", which, understood in their correct sequence, also provided a framework for a critical history of Israel's religion. These sources are traditionally identified as follows: J (the "Yahwist", who uses the divine name Yhwh), who wrote in the ninth century BCE; E (who uses *'elohim*, "God"), dated a little later; D (mostly the book of Deuteronomy), in the seventh century; and P (the Priestly writer), who dates from the exile. This approach was known as the Documentary Hypothesis. While working within these sources, however, scholars had become accustomed to tracing a pre-history of some of the contents, going back to shorter and often oral compositions. A great climax was reached in the work of Gerhard von Rad and Martin Noth in Germany in the 1930s and 1940s, each of whom produced an account of the history of the composition the Pentateuch from its very beginnings to its final form. Noth argued that five originally independent themes — "promise to the patriarchs", "guidance out of Egypt", "guidance into the arable land", "guidance in the wilderness", and "revelation at Sinai" — had been combined into a continuous history before J and E wrote, while P was seen as a final editor, rather than merely another source-document. Von Rad, on the contrary, saw the Pentateuch as growing up around a kernel which contained nearly all the main components — promise to patriarchs, exodus, and land occupation — and which was filled out with stories until the outline of the Pentateuchal story was achieved. Only the Sinai story, in his view, was originally independent. For Von Rad, J, the Yahwist, was the author of the earliest draft of the Pentateuch. Working in the reign of Solomon, J wrote down the emerging national tradition of Israel's beginnings and history up to the occupation of the land after the Exodus, and prefaced it with an account of the origins of the world and humanity (Genesis 1–11).

Neither of these scholars (whose work dominated German and Anglo-American scholarship for decades) cast doubt on the existence of the four component documents. For them, although the final composition was late, the first complete draft was early: at the beginning of the monarchy, if not before. The only major alternative to this view (apart from the fundamentalist one) was in Scandinavia, where many scholars preferred to think of two circles of tradition (corresponding to D and P) who committed their stories to writing relatively late.

In the last twenty years, however, Pentateuchal criticism has taken some new directions. Many of the above conclusions are now being abandoned. Of the original sources, the only one that is not hypothetical is the book of Deuteronomy (discussed in chapter 16). Of the three other sources postulated in the New Documentary Hypothesis, as it is called, the E source is considered, at best, to be represented only intermittently and, at worst, never to have existed. The Priestly writer has tended to be seen as the final or near-final creator of the Pentateuch in its present form, and thus becomes less of a source and more of an author/reviser of the final product. It is the Yahwist, the J source, which in recent debate has proved to be the key issue. Among scholars who still accept the existence of a Yahwist, several date him to the exilic period. Many other scholars are now doubting the existence of any of the documents (see Whybray 1987). Unlike Noth's "themes" combining at an early stage to form the "Pentateuchal tradition", these themes are seen as developing independently and being combined only at a relatively late stage to form the connected Pentateuchal narrative. (Conceivably, Noth might have adopted this view had he not inherited the "Documentary Hypothesis"). Whybray, without denying the existence of some sorts of sources, assigns the compilation of the Pentateuch to a single author.

Some possible outlines

It is simply no longer possible to chart with any confidence the process by which the Pentateuch was composed. The problem is, essentially, that it can be sliced up in two ways: the existence of passages spread across the Pentateuch that share linguistic and ideological features provides a basis for a horizontal division, such as the Documentary Hypothesis provided; on the other hand, form-critical and tradition-critical analysis has suggested an equally cogent vertical segmentation into blocks of materials strung together to create a continuous history.

Another complicating factor is the relationship between the Former

Prophets (the "Deuteronomistic History") and the Pentateuch. Most adherents of the Documentary Hypothesis were inclined to think that the Pentateuchal sources originally told of the conquest of the land. These sources, it was usually argued, could sometimes be discerned, but on the whole they had been submerged by the authors of Joshua and Judges. Noth's thesis of a Deuteronomistic History (see chapter 16) argued that Joshua-Kings belonged to an independent work, of which Deuteronomy was the first part. Only when this work was placed after the equivalent of Genesis-Numbers did Deuteronomy get detached and integrated into what became the "Pentateuch". If, as is now thought, Joshua-Kings or Deuteronomy-Kings is older as a unit than the Pentateuch, new perspectives on their relationship are needed. Possibly the two collections of Pentateuch and Former Prophets were once seen as continuous. At the opposite extreme, perhaps Genesis-Kings is formed of nine or even eleven separate works, which, over the course of being added to, grew naturally to fill the chronological gaps between each other to produce a single narrative, though retaining the division into books. It pays to remember that we are not talking about "books" but "scrolls", and whereas we can buy *War and Peace* or even the Bible, in a single volume, the Pentateuch and Former Prophets were always sets of scrolls. How can we know what it meant for several scrolls to form a single "work"? How does this differ from a single scribe deciding to copy them all (for his own use, even) and at the same time insert his own comments into them. Was he producing a single "work"?

The present state of uncertainty about the composition of the Pentateuch is in some ways welcome to the scholar, but is highly unsatisfactory to the general reader, or even the student. So let us present a hypothesis — even though it is neither complete nor very certain (hardly even probable, given the range of possibilities!) To begin with, we can assume that the Pentateuch, in its present form, came into existence in the Persian (that is, post-exilic) period by a process which was perhaps relatively rapid but also complex. Let us begin to construct our hypothesis by noting two processes which seem to have occurred during the formation of the Pentateuch. One is the production of a *continuous historical narrative*, either in two stages (creation to land entry, conquest to exile) or perhaps even one stage. The other is the incorporation of blocks of legal material, probably already in existence, into that narrative. The first process created, in effect, a continuous story, in however many scrolls; the second created the Torah and Former Prophets, distinct from one another in character and status.

Now for more detail. The earliest components of the Pentateuch will have included two collections of law: one, pre-exilic, represented in Deuteronomy, the other, with its roots in the pre-exilic period later inserted into the Pentateuchal narrative as what documentary critics would call "P". Additionally, we may suppose the existence of cycles of origin stories, including probably four different explanations of how Israel came to be — and, in particular, came to be in Canaan.

One explanation had Yhwh summon the ancestor Abra(ha)m from Syria (Haran) to the land in which he settled with his family. Another had the Israelites finding refuge in Canaan after having escaped from Egypt. A third had them coming from outside, from the "wilderness" to conquer the land by warfare. There may have been a fourth one which had individual tribes wandering in from different directions and either defeating, or living alongside, or living under the existing occupants.

At some point in the Persian period, perhaps among those in Babylonia, perhaps in Palestine, these various stories were connected into a single narrative. Whether the story went as far as Deuteronomy and conquest we cannot say; but if not, no account of the occupation of the land was needed, since occupation of the land presented no problem. The Israelites would have been assumed to have returned to the land of the patriarchs without any difficulty, rich after their departure from Egypt.

The next stage in the development of the Pentateuch is the incorporation of the legal codes of Deuteronomy and "P". With their inclusion came also enlargement of the narrative. Deuteronomy introduced the theme of land conquest and expulsion of the Canaanites, while "P" attracted some additions such as Genesis I and a number of genealogies (Genesis 5, 10).

To explain how these processes occurred, a comment is needed, by the way, about "editing" and "copying", just as it was needed earlier about the idea of a "single work". It is common, but erroneous, to imagine an ancient process of scribal copying which did not also entail revision. There is very little evidence that any ancient scribe normally copied an earlier document without altering it, unless he was ordered to produce multiple copies of a single decree or inscription; conversely, there is plenty of evidence that scribes *did* change as they "copied". So we ought to suppose that every time the "Pentateuch" or its components were copied, the opportunity was taken to "update" it. This process no doubt happened at least every generation, probably every decade, possibly sometimes even more frequently. Accordingly, we ought not to oversimplify the process by which the Pentateuch was formed. Many small and imperceptible changes no doubt occurred whenever a scribe made a copy. We can only identify major revisions which represent conscious efforts to amend the overall shape or ideology. Like the prophetic books, this Pentateuch is the product of many anonymous writers, not just the occasional inspired individual who produced a new "edition". Every copy made was, in itself, a new "edition".

THE ADOPTION OF THE "LAW OF MOSES"

When did the present form of the Pentateuch, or Torah, become the definitive written (i.e. "scriptural") text of the "law of Moses"? In Joshua 23: 6; 1 Kings 2: 3; and 2 Kings 14: 6 and 23: 25, the "law of Moses" probably refers to some form of Deuteronomy. As we have noted above, Joshua and Kings are all "Deuteronomistic" (i.e. utilizing the ideas and language of Deuteronomy), and it would be expected that their understanding of the Mosaic law would correspond to that book, which was perhaps the earliest written codification of a "Mosaic law". In Chronicles, Ezra, and Nehemiah, however, which are not "Deuteronomistic", it is not clear whether Deuteronomy, "P", or the Pentateuch as a whole is meant when the law is referred to. The laws of P, though now attributed to Moses, represented the theory and practice of the Jerusalem Temple priesthood, and were probably at first not associated with Moses. However, the formation of the Pentateuch brought all divine law under the general rubric of "Mosaic" law — that is to say, it was all assigned to the revelation at Sinai.

Had this process of amalgamation taken place by the time of Ezra in the fifth century BCE? Most scholars think so, but we cannot be certain. In Nehemiah 8: 1, Ezra is said to have brought "the book of the law which the Lord has given to Israel". This law book, we can deduce from the second verse, contained prescriptions for celebrating the Feast of Booths. But of the rest of its contents we are told nothing. Nevertheless, the prayer in the following chapter of Nehemiah includes a history of God's deeds, beginning with Creation (reminiscent of Genesis 1 though with few verbal parallels), proceeding to the calling of Abraham from Ur of the Chaldeans (cp. Genesis 11: 28) and the giving of his name (cp. Genesis 17: 5), the covenant to dispossess the Canaanites (unmistakeably from Deuteronomy), the crossing of the Red Sea, the law-giving (*not* the covenant!) at Sinai, the provision of manna in the wilderness (cp. Exodus 16 or Numbers 11), and the entry into Canaan. Thus, at least by the time of the composition of the prayer — whether by Ezra or the author of the book of Nehemiah — the present form of the Pentateuch, narrative and laws, Deuteronomic and Priestly, seems to have been known. It seems plausible, in any case, that the formation of the religious community under the Persian rule would have required a fairly definitive code of religious law. The adoption of the "law of Moses" as Torah in the fifth century BCE thus seems likely.

THE PROPHETIC COLLECTIONS

Apart from an allusion to judges, the events recounted in Nehemiah 9 refer only to the Pentateuch, as do those early events mentioned in psalms 78, 105, 106, 135, and 136. By contrast, Ben Sira, in the third century BCE, (chapters 44–49) knows and recounts the whole story from Adam to Nehemiah, (not Ezra!), and mentions Isaiah, Jeremiah, Ezekiel, and the book of the twelve minor prophets (see below). By the time of Ben Sira, then, the collection of scriptural texts had been extended to include all of the prophets and some of what were to be called the Writings.

The origins of the Former Prophets (the "Deuteronomistic History") have been treated in chapter 16, and here we need only explain how these books came to carry the name "Prophets". The Chronicler, who uses the books of Samuel and Kings quite extensively and often verbatim, probably alludes to them as the "Book of the Kings of Israel and Judah" (e.g. 2 Chronicles 25: 26). The fact that he uses them, of course, does not imply that they had any scriptural status — possibly the reverse! Now, contemporary with the work of the Chronicler, a process of compiling prophetic books was taking place. It has been suggested that this process seems to reflect the sort of interests of those influenced by the ideas and language of Deuteronomy and the Deuteronomistic history. Perhaps we should think of two groups in Jerusalem: one interested primarily in the cultic reinterpretation of Israel's past, present, and future (the Chronicler and the framers of the priestly laws in the Pentateuch); the other interested in the prophetic reinterpretation of past, present, and future — whom we often loosely call "Deuteronomists". (Incidentally, it is worthwhile considering that although the former group were essentially priestly and the latter scribal, Jerusalem was a small place, and these two groups can hardly have remained entirely separate. Possibly they overlapped to a large extent.)

The Latter Prophets do show clear signs of collection and formation by "Deuteronomists", as we shall presently see. Thus, they were made in some kind of association with those responsible for the Deuteronomistic History. In the light of this, we can understand how both bodies of literature became associated, and how the name "Former Prophets" was applied to the Deuteronomistic History. But more than a change of nomenclature took place. Understanding the story of Israel's pre-exilic history as "prophecy", or as an account of prophecy, gave depth and vindication to the collections in the Latter Prophets — although these prophets were not (with the exception of Isaiah) "written back" into the Former Prophets. But both Jeremiah 52 and Isaiah 36–39 contain excerpts from the Deuteronomistic History.

As we have said, by the beginning of the second century BCE the prophetic books had a scriptural status. Daniel, in the middle of the second century BCE, finds Jeremiah "in the books" (Daniel 9: 2). At the end of the second century BCE (or a little later), we find in 2 Maccabees the term "Law and Prophets".

The Books of the Latter Prophets

We have looked in some detail, in chapter 12, at the composition of Isaiah, as an example of how the prophetic books were assembled. Here we shall look at the remaining books individually. For they are certainly in most cases "collections" which took place over a period of time, almost entirely in the exilic and post-exilic periods.

Jeremiah

A brief description of the book of Jeremiah and of its author/subject is given in chapter 12. Here we shall look at the content.

The prophet Jeremiah — here represented in a fifteenth-century stained glass window — was, with Isaiah, a favourite Old Testament prophet for Christians on account of his personal anguish and rejection by his contemporaries, which prefigured the suffering of Christ.

Scholarship on the book offers little consensus. There is widely accepted classification of the materials into four kinds: (a) poetry attributed to Jeremiah himself, found in chapters 1–25; (b) historical tales about him (sometimes attributed to Baruch) in chapters 26–45; (c) prose speeches attributed to Jeremiah but not authentic, in chapter 1–45; and (d) a "book of consolation" in chapters 30–31. The remaining chapters, 46–52, are usually considered secondary (though secondary to *what* remains an open question). But there is little consensus on how these relate to each other or to Jeremiah. Among the material in (a) are the so-called "confessions" (11: 18–12: 6; 15: 10–21; 17: 14–18; 18: 18–23; 20: 7–18, possibly more). Are these Jeremiah's own experiences, his words, or are they psalms (perhaps derived from the prophetic office in the cult (Reventlow 1963) or, at least, used by later editors of the book to create the prophetic character? The prose speeches, the most coherent body of material in the book, are thoroughly Deuteronomistic in style and ideology. Yet how close are these speeches to Jeremiah? Some scholars hold that Jeremiah himself wrote them; others, that they are a development and application of the prophet's thought; still others, that they are an outright invention, having nothing to do with Jeremiah. No simple answer presents itself. There are certainly internal contradictions. Material in (a), which is most likely to contain original sayings of

Jeremiah, opposes prophets in general, thinks little of the Temple, and calls for submission, rather than repentance. The speeches assigned to (c) are dominated by criticism of cultic impurity, and by calls to repentance. The book also offers hope and consolation, and presents Jeremiah to us as a prophet who speaks to those exiled, perhaps also those who have returned. A good example is 24: 4–10:

Like these good figs I will regard as good the exiles from Judah, whom I have sent away from this place to the land of the Chaldeans . . . like the bad figs . . . so will I treat Zedekiah the king of Judah, his princes, *the remnant of Jerusalem who remain in this land* and those who dwell in the land of Egypt . . . .

Here Jeremiah's own political situation is reinterpreted into the "restoration" community, where the *golah* (Hebrew "exile", those priding themselves on having been in exile and preserving their religion intact) is turning upon those who remained in the land, using Jeremiah, the successful prophet whose words were fulfilled as a sanction.

If to many readers Jeremiah seems the most immediately accessible of all the prophets, scholarship deems otherwise. While scholarly attempts continue to be made (Holladay 1986, 1988) to write Jeremiah's biography from the contents of his book, analysis of the way the contents have been put together suggests a long, even tortuous process. The book of Jeremiah, then, is a collection that has grown around the words and the figure of one who interpreted the Babylonian invasion as divine punishment and was persecuted by the leaders of the community. Around that core have developed sermons which create of this figure a Deuteronomistic prophet *par excellence*, who can provide a lesson for exiles. He himself, as much as his words, is the object of interest. McKane (1986) has argued that the book constitutes a "rolling corpus" in which bits of existing text, poetry, or prose have generated comments or expansions, but not so as to create an overall unity. McKane sees the growth of the book as a *literary* and organic one, not one tied to external events or historical "occasions". Carroll (1986), who likewise finds little overall coherence, believes that the context of any passage can be gained only by investigating the theological interests that inspire it, and finds many different circles in the exilic and Persian periods to have been responsible. If these views are right — and they are argued in great detail — then the book of Jeremiah is a supreme post-exilic *collection* in its own right.

Ezekiel

Quite apart from its intriguing psychological dimension, the book of Ezekiel (see also chapter 12) is also distinctive as literature. First of all, it is written largely in prose. It also has a tighter structure than either Jeremiah or Isaiah: chapters 1–24 contain speeches of denunciation; chapters 25–32 deal with foreign nations, and 34–48 with salvation. (This overall arrangement is like that of Isaiah.) The whole book is written in the first person, and there are frequent datings (based on the reign of Jehoiachin), which assign the contents between the years 593 and 571 BCE; these, together with the formula "the word of the Lord came to me: 'son of man . . . .' " (or some element of this) divides the book into exactly fifty units. The initial impression of an orderly autobiographical sequence disintegrates under scrutiny, however: there are signs of revision (e.g. 1: 15–21 actually amends the description that surrounds it), and some individual groups of units can be discerned (e.g. chapters 29–32). These units are more extended, more impersonal and abstract, and more developed in their imagery and argument than the shorter pieces of Isaiah or Jeremiah. Both the judgement and restoration of the nation are much more dramatically depicted — e.g. in chapter 16, where Judah and Israel are described as whores, and in chapter 37, where dried-out bones come to life. The conscious literary creation of "prophecy" also takes place in the re-use of older texts (such as Isaiah 5, Psalm 46, and Jeremiah 4–6) in chapters 38–39; the "call" of Isaiah and Jeremiah — as well as Exodus 24 — is evoked in Ezekiel's own "call" (1: 1–3: 15). The process of what is now called "inner-biblical exegesis", or interpretation of one biblical text in another, can be seen in Ezekiel. This even happens *within* the book (compare chapters 16 and 23). The book has, much more than Isaiah or Jeremiah, the marks of a coherent literary shaping, though not of an individual author. The autobiographical style, weird imagery, use of angelic guides (chapters 40–48), re-use of Scripture, appropriation of mythical motifs, speculation about the end of history, and many other features point towards the kind of scribal activity that produced apocalypses (see chapter 14).

As for the major ideological features of the book, they are much concerned with holiness, the cult and the Temple. The ability of Yhwh to vindicate himsef, to demonstrate his power, both to Israel and to other nations, is emphasized; and the final assault of the nations on Jerusalem (38–39) is the ultimate demonstration of this. The book is also concerned to counteract the notion among the exiles that they were suffering for the sins of a previous generation, rather than for their own. The overwhelming impression of God's distance, emphasized by Israel's wretchedness, by the elaborate imagery of the prose, the reiteration of Yhwh's holiness, and the culmination of the book in a description of a new Jerusalem dominated by a new Temple, points to priestly ideology.

The signs are, then, that the book is the product of several authors, who share a common outlook and even a common literary style. It is certainly a complex, highly artistic, and, above all, *literary* product. It does not describe the outward activity of a prophet of the kind that a reader of Kings, Amos or Jeremiah would expect. Is the real Ezekiel, like Jeremiah, mainly a vessel of later writers? What purpose does this collection serve? It certainly reflects the attitudes of those exiled against those not exiled, and particularly those of the priests.

The Minor Prophets

The Minor Prophets were originally considered to be a single book. Of the origin and composition of most of the individual books we know, in fact, very little. The arrangement is apparently chronological, according to the superscriptions (and in the case of Jonah, his dating in 2 Kings 14: 25). Other signs of unity are repeated phrases such as "the word of Yhwh which came to" and "which he saw"; and the collection ends with three sections called "saying" in Zechariah and Malachi (Zechariah 9: 1, 12: 1; Malachi 1: 1). Since the title of the last-named book means "my messenger" and may therefore be a pseudonym, Malachi may even be an artificial prophet, invented to make the number of minor prophets up to twelve, and is credited with a "saying" that once belonged at the end of the book of Zechariah.

What principle, if any, controls the assembly of this multiple book, and of the Latter Prophets taken together? One clear answer is that all of these books point towards the *eschaton* (Greek "last things") — the definitive act of God at some time in the future which will resolve all the tensions of history and fulfil the act of Creation and the election of Israel. The final chapters or passages of all the prophetic books give, in different ways, a picture of how things will be. Much of Isaiah 40–66 dwells on this theme, while the last chapter, for example, speaks of gathering the exiles of Israel to the "holy mountain" of Jerusalem, "all flesh" worshipping Yhwh, a new creation of heaven and earth, and the destruction of all those who rebelled against Yhwh. Jeremiah 46–51 contains oracles against foreign nations, promising their punishment or destruction, though in most cases a short statement at the end of each oracle promises their restoration (Egypt, 46: 26; Moab, 48: 47; Ammon, 49: 6; Elam, 49: 39). (Chapter 52, which repeats material from the last two chapters of 2 Kings, may have been added later, though it ends with what sounds like a note of promise about the Davidic line, and can thus be taken also as eschatological.) Ezekiel also ends with oracles against foreign nations, but these in turn are followed by a description of the final battle with Gog and then with a picture of the New Jerusalem.

Among the minor prophets, we also find signs of an eschatological message. Hosea, Amos, Micah, Malachi, though not books of promise about Israel's future, nonetheless all end with such passages. Joel, Obadiah, Nahum, Habakkuk, Zephaniah, Haggai, and Zechariah are all based predominantly on eschatological themes. Jonah, in this perspective, can also be seen to be a book about the future, raising the possibility of repentance and salvation for Israel's enemies. Of course, many of these books were written on other themes and for other purposes. But it can be no accident that nearly all of the prophetic books end on a note of promise for the future of Israel or of woe to its enemies. It is here that we must see the function of the Latter Prophets as a *collection*. According to such texts as Ben Sira 48: 17ff; Acts 3: 24; and 1 Peter 1: 10–12, Old Testament prophecy was seen cumulatively as a message of salvation for Israel. But we cannot consider the formation of individual books as being always prompted by such concerns. Research done on the individual books underlines their disparate origins: Isaiah and Micah may come from the same circles, but Amos and Hosea do not. Haggai might be associated with circles that produced Chronicles. The ideology of the various books also differs widely. The three major prophetic books each have a distinctive character, whereas the Minor Prophets vary in their attitude towards non-Israelites, the cult, the law, and almost every other criterion by which we might assess their authorship.

A final point of interest is the last verse of Hosea, which begins,

Whoever is wise, let him understand these words; whoever is discerning, let him know them.

Why does this book in particular end with such a comment? Is it the allegory which attracts attention? Or the sexual language which invites decoding? Whatever the answer, it shows us one way in which the prophets were understood to function as literature for the "wise" to study — and thus, since wisdom and the law were to be equated, to bring what were to become the three parts (Torah, Prophets, Writings) of the canon together, unifying the Jewish Scriptures and, to an extent, also de-historicizing and individualizing them. Both of these, together with the levelling of overall meaning which occurs, are functions of an authoritative body of Scripture, finally of a canon. Those who look to the vitality of the individual "men of God" who challenged their contemporaries in the face of historical crises are seeking to undo the process of creating Scripture and canon, which needs to emphasize universality against particularity, unity against diversity. Is it good or bad that Hosea the poet became Hosea the book of Scripture?

WRITINGS

The Writings comprise Psalms, Proverbs, Job, Ruth, Song of Songs, Lamentations, Ecclesiastes (Qoheleth), Esther, Daniel, Ezra, Nehemiah, and Chronicles. This section of the Old Testament appears, both by arrangement and name, to have no unity of genre or content. This section of the canon was apparently created when the canon itself was declared, and the arrangement of its contents in the Hebrew Bible remained fluid long afterwards.

As we have noted earlier in this book, Psalms contains five books (1–41, 42–72, 73–89, 90–106, and 107–150, each of the first four ending with a short doxology. Psalm 1 is generally seen as an introduction to the entire Psalter, and there is evidence that in many mediaeval Hebrew Bibles it was unnumbered (see Wilson 1985, p. 204f.). This psalm places the psalms as a whole within the orbit of obedience to the law. But it also seems to presuppose not public performance of the psalms, but private meditation on them. Wilson has suggested that the five books of Psalms exhibit a clear shape: book 1 (starting with Psalm 2) concentrates on the relationship between King David and God; book 2, on David's royal descendants; book 3 on the Davidic covenant, but ending on a note of despair (Psalm 89: "How long, O Lord?"). The fourth book, where Wilson sees a good deal of editorial activity having taken place, offers assurance that Yhwh, who is Israel's king, will be its refuge, thus answering the cry of Psalm 89. The final book, where the overall theme is least explicit, nevertheless emphasizes obedience to Yhwh's law and reminiscence of his great acts for Israel in the past. The Psalter ends emphatically with hymns of praise.

Three other books in the Writings also have royal associations; Proverbs, the Song of Songs, and Ecclesiastes are attributed (partly or entirely) to Solomon. His reputation as the representative of wisdom explains two of these, but why the Song? Why, in any case, was this erotic composition preserved as a religious writing? The best answer seems to lie not in its attribution to Solomon, but in an allegorical interpretation: perhaps the lovers represented Solomon and wisdom at first, but later Israel and God (and, in Christian interpretation, Christ and the Church). The book of Ruth also has a royal association, being about the ancestry of David, at least, as the text now stands. Esther and Daniel are also books about kingship; Esther and the first six chapters of Daniel probably belong to the late Persian-early Greek period, while Daniel 7–12 *may* be the latest part of the Old Testament.

THE CANON

The formation of the canon — also known as canonization — entails the use of some tricky terms. A canon may be defined as a list of books sanctioned for religious use. In the strict sense, then, there was no *process* of canonization, but an act of drawing up such a list, at a point when a "canon" was needed. The declaration of a canon was one of the tasks undertaken by the rabbis in their reformation of Judaism. Their tradition has it that at Yavneh (formerly Jamnia), where Rabbi Yohanan ben Zakkai set up his academy after the first Jewish War of 66–74, it was discussed which books were holy, and which not.

It is anachronistic to speak of a canon before this time. Indeed, even the word "canon" is never used in Jewish sources. What makes it appropriate, if at all, is that only after 70 CE was Judaism so formally constituted that an official "canon" could exist. But "scriptures", of course, were already in existence. In Palestine, by the first century CE, their extent was not much disputed, it seems. Discussion at Yavneh was apparently confined to the Song of Songs, Ecclesiastes, and Esther. Luke 24: 44 speaks of "the Law of Moses, the Prophets, and the Psalms". Josephus (*Against Apion* 1: 8), a contemporary of Yohanan ben Zakkai, mentions twenty-two books "justly believed to be divine". 4 Ezra, a Jewish apocalypse, also from the end of the first century CE, enumerates twenty-four (14: 18ff.). However, different Jewish groups had other scriptural books besides these. The Qumran caves contained fragments of probably every biblical book (except Esther), but also other books, which may have been regarded as of equal authority, such as Jubilees (which is part of the scriptures of the Ethiopian Church). Outside Palestine, Jewish Scriptures in Greek contained additional books, namely those now included in the Apocrypha. However, as we have seen, the Prophets were probably fixed as a collection by the beginning of the second century BCE, and the Torah by the fourth.

If we now trace the history of the canon forwards rather than backwards, we can reconstruct the following process. The impetus for the creation of Scripture begins with the law, and the authority of the Torah derived not from any concept of "canon" but because, simply, it was the law and thus the supreme authority for the governing of the religious community in Judea. The addition of the prophetic books is an intriguing process. We may assume that parts of this section, notably the Former Prophets, were already venerated because of a different reason — their *historical* reportage. Other prophetic collections were venerated because the prophets concerned had warned Israel of the catastrophe which had indeed befallen, and which had even now not been fully reversed. Their authority lay in their claim to be messages from God, proved as such by their fulfilment. But the promotion of this whole collection *alongside the Torah*, suggests that "prophecy" had become established as a theological category and enshrined in a literary repository of reminders about the past history of Israel's disobedience to the Torah, and of divine promises about Israel's glorious future if — implicitly — it remained true to that Torah. The book of Malachi closes with an exhortation beginning (4: ff.):

Remember the law of my servant Moses, the statutes and ordinances that I commanded him at Horeb for all Israel . . . .

Thus, Law-and-Prophets together constitute a mutually reinforcing system of law plus commentary — the commentary being the lessons of history and the moral exhortations, and promises, of the prophets.

With the third canonical collection, likewise, we have to reckon with books enjoying at first some independent authority, and again for different reasons. The psalms had long existed as a growing collection of religious poetry, used publicly and, more recently, privately too. Other collections were attributed to Solomon, or, in the case of Lamentations, to Jeremiah. The decision to make of these a formal collection, and to declare them, together with Law and Prophets, as books which were of divine origin, or at least of divine inspiration, constituted the creation of a new entity.

In recent years there has been an increasing emphasis on the "canonical process" as a level of theological exegesis of the Old Testament. This has been pioneered in the United States by James Sanders and Brevard Childs. It is an attempt to marry a method that acknowledges the canonical — i.e. religiously authoritative — status of the Old Testament for contemporary Christians to one that acknowledges the historical dimension of its formation. Both Sanders and Childs emphasize the canon as a creation of a community and imply a continuity between the community that created the canon and the church that now possesses it. For the historian working from a secular viewpoint, this approach has validity to the extent that there existed a process of organization within the Old Testament which goes beyond the production of the individual books. Even after Torah and Prophets, for example, had reached a position of some authority, the process of adapting them to the roles which we outlined in the previous section continued. But the "community of faith" which, according to Childs, is the true author of the canon, remains a dubious entity. The community of faith that created the *canon* is the rabbinic academy. Earlier communities likewise had a hand in producing the Old Testament books as books, as collections, as Scripture. But we can see in the accumulation of Scripture, as well as the declaration of a canon, a kind of narrowing down of the meaning, a levelling, in which disparate elements are harmonized and tensions resolved. The decision to elevate the canonizers over the earlier authors and editors is purely a theological decision; and other decisions, even different theological ones, are equally valid. There is no reason why the community which has *received* a canon should not wish to pay as much attention to the entire *process* as to the product. The Church has a claim to the Bible as canon; as literature, however, the Old Testament books belong to everyone, and their authority derives from their own artistic, aesthetic, and religious merit, as much as from any "confession" or creed.

TEXT AND VERSIONS

It is wrong to think that once a book — or, in this context, "scroll" — has come into existence, its form remains fixed. The composition of the biblical scrolls came to an end only with the concern to *preserve* the form already in existence. On the whole, this concern manifests itself when a scroll becomes "scriptural", acquiring the kind of authority that does not permit further revision. Up to that point, however, different forms of a biblical scroll might exist, and these different forms might all be preserved as "scriptural". The form of the Hebrew text we have is called the Masoretic text, after the Masoretes or "Traditionists" who produced the definitive edition — complete with notes, signs to indicate the vowels (omitted in written Hebrew), punctuation, and, generally, all that was necessary to ensure the correct reading or singing of the Bible. Our earliest Masoretic Bibles date from the ninth century CE. In fact, this is much later than our earliest Christian Bibles, which include the Old Testament in Greek. The Greek translation sometimes differs from the Masoretic text (MT). It is not a Christian translation, but a Jewish one, produced, according to Jewish tradition, by seventy-two elders in Egypt at the command of Ptolemy Philadelphus (285–247 BCE). Hence it is called the Septuagint ("Seventy", commonly abbreviated to LXX). In truth, the translation was not a single process, and we know of several other Greek translations in antiquity. Some of these presuppose a third kind of Hebrew text, and some are translations of the text that became the MT, made after the MT had been adopted as the standard. The Hebrew text of the Torah from which the Greek translations were made was very similar to the MT. But the Prophets and Writings show a much greater range of deviation, and show that Hebrew texts other than those represented by the MT were known. In the case of Jeremiah, the most notorious example, we have, in effect, a different edition of the book. Finally, we have the scriptures of the Samaritans. They separated from the Judeans at a time when only the Torah was scriptural, and so have only what we refer to as the Samaritan Pentateuch. This has about 6,000 differences from the MT, about a third of which agree with the LXX.

The biblical texts discovered in the caves at Qumran, dating from the third century BCE–first century CE, represent both the MT and the other text-types implied by the Greek. There are also some texts agreeing substantially with the Samaritan Pentateuch, which suggests that the text was not necessarily Samaritan in origin or exclusive to them. No single authoritative text had been established by this time. The history of these different forms of the Hebrew text is currently in dispute. One dominant theory, that of Frank M. Cross, is that there were three major text types prevalent in Egypt, Babylonia, and Palestine. But, according to Emanuel Tov, the existence of texts from Qumran which fall between these three, and the fact that the three so-called ''text types'' do not exhibit consistently *typical* features, means that the LXX, Samaritan Pentateuch, and MT, at any rate, are three actual texts from a number of ancient texts, which varied from and agreed with each other in a multitude of ways — in effect, that the text was, if not fluid, at least elastic.

There are a few other translations worth mentioning here. The targums are Aramaic versions, preserved, for the most part, in mediaeval manuscripts. However, Aramaic translations go back at least as far as the first century BCE, as we know from a targum of Job found at Qumran, and were in use in synagogues at least by the second century CE. These are sometimes very literal, sometimes very paraphrastic. From about the first century CE comes the translation into Syriac, an Aramaic dialect of northern and northeastern Syria. Although perhaps Jewish in origin, it was later revised by the Syrian Christian Church and has been influenced by the LXX. Two Latin versions are also known: the Old Latin is a general term for early Latin translations, while the Vulgate is the work of St. Jerome (fourth–fifth century), translated from the Hebrew. Jerome's resorting to the Hebrew rather than the LXX, which the Church regarded as its sacred text, met with opposition, raising as it did the question of whether it was the Jewish or ''Christian'' Old Testament text which was truly inspired. It is fortunate that Jerome and his antagonist (on this issue), St. Augustine, were unaware of, and thus undistracted by, other Hebrew and Greek translations of the text which had existed only a few centuries earlier!

The impression must not be given that all these ancient versions differ very widely; many of the deviations are slight. In places, however, they are significant, and they raise an important question: what is the "original text" of any biblical book? The theory of one original from which all others eventually derive provides a useful template for evaluating the comparative antiquity of biblical texts. And indeed, since all texts suffer from accidental as well as deliberate corruption, the existence of other ancient forms of the text can often enable the text-critic to identify and correct these. The corruptions in a text generally involve *expansions* (e.g. to remove ambiguity, enhance clarity, or eliminate accidental writing of words or phrases twice); *conflations*, where a scribe adds extra words from another text or passage; *omissions*, where a scribe's eye jumps accidentally from one group of letters or words to another group a little later, missing the text in between; or *misreadings*, where a letter is incorrectly written (scribes did not always read carefully what they were copying). For examples of these (and a readable guide to text criticism generally), see McCarter 1986. By comparing versions, one can suggest more primitive, as opposed to later, forms of a text. But to reconstruct the "original copy" of any biblical book is something else altogether and can never be a realizable goal. It is important to bear in mind, however, that the history of a book is not finished when the contents have all been supplied. Even if only in small ways, the copyist can frustrate the author. And furthermore, although some modern readers may attach immense importance to the precise words of the Bible, the early scribes did not, being often happy to alter the words intentionally in order to clarify what they took to be the sense. Adherence to the "literal truth" or "literal inspiration" of Scripture, whatever its *theological* merits or demerits, is based on a delusion about how the text has reached us.

BIBLIOGRAPHY

ANET	*Ancient Near Eastern Texts relating to the Old Testament*, (see Pritchard, 1955)
BLS	Bible and Literature Series
BMI	The Bible and its Modern Interpreters
BWANT	Beiträge zur Wissenschaft vom Alten und Neuen Testament
BZAW	Beiheft zur Zeitschrift für die alttestamentliche Wissenschaft
CBC	Cambridge Bible Commentary
CBQMS	Catholic Biblical Quarterly Monograph Series
HTIBS	Historic Texts and Interpreters in Biblical Study
JSOT	Journal for the Study of the Old Testament
JSOTSS	Journal for the Study of the Old Testament Supplement Series
NCB	New Century Bible

OTG	Old Testament Guides
OTL	Old Testament Library
OTS	Oudtestamentische Studiën
SBLCP	Society of Biblical Literature Centenary Publications
SBLDS	Society of Biblical Literature Dissertation Series
SBLTTSPS	Society of Biblical Literature, Texts and Translations Series; Pseudepigrapha Series
SJLA	Studies in Judaism in Late Antiquity
SVT	Supplements to Vetus Testamentum
SWBA	Social World of Biblical Antiquity
TB	Theologische Bücherei

Except where the authors have made their own translations, all quotations from the Bible are from the Revised Standard Version.

ALT, A., 1970, "Der Anteil des Königtums an der sozialen Entwicklung in den Reichen Israel und Juda", *Zur Geschichte des Volkes Israel* (ed. S. Herrmann), Munich: C.H. Beck. See also vol. 3 of Alt's *Kleine Schriften zur Geschichte des Volkes Israel*, 1959.

AULD, A.G., 1983, "Prophets Through the Looking Glass: Between Writings and Moses", *JSOT* 27, pp. 3–23.

BEYERLIN, W., 1978, *Near Eastern Texts relating to the Old Testament*, London/Philadelphia: SCM Press/Westminster Press.

BICKERMAN, E., 1979, *The God of the Maccabees.* *Studies on the Meaning and Origin of the Maccabean Revolt*, (SJLA 32), Leiden: E.J. BRILL.

BOHANAN, P. (ed.), 1967, *Law and Warfare.* *Studies in the Anthropology of Conflict*, New York: The Natural History Press.

BOROWSKI, O., 1987, *Agriculture in Ancient Israel.* *The Evidence from Archaeology and the Bible*, Winona Lake: Eisenbrauns.

BRIGHT, J., 1981, *A History of Israel*, 3rd edition Philadelphia/London: Westminster Press/SCM Press.

BRUEGGEMANN, W., 1977, *The Land. Place as Gift. Promise and Challenge in Biblical Faith*,

Philadelphia/London: Fortress Press/SPCK.

CARROLL, R.P., 1986, *Jeremiah. A Commentary* (OTL), London: SCM Press.

CAROLL, R.P., 1983, "Poets not Prophets", *JSOT*, pp. 25–31.

CARROLL, R.P., 1979, *When Prophecy Failed. Reactions and Responses to Failure in the Old Testament Prophetic Traditions*, London: SCM Press.

CHARLESWORTH, J.H., 1984–5, *The Old Testament Pseudepigrapha*, 2 vols., Garden City, New York/London: Doubleday/Darton, Longman & Todd.

CHILDS, B., 1985, *An Introduction to the Old Testament as Scripture*, Philadelphia: Fortress Press.

CLEMENTS, R.E., 1980, *Isaiah 1–39*, (NCB), Grand Rapids/London: Eerdmans/Marshall, Morgan & Scott.

COGGINS, R., 1975, *Samaritans and Jews. The Origins of Samaritanism Reconsidered*, Oxford/Atlanta: Blackwell/John Knox Press.

COLLINS, J.J. 1984, *The Apocalyptic Imagination: An Introduction to the Jewish Matrix of Christianity*, New York: Crossroads Publications.

CROSS, F.M., TALMON, S. 1975, *Qumran and the History of the Biblical Text*, Cambridge, Mass: Harvard University Press.

DAVIES, P.R., 1982, *The Damascus Covenant. An Interpretation of the "Damascus Document"*, (JSOTSS 25), Sheffield: JSOT Press.

EISSFELDT, O., 1965, *The Old Testament: An Introduction*, Oxford: Blackwell.

FISHBANE, M., 1985, *Biblical Interpretation in Ancient Israel*, Oxford: Oxford University Press.

FLANAGAN, J.W. 1981, "Chiefs in Israel", *JSOT*, 20, 47–73.

FOX, M.V. 1988, *Meanings and Values in Qoheleth*, (BLS 18), Sheffield: Almond Press.

FOX, R., 1967, *Kinship and Marriage*, Harmondsworth: Penguin.

FRANKENA, R., 1965, "The Vassal-Treaties of Esarhaddon and the Dating of Deuteronomy", *OTS*, 14, 122–154.

FRICK, F.S., 1985,. *The Formation of the State in Ancient Israel* (SWBA 4), Sheffield: Almond/JSOT Press.

GARBINI, G., 1988, *History and Ideology in Ancient Israel*, London: SCM Press.

GOTTWALD, N.K., 1985, *The Hebrew Bible: A Socio-Literary Introduction*, Philadelphia: Fortress Press.

GUNKEL. H., 1988, *The Folktale in the Old Testament* (HTIBS 5), Sheffield: Almond/JSOT Press.

HANSON, P.D. 1975, *The Dawn of Apocalyptic. The Historical and Sociological Roots of Jewish Apocalyptic Eschatology*, Philadelphia: Fortress Press.

HAYES, J.H., MILLER, J.M. 1986, *A History of Ancient Israel and Judah*, Philadelphia: Westminster Press.

HEIDEL, A., 1963, *The Babylonian Genesis*, 2nd edition, Chicago and London: University of Chicago Press.

HEIDEL, A., 1963a, *The Gilgamesh Epic and Old Testament Parallels*, 2nd edition, Chicago and London: University of Chicago Press.

HOLLADAY, C.R., 1983, *Fragments from Hellenistic Jewish Authors*, (SBLTTS 20; PS 10), Chico, California: Scholars Press.

HOLLADAY, W., 1986, *Jeremiah 1: A Commentary on the Book of the Prophet Jeremiah Chapters 1–25* (Hermeneia), Philadelphia/London: Fortress Press/SCM Press.

HOPKINS, D.C., 1985, *The Highlands of Canaan. Agricultural Life in the Early Iron Age* (SWBA 3), Sheffield: Almond/JSOT Press.

JACKSON, B., 1972, *Theft in Early Jewish Law*, Oxford: Clarendon Press.

JACKSON, B., 1975, *Essays in Jewish and Comparative Legal History*, (SJLA X), Leiden: E.J. Brill.

KARSTEN, R., 1967, "Blood Revenge and War among the Jiboro Indians of Eastern Ecuador", in Bohanan, 1967.

KIPPENBERG, H.G., 1982, *Religion und Klassenbildung im antiken Judäa*, 2nd edition, Göttingen: Vandenhoeck & Ruprecht.

KNIGHT, D.F., TUCKER, G. (eds.), 1985, *The Hebrew Bible and its Modern Interpreters*, (SBLCP), Philadelphia/Chico, California: Fortress/Scholars Press.

KRAFT, R.A. & NICKELSBURG, G.W. 1986, *Early Judaism and its Modern Interpreters*, (BMI 2), Philadelphia/Atlanta: Fortress/Scholars Press.

LEMCHE, N.P., 1985, *Early Israel. Anthropological and Historical Studies on the Israelite Society before the Monarchy*, (SVT XXXVII), Leiden: E.J. Brill.

MCCARTER, P.K., 1986, *Textual Criticism: Reconstructing the Text of the Hebrew Bible*, Philadelphia: Fortress Press.

MᴄKANE, W., 1983/1965, *Prophets and Wise Men*, London: SCM Press.

MᴄKANE, W., 1986, *Jeremiah 1–25*, (ICC), Edinburgh: T. & T. Clark.

MARKS, J.H. 1985, *Visions of One World: Legacy of Alexander*, Guildford, Connecticut: Four Quarters Publishing House.

MAYES, A.D.H., 1979, *Deuteronomy*, (NCB), Grand Rapids/London: Eerdmans/Oliphants.

NOTH, M., 1972, *A History of Pentateuchal Traditions* (Translated by B.W. Anderson), Englewood Cliffs, N.J.: Prentice Hall.

OTTO, E., 1979, *Jakob in Sichem. Überlieferungsgeschichtliche, archäologische und territorialgeschichtliche Studien zur Entwicklung Israels*, (BWANT 110), Stuttgart: Kohlhammer Verlag.

PAUL, S.M. 1970, *Studies in the Book of the Covenant in the light of Cuneiform and Biblical Law* (SVT XVIII), Leiden: E.J. Brill.

PETTINATO, G., 1971, *Das altorientalische Menschenbild und die sumerischen und akkadischen Schöpfungsmythen*, Heidelberg: Abhandlungen der Heidelberger Akademie der Wissenschaften, Phil-Hist. Klasse.

PHILLIPS, A.C.J., 1984, ''The Laws of Slavery'', *JSOT 30*, 51–66.

POOLE, M., 1962, *A Commentary on the Holy Bible*, vol. 2, Edinburgh: Banner of Truth Trust (reprint of 1st edition, 1700).

PRITCHARD, J.B., 1955, *Ancient Near Eastern Texts relating to the Old Testament*, 2nd edition, Princeton: University of Princeton Press.

PRITCHARD, J.B., 1969, *The Ancient Near East in Pictures*, 2nd edition, Princeton: Princeton University Press.

PROPP, V., 1968, *Morphology of the Folktale*, Austin, Texas and London: University of Texas.

RAD, G. VON, 1966, *The Problem of the Hexateuch and Other Essays*, Edinburgh: Oliver & Boyd.

REVENTLOW, H. GRAF, 1963, *Liturgie und Prophetisches Ich bei Jeremiah*, Gütersloh: Gerd Mohn.

ROGERSON, J.W., MᴄKAY, J.W., 1977, *Psalms*, (CBC), 3 vols, Cambridge: Cambridge University Press.

ROGERSON, J.W., 1978, *Anthopology and the Old Testament*, Oxford/Atlanta: Blackwell/John Knox Press, (reprint 1984, Sheffield: JSOT Press).

ROGERSON, J.W., 1985, *The (New) Atlas of the Bible*, London/New York: Macdonald/Facts on on File.

SAGGS, H.W., 1962, *The Greatness that was Babylon*, London: Sidgwick & Jackson.

SANDERS, E.P., 1977, *Paul and Palestinian Judaism*, London: SCM Press.

SANDERS, J.A., 1984, *Canon and Community: A Guide to Canonical Criticism*, Philadelphia: Fortress Press.

SASSON, J.M., 1979, *Ruth. A New Translation with a Philological Commentary and a Formalist-Folklorist Interpretation*, Baltimore/London: Johns Hopkins University Press.

SETERS, J. VAN, 1975, *Abraham in History and Tradition*, New Haven and London: Yale University Press.

SETERS, J. VAN, 1983, *In Search of History. Historiography in the Ancient World and the Origins of Biblical History*, New Haven and London: Yale University Press.

SMITH, G., 1876, *The Chaldean Account of Genesis*, London: Sampson Low, Marston, Searle, & Rivington.

SMITH, G.A., 1931, *The Historical Geography of the Holy Land*, 25th edition (1st edition 1894), London: Hodder & Stoughton.

SMITH, M., 1971, *Palestinian Parties and Politics that shaped the Old Testament*, Columbia: Columbia University Press (1987 edition, London: SCM Press).

STONE, M., 1976, ''Lists of Revealed Things in Apocalyptic Literature'' in F.M. Cross, W.E. Lemke and P.D. Miller (eds), *Magnalia Dei: The Mighty Acts of God*, Garden City, New York: Doubleday, pp. 414–452.

SODEN, W. VON, 1985, *Bibel und Alter Orient. Altorientalische Beiträge zum Alten Testament*, Berlin and New York: W. de Gruyter.

THOMPSON, T.L., 1987, *The Origin Tradition of Ancient Israel. 1. The Literary Form of Genesis and Exodus 1–25*, (JSOTSS 55), Sheffield: JSOT Press.

TIGAY, J.H., 1982, *The Evolution of the Gilgamesh Epic*, Philadelphia: University of Philadelphia Press.

VANDERKAM, J.C., 1984, *Enoch and the Growth of an Apocalyptic Tradition*, (CBQMS 16), Washington: Catholic Biblical Association of America.

VERMES, G., 1973, *Jesus the Jew. A Historian's Reading of the Gospels*, London: Collins.

WEINFELD, M., 1972, *Deuteronomy and the*

Deuteronomic School, Oxford: Clarendon Press.

WESTERMANN, C., 1964, "Arten der Erzählung in der Genesis", *Forschung am Alten Testament. Gesammelte Studien*, (TB 24), Munich: Chr. Kaiser Verlag.

WHYBRAY, R.N., 1974, *The Intellectual Tradition in the Old Testament*, (BZAW 135), Berlin and New York: W. de Gruyter.

WHYBRAY, R.N., 1987, *The Making of the Pentateuch: A Methodological Study*, (JSOTSS 57), Sheffield: JSOT Press.

WILLIAMSON, H.G.M., 1987, *Ezra and Nehemiah*, (OTG), Sheffield: JSOT Press.

WILSON, G.H., 1985, *The Editing of the Hebrew Psalter*, (SBLDS 76), Chico, California: Scholars Press.

WILSON, R.R., 1977, *Genealogy and History in the Biblical World*, New Haven and London: Yale University Press.

WILSON, R.R., 1980, *Prophecy and Society in Ancient Israel*, Philadelphia: Fortress Press.

WISEMAN, D.J. (ed.), 1973, *Peoples of Old Testament Times*, Oxford: Clarendon Press.

ZIMMERLI, W., 1979–83, *Ezekiel 1 & 2. A Commentary on the Book of the Prophet Ezekiel*, (Hermeneia), Philadelphia/London: Fortress Press/SCM Press.

CREDITS

The authors and publishers wish to acknowledge, with thanks, the following photographic sources:

Ancient Art and Architecture Collection, Ronald Sheridan: 13, 15, 22, 66–67, 73, 74 (below), 75 (above), 76, 115, 131, 152, 164, 172, 179, 188 (above), 253, 295, 340;
Jon Bartlett: 88 (above);
Bible Scene: 9 (above), 9 (below), 12, 20, 65 (above), 85, 74 (above), 125, 138, 155, 258 (right), 265;
Bibliothèque Nationale, Paris: 221;
Daniel Blatt: 10–11 (above and below);
The Bridgeman Art Library: 137, 151, 163, 325 (above), 366;
British Museum: 92, 98, 101, 150 (above), 210, 266;
Peter Clayton: 21, 162, 173, 177;
Werner Forman Archive: 93, 111;
Sonia Halliday Photographs: 29 (below), 68, 87, 95, 123, 126, 128, 156, 167, 188 (below), 208, 214, 283, 284, 365 (below), 326, 328 (below), 349; photographs by Jane Taylor: 105, 108, 142, 166, 168, 258 (left);
Robert Harding Photograph Library: 106–107, 165, 232;
Michael Holford: 18, 99, 100, 147, 148, 150 (below), 153, 195, 206;
Hutchison Photograph Library: 193;
Israel Museum, Jerusalem: 171, 181, 336;
JCK Archive: 2, 54, 104, 199, 207, 234, 235, 338, 345, 352;
Behram Kapadia: 231;
Mansell Collection: 215, 236;
Zev Radovan: 30–31, 75 (below), 88 (below), 127, 192, 213, 264, 328 (above);
John Rogerson: 29 (above), 65 (below);
Zefa: 186.

The publishers have made every effort to trace the copyright holders, but if any have been inadvertently overlooked, they will be pleased to make the necessary arrangements at the first opportunity.

INDEX

Page references in italics refer to illustrations.

Abel, murder by Cain *209*
Abimelech 350
Abner 124, 129
Abraham 52, 243, 345, 346–347, 352, 356
  oral material 351–352
  story, date 55
Absalom 37, 48–49
  revolt of 131
Achish, King of Gath 124
Ahab 39, 143, 144–145
Ahaz 150
Ahijah 135
Ahiqar 296
Alexander the Great 61, 111, 113, 172
  coin depicting *172*
Alexander Jannaeus 83, 184–185
Amalekites 81–82
Amarna, letters 72
  wars 76
Amaziah of Judah 149
Amen-em-ope, instruction of, 94, 294
Amenhotep IV, (Akhenaten) 92, *93*, 94
Ammon 79
  descent of 77
Ammonites 78–79
Amorites 71
Amos 23, 40, 56, 57, 72, 81, 254, 279, 289–290
Animals, laws on keeping 240
Animal Apocalypse 319

Antigonus 191
Antiochus III 113, 173
Antiochus IV 177–179
Antipater 191
Apocalypses
  Enoch 315–20
  Jewish 315
  Knowledge 311–312
  see also Animal Apocalypse
Apocalypse of Weeks 319
Apocalyptic
  definition and usage 310–311
  literature (Daniel) 320–321
Apocrypha
  Judith 230
  Tobit 230
  Wisdom of Solomon 307–309
Apollonius 172, 179
Aram 70, 89–90
Arameans 84
Aretas I 83
Aristobulus I 184
Aristobulus II 189, 191
Artaxerxes 163
Asa, King of Judah 141
Ashtoreth, (Istar, Astarte) *75*
Ashur, text from 203,
Ashurbanipal 98, 100
  inscriptions 83
Assyria 97
  religion of 102
Assyrians 97–102
Assyrian relief, Nineveh *99*
Aten 94
Athaliah, Queen 149
Atrahasis, Epic 202, 210–211
Azazel 318

Baal 145
  epic, (Ugarit) 75
Baasha 141
Babel, Tower of 201, 202
Babylon 102–104, 109
  cylinder seal *163*
  Ishtar Gate *104*
  Persian conquest of 215
  religion of 103–104
'Babylonian Chronicles' 109
'Babylonian Job' 296
Bashan 23
Ben Hadad 144, 149
Benjamin, tribe of 47
Ben Sira 315, 319, 364
Bet av 56
Bet avot ('sons of') 59–60
Bethel *265*
Beth Shan, clay coffins *76*
Beth Shean 69
Book of Law 154

Caesarea Maritima, aqueduct *188*
Cain and Abel 209
Cambyses 91, 110
Canaan
  city states 75
  conquest of 133
  Egypt as sovereign of 77
  feudal system 76
Canaanites 70–71
  Amorites 71
  Philistines 72
  Phoenicians 72
  racial distinction 70–71
  religion of 73

temples 75
Canon, formation of 371–373
Capernaum, synagogue *264*
Carchemish 91
   Battle of 155
Carmel, Mount 64
Chronicler 55, 223
I Chronicles 48, 55, 82, 123,
   223, 224, 227, 281
2 Chronicles 15, 38, 39, 143,
   149, 150, 151, 152, 154,
   223, 237, 281, 297
Coastal plain, Israel 16
Counsels of Wisdom 295
Covenant, Ark of 124
   Book of 223, 235, 238–241,
   242
Creation
   Akkadian texts 198–199,
   201–202, 208
   early theories of 196
   Genesis story 200–205
   Sumerian texts 198–199,
   201–202, 208
Cyrus 110
   'Cylinder' 162, *162*
   Edict of 41, 162
   reputed tomb *106–107*

Damascus 89
'Damascus Document' 61
Damages, law on 241
Dan, tribal migration of 121
   area occupied by *125*
Daniel, Book of 112, 158, 174,
   178, 227, 296, 314,
   320–322, 331
Darius I 110, 112
   seal impression *111*
David 48–49, 123–124, 129,
   131, 132, 223, 257,
   268–269, 350–351
   captures Jerusalem 37
   Oscott Psalter *266*
Dead Sea 23, 33, 353
Deborah 120, 121, 241, 278
Decalogue 250
Deir Alla inscription 276
Deuteronomy 44, 71, 79, 81, 82,
   89, 96, 135, 154, 237,
   245–250, 262, 280, 313,

332, 336, 343
   beginnings of 245–247
   humanitarianism 249
   war 248
   women 248
Deuteronomistic history 362, 365
Divination 313, 314
Documentary hypothesis 361,
   362
Dumuzi and Enkimdu 208

Ecclesiastes, *see* Qoheleth
Eden, garden of
   expulsion from 207
   story 222
Edom 77, 78, 80–81, 89, 349
Egypt 70, 90–94
   under Rome 91
   religion 92
Egyptian Judgement scene *92*
El 74
   see also Canaan
Elah 141
Elephantine 91, 171–172
   papyri 171
Elijah 282
Elisha 151, 282, 285
Elohim, use of 199–200
Enki and Ninhursag 206
Enkimdu, *see Dumuzi and
   Enkimdu*
Enmeduranki 316
Enoch 315, 317–318, 320
Enuma Elish 197–198, 204, 212
Esau 81, 319, 354
Eshbaal 122, 129
Essenes 340–342
Esther 112
Etemenanki
   temple at Babylon 212
Euphrates, river *165*
Exile, Babylonian
   Judaism under 158–160
   the return 161
   social change during 60
Exodus 43–44, 132–133
   Book of 73, 81–82, 139,
   233–242, 250–252, 256,
   276, 297, 332, 354–355
Ezekiel 291, 292, 328
   Book of 64, 79, 158, 205,

291, 367–369
Ezra 41, 79, 158, 161, 162,
   163–164, 169–171, 338

Festivals
   agricultural 35
   Temple 332–335
Flood Story
   Assyrian tablet depicting *210*
   Genesis 211–212
   Narrative 199
'Fourth Philosophy' 342

Galilee, sea of 22
Gedaliah 41, 51
Gemariah 50, 51
Genealogies, function 51
Genesis 20, 26, 43, 48, 52, 53,
   55, 56, 70–72, 74, 77,
   81–84, 89, 96, 102, 109,
   114, 118, 132, 134, 164,
   196, 198, 199, 200,
   201–206, 208–216, 226,
   278, 316, 331, 351–354,
   346, 347
Gezer 84
   calendar 34
   gold dagger from *75*
Gideon 120
Gilboa, Mount 73
Gilead 78
Gilgamesh
   death of 199
   Epic of 197, 199, 200, 202,
   204, 206, 211
   King of Erech *195, 199*
Golan Heights *29*

Haggai 41, 291
Hammurabi
   Law Code of 233, 235, 239
   stela of *235*
Hanamel 40
Harran 89
Hasidim 180–181
Hasmoneans 180
   dynasty of 182
   see also Maccabean Revolt
Hatti 95
Hazael 146, 149

Hazor *128*
   gate *131*
Hebrews, early history 43
Hebrew text 373
   see also Masoretic
Hebron 125, 181
   hills 20, 21–22
   vineyards *29*
Hellenism
   'Hellenistic Crisis' 174
   Hellenizers' 177–180
   political context 176
Herod the Great 169, 191–194
Herodium *168, 184*
Hezekiah 151–153, 286
   water tunnel 152, *156*
Highlands, Israel 19–22
Historiography
   Greek 220
   Israelite 222–223
   Narrative 218, 220–223,
     223–225
Hittites 94, 95, 96
Hittite relief *95*
Holiness Code 242–245
   festivals 244–245
Hosea 132, 133, 289
Huldah 278
Hurrians 94, 95, 96–97
Hyrcanus II 83, 191–192
Hyrcanus, John 184, 331

Isaac, blessing Esau *349*
Isaiah 16, 40, 44, 72, 98, 100,
    102, 197, 206, 259, 279,
    285–287, 314, 324, *325*,
    365
   Second 112, 114, 158,
     287–288
   Third 288
Ishmaelites 83
Israel
   fall to Assyria 39
   land use 35
   League of Twelve Tribes 132
   location of 118
Israelites
   crossing Red Sea *328*
   early 117
   social groups 56, 57
   village settlements 28, 35

Jabesh Gilead 46–47
Jacob 243, 348–*349*, 354, 355
Jason 177–179
Jehoahaz 144
Jehoiachin 157, 158
Jehoiakim 155, 157
Jehoram 143, 145, 146
Jehoshaphat 143, 146, 237, 280
Jehu, dynasty of 146
Jephthah 118, 349–350
Jeremiah 41, 44, 50–51, 79, 155,
    157, 158, 160, 254, 278,
    281, 290–291, 297, 313,
    319, 365–367, *366*
Jericho *115, 213*
Jeroboam 134–135, 141
Jeroboam II 149
Jerusalem *20*, 21, 41, 61,
    177–178
   citadel 179, *193*
   City of David *164*
   Herodian, model *192*
   Old City *21*
   road to Jericho *8*
Jezebel 143, 145
Jezreel, valley 19
Joab 48–49, 129
Joash, King of Judah 146, 149
Job 301–305, *325*
Joel 114, 120
Johanan, High Priest 171
Jonah 16, 229
Jonathan 183–184, 350–351
Joram, *see* Jehoram
Jordan valley 22–23
Joseph *54*
Josephus *221*, 329–330
Joshua 26, 58, 71, 78, 80, 113,
    358
Josiah 154–155
   reforms of 246, 258
Jubilee Year 42, 245, 333
Judah 121, 152, 160–161
   Kings of 149–157
Judaism 323, 324, 330–333,
    335–337
see also Sadducees, Pharisees,
    Essenes, Samaritans,
    Temple
Judas, 'Maccabee' 180
Judean wilderness *13*, 22

Judges, Book of 16, 18, 19, 23,
    35, 36, 47, 56, 58, 59,
    70, 74, 77, 78, 81–83, 118,
    120–122, 133, 164, 237,
    257, 260, 349, 350,
    357–359
Judges, Minor 120
Judith 230

King's highway 79, 81
I Kings 18, 19, 38, 39, 91, 96,
    123, 131, 132, 134, 135,
    141–145, 237, 258, 278,
    280, 295
2 Kings 28, 41, 50, 79, 89, 96,
    102, 109, 143–146, 148,
    149, 151, 152, 154, 157,
    160, 227, 276, 278, 279,
    357, 358

Laban 354
Lachish 19
   reliefs 99, *18, 100, 153*
Land, acquisition of 39
Land, use of 35–43
Land of Israel
   agriculture 34, 42
   ancient neighbours 63–64, 70
   climate 24, 26
   forests 26, 28
   geography 16, 18, 19, 22, 23
   history 116
   justice 47–48
   population 28, 34–35
   social organisation 45, 51
   vegetation 61–62
Latter Prophets 365
   see also Prophets
Law 235–238, 336–337
   Book of 50
Law of Moses 363–364
Leah 354
Leviticus 14, 42–43, 96,
    242–245, 253–262
   laws in 242–245, 259–263
Lineage, blood ties 45–51

Maccabean Revolt 43, 61, 180
   see also Judas Maccabee
1 Maccabees 180, 224–225
2 Maccabees 61, *179*

Magi 314
Mamu, Temple of *148*
Manasseh 153–154
Manticism 296, 314–315
  see also Wisdom
Maps
  Alexander the Great, empire
    113
  Assyrian empire *110*
  Conquests of Herod *190*
  David's empire *130*
  Divided monarchy *140*
  Forested areas *27*
  Hasmonean kingdom *183*
  Israel, era of Judges *119*
  Median and Babylonian
    empires *103*
  Persian empire *110*
  Settlements, Iron Age *33*
  Six 'strips' of Israel *17*
Mari 275, 276
Mariamne 191–193
Marriage 243
Masada 187, *188*, 189
Masoretic text 373
Mattathias 180
Megiddo *86*, 155
  gate, model *74*
  stone altars *73*
  water tunnel *142*
Menelaus 179, 181
Mephibosheth 37
Merneptah 91
  stela 91, 117
Mesha, Inscription of 80, 142
Messianic expectation 343
Micah 281, 290
Micaiah 280
Midianites 82
Minor Judges, *see* Judges
Mišpahah 56
Moab 23, 77, 80
Moabites 79
Moses 57, *231*, 236, 346–347
Murašu, archive 158
Myth 200–201

Nabateans 83–84
Nabonidus 227
Nadab 141
Nahash 49–50

Nahum 102
Narrative 217–228
  see also Historiography
Nebuchadrezzer 109, 155, 227
Neco 91
Neco II 155
Nehemiah 41, 42, 43, 59, 60,
    61, 163, 164, 169–171
New Testament
  Luke 14, 333
  Matthew 194
Nimrud, palace *150*
Nineveh, palace *101*, 295
Nineveh 154–155
Ninhursag, *see* Enki and Ninhursag
Noah *214*
Nob, sanctuary 120
Numbers 47, 57, 78, 82, 83, 180
Nuzi, archive *96*

Octavian (Augustus) 192–193,
    194, 330
Old Testament
  composition 357–359
  oral tradition 347–349
  political considerations 356
  text translations 374
  written material 355–359
Omen literature 313
Omri 141–143, 146

Patriarchal narratives 226, 347,
    348
Patriarchal traditions 132
Pekah 150
Pentateuch 360–364
Persians and Medes 109–111
Persian Art 112
Pesher, commentary *336*
Petra 83, 84, *105, 108*
Pharisees 62, 339–340
Philistines 35, 72, 77, 121
Phoenicians 72
Pompey 189
Priest, priesthood 243, 334–335
Priestly writer, 'P' 360
Prophecy 274, 275, 279
Prophetic groups 135
Prophets 276–282
  Latter 365–369
  Minor 369–370

Proverbs, 72, 294, 298–301, 358
Psalms 270, 271–273
  royal ceremonies 263–264,
    367–369
Psalms, Wisdom, *see* Wisdom
Ptolemies 172–173

Qarqar, Battle of 144
Qoheleth 303–305
Qumran 325, 341–342
  texts *340*, 374
  War Scroll 180, *181*

Rachel 354
Ramah 141
Ramoth Gilead 143
Ras Shamra 73–74
  texts 74–75
Rehoboam 38, 132, 134
Return, The (Exile) 162
Ritual, in Leviticus 259–263
Rome, rule of Palestine 61
Ruth 23, 26, 35, 39, 124, 229,
    237
Rezon 150

Sacrifices 254–255
  criticism of 259
  types of 255–257
Sadducees 339
Saga 225–226
Salome Alexandra (Shelomzion)
    189
Samaria 143, 150, *155*
  (Sebaste) *138, 166–167*
Samaritans 14, 62, 343
Samaritan Pentateuch 374
Samson 120, 350
Samuel 121, 241
  Books of 350–351
  I Samuel 16, 19, 36, 37, 45,
    46, 77, 82, 96, 121–124,
    129, 256, 268, 133, 135,
    276, 278, 357
  2 Samuel 19, 23, 24, 26, 37,
    38, 39, 48, 49, 50,70, 84,
    124, 129, 131
Sanctuaries 257
Sargon 152

Saul 36–37, 45–47, *126*, 350–351
    rise to Kingship 122–123
    length of reign 122
Scribes 297, 314–315
Seleucids 177, 182
Seleucus 91
Seleucus IV 178
Sennacherib 98, 152
Septuagint 373–374
Ševet 57
Shalmaneser II 110
Shalmaneser III 98, 144
    black obelisk of *98, 147*
Sheba 131
Shechem 20
Shephelah *15*, 18–19
Sheshbazzar 162
Sheshonk 1, (Shishak) 91, 139
Simon 182, 184
Sinai, Moses at *231*
Sinai, Mount *232*
Slavery, laws concerning
    238–239
Solomon 38, 131–132
    Wisdom of, *see* Wisdom
Sumerian king lists 209, 210,
    316
Syria 95

Tabor, Mount 19, *65*
Temple, Jerusalem *131, 137*,
    258, 334
    community 169–170
    'Desolation' 179–180
    liberation of 61
    rededicated 181
Temple Scroll 341
Tent of Meeting 253–254
Tibni 141–142
Tiglath Pileser III 98, 110,
    149–*150*, 152
Time charts
    Israel and Judah 136
    Persian Kings and main
        events in Judah 159
    Syria and Judea 175
Timnah 81, 82
Tobit 230
Transjordan 77
    highlands 23
    see also Ammon, Moab, Edom
Tribes 55
Tyre *66*, 72
    king of 205

Ugarit, cuneiform tablet *74*
Utnapishtim 206, 211

Utu 206
Uzziah 149

Wadi Daliyeh papyri 172
Wadi Mojib *88*
Wadi Qelt *31*
Wisdom literature 293–309
    folk wisdom 297–298
    Job 301–302
    manticism 296–297
    Psalms 305–306
Wisdom of Solomon 307–308
Writings, books comprising
    370–371

'Yehud' coin *171*
Yhwh, use of 8, 199, 331

Zakir inscription 276
Zechariah 41, 72, 163, 292
Zelophehad 57
Zenon papyri 172
Zephaniah 72, 280, 281
Zerubbabel 163
Ziasudra 210
Zimri 141